CALVIN

FRANÇOIS WENDEL is Professor of
the History of Christianity and Dean
of the Faculty of Protestant Theology
at the University of Strasbourg. He
is one of the greatest European
experts on the history and literature
of the Reformation.

FRANÇOIS WENDEL

CALVIN

THE ORIGINS AND DEVELOPMENT OF HIS RELIGIOUS THOUGHT

translated by
Philip Mairet

COLLINS

THE FONTANA LIBRARY
THEOLOGY AND PHILOSOPHY

First published in English translation Wm. Collins, Sons & Co. Ltd., 1963
First issued in the Fontana Library, 1965
Second Impression, September 1965
Third Impression, November 1969
Fourth Impression, February 1972

Copyright by Presses Universitaires de France, 1950
© in the English translation by William Collins, Sons & Co. Ltd., London
and Harper & Row Inc., New York, 1963

Printed in Great Britain
Collins Clear-Type Press
London and Glasgow

CONTENTS

Contents

FOREWORD

Since the completion of the monumental edition of Calvin's works at the beginning of this century, studies of all kinds concerning the personality and the work of the French reformer have multiplied. The fourth centenary of his birth, which came soon after that publication, gave a fresh impetus to the production of works that sought to grasp Calvinist thought as a whole, or to reconstitute this or that chapter of Calvin's biography. Besides these publications, mostly rather brief or even summary, appeared the *Jean Calvin* of the doyen Emile Doumergue, celebrating the glory of its hero in seven big volumes: a considerable work, not only for its amplitude, but also for the infinite care with which its author elucidates the smallest details of the life of Calvin. Doumergue's work remains to this day a mine of information, even for those who deprecate its hagiographic and apologetic bias or hesitate to accept its theological prejudices, traces of which too often tend to falsify its interpretation of Calvinist doctrine.

Notwithstanding all these studies, which appeared to indicate a renewal of interest in Calvin, P. Wernle thought he could affirm, at the beginning of the remarkable summary of Calvinist theology he published some thirty years ago, that 'the *Institutes* of Calvin will probably be read even less in the twentieth century than they were in the nineteenth.' This was a prediction of a kind that historians should be careful to avoid, and was the reverse of what was really happening. It is even probable that Calvin's writings never found so many readers since the seventeenth century as they do today. Innumerable monographs and articles in reviews have been published during the last twenty years, all with the object of clarifying some special aspect of

Calvin's religious thought or pastoral activities. As one would expect, these studies are of unequal value, and it is certain that Calvin himself would have found it difficult to recognize his own ideas in the expositions of a good many of his disciples. It remains no less true that some others have known how to render genuinely scientific service, and have shed light upon a number of hitherto little-known aspects of the reformer's teaching.

The aim of the present work is at once more modest and more ambitious. It does not claim to adduce any sensational novelties or unprecedented interpretations. It seeks to supply, in some measure, a genuine need, to fill a rather surprising gap. Apart from the volume of Doumergue that deals with Calvin's religious thinking—a volume no longer obtainable in bookshops and liable to be judged out-of-date in its historical method—there is no exposition of the Calvinist doctrine as a whole in existence. A new historical study, founded upon careful examination of the texts and upon the results of the most recent research, seemed therefore to be justified. It was not a question of presenting Calvin's religious thought in a fully complete and exhaustive manner by entering into every detail of the problems and controversies it has given rise to: for that a huge volume would be insufficient. My intention has been to give a correct and succinct account of the essential points of this teaching, the historical importance of which needs no underlining. So far as possible I have emphasized those aspects of it which demonstrate the originality of Calvinism. At the same time, the points upon which Calvin did no more than accommodate himself to the conceptions of the ancient Church or of the reformers who preceded him have not been neglected.

Here we are touching upon the problem of the sources of Calvin's thought, which is of considerable importance for the history of ideas in the sixteenth century. Nor is this, as some have thought, merely a matter of erudition. It seems to me, indeed, that in trying to become clear about the intellectual formation of Calvin, and the family of minds to which he relates himself by his choice of reading, we have some chance of discovering the very basis of his thought, and of reaching a better understanding of its contours. But whatever relations can be established between Calvin and his predecessors, they are not those of a disciple eager to reproduce the thought of his masters and alarmed at the very thought of changing the smallest feature of it. From his very first publication he showed his independence, as he did again in regard to Erasmus. This somewhat lofty independence he maintained throughout, even towards authors from whom he was borrowing with both hands, such as Luther, Augustine or Bucer. We have found it easy to accumulate precise references upon this point. Innumerable parallels can be established between this or that doctrine of Calvin and a particular teaching of one of his favourite preceptors; one could point out many more of them than I have. But these borrowings take on another colour under his pen; they are, as it were, suffused by another light. And I hope I have been able to show that in all his writings and commentaries—up to and including those on the Bible, which he did not scruple to interpret in a highly personal manner— Calvin remained himself.

The subject of this work excluded any complete account of Calvin's life; but it has not been possible to exclude all biographical considerations. Just as it would never occur to anyone to separate the biographical data from an exposition of the thought of Luther, it would be contrary to historical truth to try to explain Calvin's thought in abstraction from some of the most important events that marked his life. His intellectual formation, his experiences at Geneva and Strasbourg, and some at least of his doctrinal controversies, left a deep imprint upon the development of his ideas. It is in function with these that I have shaped the biographical sketch that forms the first part of this work.

As for the doctrinal exposition itself, the plan that has imposed itself is that which was chosen by Calvin for his *Institutes*. And it is also from the various editions of the *Institutes* that the majority of the references and quotations have been taken. Concern for objectivity has led me to multiply the latter, in order to put the reader into direct contact with the texts themselves.

There could obviously be no question of mentioning all the modern works; to do so would almost have transformed this survey into a bibliographical catalogue: only the most important studies have been retained. The reader is asked to forgive some involuntary omissions, at least any omissions of more recent works which I have not been able to consult.

Need it be added that in this exposition I have tried to conform to as strictly historical a method as possible? My intention was to present Calvin's thought just as it emerges from the documents and the historical surroundings, and not according to any ideological preferences. Such an effort requires a certain effort of adaptation, perhaps even of sympathy, but it does not necessarily imply adherence without reservations. If it did, we should end by having to condemn all history of philosophical or religious ideas.

PART ONE

Biographical Outline

CHAPTER ONE

The Young Calvin

Although the life of Calvin has not been the subject of so imposing a list of works as the life of Luther, the researches made in this domain during the last half-century are nevertheless considerable. It is true that numerous details of the French reformer's biography are still unknown, or imperfectly known, for want of precise documentation. Calvin was by nature uncommunicative about his personal history: a certain timidity, an aristocratic inclination to screen himself from the public, and finally his conviction that the individual is nothing in himself but only in so far as he is an instrument of the Divine will, caused him to remain silent about many events that would have interested biographers. The few sources that we possess, especially those that concern the youth of Calvin, have been all the more attentively and minutely scrutinized. Historians have wellnigh exhausted their wisdom and ingenuity in trying to reconstitute the succession of events that marked the earliest years of Calvin. All in all, what we know today is as much as it is possible to know, but for a few details, unless and until new documents are discovered.[1]

[1] Besides E. DOUMERGUE, *Jean Calvin, les hommes et les choses de son temps*, 7 vols., Lausanne, 1899-1917 and Neuilly 1926-7, we must mention, among the biographies of Calvin that retain value to this day, F. W. KAMPSCHULTE, *Johann Calvin, seine Kirche und sein Staat in Genf*, 2 vols., Leipzig, 1869-99; W. WALKER, *John Calvin, the Organizer of Reformed Protestantism*, New York, 1906, and the small volume by AUG. LANG, *Johannes Calvin*, Leipzig, 1909. Chief among the general works that have appeared recently are those of R. N. CAREW HUNT, *Calvin*, London, 1933, and P. IMBART DE LA TOUR, *Calvin et l'institution chrétienne*, Paris, 1935. We would add the two studies by J. D. BENOÎT, *Jean Calvin, la vie, l'homme, la pensée*, 2nd edition, 1948, and *Calvin, directeur d'âmes*, Strasbourg, 1947, which constitute a valuable and often

I. THE YEARS OF STUDY

Jean Calvin, or Cauvin, was born at Noyon on July 10th, 1509. His native town was an old cathedral city whose bishop was its ruler and was at the same time one of the Twelve Peers of France. At the time of Calvin's birth and until 1525, the throne of Noyon was occupied by Charles de Hangest, who belonged to the nobility of the neighbourhood.[2] This detail has some importance, for Calvin, from his childhood, was to be in contact with several members of this family, with the branch of Montmor in particular: it was in company with three young men of the Hangest family that he went to Paris as a student, and to one of these, Claude, Abbé of St-Eloi, that he was to dedicate his commentary on the *De Clementia* of Seneca in 1532. Such connections were not without effect upon the formation of the young Calvin. If he shared with the generality of his Picard compatriots their sense of logic and quickness of sensibility, he certainly owed his aristocratic tastes and manners to the familiar terms on which he was admitted to the Montmors' family circle.

His own family had risen to the petty bourgeoisie through the tenacity and ambition of his father, Gérard Cauvin, who had emerged from among the artisans and boatmen. In 1481 Gérard had become one of the town's registrars; later on, he added to this responsibility, probably not very onerous, those of solicitor to the episcopal offices, of fiscal agent, of secretary to the bishop and, lastly, of procurator of the cathedral Chapter. By 1498 he had been admitted to the status of a citizen. About the same time, he married a young bourgeoise, Jeanne Lefranc, who bore him four sons, Charles, Jean, Antoine and François, and two

---

original introduction to Calvin. Upon Calvin's youth, see also A. LEFRANC, *La Jeunesse de Calvin*, Paris, 1888; J. PANNIER, *Recherches sur l'évolution religieuse de Calvin jusqu' à sa conversion*, Strasbourg, 1924; and the same author's *Recherches sur la formation intellectuelle de Calvin*, Paris, 1931; QUIRINUS BREEN, *John Calvin, a Study in French Humanism*, Grand Rapids, Mich., 1931; MARG. MANN, *Erasme et les débuts de la Réforme française*, Paris, 1934; A. MITCHELL HUNTER, 'The Education of Calvin' in the *Evangelical Quarterly*, 1937, pp. 20 ff.

[2] Cf. A. LEFRANC, *La Jeunesse de Calvin*, pp. 34 and 186 ff.; E. DOUMERGUE, *Jean Calvin*, vol. I, pp. 13 ff. and 536.

daughters, Marie and another whose name is unknown. François died at an early age. Charles became a priest, and died excommunicated in 1537. Marie and Antoine followed the reformer to Geneva, where Antoine assisted his brother in his literary work, but achieved celebrity chiefly by his conjugal misfortunes.[3]

Calvin very soon lost his mother, about whom we know almost nothing except that she had a great reputation for piety. As for the father, he had, it seems, great ambitions for his sons and especially for Jean. His good relations with the bishop and the Chapter enabled him to obtain for Jean a chaplaincy to the altar of La Gésine in Noyon Cathedral. Jean Calvin was then twelve years of age: this benefice must have enabled him to pursue his studies without drawing too heavily on his father's revenues: he resigned it, for unknown reasons, in 1529, but resumed it in 1531. In 1527 he became the occupant of another benefice; this time it was the curacy of St-Martin-de-Martheville, which he afterwards exchanged for that of Pont l'Evêque, the place from which the Cauvin family had come.[4] In procuring these benefices for his son, Gérard Cauvin was only doing what was customary at the time. He may have had to commit himself to guide Jean towards the study of theology, which however would not be surprising on the part of an episcopal official. Some have tried to explain Calvin's delay in pronouncing himself openly in favour of the Reform by the fact that he would then have put himself under an obligation to renounce indispensable revenues; but there is nothing to justify that hypothesis.

After having followed the courses of the college of the Capettes in his native town, Calvin was sent to Paris to continue his studies. This was in 1523, when he was just fourteen years old. At first he lodged with one of his uncles, an ironsmith, at whose house he received lessons from a master who must have made a poor impression on his pupil, for in after life Calvin described him simply as incompetent.[5] But very soon Calvin obtained entry to

---

[3] E. DOUMERGUE, op. cit., vol. 1, pp. 22 ff.; W. WALKER, *John Calvin*, pp. 30 ff.

[4] DOUMERGUE, op. cit., vol. 1, pp. 37 ff.; p. 13; BREEN, *John Calvin*, p 13 ff.; LEFRANC, op. cit., pp. 193 ff.; K. MULLER, 'Calvins Bekehrung,' pp. 220 ff.

[5] LEFRANC, op. cit., p. 59; *Opp.*, 13, 525.

the Collège de la Marche, where he found himself under the direction of the famous Mathurin Cordier, one of the founders of modern pedagogy. Although the young Calvin had the benefit of Cordier's lessons in Latin only for a little while, it was the beginning of an enduring friendship, which Calvin was to express many years later by the appeal which he addressed to his old master before entrusting him with the organization of education at Geneva and Lausanne.[6]

From the Collège de la Marche, Calvin went on, for reasons we do not know, to the Collège de Montaigu, which was regarded by everyone as one of the strongholds of orthodoxy, and by its students with terror. At the end of the fifteenth century Standonck had introduced at Montaigu something of the spirit and method of the Brothers of the Common Life. His successor had been the celebrated Béda, or Bédier, who in the Faculty of Theology was leading the struggle against the Lutheran 'heresies' and against the methods of the humanists. Several years before Calvin was enrolled at Montaigu, Béda had been replaced by a certain Tempête, the man who was nicknamed '*horrida tempestas*' and was the terror of the students. Béda, however, continued to supervise the teaching. The sarcasms of Rabelais and Erasmus are hardly to be relied upon for a correct impression of what that teaching was like.[7] In spite of the iron discipline that ruled at Montaigu and in spite of the retrograde mentality of most of the masters who taught there, a little of the spirit of Standonck still survived in the school. Calvin does not seem to have suffered seriously there during his five years of residence; he was even able to enjoy some freedom. Among his masters there happened to be a Spaniard, Antonio Coronel, who must have made a certain impression upon the young Picard by his teaching of

[6] DOUMERGUE, op. cit., vol. 1, p. 60. Upon Cordier, cf. the work of J. LE COULTRE, *Mathurin Cordier et les origines de la pédagogie protestante*, Neuchâtel, 1926.

[7] ERASMUS, *Colloqia: Ichtyophagia*, edn Le Clerc, vol. 1, p. 806; RABELAIS, *Gargantua et Pantagruel*, liv. 1, chap. 37 and liv. IV, chap. 21. Upon the history and organization of Montaigu see M. GODET, 'Le Collège de Montaigu' (*Revue des Etudes Rabelaisiennes*, 1909, pp. 296 ff.) and the same author's 'La Congrégation de Montaigu', Paris, 1912, and particularly pp. 59-68; A. RENAUDET, *Préréforme et humanisme à Paris*, Paris, 1916, pp. 172 ff., 267 ff., 309 ff.

philosophy;[8] and a little after Calvin's arrival, the celebrated nominalist theologian John Mair, or Major, resumed his position on the teaching staff of Montaigu; it is likely that he, too, exercised a deeper influence upon the future reformer than is generally admitted. Since John Mair published, in 1529, a commentary upon the four Gospels in which he sought to defend the Roman teaching against the innovations of Wycliffe, Huss and Luther, it is not improbable that he had previously made this the subject of one of his courses which Calvin may have attended, and which would have made him aware of certain Lutheran theses from that time.[9] In any case, John Mair gave him direct knowledge of the *Sentences* of Peter Lombard and of the Occamist interpretation that he put upon them. It was at Montaigu, lastly, that he seems to have made contact with the Fathers of the Church and notably with St Augustine, which would explain the precocious knowledge of them that he showed in his earliest publications.

In the intervals of his scholarly occupations Calvin was able to carry on friendly relations with young men of his age such as the Montmors or his cousin Olivétan, who had already been won over to the Reform and showed a lively interest in the humanism then in fashion. Even more important was the friendship of advanced men such as Fourcy de Cambrai, who had some influence in the Faculty of Theology. But de Cambrai's influence upon Calvin was far less considerable than that of King Francis I's chief physician, Guillaume Cop, of Basle, one of whose three sons, Nicolas, pronounced the famous rectoral discourse of 1533. Cop was himself a friend of the best-known humanists; he was frequenting Guillaume Budé and was in correspondence with Erasmus on the subject of the institution of Royal Readers.[10] In

[8] Cf. IMBART DE LA TOUR, *Calvin et l'Institution chrétienne*, p. 10. The mention of this 'Spaniard' in the *Vita Calvini* of TH. DE BÈZE (*Opp.*, 21, 121) can come only from Calvin himself. Coronel's teaching was worth more than one would be led to suppose by the contemptuous remarks in PRANTL, *Geschichte der Logik im Abendland*, vol. IV, pp. 252 ff.

[9] Upon the tendencies of J. Mair, see RENAUDET, op. cit., pp. 366 ff., 463 ff., 470, 593, 658; see also *Dictionary of National Biography*, art. 'Major (John).'

[10] On the subject of these associates of the young Calvin, refer to the bibliographical indications in BREEN, op. cit., pp. 23 ff.

these surroundings, open to all the new ideas, Calvin undoubtedly learned to know the writings of Lefèvre d'Etaples, of Luther and of Melanchthon; at the very least he must often have heard them spoken of. For all that, it must not be imagined that he had at this time the smallest inclination to range himself with the partisans of Lefèvre's reformism, still less to embrace Lutheran ideas. He tells us himself that he was 'obstinately addicted to the superstitions of the Papacy', which implies that he had resisted efforts to turn him away from them.[11] But on the other hand, he says that the polemics of Luther against Zwingli and Oecolampadius concerning the Holy Communion had dissuaded him from reading the latter, perhaps at a period prior to the Colloquy of Marburg (1529).[12] Be that as it may, it seems certain—and it is the contrary that would surprise us—that he had the opportunity of reading certain 'Lutheran' writings, but did not therefore remain any the less attached to the Roman Church. Even up to 1530 there is not the slightest indication that he had gone beyond the humanist positions or shown any susceptibility to the arguments of advocates of a break with Rome. And even after that date, there are no real grounds for supposing that there was any relationship between Calvin and the Reform movement until 1533 at the earliest.[13] The influence that Olivétan, the future translator of the Bible, may have had upon Calvin's religious life left no immediate traces. In 1528 Olivétan had fled to Strasbourg; he could not, therefore, have affected Calvin's later development. That he may indeed have tried to do so, I think we can find some indication in the fact that Calvin, shortly after his conversion, wrote a preface for Olivétan's French Bible in order to recommend it to the public.

Towards the end of his sojourn in Paris, we must imagine Calvin to have been very like one of those Catholic humanists who were then gravitating around Guillaume Budé, for whom the re-establishment of good literature was infinitely

---

[11] *Opp.*, 31, 22 (Preface to *Commentary on the Psalms*).

[12] *Opp.*, 9, 51. The interpretation of the text is controversial.

[13] For the opposite opinion, see DOUMERGUE, op. cit., vol. I, pp. 155 ff., 181 ff.; PANNIER, *Evolution religieuse de Calvin*; K. HOLL, *Johannes Calvin, Gesammelte Aufsätze*, vol. III, p. 255, n. 1. Most recent authors have abandoned Doumergue's point of view; cf. below, pp. 37 ff.

more important than any attack upon Roman dogmatics. That tendency became even more marked in the following years.

Calvin's father had at first intended him to enter the priesthood, and he was studying theology with that end in view. But in 1528 or 1529 the young man gave up his first ambition.[14] He had just gained the degree of Master of Arts, which terminated the course of his philosophical studies. Of this very important moment in his intellectual formation we have his own account. In his *Commentary on the Psalms*, he writes:

> Ever since I was a child, my father had intended me for theology; but thereafter inasmuch as he considered that the study of the law commonly enriched those who followed it, this expectation made him incontinently change his mind. That is the reason why I was withdrawn from the study of philosophy and put to the study of the law, to which I strove to devote myself faithfully in obedience to my father. God, however, in his hidden providence, at last made me turn in another direction.[15]

That the dream of finding a remunerative and brilliant position for his son was among the reasons for Gérard Cauvin's decision, we are led to believe by all that we know of his character. But it was not the only reason. He caused his son to abandon theology because he was no longer assured of the support of the Church dignitaries of Noyon, upon whom he had been counting to provide Jean with a first-class appointment. In consequence of his management of the winding-up of an estate, of which he had not been able to render an acceptable account, Gérard was now embroiled with the Chapter of Noyon.[16] He thought therefore that he was obliged to seek a career for his son elsewhere, and, relying upon the celebrity of Pierre de l'Estoile, he sent Jean to pursue legal studies at Orleans.

The Faculty of Law at Orleans was then justly famous; it

[14] We remain uncertain of the precise date of Calvin's change of professional orientation. The first document in which he appears as Master of Arts is of 30th April 1529. Cf. LEFRANC, op. cit., p. 197.

[15] *Opp.*, 31, 32.

[16] LEFRANC, op. cit., p. 17; WALKER, op. cit., p. 51.

numbered no less than eight professors, among them this Pierre de l'Estoile, who with good reason was regarded as the best French jurist of the time.[17] By leaving the College of Montaigu, Calvin escaped not only from the inhuman discipline of that establishment but also from the finicky orthodoxy that prevailed there. It is true that Pierre de l'Estoile and his colleagues were also sincerely attached to the traditional faith, and their conservatism was well known: but with this they retained some degree of open-mindedness towards the efforts of the humanists, with a readiness to appropriate their results and make use of them in their juridical science. Furthermore, in the atmosphere of the Orleans University there was no possible question of students being subjected to the continual bullying that was customary in some of the Parisian colleges. Pierre de l'Estoile made a profound impression upon Calvin: he was a man of integrity, very religious and scrupulous. It was after the death of his wife that he had entered into orders. But what Calvin appreciated in him above all was his intelligence: in Calvin's own words, he had been struck by 'his penetrative mind, his skill, his experience in law, of which he is the unchallenged prince of our epoch'.[18] And it is true that Pierre de l'Estoile was the only French jurist that they dared oppose to Alciat, the famous Italian Romanist whose acquaintance Calvin was to make soon afterwards at Bourges, but with whom he had no continued relations. In Calvin's opinion the glory of Alciat could never obscure the less brilliant but more solid merits of his first master in law: his own juridical conceptions remained always clearly dependent upon the teaching of Pierre de l'Estoile, in spite of the latter's hostile attitude towards the Protestants.

But though Calvin applied himself strenuously to his legal studies, at Orleans he found the means to pursue other studies too, and these nearer to the humanist ideal. At the cost of arduous toil, which was the cause of an incurable disease and may have contributed to his premature death, the young student acquired

[17] J. BOUSSARD, 'L'Université d'Orléans au XVIe siècle,' (*Humanisme et Renaissance*, vol. V, 1938, pp. 223 ff.); K. MULLER, ' Calvins Bekehrung ', p. 201; G. BEYERHAUS, *Studien zur Staatsanschauung Calvins*, pp. 27 ff.

[18] *Opp.*, 9, 785 (Preface to the *Antapology* of Nicolas DUCHEMIN).

the rudiments of Greek within a few months. His teacher, the German Melchior Wolmar of Rothweil, had gained his Hellenic learning in Paris and had lately published some notes on Homer. A convinced Lutheran, he made himself conspicuous by his religious propaganda, no less at Orleans than later at Bourges, where he established himself in 1529 at the request of Marguerite of Navarre.[18b] All that we know of this personage makes it seem unlikely that he made no efforts to convert Calvin to his views; it is all the more remarkable that Calvin has not left us a single line of allusion to Wolmar's having had any influence at all in the sphere of religion. Nor has any other document been found to fill this lacuna; so it must be admitted that there are no grounds for the hypotheses that have been put forward to show that the conversion of Calvin dated back to his stay at Orleans and was principally due to Wolmar.[19] On the contrary, we shall see that Calvin did not noticeably modify his religious attitude in any way during that period. On the other hand, he yielded more and more to the humanist ideal. And the majority of the friendships he then contracted could only have attached him still more to the humanist cause. Such, for instance, were his friendships with François Daniel (through whom he perhaps came to know Rabelais[20]), with François de Connan, and above all with Nicolas Duchemin; all three were enthusiastic humanists who yet remained faithful to the ancient Church. Among them Calvin found the same preoccupations and the same atmosphere as with Cop or Budé.[21]

In the course of the year 1529, he left Orleans to present him-

[18b] Cf. D. J. DE GROOT, 'Melchior Wolmar' in the *Bulletin de la Soc. de l'Hist· du Prot. français*, vol. 83, 1934, pp. 416 ff.

[19] Cf. LEFRANC, op. cit., p. 39. If Calvin had been under the religious influence of Wolmar, he could not have failed to allude to it in the dedication to Wolmar of his *Commentary* on the *2nd Epistle to the Corinthians* (*Opp.*, 12, 364); but he speaks only of lessons in Greek he had had from him. It was FLORIMOND DE RAEMOND, a Catholic historian contemporary with Calvin, who first attributed a decisive part in Calvin's conversion to Wolmar, in *l'Histoire de la naissance, progrès et décadence de l'hérésie de ce siècle*, Rouen, 1623, p. 882.

[20] Cf. H. CLOUZOT, 'Les Amitiés de Rabelais en Orléans' in the *Revue des Etudes Rabelaisiennes*, vol. III, p. 174 ff.

[21] LEFRANC, op. cit., pp. 74 ff.; DOUMERGUE, op. cit., pp. 133 ff.

self at Bourges, where the famous Alciat had just established himself as professor of Roman law. Calvin had doubtless heard much about him, and wanted to experience and verify for himself all the wonders he had been told. Besides, Roman law had been the speciality of Bourges ever since Louis XI had founded the University in 1463 in order to encourage the study of the *Digests* and the *Authentica*, which he regarded, not without reason, as juridical foundations capable of supporting the theory of absolute monarchy. Marguerite of Navarre, who had become the Duchess of Berry, interested herself personally in this centre of studies, which had hardly justified its promise thus far. We have noted that it was she who invited the Hellenist Wolmar to Bourges: and to endow this University with still greater lustre she brought thither the Milanese Alciat, who then passed for one of the best jurists in Europe and was also an accomplished humanist.[22] Alciat was to remain five years at Bourges, where he regarded himself somewhat as an ambassador of Italian humanism to the barbarians, allowing no opportunity to pass without loftily proclaiming his superiority and that of his nation as a whole in the things of the spirit. However, in order to circumvent the jealousy of the French colleagues, still faithful to the methods of the old glossators, he began by making use of their rather heavy and cumbersome exegesis and of their peculiar Latin, which it would have given Cicero some trouble to understand. This was not at all what was expected of him by the numerous students assembled from almost everywhere to listen to him. They protested with considerable vivacity.[23] This was just the pretext Alciat had been waiting for in order to justify his display of the humanist method—indubitably more literary and elegant, though he practised it with a kind of superficial breeziness which we now find slightly comic, especially if we compare it with the perhaps less brilliant, but infinitely sounder and more conscientious, methods of the great French jurists of the end of that

[22] See the bibliographical indications given by BEYERHAUS, op. cit., pp. 31 ff., and BREEN, op. cit., p. 45.

[23] Cf. LECOULTRE, 'Une Grève d'etudiants au XVIème siècle' (*Mélanges*, pp. 69 f). There is, however, nothing to show that Calvin played any part at all in this incident.

century. Calvin was deeply displeased by Alciat's pompous discourses. This first direct contact with an authentic representative of Italian humanism nevertheless left its mark on the future reformer. It seems to have awakened his interest, as Pierre de l'Estoile had never succeeded in doing, in a number of juridical problems, and it convinced him of the value of an impeccable and elegant style. It was partly to this impulse from Alciat that Calvin was indebted for his precise and harmonious Latin. But the aversion he felt for the man remained; it became intensified by the criticisms and raillery that Alciat permitted himself when referring to his rival at Orleans. And when an intimate friend of Alciat, Aurèle Albucius, made use of these criticisms in a pamphlet aimed against l'Estoile, Calvin's friend Nicolas Duchemin undertook to refute them in his *Antapologia*. Calvin associated himself with this defence by writing a preface to it; he also agreed to see to the printing of it when he went to Paris in 1531.[24]

Calvin had been obliged to leave Bourges rather suddenly, upon learning that his father had fallen seriously ill. He went in haste to Noyon, where he was present at the last moments of Gérard Cauvin, and at the painful arguments that took place with the Chapter in an effort to obtain remission of the excommunication which had weighed upon his father for more than two years. Although it was his brother Charles who led the discussion, it is by no means impossible that this dispute, further embittered by the excommunication of Charles himself, helped to detach Calvin from the Roman communion, or at least prepared his feelings for the ultimate rupture.[25]

The death of his father made Calvin master of his own destiny, free to pursue what career he chose. And as soon as he had disposed of the affairs left in suspense at Noyon he went to Paris, meaning to devote himself to literary studies, though without completely giving up the law. In Paris, Francis I had just

[24] See the analysis, with examples of this work, by BREEN, op. cit., pp. 52–60—to be corrected by J. BOHATEC, *Budé und Calvin*, Graz, 1950, p. 439, n. 6.

[25] LEFRANĆ, op. cit., pp. 17 ff.; the author probably gives too much weight to the incidents at Noyon; nevertheless it would be wrong to leave them wholly out of account.

founded, in imitation of the trilingual college that had been created at Louvain in 1518, a college of a new type, entirely independent of the ancient University, one in which the teaching was entrusted to Royal Readers. Several attempts had been made by Budé to attract Erasmus to Paris by offering him the direction of this new establishment. But Erasmus declined, pleading his health and his age. The new institution, after some initial difficulties, showed itself none the less viable; indeed, it was destined to win enduring glory, for out of it the great Collège de France was born.[26] It is easy to understand how Calvin was fascinated by this new creation. For it was conceived in the purest spirit of humanism, complete freedom being allowed to its professors in their research and teaching, and to the students in their choice of courses. Calvin, having already acquired some Greek under Wolmar, decided to pursue Hellenic studies by following the courses of Pierre Danès, who was one of the most illustrious of the new Royal Readers.[27] He also attached himself to the scholar in Hebrew, Vatable, and it was then perhaps that he began to learn the elements of Hebrew; though the traditional view is that his real learning in that language was gained at Basle and at Strasbourg.[28] In any case, Hebrew was then in fashion; it was also disesteemed at the Sorbonne, which gave it an additional attraction in humanist circles.

During the winter of 1531-2 Calvin was also working at the completion of his first book, a commentary upon Senaca's *De Clementia* which was published on April 4th, 1532, and was soon to place its author among the humanists of renown. As soon as he had finished this labour, he seems to have returned to Orleans for some months, in order to crown his studies in law with a degree.[29]

[26] Cf. A. LEFRANC, *Histoire du Collège de France*, Paris, 1893.

[27] Ibid., p. 172.

[28] A. BAUMGARTNER, *Calvin hébraïsant et interprète de l'Ancien Testament*, Paris, 1889, pp. 8, 14 ff., and the review of this work by VUILLEUMIER, *Revue de Théologie et Philosophie*, Lausanne, 1889.

[29] The chronology of Calvin's various sojourns in Orleans is somewhat confused. In May and June 1533 he was performing the functions of annual substitute for the Picard national procurator; Cf. DOINEL, 'Jean Calvin à Orléans', *Bulletin de la Société de l'Histoire du Protestantisme français*, vol. XXVI,

II. THE COMMENTARY ON THE 'DE CLEMENTIA' of SENECA: CALVIN'S HUMANISM

Biographers of Calvin usually devote no more than a few pages or even only a few lines to this first work of his. At the most, they examine it for indications of his future religious orientation.[30] But the *Commentary on the De Clementia* is much more than the 'very good work of a serious student'.[31] It is a work that deserves to arrest attention by its erudition and style, and, no less, by the author's employment of the method which had been perfected by Valla, Erasmus, Budé and others. It will repay us to spend a little time upon it.

Readers have often wondered why Calvin chose precisely this treatise of Seneca, and have had no difficulty in arguing that he did so in the hope of bringing Francis I to consider a policy of flexibility and clemency towards the Protestants, much as Seneca wrote this same treatise in order to persuade Nero to be more benevolent to his subjects.[32] It is possible, of course, that Calvin did feel a concern of this kind while writing his commentary; but there is nothing to confirm that hypothesis. There is not a line that is clearly interpretable in that sense, unless one makes Calvin say what he did not.[33] That he had been opposed to

---

1877, p. 174. The second stay at Orleans may have been prolonged to a year: WALKER, op. cit., p. 70; also LANG, *Johannes Calvin*, p. 14, and PANNIER, *Evolution religieuse*, p. 31.

[30] Exception must be made, however, for the remarkable article by H. LECOULTRE, 'Calvin après son commentaire sur le De Clementia de Sénèque' in the *Revue de Théol. et Philos.*, Lausanne, 1891, pp. 51-77; and the work of BREEN, which has two substantial chapters on this subject, op. cit., vol. I, pp. 67-99. DOUMERGUE's chapter., op. cit., vol. I, pp. 210 ff., contains nothing new: but account must be taken of the remarks of BEYERHAUS, op. cit., pp. 1-25, concerned mainly with the political content of the *Commentary*. Recently A. M. HUGO has devoted an interesting thesis to the *Commentary*. One can commend especially the pages upon Calvin's relations with Stoicism.

[31] PANNIER, *Evolution religieuse*, p. 23.

[32] Cf. finally, ibid., p. 20. For comparison, DOUMERGUE, op. cit., pp. 213 ff.

[33] LECOULTRE, op. cit., p. 72; WALKER, op. cit., p. 69; M. MANN, op. cit., p. 163.

violent persecution even before he rallied to the Reform, his humanist convictions are a sufficient guarantee. But again, nothing of this appears in the erudite notes he adds to Seneca's text.

The external motive for this *Commentary* seems to have been a much simpler one. Erasmus had published the works of Seneca twice over: his second edition came out in 1529; but Erasmus was only partly satisfied with it, and invited the readers to do better. And this appeal—perhaps only half sincere—must have been a challenge to Calvin's ambition, for he asserts in his preface that he has found all kinds of things in Seneca which Erasmus has not noticed.[34] Such self-confidence on the part of a young man of twenty-three looked highly presumptuous, and incurred rebukes from Erasmus's admirers.

But the question is, more generally, why Calvin should have chosen to write about Seneca. Here too, the answer presents no difficulty. It is enough to recall the fact that the Stoic authors, and Seneca in particular, were then enjoying a vogue which we may now find difficult to understand.[35] The Stoic ethic was regarded by Calvin's contemporaries and for a long while afterwards as a superior teaching, accessible only to select souls, and therefore all the more precious. On the other hand, the Italian Renaissance had been very willing to extol individual virtue and happiness in their most terrestrial, even their most earthy, sense. Whatever real elevation of thought there may have been in some of the Italian Epicureans, there were others who did not scruple, either in their behaviour or in their writings, to lend colour to the evil reputation—incidentally quite unjustified—that attached to the name of Epicurus. Against such Epicurean hedonistic tendencies Christian humanists thought they had found an effectual counterpoise in Stoicism. But the remedy was not without its own danger: by placing the centre of the moral life in the consciousness it tended to efface the opposition between the natural and the supernatural. On the other hand, the importance that the Stoics attributed to man as man brought

[34] *Opp.*, 5, 6.

[35] Upon Stoicism during the Reformation the best study is still that of L. ZANTA, *La Renaissance du stoicisme au XVIe siècle*, Paris, 1914, to which we may add BREEN, op. cit., pp. 67 ff.

them into line with the essential aspirations of the humanists. To ascribe such significance to the human being was also to imply a belief in the underlying unity of humanity and in equality between all men; and here again, Stoicism must have found a sympathetic response among humanists, the most notorious of whom were demanding the abolition of all national and religious divisions. Lastly, there was the Stoic love for truth and scientific research, in which humanism recognized characteristics of its own. In religious matters the points of contact are no less numerous, whatever may then have been thought about them. Against the half-ceremonial, half-magical religions of antiquity, the Stoics had set up a religious ideal which many humanists had no difficulty in admitting in their turn, without even feeling obliged to renounce their Christianity. They knew that the Stoic ethic had made a great impression upon some Fathers of the Church in ancient times, and in later days Seneca, in whom they found the essentials of Stoicism expressed in the most accessible manner, had always been one of the authors most readily quoted by the theologians and moralists. The humanists were only following, albeit accentuating, a much earlier tendency.

We have seen how much interest Erasmus took in Seneca, yet Calvin thought his eulogies far too cool. Zwingli, incidentally, had taken the writer of the *De Clementia* to heart as one of his favourite authors, and remained attached to him even after joining the camp of the Reformers; in fact, Zwingli's *Sermon on Providence* sometimes reads almost like a commentary on chosen passages from Seneca. The more he associated himself with the humanists, the more Calvin must have been inclined to share this enthusiasm. He takes care, however, in his *Commentary*, to underline resemblances between Stoicism and Christianity. He is sure that Stoics and Christians are at one in affirming the existence of a supernatural providence which excludes chance and over-rules princes;[36] and it is quite possible that the importance he afterwards attributed to this notion of providence was at least partly of Stoic origin. With regard to the submission of governments to providence, which Seneca's treatise invited Calvin to insist upon, he says in the *Commentary* that 'this is also the teaching

[36] *Opp.* 5, 18.

of our religion, that there is no power but of God and that everything is ordered by him, according to Romans 13.'[37] On the
other hand, Calvin's fundamentally aristocratic character appears
at every opportunity; he shows himself to be hostile to the crowd,
which he thinks is naturally seditious, destitute of reason or discernment.[38] The frequent allusions to politics in the *De Clementia*
provide him with opportunities to present himself as a champion
of royal power—provided it be legitimate and moderated by
moral considerations—and at the same time as an enemy of
tyranny. We do not know whether he had as yet read Machia-
velli's *The Prince*, but it is highly probable, since Calvin's *Commentary* runs counter to the argument of the Italian theorist in
stating the case against the tyrant, 'who governs against the will
of his subjects, or exercises power in an immoderate manner'.[39]
The former pupil of Pierre de l'Estoile reveals himself in his
defence of the traditional thesis that the king is he who accedes
to power by legitimate means and who serves the public good,
while the tyrant is either a usurper or an enemy of the public
good. Calvin employs to his own purpose the definitions of
public power accepted in Roman law; in particular, he follows
the Roman jurists in admitting that the sovereign is above the
civil law, that he is *a legibus solutus* because he is himself the living
law, *lex animata*.[40] But he limits the domain to which this is
applicable by interposing, as Seneca and the Stoics did, the
notions of justice and equity.[41]

The humanist with a Stoical tinge appears also, as one would
expect, in the way he insists upon the 'natural law'.[42] It is here,
when he is speaking of legitimate sovereigns, that Calvin says
they are to be recognized also by the fact that they bequeath a
hereditary kingship to their family, conforming in that respect
to the laws of nature.[43] Here the heredity of the crown is no
more than an aspect of Calvin's traditionalism; what is, however,

[37] *Opp.*, ibid. [38] *Opp.*, 5, 16.
[39] *Opp.*, 5, 90; BEYERHAUS, op. cit., pp. 8 ff.
[40] *Opp.*, 5, 23, 53, 67; BEYERHAUS, op. cit., pp. 12 ff., 24.
[41] Ibid., pp. 6 ff., 16. [42] Ibid., p. 5.
[43] 'Tandem quum naturae legibus cedendum est, regnum relinquunt
familiae suae haereditarium.' *Opp.*, 5, 89.

clearly humanist is his insistence upon the natural law to which all must conform.

Lastly, Calvin's humanism is evident in his method properly so called. In his *Commentary* he shows a remarkable knowledge of classical antiquity and a hardly less accurate knowledge of some of the Fathers of the Church.[44] St Augustine, whose *City of God* he had lately read, is mentioned fifteen times. But Calvin had also read Erasmus, Budé, Laurent Valla and a number of other French and Italian humanists, of whom he did not spare his praises.[45] In reading his *Commentary* one can hardly refrain from comparisons with the method used in the *Paraphrases* of Erasmus, and above all in the *Annotations* of Guillaume Budé on the Pandects. Like Budé, Calvin begins with a rather long philological explanation, he appeals to grammar and logic, he points out the figures of rhetoric, draws upon his knowledge of antiquity to collect parallel quotations from other ancient writers and from Seneca himself.[46] This might seem to be merely a commonplace observation, seeing that the procedure of the humanists in general was not very different. But Calvin further refined this method and, after his conversion, applied it to the Scriptures themselves. True, Valla had already employed the humanist method in his *Annotations upon the New Testament* and Erasmus was following him along that path: but it was Calvin who first made it the very basis of his exegesis and in doing so founded the modern science of exegetics.

It would of course be a misconstruction to present Calvin, even at the epoch of the *Commentary on the De Clementia*, as a blind admirer of Stoicism. On the contrary he gives proof, even in this first publication, of an independence of thought which is surely surprising in so young an author, and gives us a glimpse of the way he can make use of sources at his disposal. Just as, when writing the *Institutes* three years later, he knew how to draw freely upon his forerunners without assimilating any of their particular conceptions, here also he knew how to keep his

---

[44] See the list of authors cited in LECOULTRE, op. cit., p. 76.

[45] 'Erasmus literarum alterum decus ac primae deliciae.' *Opp.*, 5, 6. 'Guilelmus Budaeus primum rei literariae decus et columen, cujus beneficio palmam eruditionis hodie sibi vendicat nostra Gallia.' Ibid., 54.

[46] Cf. DELARUELLE, *G. Budé*, Paris, 1907, pp. 103 ff.

distance. His principal complaint against the Stoics, and more generally against the philosophers, is of their inability to come to reliable conclusions and their indifference towards the real needs of man. 'We know,' he says, 'that nature is so made that we are more affected by the prospect of utility or pleasure than by these paradoxes of the Stoics, which are so remote from general feeling.'[47] The famous apathy of the wise, so much praised by the Stoics, is only a lure.

> We should be fully persuaded that pity also is a virtue; that a man cannot be good if he is not merciful, whatever may be argued by these sages, idle in their ignorance; I know not whether they be wise, as Pliny would say, in any case these are not men. It is of the nature of man to feel pain, to be moved by it, to resist it nevertheless, and to accept consolations, but never to have no need of them.[48]

Similarly, Calvin rejects the Stoics' indifference to what 'other people will say'; he does so in the name of 'our religion', and of the opinion of St Augustine.[49] But the few allusions to Christian principles that we find here and there must not mislead us. Calvin certainly takes up Christian positions as his own; but among all the innumerable quotations there are only three from the Bible, and as W. Walker says, 'it would be embarrassing to have to prove, from this *Commentary*, that the author had any special interest in religious problems.'[50] All in all, this Calvin appears far more like a humanist, intent upon giving a faithful rendering of ancient thought and sincerely attached to it, than like a Christian concerned to emphasize the originality and transcendent value of his religion.

If he had retained no more of his humanism than this exegetical method when he went over to the Reformers, we might well endorse the opinion that there was a gulf between the Calvin before and the Calvin after conversion. His humanism, in that

---

[47] *Opp.*, 5, 39.   [48] *Opp.*, 5, 154.
[49] *Opp.*, 5, 112; Cf. ZANTA, op. cit., pp. 62-4; IMBART DE LA TOUR, op. cit., pp. 15-18.
[50] WALKER, op. cit., p. 69.

case, would have been but a passing episode in his life. But in reality things present themselves rather differently. We must not forget that Calvin's conversion to the Reform took place relatively late, during his twenty-fourth year; and, considering his intellectual precocity, we can be sure that his mentality had by then assumed its definitive character. Just as Luther never managed completely to efface the intellectual imprint of Occam, so Calvin remained always more or less the humanist he had been in 1532. As R. Seeberg says of him,

> Humanist culture was not only, in Calvin's eyes, a torch bearing the light of the Gospel, but in spite of his strict Biblicism, his humanist mind was in some degree harmonized with the Gospel. The mental formation and the religion, the culture and the morality, went hand in hand. Calvin really arrived at that union to which Melanchthon aspired but never attained except in a rather external manner.[51]

One could cite numerous instances of this persistence of humanist tendencies. Whatever has since been said of it, Calvin retained the notion of natural law that he had acquired from the Stoics, and did no more than accommodate it to Christian principles.[52] Though he defended himself, with good reason, against those who accused him of having brought the Stoic notion of fate into his doctrine of predestination,[53] we have been

[51] R. SEEBERG, *Lehrbuch des Dogmengeschichte*, 2nd edn, 1920, vol. IV, 2, p. 558. The author thinks that Calvin's humanism was the cause of his success with the intellectual elite.

[52] J. BOHATEC, *Calvin und das Recht*, Feudingen 1934, pp. 1-93. The same author, in his magistral work *Budé und Calvin*, has reopened the whole problem of the humanist elements in Calvin's thought and work. In his eagerness to uphold the originality of Calvin at all cost, F. J. M. POTGIETER, *De Verhouding tussen die teologie en die filosofie by Calvyn*, Amsterdam, 1939, comes very near denying that humanism influenced Calvin at all. Per contra, J. BOISSET, *Sagesse et Sainteté dans la pensée de Jean Calvin*, pp. 225 ff., assumes the defence of Calvin's humanism, but of a humanism so strongly coloured by Platonism as to have tinged his theological teaching too, which seems at least contestable. The limits of the Platonic influence are well drawn by J. BOHATEC, op. cit., p. 417.

[53] *Inst.*, I, 16, 8.

able to discover a whole series of passages, even in the *Institutes*, which are manifestly inspired by texts of Erasmus.[54] His conversion no doubt lowered the ancient authors in the hierarchy of values he admired, to the advantage of the Scripture; but it did not cause him to condemn them without reservation. In his commentaries and dogmatic treatises he continued to quote them abundantly, and with a mastery that betokens long familiarity.[55] As early as the *Institutes* of 1539, he thought it useful to make his position clear upon this point:

> When we read Demosthenes or Cicero, Plato or Aristotle or some others of their kind, I confess indeed that they wonderfully attract, delight and move us, even ravish our minds. But if from them we turn to the reading of the Holy Scriptures, whether we will or no they so pierce us to the heart and fix themselves within us that all the power of the rhetoricians and philosophers, compared with them, seems no more than smoke.[56]

No comparison is possible, Calvin means to say, between the profane authors and the Scriptures in point of efficacy, yet these great writers nevertheless ravish our minds. He even goes so far as to credit them with 'an admirable light of truth'.[57] With advancing age, this influence from antiquity may have become attenuated, but it never disappeared. We can subscribe to the considered opinion of J. Neuerhaus that 'Calvin, while absorbing all the elements of humanist culture, endeavoured to use them to the service of his faith, and avoided the dangers which might have arisen from them. The Hellenic spirit faded little by little before the Christian spirit; nevertheless, Calvin preserved to the end the reputation of an excellent humanist.'[58]

The attacks that the reformer launched against the humanists must not lead us into error upon this point. In his *Treatise upon*

[54] M. SCHULZE, *Calvins Jenseitschristentum*, Görlitz, 1902; cf. especially p. 55.

[55] See references to quotations contained in the commentaries of Calvin, in L. GOUMAZ, *La Doctrine du salut*, Nyon, 1917, p. 94.

[56] *Inst.*, I, 8, 1.

[57] *Inst.*, II, 2, 15; H. STROHL, *Bucer, humaniste chrétien*, Paris, 1939, pp. 28 ff.

[58] J. NEUENHAUS, ' Calvin als Humanist,' *Calvinstudien*, Leipzig, 1909, p. 2.

Scandals in particular, he reproaches some humanists for pride and vanity, and others for being disciples of Lucian and Epicurus, 'who ever proudly despised the Gospel' or who 'in their diabolical presumption profaned the holy and sacred promise of eternal life'; and yet others again[59] who 'wish to be considered very wise' but 'pretend they dare not accept the Gospel because they see none of the agreement that they would desire among those who make profession of it'.[60] These complaints are aimed at the personal attitudes of certain humanists, not at humanism as such.

Even if he had to deny some of its essential doctrines he at least retained, besides scientific method, that concern for external form which distinguishes him among all the reformers. In all his works he remains respectful to well-conducted reasoning, to chaste style and good taste. We know that Calvin was one of the best Latinists of the sixteenth century;[61] and when he wrote French, too, his language was of a range and elegance comparable to Pascal's or Bossuet's.[62] In refinement of taste he comes very near to Erasmus.[63]

Negatively too, he remained subject to a good many humanist reactions. His attitude to tradition, for instance, was largely

[59] But were these humanists, as BOHATEC believes in 'Calvin et l'humanisme' in the *Revue Historique*, 1938, p. 212? The same author re-states the question in full, in his *Budé und Calvin*, a good deal of which is devoted to the humanist adversaries of Calvin (pp. 121-240).

[60] *Opp.*, 8, 20, 42, 57.

[61] It is hard to understand the reservations of P. VAN TIEGHEM in 'La Littérature latine de la Renaissance', *Bibliothèque d'Humanisme et Renaissance*, vol. IV, p. 379.

[62] Cf. A. BOSSERT, *Calvin*, pp. 211 ff.; A. LEFRANC, *Grands écrivains français de la Renaissance*, pp. 350 ff.; and the evidences collected by PANNIER, *Calvin écrivain*, Paris, 1930, to which one might add this curious remark by DE RAEMOND in his *Histoire de la naissance*: 'No man who preceded him exceeded him for good writing, and few have since come near the beauty and facility of language that he had . . .' (Quoted by BUNGENER, *Calvin*, p. 23.)

[63] BREEN, op. cit., p. 150, even suggests that in his controversy with Heshusius over the Eucharist, Calvin allowed himself to be guided as much by considerations of good taste as by logical argument. Whether true or not, this is credible from what we know of Calvin's humanistic training.

determined by the humanist contempt for scholasticism. For the traditions he rejected were primarily those that were formed in the medieval schools and which he knew well. Towards the Christian authors of antiquity he was much more indulgent; whatever reservations he had about them, he loved to quote them in support of his own opinions. Naturally, this does not mean that he thought it possible to accept even the oldest traditions as normative in matters of faith.

Everything, even including the limitations of his knowledge, betrays the previous humanist in Calvin. His erudition was immense, but all within the domains that the humanists had made their own—political, ecclesiastical and literary history, philology, exegesis, law and philosophy. He seems never to have been seriously interested in the physical or natural sciences nor in mathematics—very unlike Melanchthon, who in that respect widened his horizon considerably.[64]

One could follow even further, in the light of this *De Clementia* commentary, the survivals of Calvin's humanism in other directions and throughout his subsequent writing. We should undoubtedly find only confirmation of what has already been indicated; which at the very least would demonstrate the importance of this first work of Calvin for an understanding of his thought. The contemporaries of course had no inkling of this. The readers for whom Calvin's book was intended could see little in it but the work of a young man, highly gifted, of course, but much too young to presume to teach the venerable Erasmus. Instead of showing a becoming modesty and pleading indulgence for a beginner, this author's preface (addressed to his old fellow-student Claude de Hangest) rejected in advance the excuses he might have claimed on the score of youth and inexperience.[65] With a touch of arrogance, he presented his work to the humanists as though he had been their equal. They judged him presumptuous, self-important; and when Calvin redoubled his efforts to sell the book, which had been printed at his own expense, the reaction almost everywhere was one of cold disapproval. By this

[64] This opinion is confirmed rather than weakened by the study by CHOISY, ' Calvin et la science ', Geneva, 1931.

[65] *Opp.*, 5, 5 f.

he was more disappointed and annoyed than they may have thought. His literary self-esteem, which remained with him all his life, had suffered its first—and last—humiliation.[66]

III. CONVERSION

Calvin's conversion has been the topic of innumerable and not very interesting controversies.[67] It used to be assumed, on the evidence of a letter of Calvin's to Bucer, that he took the side of the Reform as early as 1532,[68] until one day it turned out that the date of that letter was wholly uncertain, and in any case must have been later than 1532. The one and only document we have from Calvin himself attaches no date to the event in question, but contains some no less interesting information about it. This is a passage in the preface to the *Commentary on the Psalms* of 1557:

> And at first, whilst I remained thus so obstinately addicted to the superstitions of the Papacy that it would have been hard indeed to have pulled me out of so deep a quagmire by sudden conversion, [God] subdued and made teachable a heart which, for my age, was far too hardened in such matters. Having thus received some foretaste and knowledge of true piety, I was straightway inflamed with such great desire to profit by it, that although I did not attempt to give up other studies I worked only slackly at them. And I

[66] Cf. the letters addressed to François Daniel, *Opp.*, 10b, 19 ff., and the prefaces to various later writings.

[67] The following studies are among the most thorough: LECOULTRE, 'La Conversion de Calvin,' in the *Revue de Theol. et de Philos.*, Lausanne, 1890; A. LANG, *Die Bekehrung Calvins*, Leipzig, 1897; K. MULLER, 'Calvins Bekehrung' in the *Nachrichten der Gesellsch. der Wissensch.*, Göttingen, 1905; K. HOLL, *Johannes Calvin, Gesammelte Schriften*, vol. III, p. 255, n. 1; WALKER, op. cit., pp. 78 ff.; P. WERNLE, 'Zur Bekehrung Calvins' in the *Zeitschr. für Kirchengeschichte*, 1906 and 1910; A. LANG, *Johannes Calvin*, pp. 14 ff.; DOUMERGUE, op. cit., vol. I, pp. 327 ff.; PANNIER, *Evolution religieuse (passim)*; IMBART DE LA TOUR, op. cit., pp. 20 ff. It is needless here to go over the whole of this discussion.

[68] *Opp.*, 10b, 22.

was wonderstruck when, before the year was out, all those who had some desire for the true doctrine ranged themselves around me to learn, although I was hardly more than a beginner myself.[69]

In this passage Calvin himself says that he had shown obstinacy in his attachment to the Roman Church. We can surely see in this a direct allusion to the reading of the Protestant writings that he had been able to procure up to that time, to the (at least very probable) attempts by Olivétan, Wolmar and others to win him over to the Reformation, and his resistance to them. Calvin affirms later on that his conversion was sudden. There is no need to quibble over the term; it must have been one of those abrupt changes of direction such as Luther had known, which are usually the result of a long unconscious preparation. Even if, a quarter of a century later, Calvin was simplifying the story, the expression he uses does not exclude his having had previous knowledge of the leading ideas of the reformers, nor even his having been an advocate of a moderate reformism before he adhered openly to the Reform and at the same time broke with Rome.

On the other hand it seems impossible not to apply to Calvin himself the well-known passage in the *Epistle to Sadolet* where he makes an advocate of the Reform describe his conversion:

'The more closely I considered myself, the more my conscience was pricked with sharp goadings; so much that no other relief or comfort remained to me except to deceive myself by forgetting. But since nothing better offered itself, I went on still in the way I had begun: then, however, there arose quite another form of teaching, not to turn away from the profession of Christianity but to reduce it to its own source, and to restore it, as it were, cleansed from all filthiness to its own purity. But I, offended by this novelty, could hardly listen to it willingly; and must confess that at first I valiantly and bravely resisted. For since men are naturally obstinate and opinionated to maintain the institutions they have once received, it irked me much to confess that I had been fed upon error and ignorance all my life. One thing especially there was that prevented me from believing in those people, and that was reverence for the Church. But after I had listened for some time with open ears and suffered myself to be taught, I saw very well that such a fear, that the majesty of the Church might be diminished, was vain and superfluous.'[70]

Apart from the evidence of Calvin himself, there are some indications that enable us to date his conversion approximately.[71] On August 23rd, 1533, he was present at a session of the general Chapter of Noyon, in the course of which it was decided to organize a procession against the plague.[72] The insistence with which Calvin in later days denounced 'nicodemism'—that is, the attitude of members of the Reform who lacked the courage of their opinions and continued in the outward observance of Roman practices—and his own ever-watchful conscience in this respect, render it unthinkable that he already considered himself one of the reformed at that time.[72b] On the other hand, we find him again at Noyon in May 1534, which is less than a year later, and this time he journeys thither in quite another state of mind,

[70] *Opp.*, 5, 412—*Opusc.* 194.

[71] P. BARTH, '25 Jahre Calvinforschung' in the *Theologische Rundschau*, 1934, and J. CADIER, *Calvin*, Geneva, 1958, have resumed the thesis of E. DOUMERGUE and of K. HOLL, according to which Calvin's conversion occurred before the Marburg Colloquy. This is founded upon the frequently quoted passage in the *Second Defence against Westphal* (*Opp.*, 9, 15) and upon Bèze's *Life of Calvin*, which make the conversion coincide with the commencement of the studies in law in 1528. But Calvin's text signifies only that he had begun to detach himself from the Papacy (Quum enim a tenebris papatus emergere incipiens) and had read Luther's writings (legerem apud Lutherum); he does not say he had broken with the Roman Church and he gives no precise date. The sentence about the Marburg Colloquy simply introduces the statement that these 'conversations' had taken place before Calvin began to write (porro antequam scribere aggressus sum, Marpurgi . . .). P. SPRENGER, *Das Rätsel um die Bekehrung Calvins*, Neukirchen, 1960, places the *subita conversio* in 1527-8, but at the same time reduces its significance to little more than a point of departure for a new spiritual orientation.

[72] LEFRANC, op. cit., p. 200.

[72b] Cf. his letter to Marguerite of Navarre of 28th April 1545, *Opp.*, 12, 67.

for he is returning to his native town to surrender his ecclesiastical benefices.[73] That is, he regards his enjoyment of them as incompatible with his severance from Rome. Necessarily, therefore, his conversion must be placed between these two dates.

In the course of the year 1533 the partisans of the Reform had had the impression that the King and his advisers would support their cause in the end. Lefèvre d'Etaples, and with him the advocates of a moderate reformation, were openly enjoying the royal favour and allowing themselves some rather unexpected liberties. Sermons of an evangelical character were delivered in the Louvre itself at the request of Marguerite of Navarre, and Francis I allowed it. But on All Saints' Day, 1533, the new rector of the University, Nicolas Cop, had to pronounce the customary discourse in the Church of the Mathurins. For the text of this harangue he chose the beatitude 'Blessed are the poor in spirit', and in one part of his sermon he extolled certain ideas cherished by the Reformers concerning the function of the Gospel and justification by faith. This discourse was long held to be the work of Calvin:[74] and it must be admitted that arguments are not lacking in favour of that hypothesis. Nicolas Cop was one of the sons of the King's physician and one of Calvin's intimate friends ever since he first came to Paris; moreover, it was believed that a part of the original draft had been discovered, written in Calvin's own hand. Calvin also seems to have been in danger at the same time as Cop—on the day after this outburst; anyhow he took to flight under some disguise or other, and this could have been regarded as an admission of paternity. Calvin would then have been making his opinions known for the first time through the mouth of Cop, and would have been already, by 1533, so far committed to the Reform as to avow it in public. But if the last point can hardly be contested, that cannot be said of the rest. Although some have thought they could assert that 'the whole discourse sounds very much like the authentic Calvin,'[75]

[73] Ibid., p. 201.

[74] Ibid., p. 112; LANG, *Die Bekehrung Calvins*, pp. 43 ff.; the same author's *Johannes Calvin*, p. 205.

[75] J. Vienot, *Histoire de la Réforme française*, vol. i, p. 117.

it has now been demonstrated that the opening is borrowed almost literally from the *Paraclesis* that Erasmus put at the front of the third edition of his New Testament, and that the interpretation of Matthew v: 3 reproduces entire passages from a sermon by Luther which had been put into Latin by Bucer in 1525.[76] As for the rest of the discourse, it is much more in line with Lefèvre than with Calvin.[77] Besides, it has recently been established that, in his own later sermons on the same text, Calvin gives a very different interpretation of it, and openly argues against Cop's exegesis.[78] There remains the problem of the existence of a manuscript in Calvin's hand; but the researches of A. Lang and K. Müller enable us to conclude that this could only be a copy of an original which has disappeared.[79] All that remains, then, of the hypothesis that Calvin was the author of the discourse, is that Calvin was a friend of Cop and seems to have been sufficiently interested in his oration to have copied out a part of it. That he was also 'wanted' after the Cop scandal is not surprising either, when we remember that the friendship between the two men was notorious, and that it was common form to proceed against everyone who could possibly have been confederate with a chief culprit: so much so indeed, that when Cop and Calvin had taken flight, some fifty other persons were arrested—which does not mean that they had all collaborated in Cop's discourse.

It is anyhow probable that Calvin had approved his friend's intention. We may well suppose that by that time he had already reflected seriously upon the religious problems which were present to all his contemporaries, and even that he had overcome the 'obstinacy' which had so long kept him in the bosom of the Roman Church. At the least he had been drawn into the reformism of Lefèvre and his following. And the very structure

---

[76] For the texts, see LANG, *Bekehrung*, pp. 46 and 49 ff.

[77] R. STAEHELIN, art. 'Joh. Calvin' in the *Realencyclopädie für prot. Theolog. und Kirche*, 3rd edn, vol. III, p. 657; K. MULLER, 'Calvins Bekehrung,' pp. 224-42; NOESGEN, 'Die bei der Entstehung der Theologie Calvins mitwirkenden Momente' in the *Neue kirchliche Zeitschr.*, vol. XXII, Erlangen, 1911, p. 566, n. 3. M. MANN, op. cit., pp. 164 ff.

[78] E. MUELHAUPT, *Die Predigt Calvins*, Berlin, 1931, pp. 4 ff.

[79] The same is true of the complete version preserved in the Archives of the Chapter of St Thomas at Strasbourg.

of his discourse suggests that Cop still believed in the possibility of a peaceful reformation of the Church which would find room for an Erasmus as well as a Luther.

After leaving Paris on the day after the famous oration, under the threat of pursuit, Calvin took refuge at Angoulême with one of his friends, Louis du Tillet, curé of Claix, who sheltered him under a pseudonym and also put the three or four thousand volumes of his father's library at his disposal.[80] This was too timely a godsend for Calvin not to have profited by it in order to perfect his theological knowledge, and already perhaps to lay the foundations for the future *Institutes*. From there he went on as far as the court of Marguerite of Navarre at Nérac, where he met Lefèvre. We know nothing of what passed between the two men at that meeting; but the reserved attitude of Lefèvre entitles us to think he did nothing to persuade Calvin to break with the Church. Indeed, after an impartial examination of Lefèvre's writings, whatever has been advanced to show that Lefèvre ever really adhered to the Reform or to its theological principles[81] can be cast out into the limbo of tendentious legend.

Under these conditions it becomes possible, without great risk of error, to determine the time of Calvin's sudden conversion—that is, of the radical change which he says took place within him immediately before the brief visit he paid to Noyon in order to surrender his benefices to the Canons there. What we know otherwise of the reformer's scrupulous character obliges us to believe that he cannot have waited long before renouncing the material advantages that attached him to the Roman Church when once he had become clear about his new orientation.

[80] DOUMERGUE, op. cit., vol. i, p. 369. A. AUTIN, *L'Echec de la Réforme en France*, pp. 120 ff. and 272.

[81] In this sense, cf. GRAF, 'Faber Stapulensis' in the *Zeitschrift für hist. Theol.*, 1852; DOUMERGUE, op. cit., vol. i, pp. 400 ff., and 542-51; H. DORRIES, ' Calvin und Lefèvre ' in the *Zeitschr. für Kirchengeschichte*, 1925, pp. 544-81, has shown convincingly that Lefèvre remained outside the Reform and cannot be counted one of the real inspirers of Calvinist thought. At the most he had only a temporary influence upon Calvin before his conversion. See also the study by J. BARNAUD, 'Jacques Lefèvre d'Etaples' in the *Etudes Théologiques et Religieuses*, Montpellier, 1936.

The steps he took after this visit to Noyon are not too difficult to follow.[82] He returned by way of Paris, stopped at Poitiers and Angoulême, and re-entered Orleans for the last time. It was there that he wrote or finished his treatise *De Psychopannychia* (Upon the Sleep of Souls).[83] In this he attacked a certain Anabaptist teaching to the effect that the souls of the dead went to sleep at death and until the Last Judgment. The work may have been published in 1534,[84] but it is more likely that, on Capiton's advice, Calvin postponed publication of it until 1542.

The affair of the placards (October 1534), by provoking a violent reaction from the authorities against everyone who was either directly or distantly suspected of complicity in the plot——which the 'Lutherans' were accused of having fomented against religion and the public order—put an end to Calvin's days of tranquil study.[85] It became dangerous for him to remain in the country now that he had been brought to the attention of the authorities by his propagandist activity in favour of the new faith. Moreover, he was anxious to find a refuge where he would be sheltered from persecution, able to pursue his studies in theology, and have sufficient calm to write the 'catechism' that he intended to compose for the Reform in the French language. He decided in favour of Basle, which was then, as now, one of the chief intellectual centres of Europe and was celebrated for its printers as well as for Erasmus's recent sojourn there.

[82] On this subject, consult the data collected by DOUMERGUE, op. cit.. vol. 1, pp. 441-68, with a great wealth of detail.

[83] A re-edition of this was published by W. ZIMMERLI in 1932 in the collection *Quellenschriften zur Geschichte des Protestantismus*. It is preceded by a useful Introduction.

[84] This is the opinion of the publishers of the *Opera Calvini*, vol. 5, pp. xxxv. ff. The title of the edition of 1542 is *Vivere apud Christum non dormire animis sanctis, qui in fide Christi decedunt, Assertio*. The end of the *Psychopannychia* does not appear except in the edition of 1545.

[85] Upon the affair of the Placards, cf. V. L. BOURRILLY and N. WEISS, 'Jean du Bellay: les protestants et la Sorbonne' in the *Bulln de l'Hist. du Protest. français*, vol. LIII, 1904, pp. 106 ff. and IMBART DE LA TOUR, *Origines de la Réforme*, vol. III, pp. 552 ff. On the contents of the placards, L. FEBVRE, ' L'Origine des Placards de 1534 ' in the *Bibliothèque d'Humanisme et Renaissance*, vol. VII, pp. 62 ff.

For Calvin, conversion had meant a break with his previous studies, and—or so at least he thought—a break with the humanism which had hitherto been the aim of his life. And indeed it would be a falsification of this conversion to suppose that after the event Calvin became simply a Protestant humanist. Deeply though he had been impressed by humanism in his younger days —and as we have seen, this impression was deeper and more durable than is often recognized—Calvin must necessarily have interpreted his conversion as a total change of orientation. Until that moment, the humanist values had constituted, to his mind, the highest attainment possible to man. In relation to religion, humanism, to the extent that it included the cult of the ancient wisdom, had appeared to be a preparation and approach to the truths of Christianity. But now he realized that there was a break in continuity between the philosophy of the ancients and the Christian faith. To humanism, which by definition rested upon the greatness of man, he had now and henceforth to oppose the corruption of mankind by its sinfulness and alienation from God. To the partisans of free will and human autonomy he must now reply by preaching man's dependence and his ineluctable submission to the decrees of predestination. As in the conversion of Luther, though in a far less dramatic manner, an awakening to the consciousness of sin was the decisive moment in Calvin's conversion. The humanists, even Christian humanists, had never had more than a formal or impersonal notion of sin. For the Reformers it was a reality that concerned every individual and was determinative of his most intimate being.

Calvin could therefore no longer believe in the humanism he had known. But although, after 1534, he laid deliberate emphasis upon all that henceforth separated him from it, we know that he remained no less humanistic in method and in his particular type of intellectual outlook. Before his conversion he took humanism to be the end in itself; after that event it was no more than a means; and as has been said of him, no less correctly than tersely, 'he employs humanism to combat humanism.'[86] He continues to admire the philosophers of antiquity, he still

[86] M. MANN, op. cit., p. 171.

respects Erasmus and his disciples, and all his life he will never cease to admire and make use of their labours and their writings: but he will always take care never to go too far with them; he will always point out that it is better 'not to follow the philosophers farther than is profitable'.[87]

[87] *Instit.*, II, 2, 4.

CHAPTER TWO

From the First to the Second Period
at Geneva

The Preface to the first edition of *The Institutes of the Christian Religion* is dated August 23rd, 1535; but it was not until March 1536 that the printing of the work was completed. After leaving France, Calvin lived in Basle during the first weeks of 1535.[1] He had once again taken a pseudonym to protect his liberty, and he disclosed to no one that he was the author of the Latin catechism which was to be the first of the *Institutes*. Now entirely pre-occupied with theology, he forced himself, at the cost of the most strenuous labour of which even he was capable, to attain a mastery of this science, which, for all his previous studies, was largely new to him. He seems at the same time to have been busy with the publication of his book and the reading of the Scriptures, of the Church Fathers, of Luther, Melanchthon and Bucer: incidentally, he must sometimes have had to refresh his memories of Montaigu by consulting the scholastics in the interests of his polemic. All this reading, which the text of the *Institutes* itself gives us to think was very extensive, did not, however, prevent him from entering into relations with the Basle theologians, or from beginning to correspond with men such as Bullinger and Paul Viret, or again with Capiton and Bucer at Strasbourg.[2]

[1] DOUMERGUE, *Jean Calvin*, vol. I, pp. 487 ff.; WERNLE, *Calvin und Basel bis zum Tode des Myconius*, Tubingen, 1909. Upon the Basle circles, and tendencies that the Reform assumed there, cf. R. WACKERNAGEL, *Humanismus und Reformation in Basel*, Basle, 1924; E. STAEHELIN, *Das Buch der Basler Reformation*, Basle, 1929; and the same author's *Das Theologische Lebenswerk Johannes Oekolampads*, Leipzig, 1939.

[2] KOLFHAUS, 'Der Verkehr Calvins mit Bullinger': *Calvinstudien*, Leipzig, 1909, p. 28; A. BOUVIER, *Henri Bullinger*, Neuchâtel, 1940, p. 49; HERMINJARD, *Correspondence des Réformateurs*, vol. III, p. 373, n. 2; *Opp.*, 10b, 45.

As soon as he was free of the proof-correcting of his *Institutes* he left Basle, in company—it is generally said—with his friend du Tillet, who had followed him into exile, but who was afterwards to disappoint him by reverting to the Roman Church.[3] Under an assumed name, he made his way into Italy to visit the Duchess of Ferrara.[4] The reasons for this journey are little known. No doubt Calvin had heard, before his flight, about this Renée of France who was a daughter of Louis XII and had married Hercules D'Este. She was living on bad terms with her husband, who understood nothing of his wife's refined sentiments, and she had turned to religion for consolation. She favoured the Reformation, and had attracted a number of Protestant refugees to her court, including the poet Clément Marot. Calvin spent only a few weeks at Ferrara; enough, however, to have tried to strengthen the princess in her faith and to make some friends in her circle.

Meanwhile he did not forget his earlier connections: he addressed letters to Duchemin and to Gérard Roussel, which were published a year later at Basle. In these he condemned the attitude of the waverers, those whom he afterwards called Nicodemites—the people who had leanings towards the Reform but continued to attend the Roman ceremonies or to accept ecclesiastical benefices and offices. This was precisely the case with his two correspondents; in these letters Calvin was already exhibiting the frank and imperious tone which was to characterize a good deal of his correspondence.[5] With Renée of France also he exchanged several letters after his return to Basle, but it was not until and after 1548, therefore much later, that he became in the full sense of the word her spiritual director.[6]

---

[3] DOUMERGUE, op. cit., vol. II, p. 8.

[4] This journey into Italy has excited a lively curiosity among historians. Cf. DOUMERGUE, op. cit., vol. II, pp. 3-84; RODOCANACHI, *Renée de France, Duchesse de Ferrara*, Paris, 1895; and his *La Réforme en Italie*, vol. I, Paris, 1920, pp. 337 ff.; PANNIER, 'Renée de France' in *Études Theol. et Relig.*, Montpellier, 1929, pp. 135 ff. See also the account given by C. A. MAYER, 'Le Départ de Marot de Ferrare', *Bibliothèque d'Humanisme et Renaissance*, vol. XVIII, 1956, pp. 198, 203 and 209.

[5] Opp., 5, 233-312; cf. DOUMERGUE, op. cit., vol. I, pp. 22 ff.

[6] Ibid., pp. 729 ff., BENOIT, *Calvin, directeur d'âmes*, pp. 36-41.

Another journey, this time into France, was soon afterwards to interrupt his stay at Basle:[7] it seems that something to do with the paternal heritage had to be put in order. Calvin took the risk of going as far as Paris, where he saw his brother Antoine and his sister Marie, whom he persuaded to follow him abroad. His intention then was to go to Strasbourg.[8] But people could not travel as they chose in those troubled times. The reopening of hostilities between Francis I and the Emperor Charles V obliged Calvin to take the roundabout way through Geneva— a circumstance of immense consequence for the rest of his career.

It was here, in fact, that the famous interview between Calvin and Farel took place. Let us quote the reformer's own words as he recounts it in the preface to his *Commentary on the Psalms*:

> Because in order to go to Strasbourg, whither I now wished to retire, the most direct road was closed by the wars, I had planned to come this way quietly without stopping more than one night in the town. Only a little while before, the Papacy had been expelled from it by the means of this good person I have named [Farel] and of Master Pierre Viret: but things had not as yet been settled as to their form, and there were bad and dangerous divisions between those of the town. Thereupon a certain person, who has now basely revolted and turned back to the Papists [du Tillet], discovered me and made me known to the others. Upon this Farel (burning as he was with a marvellous zeal to promote the Gospel) instantly put forth all his efforts to detain me. And after having heard that I had several particular studies for which I wished to keep myself free, when he saw that he was gaining nothing by entreaties, he went so far as an imprecation, that it might please God to curse the rest and quietness I was seeking, if in so great a necessity I withdrew and refused aid and succour. Which word so horrified and shook me that I desisted from the journey I had undertaken: in such a way, however, that,

[7] DOUMERGUE, op. cit., vol. II, pp. 173 ff.
[8] *Opp.*, 31, 26

feeling my shame and timidity, I did not want to commit myself to discharge any particular duty.[9]

The succinct account that Calvin gives of the situation in Geneva agrees with what we know from other sources. Truly 'circumstances had made Farel the spiritual leader of Geneva. Nothing was being done there in spite of him or without him.'[10] But the Reformation was not yet firmly established; it was suffering, as it was long to suffer still, from the fact that it had been introduced partly with political motives. The Catholic party, beaten for the moment, was still considerable. Above all, what the party of the Reform needed was a leader capable of organizing the Church and setting it upon firm foundations. From this point of view, everything still remained to do, and it was Calvin's fortune to be able to build upon new ground which no traditions had as yet overgrown.[11]

Nevertheless, one should be careful not to underestimate the work that Farel had already done. In most of the directions which were to claim Calvin's activity, Farel appears as the precursor. Less gifted, and no doubt less systematic, he had at least the merit of having staked out the ground and picked the first teams, and of having brought Calvin into the work. His shortcomings prevented him from accomplishing by himself what

[9] Ibid.; DOUMERGUE, op. cit., vol. I, p. 177. Cf. the farewell discourse in which Calvin again calls himself 'timid and fearful', *Opp.*, 21, 43.

[10] CH. BORGEAUD, 'La Conquête religieuse de Genève' in the symposium *Guillaume Farel*, Neuchâtel, 1930, p. 336. Upon the beginning of the Reformation in Geneva, see, besides the work just cited, H. HEYER, *L'Eglise de Genève*, Geneva, 1909; BORGEAUD, *L'Adoption de la Réforme par le peuple de Genève*, Geneva, 1923, and H. NAEF, *Les Origines de la Réforme*, Geneva, 1936. Upon Calvin's activities during the years 1536-8, one must still consult the 'Notice sur le premier séjour de Calvin à Genève' by A. RILLIET, which serves as Introduction to the republication of the *Catéchisme* of 1537 by RILLIET and DUFOUR, Geneva, 1878: as well as CORNELIUS, *Die Verbannung Calvins aus Genf im 1538*, Munich, 1886.

[11] Calvin had so vivid a sense of the inadequacy of what had been done before his arrival, that upon his deathbed he could not refrain from reminding his colleagues of it: 'When I first came into this Church there was almost nothing there. They preached and that was all. They sought out the idols indeed, and burnt them, but there was no reformation. Everything was in tumult.' *Opp.*, 9, 891.

Calvin was to succeed in doing with so much brilliance (though not without difficulty). In his meeting with Calvin he had the insight to recognize the man who could realize his designs better than he could himself. And, in despite of his own authoritarian character, he had the wisdom to efface himself before the new-comer.

Calvin began his career as a reformer at Geneva with the status of Reader in Holy Scripture to the Church in Geneva.[12] Before being a preacher, then, he was a professor. But he was very soon commissioned to preach sermons and to take part in the ecclesiastical organization. Thus, from the beginning, the four domains in which he was to do really original work—exegesis and dogmatics, preaching and the reconstitution of the Church—were open to his initiative. At the beginning of October 1536 he was called upon for the first time to intervene in the affairs of other churches elsewhere: he took part in the dispute at Lausanne which was to pave the way for the organization of the Church in the district of Vaud, which the Bernese had lately annexed.[13] But it was to the Genevan Church that he naturally devoted the greater part of his time.

Strengthened by the experience he had just gained, he submitted to the various councils of the town, on January 16th, 1537, a series of Articles which were to serve as a foundation for the new ecclesiastical organization.[14] And in this text we already

[12] This is the title he gives himself at the head of the two epistles to Duchemin and to Roussel, see *Opp.*, 5, 233.

[13] H. MEYLAN and R. DELUZ, *La Dispute de Lausanne*, 1936; H. VUILLEUMIER, *Histoire de l'Eglise réformée du pays de Vaud*, Lausanne, 1927, vol. I, pp. 153 ff.

[14] WALKER, op. cit., pp. 202 ff.. *Opp.*, 10a, 5-14. ——The Republic of Geneva was administered by four Syndics (chief magistrates) and several Councils. The 'Little Council' consisted of 25 members, including the four Syndics: it had the right of initiative in executive and legislative matters and extensive rights of jurisdiction. The 'Council of the Sixty' (LX) was consulted by the Little Council upon questions judged to be particularly grave, and principally on those of foreign policy. 'The Council of the Two Hundred' (CC) or Great Council had powers of decision in current legislative business and functioned, if the case required, as the court of appeal or of last resort. The 'General Council' was the assembly of all the citizens, which since the end of medieval times had assumed a certain amount of political and legislative power, but was more and more rarely consulted. It lost the right to elect the Little Council and the Council of the Sixty, giving way before a

find some of the cardinal ideas which were to characterize the work of the Calvinists.[15] First of all, that of the Church, which, though it was not to be a community of the elect in the Anabaptist style, was none the less to base itself upon the adherence of its members. Here too, Calvin proposes to submit a formal confession of faith to all the inhabitants, 'to make known those who agree with the Gospel, and those who love better to be of the kingdom of the Pope rather than of the Kingdom of Jesus Christ'.[16] In practice, now that unity of belief was thus broken, the Confession offered to the Genevans became obligatory upon all who wished to remain in the town.[16b]

But it was not only a question of separating the Reformed from the Catholics. The Church constituted by the advocates of the new confession of faith had other things to do, in Calvin's view, besides ensuring the preaching of the Word and the administration of the sacraments, although according to him these were the marks by which the true Church was to be recognized. It also had to be a living community, a Kingdom of Christ upon earth. It had therefore to approach as nearly as possible to the ideal of sanctity that this implied, without thereby becoming a church reserved to an élite of 'the perfect'. Positively, its mission was to contribute by every means at its disposal to the progressive sanctification of its members. Negatively, it must have the right to exclude impenitent sinners. Thus excommunication became for Calvin, as it was for Bucer, one of the prerogatives of the true Church: Calvin insisted upon this in his Articles and devoted a

---

system of plainly aristocratic tendency: the Two Hundred thenceforward nominated the Little Council, which in its turn appointed the Sixty and the Two Hundred. This evolution, which had begun before Calvin's arrival, continued during his residence—in some degree with his approval—and it ended by concentrating the reality of power in the hands of the self-perpetuating Councils.

[15] W. KOEHLER, *Zürcher Ehegericht und Genfer Konsistorium*, vol. II, Leipzig, 1942, pp. 508 ff.

[16] *Opp.*, 10a, 11.

[16b] However, as M. P.-F. GEISENDORF has noted, two months before Calvin's arrival, 'the votes of the people had made attachment to the Reformed faith the condition *sine quâ non* for belonging to the city newly declared an autonomous republic'. *Biblioth. d'Humanisme et Renaissance*, vol. XIII, p. 113, n. 2.

whole chapter to it in his *Confession of Faith*.[17] His further demands were: that the singing of the Psalms should be included in the order of worship; that an education in the catechism should be instituted; and that commissioners should be nominated to elaborate the ordinances of marriage.

The *Articles* were completed, shortly afterwards, by a projected *Confession of Faith* and a *Catechism*, both of which seem to have been drawn up by Calvin and Farel in collaboration.[18] The substance of the *Catechism* is taken from *The Institutes of the Christian Religion* published a year before: as for the *Confession*, this was itself a sort of summary of the *Catechism*.

The Magistracy seemed in no great hurry to adopt Calvin's proposals, but finally, in March, the *Articles* were accepted.[19] Then, after some delay, so was the *Confession*, the members of the Magistrature undertaking to be the first signatories, in order to set an example. The real difficulties did not arise until they set about the submission of the *Confession* to the population. At first they did this by sending officials round from house to house to obtain the assent of the head of each household. This was a total failure. Then the inhabitants of each quarter in turn were assembled in the Cathedral of St Peter, in the hope that recalcitrants would not dare to put up an opposition in public. But again, the number of defections and abstentions was very large. The Councils themselves began to show more and more reserve. In July they rejected the plan for discipline, reserving to themselves the supervision of public morals, holding that this was within the competence of the political authorities.[20] As previously at Basle, at Strasbourg and other towns in which people had wanted to introduce an ecclesiastical discipline, in Geneva too the civil authorities had no wish to find themselves confronted by a new ecclesiastical authority, which would soon have tried to

[17] *Opp.*, 10a, 9; 22, 93. KOEHLER, op. cit., vol. II, p. 512, shows that 'it is not in the programme itself nor in the statement of the problem that Calvin's novelty resides, but in the personal energy with which he knew how to master them'.

[18] *Opp.*, 22, 33-74 and 85-96.

[19] WALKER, op. cit., p. 223; KOEHLER, op. cit., vol. II, p. 515.

[20] It does not seem to have been realized by the Magistracy of Geneva that Calvin's projects raised further questions, quite other than that of the public morality, although this also played its part.

make itself independent of the political power. And in fact, even in the days when Calvin's personal authority was no longer questioned, he never succeeded in withdrawing the Genevan Church from the control of the Magistracy.

For the time being, the obligation imposed upon the Genevans to sign the *Confession* proved to be a mistake, due to the reformer's political inexperience. By opposing the Catholic to the Reformed factions of the population, and thus rendering the existence of any middle party impossible, the leaders of the Church had hindered the progressive formation of a strong majority in favour of their plans. The Catholic party and the waverers were surprised to find themselves so numerous, and their opposition gradually hardened. It was augmented by that of many of the reformed who did not approve of the imposition of a discipline which seemed incompatible with the liberty of the Gospel, at least as they understood it.[21] Those Councils which were thought to have been too obedient to Calvin and Farel were all included in the same reprobation; and at the elections of February 1538 the parties in opposition easily carried the day.

It was not long before other anxieties overtook the leaders of the Genevan Reform. Calvin had hardly been more than a few months in the town before the Anabaptists were creating difficulties for him.[22] Then there was Caroli, who, some fifteen years earlier, had been one of the 'group at Meaux' gathered around Lefèvre and Briçonnet, and who had now become a preacher at Lausanne.[23] His ideas were regarded with suspicion by the Genevan Reformers from the moment when he began preaching

[21] In the same way, at Strasbourg, the disciplinary measures of Bucer, three years earlier, had incurred the hostility of those who saw them as signs of a 'new popery'.

[22] DOUMERGUE, op. cit., vol. II, p. 242.

[23] The most complete study of Caroli is that of E. BAEHLER, 'Petrus Caroli und Johann Calvin', in the *Jahrbuch für Schweitz. Geschichte*, vol. 29, 1904, pp. 41-169; but the author may be reproached with having reacted against the Calvinist historiography by insisting too one-sidedly upon what is in Caroli's favour. Cf. DOUMERGUE, op. cit., vol. II, pp. 252-68. H. VUILLEUMIER, op. cit., vol. I, pp. 165-71, and E. CHOISY, 'Farel à Genève avec Calvin', in the collection *Guillaume Farel*, pp. 354 ff. Upon the incidents at Strasbourg, E. STRICKER, *Johann Calvin als erste Pfarrer der reformierten Gemeinde zu Strassburg*, Strasbourg, 1890, pp. 31-9.

in favour of intercessions for the dead while at the same time expressing hostility to the Roman doctrine of Purgatory. Prayers for the dead, almost as much as taking part in the Mass, were regarded as a definite sign of allegiance to Roman Catholicism. But it was worse still when Caroli, claiming evidence from Farel's *Summary* and Calvin's *Institutes*, accused the two leaders of the Genevan Church of complicity with Arianism. The aspersion was grave, and Calvin was well aware that it might undermine all his work. Very animated discussions were held, in the course of which Viret did his best to help his Genevan colleagues. Calvin was not good at putting up with contradiction, still less personal attack. He loftily affirmed that he was an upholder of the traditional Christology, but refused to give the proof that Caroli demanded, which was his signature to the three ancient Symbols, the creeds of the Apostles, of Nicæa and of Athanasius. The reasons for his refusal are still rather obscure. Doubtless Calvin did not wish to appear to accord the least importance to tradition in dogmatic questions: did he not proclaim from the beginning of this controversy, 'we have sworn faith in one God, and not in Athanasius, whose symbol has not been approved by any legitimate Church'?[24] But it is also probable that he did not want to seem to be justifying himself before his adversary. The affair was referred to Bern, where Calvin's attitude aroused suspicions; the two antagonists went away without the Bernese arbitrators having been convinced that Caroli was in the wrong: and the dispute was renewed with added vigour at the Synods of Lausanne and Bern in May and June 1537. This time Calvin won his case, and the Bernese authorities removed Caroli from his post. However, the hostility between the two men found several more opportunities to show itself, notably during Calvin's period at Strasbourg.[25] Caroli ended by returning to the Roman Faith, and in 1545 Calvin once more took up the quarrel by publishing a pamphlet against him in which he did not scruple to drag his old enemy through the mud.[26] It is almost certain, however, that it was the painful memory of Caroli's insinuations that led

[24] HERMINJARD, *Correspondence*, vol. IV, p. 185. Cf. LANG, *John Calvin*, p. 41.
[25] DOUMERGUE, op. cit., vol. II, pp. 397 ff.
[26] Ibid., vol. VI, p. 68.

the reformer afterwards to insist so strongly upon the trinitarian dogma: perhaps it also played a part in his attitude towards Servetus.

Nevertheless, the conflict of 1537 had left a certain animosity in the minds of the Bernese towards the Reformers of Geneva, and this was soon to find plenty of material to work upon. In face of the ill-will that they opposed to Calvin and his friends, he took up an increasingly stiff and intransigent attitude towards the Magistracy of Geneva. A conflict seemed imminent, and in fact broke out at the first opportunity, which arose over the liturgical question.[27] In that domain, the Bernese had for some time been leaning towards conceptions that were more Lutheran, and to the minds of the Genevans more traditionalist. In particular, Bern had retained the use of baptismal fonts, and still used the host in celebrations of the Eucharist. These were details of no real importance in Calvin's view; but the Bernese, who were eager to extend their political influence to Geneva, attached some significance to them. They were hoping, indeed, possibly under the influence of Bucer, to unify liturgical procedures throughout the region dependent on them, and thereby to show more singleness of inspiration in their ecclesiastical polity. The introduction of the Reform in the newly-annexed territories had proclaimed their incorporation in the Bernese political system, and it followed that a uniform liturgy ought to give outward proof that no divergent beliefs divided the various countries under the Magistracy of Bern. And the Genevan authorities installed by the elections of 1538 meant to rely upon Berne in order to consolidate their still uncertain power. To ingratiate themselves with the gentlemen of Bern the Magistrates therefore hastened, of their own volition, to adopt the Bernese forms of dress, without first referring the question to the preachers. Calvin showed great indignation at what he considered a grave infringement of the autonomy he was claiming for the Church. His supporters made common cause with him and refused to submit. The retort was brutal: the Magistracy forbade Calvin and his colleagues to preach on Easter Day. They took no notice, but declared that they could not distribute the Eucharist so long as people's minds were so inflamed. Extreme measures were then

[27] CORNELIUS, op. cit., pp. 42 ff.; WALKER, op. cit., pp. 226 ff.

applied. The Little Council, the Two Hundred and the General Council held meetings in succession, and solemnly confirmed the adoption of the Bernese ceremonies. Calvin, Farel and another minister were deprived of their functions and ordered to leave the town within three days.[28]

Thus Calvin's sojourn in Geneva seemed likely to be no more than an unfortunate and transient episode in his life. In dealing with a question which he himself was ready to dismiss as practically unimportant, but which involved principles that he regarded as vital, he had intransigently preferred to run the risk of destroying the young Church of Geneva rather than make even a temporary submission.[29] The danger was indeed not imaginary, and contemporaries were well aware of it. The Roman party was still powerful, and the expulsion of Calvin and Farel encouraged some of its leaders to hope for a speedy revenge.

The banished ministers first betook themselves to Bern, to appeal against the harsh measures that had been enforced against them, and contrary to all expectation they were at first well received. The Bernese themselves were afraid of a Catholic restoration in Geneva; rather than see that happen, they would willingly have been peacemakers between Calvin and the Genevan Magistracy. Farel and Calvin then went on to Zurich in order to attend the Synod that met there at the end of April; here they naturally defended their point of view, insisting most particularly upon the necessity of imposing the ecclesiastical discipline they had recommended at Geneva,[30] of dividing the town into parishes, of providing the Church with a sufficient number of ministers appointed without the interference of the Magistracy, and of celebrations of the Eucharist at least once a month. With regard to explanations about the Bernese ceremonies, they declared that they were ready to show a conciliatory spirit. But on their return to Bern, they no longer found the

[28] CORNELIUS, op. cit., pp. 50-62, which gives a very detailed analysis of these events, needs to be corrected upon several points by the considerations advanced by CHOISY, op. cit., pp. 359 ff.

[29] The judgment pronounced by WALKER, op. cit., p. 235 and by LANG, op. cit., p. 45, remains valid, and not only if one takes a purely political point of view; cf. the letter of Bucer to Calvin in HERMINJARD, *Correspondence*, vol. v, p. 65. For the opposite opinion, DOUMERGUE, op. cit., vol. II, p. 288.

[30] *Opp.*, 10b, 190-3. CORNELIUS, op. cit., p. 63; KOEHLER, op. cit., p. 519.

benevolence with which they had lately been received there. In the meantime new reformed ministers had been appointed in Geneva, which had made the Catholic menace seem more remote. The Bernese, however, consented to have Farel and Calvin accompanied as far as the Genevan frontier by official delegates. But they were not allowed to enter the territory, so that all hope of a reconciliation had to be abandoned.

After this defeat Calvin had only one idea—to return to Basle, and there to resume his studies and literary work. As for Farel, he was recalled to Neuchâtel about the end of July, where he established himself for good. Calvin's natural timidity, his little liking for public activity, were amply confirmed in him by the unhappy experiences through which he had just lived. His friends du Tillet and Capiton, as well as Bucer, whose personal acquaintance he had made at the Synod of Bern in October 1536, had disapproved of his obstinacy during the Genevan quarrels,[31] and it was not long before he himself recognized his mistakes and persuaded himself that he was quite unfitted for public life.[32] Nothing remained for it then, he thought, nothing better to do, than to return to the studious life he had given up against his own wishes. And so, at first, he opposed a categorical refusal to the advances of the Reformed of Strasbourg, who wanted to attract him to that town and offered him the pastorate of the French Protestants who had taken refuge there.

On the advice of Bucer and Capiton he had agreed to go to Strasbourg in July, to discuss the question in person. During this brief visit he wrote to du Tillet in terms that show he was not merely disinclined, but resolute not to give up his own plans:

> I shall retire to Basle, waiting for what the Lord wills to do with me. It is not because of the folk of this town that I am not their guest. . . . I fear above all things a re-entry into the responsibilities from which I have been delivered, con-

[31] *Opp.*, 10b, 218 and 241.
[32] *Opp.*, 10b, 247. We are following the interpretation of LANG, op. cit., p. 47, which is confirmed by the words of a letter to Tillet mentioned here below, n. 34.

sidering the perplexities I had when I was enmeshed therein. For even as then I felt the calling of God which had bound me, and in which I had consolation, now, on the contrary, I am afraid of tempting him if again I take up such a burden, which I have known myself unable to bear.[33]

That seemed to settle the matter; but he was not reckoning with Bucer's friendly tenacity. Bucer went on harassing Calvin with letters; he even caused such mutual friends as he could find to intervene; and lastly, he fell back upon the means used by Farel two years earlier to keep Calvin at Geneva. 'I had decided,' Calvin tells us in the preface to his *Commentary on the Psalms*, 'to live in peace without taking any public office, until that excellent servant of Christ, Martin Bucer, by means of a remonstrance and protestation like that which Farel had pronounced before him, recalled me to another place. Being then appalled at the example of Jonah which he quoted against me, I went on again with the burden of teaching.'[34] Once more, against his wishes, Calvin finally yielded to the reproaches of his friends. He could hardly have suspected, at the time, that this acceptance would be of capital importance in his life and in the development of his thought as a theologian.

By 1538, Strasbourg had for several years been one of the most important centres of Protestantism in Europe. Thanks to the political genius of Jacques Sturm, this city had acquired a position in the politics of the Holy Roman Empire which was out of all proportion to its material importance. Its theologians, Capiton and Bucer in particular, had been able to maintain an original position, in spite of their sincere adherence to Lutheranism at the Concord of Wittenberg in 1536. By their works of exegesis and erudition, as well as of popularization, they had made themselves known far beyond their immediate field of activity and even outside the German states. Bucer especially was considered the best negotiator in the service of the new Churches and a first-rate organizer. The co-operative efforts of

[33] *Opp.*, 10b, 221; cf. DOUMERGUE, op. cit., vol. II, pp. 295 ff.
[34] *Opp.*, 31, 26. Cf. the letter to du Tillet of 20th October 1538. *Opp.*, 10b, 271.

the Magistracy and the theologians had succeeded in making Strasbourg an intellectual centre in which the gains of the Reform combined harmoniously with all that had been best in the ideals of the humanists. It was a humanist, Jean Sturm, who was about to open the new High School at the moment when Calvin arrived at Strasbourg.[35]

In accordance with their offer to him, the newcomer was entrusted with the ministry to the refugees.[36] In September, he began to preach, first at the Church of St Nicolas-des-Ondes and then in the Chapel of the Penitents of St Magdalene: later on, the Magistracy gave the French congregation the use of the choir of the secularised Church of the Dominicans. It was also by agreement with the authorities, and in conformity with the ecclesiastical legislation adopted four years earlier, that Calvin organized in Strasbourg that first French parish which was to serve, in his mind, as a model for all the parishes which were afterwards created in the chief Protestant centres of France. It is not without interest to note in this connection that Calvin was largely influenced by the organization of the Strasbourg Churches and the customs observed in them. Without restricting himself to any literal translation of the liturgies in use, it was nevertheless from them that he borrowed the general order of worship and the most characteristic formularies. The confession of sins, the prayers of thanksgiving recited at Holy Communion, and the marriage service, were thus transposed into French; moreover, these were still preserved by Calvin later on in the Genevan

[35] Upon the Reformation at Strasbourg see J. ADAM, *Evangelische Kirchengeschichte der Stadt Strassburg*, Strasbourg, 1922; J. W. BAUM, *Capito und Butzer*, Elberfeld, 1860; DOUMERGUE, op. cit., vol. II, 318-56; G. ANRICH, *Martin Bucer*, 1914; H. EELLS, *Martin Bucer*, New Haven, 1931. Upon the organization of the Church at the time of Calvin's arrival, F. WENDEL, *L'Eglise de Strasbourg, sa constitution et son organisation*, Paris, 1942.

[36] Calvin's stay in Strasbourg has been the subject of several interesting monographs: e.g., E. STRICKER, *Johann Calvin als erste Pfarrer der reformierten Gemeinde zu Strassburg*, Strasbourg, 1890; J. PANNIER, *Calvin à Strasbourg*, Strasbourg, 1925; J. D. BENOIT, 'Calvin à Strasbourg' in the symposium of the same title, Strasbourg, 1938, pp. 11-36; P. SCHERDING, 'Calvin, der Mann, der Kirche und die Bedeutung seines Strassburger Aufenthalts' in the same collection, pp. 67-96; not to mention DOUMERGUE, op. cit., vol. II, pp. 376-526.

Church, which in its turn transmitted them to all the Reformed Churches using the French language.[37]

In the Articles of 1537 Calvin had asked for the adoption of the singing of the Psalms by the congregation. That was also the custom at Strasbourg; the liturgies drawn up by Bucer or under his inspiration contain a complete German Psalter for the use of the faithful. Calvin in his turn, soon after his arrival, published a first selection of the Psalms, for which he himself put five Psalms into French, as well as the Canticle of Simeon and the Decalogue. This little book also contained eight other Psalms in the translation of Clément Marot. As for the music, it was taken from a German psalter: most of the melodies had been composed by the Strasbourg organist Matthias Greiter.[38]

In his new parish Calvin sought, as might have been expected, to apply his principles of discipline.[39] Here also he found himself in agreement with Bucer, who had made several attempts since 1531 to introduce an effective discipline into the communities he had been commissioned to organize.[40] Even at Strasbourg he had come up against the firm determination of the Magistracy to give up nothing of its power over the police. During the elaboration of the ordinances of 1534, the power of excommunication, the ultimate sanction of discipline, had indeed been written into the law, but its application had been reserved to the magistrates and some elders who were, in fact, agents of the civil power as much as of the Church. Calvin could not do otherwise than apply the ordinances of 1534; however, his tenacity and the help given him by the majority of his parishioners enabled

[37] A. ERICHSON, *Die calvinische und die altstrassburgische Gottensdienstordnung*, Strasbourg, 1894; the same author's *L'Origine de la confession des péchés dite de Calvin*, Dôle, 1896; L. BUCHSENSCHUTZ, *Histoire des liturgies en langue allemande dans l'Eglise de Strasbourg au XVIe siècle*, Cahors, 1900, pp. 106 ff.; R. WILL, 'La première liturgie de Calvin' in the *Revue d'Histoire et de Philosophie religieuses*, 1938, pp. 523-9.

[38] DOUMERGUE, op. cit., vol. II, pp. 505 ff; TH. GEROLD, *Les plus anciennes mélodies de l'Eglise protestante de Strasbourg et leurs auteurs*, Paris, 1928; PANNIER, *Calvin à Strasbourg*, pp. 24 ff.

[39] This question is specially dealt with in KOEHLER, op. cit., vol. II, pp. 519-29.

[40] WENDEL, op. cit., pp. 48 ff., 118 ff; 152-61, 179-87, 222; KOEHLER, op. cit., vol. II, pp. 400-26.

him to give this discipline a greater importance than it had in other parishes of the town. For all that has been said of this, we have no proof at all that he was ever able to go as far as an excommunication. He did, however, avail himself of all the preventive measures that the pastors of Strasbourg could imagine to give greater solemnity to Holy Communion, and to exclude the unworthy from it. He adapted to his purpose the practice recommended by Matthew Zell, pastor of the Cathedral, and by Bucer, of admitting no one to Communion except the faithful who had previously presented themselves to the pastor or his vicar. He also made instruction in the catechism obligatory for the children, who were not allowed to join in Communion until they had acquired the indispensable religious knowledge.[41]

These pastoral activities, however, absorbing as they were, represented no more than a part—and that not the most important —of Calvin's preoccupations in Strasbourg. He had hardly arrived before they entrusted him with a chair of exegesis at the new college of Sturm. There he expounded first the Gospel of John, and then the Pauline Epistles beginning with the Epistles to the Corinthians.[42] He published his lessons on the Epistle to the Romans in a volume of *Commentaries* that appeared in the winter of 1539-40, and which was the first and one of the most welcome of a long and brilliant series of exegetical works. Before this he had already found time to perfect and publish a new and completely revised edition of his *Institutes*. In this Strasbourg edition, of August 1539, Calvin went far beyond the didactic and elementary purpose he had first intended the book to serve. The *Institutes* no longer looked like an elaborated catechism; it was now a copious manual of dogmatic theology. The subjects previously outlined were now more profoundly dealt with, gaps were filled in, and almost everywhere we can glimpse the author's memories of his own experiences and of his recent conversations

[41] *Opp.*, 11, 31 and 41. WENDEL, op. cit., pp. 78, 216 n. 36; DOUMERGUE, op. cit., vol. 11, p. 412. Calvin was perhaps making use of a first sketch of what was to become the Geneva *Catechism* of 1542, which COURVOISIER, 'Les Catéchismes de Genève et de Strasbourg', in the *Bull. de la Soc. de l'Hist. du Protestantisme français*, vol. LXXXIV, pp. 105 ff., has shown to have been partly dependent upon Bucer's *Catéchisme* of 1534.

[42] J. FICKER, *Die Anfänge der akademischen Studien in Strassburg*, Strasbourg, 1912, p. 41.

with the Strasbourg theologians.[43]   A few weeks later, there appeared the *Epistle to Sadolet*, which was a response to Cardinal Sadolet's invitation to the Genevans to return to the bosom of the Church: Calvin maintained in reply that the true Church was not that of Rome, but that in which the Gospel was preached in its initial purity.   Like his previous writings, this was still written in Latin; but, no doubt at the request of his friends and parishioners, Calvin soon began to publish his principal theological writings both in the scholarly language and in French. Here we must mention the two that he completed during his stay in Strasbourg. the translation of the *Institutes* in 1539, and the *Little Treatise on Holy Communion*, in which Calvin endeavoured to clarify the point of view from which he sought to interpret the relevant Biblical data in a new way, more or less independently of the Roman, Lutheran or Zwinglian explanations.

His four sermons each week, his lectures, the publication of his works and a voluminous correspondence, did not prevent Calvin's making several journeys abroad during his years at Strasbourg, in order to attend the great Colloquies organized by Charles V in the hope of putting an end to the schism in the Church. 'So much do I continue ever to be like myself,' he wrote, 'which is to say never willing to appear at or to follow the great assemblies, they nevertheless brought me, I know not how but as if by force, to the imperial deliberations, where I found myself willy-nilly in the company of a great many people.'[44]   Then, as at the time of the analogous efforts made by Francis I, Melanchthon and Bucer were the defenders of the Protestant point of view in these controversies, where they were confronted by the cleverest and the most conciliatory of the Catholic theologians. Bucer now realized what an advantage it would be to have the presence and the advice of Calvin in these difficult and often exhausting encounters.   It was at his request that the French reformer came to Frankfurt in February 1539.   Reluctantly overcoming his own timidity as a man of learning, Calvin consented, as a matter of duty, having been told that he could intervene better than anyone else on behalf of the persecuted members of the Reform in France.[45]   His efforts were not crowned with

[43] For further details, see pp. 111 ff.   [44] *Opp.*, 31, 28
[45] DOUMERGUE, op. cit., vol. II, pp. 536 ff.

success: on the other hand, he made the acquaintance of Melanchthon during this interlude on the banks of the Main. On many
points the two men held opposing views. But how many others
were now bringing them together, and laying the foundations of
the friendship that was to last until Melanchthon's death![46]
Above all, it was the humanistic training that they shared, which
created a kind of intellectual complicity between them. No doubt
Melanchthon had remained, like Bucer, more clearly Erasmian,
or had again become so at that epoch;[47] but although Calvin
was the more clearly aware of all that separated him from the
humanist ideal, he had retained enough of the imprint of his
former training to find himself on equal terms with the friend of
Luther. Their subsequent relations were moreover to show that
it was not so much upon genuinely dogmatic questions as upon
secondary issues, such as those of the liturgy or the methods of
discussion with the Catholics, that divergences were to appear
between them.

They were permitted no more than an initial contact during
the Frankfurt conference; but at the encounters that followed
in succession during the years 1540 and 1541, Melanchthon and
Calvin came to know much of one another. At Haguenau in
June 1540, and at Worms during the winter of 1540-1, Calvin
still figured as only a brilliant second to Bucer, and was without
official status. For the great assembly of Ratisbon, however,
which met in April and May 1541, Bucer persuaded the Magistrates that Calvin, like Jacques Stein and Bucer himself, should
be accredited as a delegate of the City of Strasbourg.[48] Ratisbon
was the most important and the last of the efforts made to unite
the two Churches. It failed like the others, and for the same reason
—the impossibility of finding a ground of understanding which
would not destroy the very foundations and the reason for the
existence of one or other of the rival confessions. Concessions
were made, indeed, on both sides: Calvin soon began to think

[46] Ibid., pp. 545 ff.; and especially LANG, 'Melanchthon und Calvin' in
the *Reformierte Kirchenzeitung*, 1897, pp. 58-99.
[47] Cf. R. STUPPERICH, *Der Humanismus und die Wiedervereinigung der Konfessionen*, Leipzig, 1936.
[48] DOUMERGUE, op. cit., vol. II, pp. 625-40; PANNIER, 'Une Année de la
vie de Calvin' in the *Bulletin de la Société Calviniste de France*, No. 45, p. 2.

that Melanchthon and Bucer went too far in that direction, carried away as they were by their desire to achieve something at all costs.[49] Calvin's own optimism, which at first had been sincere, faded away quicker than Bucer's; he was cooler and more perspicuous. He had soon managed to bring to light the real intentions of the organizers of the conference; and even today, the letters that he sent from Germany to his friends are among the best documents we have concerning these last efforts, made to prevent the schism from becoming irremediable.

In the intervals between theological discussions Calvin continued, as at Frankfurt, his efforts to bring assistance to the reformed in France. He believed that Francis I, so long as he remained openly in alliance with the Protestant princes of the Holy Empire, would hesitate to commit himself deeply against the Reform in France, and would remain accessible to petitions in favour of the Reformed in his kingdom.[50] He therefore supported the negotiations of the French ambassador, which were aimed at a renewal of the alliance with the German Protestants. Calvin's proceedings in this matter were not unnoticed at the Court; a letter from Marguerite of Navarre has been preserved, in which she conveys to him the gratitude of the King for services rendered.[51]

In the course of these conferences, Calvin was not only brought into personal contact with the leading personalities of the Holy Roman Empire: he also learnt much of the internal life of the German Churches, and brought back reliable knowledge of their organization. Though this may have influenced his later work on a few points of detail, his reaction on the whole was somewhat negative. He blamed the German theologians for not according so much importance as he and Bucer did to Church discipline. In his view, the liturgical usages of the Lutherans were shaped too much upon Catholic tradition and too little upon the indications he thought he had found in the New Testament. Lastly, his ideal of a Church, not independent of the State but autonomous and free to act in its own sphere, came into conflict at every

[49] Cf., among others, the letters to Farel, *Opp.*, 11, 215 and 217.
[50] DOUMERGUE, op. cit., vol. 11, p. 592; WALKER, op. cit., p. 264.
[51] *Opp.*, 11, 62, the date should be rectified; HERMINJARD, *Correspondence*, vol. VII, p. 199.

instant with the strict dependency to which the German Churches were subjected by the political power, notably by the princes who were then trying, in defiance of Lutheran teaching, to incorporate the Churches of their territories in the general administrative framework. The example of the German Churches was to serve him as a negative example in years to come, when he was striving to organize the Genevan Church and those of France according to his own ideas.

His pastorate in Strasbourg seems to have been a definitive stage in the life of Calvin. In addition to his pastoral activities and his participation in the great conferences that he dreaded, he found in Strasbourg an intellectual and religious centre where he could work as he chose, in close collaboration with the theologians resident in the town. On July 29th, 1539, he obtained at his request the right of citizenship in the little Republic, and was inscribed, as its constitution required, in one of the occupational corporations.[52] His economic situation, which at first was so precarious that he had been obliged to sell a number of his books, improved with time. He had been endowed with the revenues of a chaplaincy, and from May 1539 the Magistracy allowed him a salary of a florin a week for his teaching. His friends were hoping to reserve to him the first vacancy that might occur in the prebendary of the Chapter of St Thomas.[53] They even thought of making his life easier by getting him to marry, which for his own part he does not seem to have considered. In an undated memorandum directed against the celibacy of the clergy, he wrote, a little earlier than this: 'I, whom you see so hostile to celibacy, have never taken a wife, and I know not if I shall ever marry. If I did so, it would be in order to devote my time to the Lord, by being the more relieved from the worries of daily life.'[54] The tone of this is somewhat lacking in warmth; like a great many of his contemporaries, Calvin looked upon marriage only as a convenient means of relieving oneself of domestic burdens. Bucer, who had been a monk, and

[52] STRICKER, op. cit., p. 44, n. 1.   [53] Ibid., p. 41, n. 1.

[54] *Opp.*, 10a, 228. DOUMERGUE, op. cit., vol. II, pp. 447 ff.; STRICKER, op. cit., pp. 44 ff.; LANG, *Das häusliche Leben J. Calvins*, Munich, 1893; N. WEISS, 'Un Portrait de la femme de Calvin', in the *Bulln. de la Soc. de l'Hist. du Protestantisme français*, 1907, vol. LVI, pp. 222 ff.

loved to surround himself with married friends—perhaps to justify his own marriage by the behaviour of other people—took it into his head to find a suitable mate for this hardened bachelor. His first attempt failed; and a second succeeded no better; but finally Calvin consented to espouse Idelette de Bure, the widow of an Anabaptist who was one of his own converts. In August 1540, Farel made the journey to Strasbourg expressly in order to bless his friend's union. And if the portraits we have of her are authentic, she was as elegant and sensitive a woman as the aristocratic tastes of the reformer would have required.

While Calvin was thus settling his personal affairs as though he were to remain permanently in Strasbourg, great changes had been taking place in Geneva, where his and Farel's departure had disorganized the life of the Church. Their friends in Geneva had soon raised their heads again and recommenced the struggle against the magistracy in power.[55] Under the leadership of Ami Perrin, a man of old Genevan stock and one of the very few who had voted against Calvin's exile, of the regent Antoine Saunier and of Maturin Cordier, they formed a considerable party which was known as the 'Guillermins', after Farel's Christian name. They began by putting up a resistance to those whom the Magistracy had appointed to succeed the exiles, and refused to recognize these as regular pastors. Calvin had to intervene to prevent a schism; he remonstrated with his partisans, urging that the Church of Geneva was a true Church so long as preaching and the administration of the sacraments were properly assured to it and the new ministers could not be accused of grave errors in respect of doctrine.[56] Saunier and Cordier, 'plus royalistes que le roi', took no notice of Calvin's disinterested recommendations and went on with their agitation, until one day the Magistracy felt outraged by it and banished them too from the town. Then Farel, who had somewhat disgruntled the Genevans, also inter-

[55] DOUMERGUE, op. cit., vol. II, pp. 653 ff.; LANG, *Joh. Calvin*, pp. 95 ff.; WALKER op. cit., pp. 267 ff.

[56] In default of the letter, now lost, which Calvin wrote to his supporters, we can refer to his letter to Farel of 24th October, 1538. *Opp.*, 10b, 273 ff.

vened and made an effort at conciliation.[57] He obtained from
the new ministers a recognizance of their mistakes and a promise
that they would be vigilant about discipline and teaching. In a
letter to the Church at Geneva, Calvin invited it to recognize the
ministers and consider that they were called by God, who had
not willed that his Church should again fall under the yoke of
the Antichrist.[58] In this there was a transparent allusion to the
efforts of the Catholics to obtain control of the town, and especially
to the insidious letter of Cardinal Sadolet.

Little by little peace was restored in the Genevan Church;
only a relative peace, however, for things were not improving
there. The Bernese were trying to profit by the situation and to
establish their own political control over Geneva. There were
troubles and risings which were alarmingly reminiscent of the
period just before the introduction of the Reform. At last the
'Guillermins' were able to convince a number of their adversaries
that the only way to restore order would be to recall Calvin
from Strasbourg as quickly as possible and entrust him with the
task of pacifying people's minds. On October 20th, 1540, an
official embassy therefore set out on the road to Strasbourg,
commissioned to solicit the return of Calvin to Geneva.

He hesitated a long while. His memories of Geneva were not
exactly happy, and there is no doubt that he was finding conversation with Capiton and Bucer preferable to disputes with
the Genevan parties. In the spring, when Farel—who had never
given up hope of securing his friend's return to Geneva—had
alluded to that event as possible, Calvin had replied: 'I would
prefer a hundred other deaths to that cross, on which I should
have to die a thousand times a day.'[59] There was nothing to
show that he had changed his mind. But once again, the friends
of Calvin joined in their entreaties. Farel, who might well have
felt humiliated by not having been invited also, showed self-
abnegation in putting himself at the service of the Genevans: he
came all the way to Strasbourg in the hope that Calvin would
once again consent to be guided by him. But Calvin obstinately

[57] J. PETREMAND, 'Les Débuts du ministère à Neuchâtel' in the symposium
Guillaume Farel, pp. 431 ff.

[58] *Opp.*, 10b, 351 ff. (letter of 25th June 1539).

[59] *Opp.*, 11, 30.

refused. He did not want to play the part of a mere instrument in the political conflict between the Guillermins and Bern. Moreover, Bucer wanted to keep Calvin near him, and sent letter after letter urging that he should be left at Strasbourg.[60] At last, weary of the strife, Calvin agreed to go back to Geneva, but only for a time and accompanied by his Strasbourg friends; he also demanded prior agreement by the Bernese. Since the latter were in no hurry to support a man whom they looked upon as an enemy to their policy of expansion, the epistolary campaign revived on both sides. Genevans and Strasbourgers mobilized all their friends elsewhere to support their respective causes. The Magistracy of Strasbourg itself remained intractable, until the day when it received letters, not only from Geneva, but from Zurich and Basle, to the effect that the return of Calvin would be the only means of restoring peace, and that not in the Church alone, but throughout the Republic of Geneva.

Calvin finally gave way, and on September 2nd, 1541, he took his departure. Eleven days later he arrived at Geneva, not, as he still believed, for a few weeks or months, but for the rest of his career.

[60] For the details, see STRICKER, op. cit., pp. 59 ff.

CHAPTER THREE

The Organization of the Church in Geneva and the Struggle for Orthodoxy

Calvin had consented to return to Geneva because he had had a glimpse of the possibility of translating into concrete reality the conception of the Church which he had outlined during his previous period in that town and had been clarifying in the course of the years he spent at Strasbourg. And it can be affirmed that, in spite of the obstacles of every kind that never permitted him to realize the whole of the ecclesiastical ideal he had conceived, still less to become the dictator that legend has invented, the Church of Geneva as he left it at his death was in fact his personal work: that is true not only of the Genevan Church, but of all the Calvinist Churches of France, of the Low Countries, of Northern Germany and of Scotland. Rarely has it been given to one man to exercise so wide and so enduring an influence as Calvin's has been in this domain. For even when his theological thinking has been under eclipse or appearing in variations, what was essential in his conception of the Church has managed to hold its own and to develop. No doubt he would have had a little difficulty in recognizing, in some modern Churches, the heritage of his work in Geneva; they have none the less retained the fundamental principles that he laid down in his *Ecclesiastical Ordinances*.

But it was not only a Church that Calvin was striving to 'train up' during the twenty-four years of his second sojourn in Geneva. He bestowed even more care, if that were possible, upon the doctrine which was to animate this Church, which in turn was to be responsible for defending it. To its elaboration, its continual buttressing by new arguments, its protection against all contamination and against the attacks made upon it, Calvin expended the best energies he had. His doctrinal work, as he has expressed it in the different editions of the *Institutes* and in his Biblical commentaries, thus went hand in hand with his properly ecclesiastical work. Like the latter, it was at least in part the result of an incessant struggle to safeguard the truth of scriptural teaching as the reformer had conceived it. It is in no way surprising, therefore, that the fight for orthodoxy, which in Calvin's eyes was a fight for the integrity of the Word of God, has left numerous traces in his writings, most of all in his *Institutes of the Christian Religion*. One cannot do justice to that treatise without taking this into account.

When he came back to Geneva, Calvin was thirty-two. He had completed his intellectual training and his theological initiation. Now his work was before him, a work that he regarded as the will of God, and to which he committed his whole existence. In the present chapter, which will conclude our brief narrative of Calvin's life, we shall recount only those incidents which directly influenced his work, or did something to give a particular turn to his thought.

When he arrived at Geneva on September 13th, 1541, Calvin was received with great demonstrations of joy, and a house was put at his disposal in the Rue des Chanoines, in which he was destined to dwell until his death.[1] The Magistrates granted him —and this was a tangible proof of the eagerness of their welcome —a salary double that of the other pastors, besides certain allowances in kind.[2] Not that a man like Calvin could be very susceptible to tokens of esteem of that description: they had called him in to restore order in the Church; that was the mission he had accepted and the rest went for little in his estimation. He also knew his Genevans, and was aware that the proposals he was about to make to them would not be met with unmixed enthusiasm. On the very day of his arrival he presented himself

---

[1] WALKER, op. cit., p. 285, n. 2; DOUMERGUE, op. cit., vol. III, pp. 568 ff. and vol. VI, p. 3. To be corrected as to date, by DE BEZE, *Vita Calvini, Opp.*, 21, 131; *Annales, Opp.*, 21, 282.

[2] DOUMERGUE, op. cit., vol. III, pp. 449 ff.; WALKER, op. cit., p. 286.

before the Magistracy, and straightway, with almost feverish haste, demanded the setting-up of a commission of pastors and advisers which was to draft 'regulations for the Church and Consistory'—a design, that is, for the ecclesiastical constitution.[3] He was in fact determined to write that constitution himself and to impose its adoption, first upon the Commission and then upon the Magistracy. By September 20th the preparatory work had been completed. Then there was a temporary standstill—for, as might have been expected, the Councils had plenty of objections to Calvin's project.[4] They were willing enough that he should organize the Church as he proposed, but on condition that this did not infringe any of the prerogatives of the civil power, or affect certain customs that the Genevan Church observed in common with the Bernese Churches, and which had to be maintained for political reasons.[5] Thus it was that Calvin was not able to obtain the celebration of Holy Communion every month as he desired, but only once a quarter. Similarly, the installation of new pastors could not be accompanied by the laying on of hands according to the example of Strasbourg; they had to be inducted simply by a prayer, and with a sermon upon the pastoral functions. These were, after all, details of minor importance, and Calvin gave way. There was more serious altercation at other points where the authority of the Magistrates seemed to be directly called in question;[6] for example, when it came to the nomination of pastors. The original plan had recognized three successive stages: first of all, the pastoral body was to conduct the examination of the candidates and present to the Magistrates those whom it thought most eligible; then came the confirmation of its choice by the Magistracy; and lastly, the community was to be called upon to pronounce its approval.[7] The councillors

[3] *Opp.*, 21, 282. E. CHOISY, *La Théocratie à Genève au temps de Calvin*, pp. 48 ff.; KOEHLER, op. cit., vol. II, pp. 555-68.
[4] Cf. WALKER, op. cit., pp. 288 ff.; LANG, op. cit., p. 108.
[5] Calvin's original plan, and the alterations that were made in it by the Councils, will be found in *Opp.*, 10a, 15-30.
[6] The pastors had asked to be given knowledge of the modifications that were made, before the project was communicated to the Two Hundred. The Little Council refused them this favour (*Opp.*, 21, 286); we find it hard to believe, however, that Calvin was not kept informed of the discussions.
[7] *Opp.*, 10a, 17.

realized that this system would amount in practice to letting the pastors choose their own colleagues. So the Council decided that it would intervene from the beginning of the procedure, and take part, together with the pastors, in the initial choice. Calvin had moreover written into his plan an obligation upon all the pastors to meet once a week, as they did in the ecclesiastical Convention at Strasbourg. The Council found nothing to say against that. But every three months the pastors thus in conference were to proceed to a mutual examination of their conduct: and here the Council scented a menace to its own judicial authority, fearing that Calvin might re-establish a juridical privilege to the benefit of the clergy: it therefore added an article stipulating that civil offences lay outside the competence of the ministers.[8] Similarly, the function of the Magistracy was reaffirmed in respect of the nomination of schoolmasters and in matrimonial matters.[9]

But the most serious divergencies were brought to light with regard to the Consistory, to which Calvin meant to entrust the ecclesiastical discipline. Originally, this Consistory was to have been composed of the pastors and of twelve Councillors nominated with their agreement. These *elders* were to have the right to convoke, to censure or excommunicate, any members of the community who had rendered themselves culpable of offences against right doctrine or against morals.[10] It therefore constituted a real spiritual jurisdiction which in the nature of things would compete with the ordinary temporal jurisdiction. But that was what the Magistracy could not allow. In its eyes, spiritual jurisdiction by the Church amounted to a trespass upon its political prerogative. To understand the hostile attitude of the Magistracy, it must be remembered that at that time the temporal power included within its competence the control of public morality to a far greater extent than in our day.[11] The regulations laid down by the civil authorities went into endless details touching the behaviour of the subjects, their private conduct, their clothing and

---

[8] *Opp.*, 10a, 20.   [9] *Opp.*, 10a, 22 and 26.

[10] *Opp.*, 10a, 22 and 29.

[11] See, in the last place, the numerous concrete examples given by KOEHLER in the work cited, and for what more especially concerns Geneva, vol. II, pp. 541 ff.

even their food. Anything might serve as a pretext for intervention by the authorities, whose power extended, through the police, into every department of life. And that was precisely the domain that Calvin was now claiming for the ecclesiastical jurisdiction, at least so far as religion and the integrity of the Church were concerned. Certainly he made no claim to withdraw the knowledge of these affairs from the Magistracy; but he affirmed that side by side with the civil justice the ecclesiastical discipline ought to know them too, in virtue of its own competence of a purely religious order, based upon the 'power of the keys' vested in the Church, and the cure of souls.[12] But in fact, the coexistence of two jurisdictions, civil and ecclesiastical, must necessarily have provoked incessant conflicts of competence, since it would amount to the subjection of the inhabitants to two jurisdictions at one and the same time in every case involving a point of doctrine or of public or private morality. However, the Genevan Councils began by taking up a conciliatory attitude. They were very willing to allow that the elders present in the Consistory, among whom the lay element would be of their own appointment, should exercise a right of supervision over the faithful, and should even go as far as admonitions. But they refused to trust them with the right to pronounce excommunications upon their sole authority. No doubt they feared that excommunication would have civil consequences, and the Consistory would thus be led to meddle with the temporal jurisdiction. Now in Calvin's eyes the right to excommunicate was the corner-stone of his whole system of ecclesiastical discipline.[13] It had been so already in 1537; and his experience at Strasbourg and his contacts with Bucer—who as we know was a determined believer in excommunication—can only have confirmed Calvin in this opinion. So on that point he refused all concession. His firmness carried the day and he won his case, at least apparently—but at the price of writing into the draft of his

[12] Calvin's point of view is expounded very fully, but perhaps in too personal a manner, by J. BOHATEC, *Calvins Lehre von Staat und Kirche*, Breslau, 1937, pp. 539-63, where there is also an interesting critique of the various interpretations to which it has given rise. Cf. also J. COURVOISIER, 'La Discipline ecclésiastique dans le Genève de Calvin' in the collection *Hommage et Reconnaissance à Karl Barth*, Neuchâtel, 1946, pp. 19 ff.

[13] KOEHLER, op. cit., vol. II, p. 509.

Ordinances a new article, designed to allay the the Magistracy's apprehensions. And this article was in fact at the bottom of all the conflicts and arguments that went on for nearly fifteen years after. Here is the text in question, as it appears at the end of the definitive edition of the *Ordinances*:

> And that all may be done in such sort that the ministers have no civil jurisdiction and use none but the spiritual sword of the word of God as St Paul empowers them; and that by the Consistory there be no derogation of the authority of the seigneury nor of ordinary justice; but that the civil power remains in its entirety; and even where there will be need to inflict some punishment or to constrain the parties, the ministers with the Consistory, having heard the parties and made the remonstrances and admonitions that are fitting, are to refer the whole to the Council, who upon their relation will decide to order and do justice according as the case requires.[14]

Such ambiguous drafting authorized a number of interpretations. Calvin saw it as a statement of the Consistory's right to excommunicate without prejudice to the exercise of the civil jurisdiction, which ought, in his opinion, to be added to it. The Magistracy, on the contrary, interpreted the text to mean that the right of excommunication was reserved to the Councils, the Consistory being restricted to the making of mere proposals. Juridically, the Magistracy's reading was undeniably correct, and it is astonishing that a jurist as well-read as Calvin could have been content with a formulation which said the opposite of what he intended. Be that as it may, it was not until 1555 that he won a definitive victory for his point of view, after incessant quarrels which more than once threatened to put an end to all relations between him and the Magistracy.[15] Nor was it until long after 1541 that Calvin was able to obtain the pronouncements of the last warning and of excommunication in the presence of the entire community—the Magistrates, who were apprehensive of such publicity, having deleted from the original draft the passages which referred to this.

[14] *Opp.*, 10a, 30, n. 1.
[15] See the convincing explanations of KOEHLER, op. cit., vol. II, pp. 655 ff.

On November 20th, 1541, the revised draft was at last adopted by the General Council of the inhabitants, and published under the title of *Ecclesiastical Ordinances*.   Inadequate though it must have appeared to Calvin, it nevertheless provided a firm foundation on which he could build his Church. For in spite of all the modifications he had been obliged to accept, it was his conception of the Church and of the ecclesiastical organization that these Ordinances prefigured; the organization which, as Calvin conceived it, was prescribed by the Lord and was therefore of Divine right. This principle is clearly laid down in the preamble to the Ordinances:

> It has seemed good to us that the spiritual government, such as our Lord demonstrates and institutes it by his word, should be set down in good form, to take place and be observed among us. And thus have we ordered and established, to obey and to maintain in our town and territory the Ecclesiastical policy, which follows, as we see it is taken, from the Gospel of Jesus Christ.[16]

Even if this passage is not by Calvin himself, it is a faithful expression of his thought. The Christ is the incontestable master of the Church, and has left in his words the rules for its government. And of this, one of the fundamental rules, according to Calvin, consists in giving each of the various members of the Church a part in its activities corresponding to his individual gifts. The Church is the body of Christ; it is an organism of which each member has the place and the functions assigned to him by the Holy Spirit.[17] Calvin distinguishes, more particularly, four ministries, the conservation of which is enjoined by the Ordinances of 1541:

> There are four orders of offices that our Lord instituted for the government of his Church: first the pastors, then the teachers, after them the elders, and fourthly the deacons. Therefore if we would have the Church well ordered and

[16] *Opp.*, 10a, 16, n. 1. Cf. BOHATEC, op. cit., pp. 382 ff.
[17] Cf. among other things, Calvin's elaboration of this idea in his Commentary on the Epistle to the Ephesians, 4, 11 and 12, *Opp.*, 51, 198; BOHATEC, op. cit., pp. 417 ff.

maintain it in its entirety, we must observe that form of rule.[18]

In the first edition of the *Institutes*, Calvin had spoken only of the pastors and deacons, and the *Articles* of 1537 mention only the pastors. Thus the four ministries upon which the reformer based the order and integrity of the Church in 1541 represented something new. Judging by the only theological justification he gave for it later, in the *Institutes* of 1543, one might think that he was the author of the theory of the four ministries. But in fact he was not: it has been effectually demonstrated that Calvin derived the outline of this conception, and even the Biblical quotations which were adduced in its support, from Martin Bucer.[19]

In what it says about the pastors, the Genevan Ordinances foresee that they will have to be subject to examination as to their doctrine and their conduct. The appointment of new ministries is to be made according to the order of the old Church. The candidate chosen by the ministers and the Magistracy is presented to the people 'in order,' says the text, 'that he may be received with common consent by the company of the faithful.'[20] An oath is required of the minister, who, according to the formula adopted in July 1542, must swear that he will serve God faithfully, keep the ecclesiastical Ordinances, maintain 'the honour and privileges of the Seigneury and of the City', and obey the laws and the Magistracy 'without prejudice to the freedom we must have to teach what God commands us and to do those things that belong to our office'.[21] Every week, the ministers must meet 'to confer concerning the Scriptures'. In the course of these assemblies they are to adjust any doctrinal differences that may have arisen between them; in case of need they are to appeal to the elders. But even in this domain, which more than any other is within the ecclesiastical competence, Calvin admits, as Bucer had done at Strasbourg, the right of the Magistracy to

[18] *Opp.*, 10a, 15 ff.; BOHATEC, op. cit., pp. 451 ff.

[19] Cf. in particular, H. STROHL, 'La Théorie et la pratique des quatres ministères à Strasbourg avant l'arrivée de Calvin', in the *Bulletin de la Société de l'Histoire du Protestantisme français*, 1935, vol. LXXXIV, pp. 123 ff.; G. ANRICH, *Strassburg und die calvinische Kirchenverfassung*, Tubingen, 1928; F. WENDEL, *L'Eglise de Strasbourg*, pp. 189 ff.

[20] *Opp.*, 10a, 17. [21] *Opp.*, 10a, 31.

the final decision.[22] Every quarter, the ministers meet in order to take 'special notice if there be any complaints between them, and to remedy these, as of right'.

As for the teachers, their 'proper office is to instruct the faithful in sound doctrine'.[23] Moreover, Calvin includes in that calling all 'the order of the schools'. The Ordinances provide for instruction in theology, but, they add, 'since one cannot profit by such lessons unless one has first been taught languages and the humanities . . . a college must be set up to teach the children, so as to prepare them for the ministry as much as for the civil government.' The teaching body for this is to be chosen with common accord by the ministers and the magistrates, and will be subject to ecclesiastical discipline in the same way as the ministers.

We have seen the importance that Calvin ascribed to the elders, and the difficulties he had to encounter in order to establish their jurisdiction. The Ordinances begin by defining their functions: 'Their office is to take care of the life of everyone, amiably to admonish those whom they see weakening or leading a disorderly life, and, where it may be advisable, to bear report to the company which will be deputed to apply brotherly correction.'[24] These elders, whom the Magistracy hastened to qualify also as 'commissioned or deputed by the Seigneury to the Consistory', met once a month under the presidency of one of the officials, in order to emphasize their secular as well as their ecclesiastical character.[25] The ordinances made it clear that they were 'to have no authority or jurisdiction to constrain' and that it was therefore necessary for them to be joined by an officer of the Magistracy, who would be charged to summon 'those whom they wish to admonish in any way'—a detail which shows what concern there was to safeguard the normal judicial power. For still better reasons, the Consistory had, properly speaking, no right to judge. According to the text which was added by the Little Council while the Ordinances were being drawn up,

[22] *Opp.*, 10a, 18: ' If they could not come to amiable agreement for the obstinacy of one of the parties, let the cause be referred to the Magistracy to be put in order'; cf. WENDEL, op. cit., pp. 171 ff.

[23] *Opp.*, 10a, 21. [24] *Opp.*, 10a, 22.

[25] KOEHLER, op. cit., vol. II, pp. 569 ff.

the elders 'must only hear the parties and make the aforesaid remonstrances'; and it belongs to the ordinary jurisdiction, if necessary and upon the Consistory's report, 'to consult and pronounce judgment'.[26] Besides, Calvin himself had never conceived the office of the elders as a repressive jurisdiction, but rather as an aspect of the cure of souls, for he declared in his draft: 'That there should be no strictness that may burden anyone, and even none but medicinal corrections, in order to recall the sinners to our Lord.'[27] He could not, in fact, prevent the ecclesiastical jurisdiction from becoming something superadded to the civil jurisdiction and preserving its purely pastoral aspect to a less and lesser degree.

The deacons, lastly, formed the fourth order of ecclesiastical government provided by the Ordinances. On close consideration, these were simply subordinates, some of them deputed to 'receive, and conserve the goods of the poor' while others had to 'watch over and tend the sick and administer the pittance of the poor'.[28] Calvin did no more than incorporate them in the Church by fixing for them rules of election, analogous to those in use for the elders, and putting them under the control of the ministers and elders.

The arrangements prescribed for the administration of the sacraments, for marriage,[29] burial, visitation of the sick and of prisoners, were of secondary importance and need not detain us here. On the other hand something must be said about the religious instruction prescribed for the children.[30] Calvin was as keen on catechism as on discipline. Of that he had given proof in the *Articles* of 1537, and in his farewell discourse to the ministers he declared once more: 'On my return from Strasbourg I made the Catechism in haste, for I would never have accepted the ministry unless they had sworn to these two points; namely, to uphold the Catechism and the discipline.'[31] By the Ordinances, parents were also obliged to send their children to religious

[26] *Opp.*, 10a, 29, n. 8. The interpretation given by WALKER, op. cit., p. 295, does not correspond to the facts.

[27] *Opp.*, 10a, 30.   [28] *Opp.*, 10a, 23.

[29] The question of the matrimonial legislation and jurisdiction has been partly reopened by KOEHLER, op. cit., vol. II, pp. 626 ff.

[30] *Opp.*, 10a, 28.   [31] *Opp.*, 9, 894.

instruction on Sundays, where they were to learn 'a certain set formulary'; and when sufficiently taught, the child had 'solemnly to recite the whole of its contents', doing so as a profession of its Christianity in the presence of the Church. Only upon this condition could the child be admitted to Communion. Just as Calvin, in his Catechism of 1542, drew inspiration from the contents and the arrangement of Bucer's Catechism of 1534, so also the rules laid down in the Ordinances reproduce, point by point, those contained in the ecclesiastical Ordinance of Strasbourg of 1534,[32] which Calvin had been able to appreciate in practice for the space of some years.

Although, in the final reckoning, the Ordinances had given the State more than Calvin had wanted to concede, one could no more speak of an annexation of the Church by the Magistracy than of a preponderance of the Church over the civil power. The distinction between the two powers was the foundation of the entire edifice. Each of these autonomous powers, State and Church, was conceived as issuing from the Divine will, and for that reason responsible for inspiring, each in its own manner, respect for the Two Tables of the Law. It is therefore inaccurate to speak, as people often do, of a theocratic confusion of powers. The Church, in Calvin's conception, had to interpret revelation and exercise spiritual jurisdiction; temporal affairs and the protection of the Church devolved upon the State. But each power had, theoretically at least, its well-defined domain. The fact that the Magistracy is a Christian Magistracy means that Church and State owe one another mutual aid and collaboration: they remain nevertheless distinct, and Calvin always took care not to intervene in political questions by virtue of his pastoral status. In so far as he was called upon to deal with them, he did so on his personal responsibility alone, and without committing the Church. If, in the sequel, conflict broke out very frequently, this was due on the one hand to the defective drafting of the Ordinances and, on the other, to the fact that the Consistory, instead of limiting its watchfulness to really grave shortcomings, allowed itself to be led further and further into inquisitorial practices, which brought it under suspicion of trespassing upon the Magistracy's domain; wrongly so, however, for it is not possible to

[32] WENDEL, op. cit., pp. 217-21.

attribute this attitude to any deliberate intention of the Church's representatives to take a hand in political affairs.

As might have been expected, the reforms concerning the liturgy and religious instruction were adopted without difficulty. In 1542 Calvin published a new liturgical compilation under the title of the *Form of the Ecclesiastical Prayers and Hymns*, which was an adaptation from the analogous collection by Bucer, and of the liturgy that Calvin himself had used in his parish at Strasbourg—at least, in everything to do with the ordinary worship of Sundays and weekdays.[33] As for the liturgy of the Eucharist, it presented the formulas in use at Geneva, with the exception of a few details and a few prayers. With the religious teaching destined for the children in view, he wrote in 1542 his second Catechism, which appeared both in Latin and in French.[34] Following Bucer's example, he wrote this in the form of dialogues, which is more suitable than dogmatic exposition for purposes of instruction. At the same time, he sought to give the greatest possible clarity and precision to his definitions, and to avoid disputed questions; though he did not succeed in avoiding certain prolixities inappropriate to the pedagogical purpose he had in mind. Nevertheless, the Catechism of 1542 played a very considerable part in the diffusion of Calvinism. It familiarized the faithful with a number of theological questions, and thereby contributed to the religious training of several generations of Protestant believers. In and after the sixteenth century numerous translations were made of it, and it served as the basis for the Catechism of Heidelberg, which, as we know, became the typical catechism of the Reformed Churches.[35]

After the adoption of the ecclesiastical Ordinances, the Genevan Councils wished to apply analogous treatment to the civil legislation.[36] They proceeded to remodel, or more exactly to codify,

[33] *Opp.*, 6, 161-210; cf. DOUMERGUE, op. cit., vol. II, pp. 497 ff. and W. D. MAXWELL, *John Knox's Genevan Service Book 1556*, Edinburgh, 1931, pp. 20 ff., 32 ff., 188 ff.

[34] *Opp.*, 6, 1-160. J. COURVOISIER, 'Les Catéchismes de Genève et de Strasbourg', in *Bulln. de la Soc. de l'Hist. du Protest. français*, vol. LXXXIV, pp. 105 ff. The oldest French edition that has been found is of 1545.

[35] Cf. A. LANG, *Der Heidelberger Katechismus*, Leipzig, 1907, pp. xxxvi ff.

[36] M.-E. CHENEVIÈRE, *La Pensée politique de Calvin*, Geneva, 1937, which illuminates, in a new way, the part played by the reformer.

the constitutional and civil laws then in force; thereby accentuating, however, the aristocratic character of the political system. They availed themselves of Calvin's legal knowledge, and he collaborated in this undertaking by various memoranda, and by taking upon himself the drafting of the edicts in their definitive form.

He also had to involve himself in the still unsettled political conflict with the adjacent canton of Bern. On February 3rd, 1544, a treaty put an end to this affair, which had been weighing heavily upon the situation at Geneva for several years. Things seemed at last to be entering upon a phase of general appeasement, especially when the political exiles were given leave to return to their homes.

Freed from the principal hindrances which had hitherto retarded his work, Calvin was henceforth able to devote himself wholly to the task he had set himself, which was to make Geneva into a city and a Church modelled as nearly as possible upon his ideal. By daily sermons, the mass of the population was to be gradually attuned to the Gospel. To ensure the recruitment of pastors for Geneva, for the surrounding regions and even for France, courses of lectures in theology were instituted, which, moreover, Calvin was at first almost the only one to deliver. Lastly, the school, which had been given an important place in the Ordinances, was to provide the general education. Calvin put it under the permanent control of the Church, and for its director he accepted Sebastian Castellion, a Savoyard humanist whom he had learnt to know at Strasbourg.[37] As one may well imagine, not all these things came to pass without difficulties, of which by no means the least were those arising from the introduction of the new discipline of the Consistory. Nevertheless, Calvin found time, in 1542, to write an important treatise upon free will, against the Catholic theologian Albert Pighius,[38] and a commentary upon the Epistle of Jude.[39] The following year saw a new edition of the Latin *Institutes*, the celebrated *Treatise*

---

[37] Cf. F. BUISSON, *Sébastien Castellion*, Paris, 1892, vol. I, pp. 138 ff.; DOUMERGUE, op. cit., vol. VI, pp. 8 ff.

[38] *Opp.*, 6, 225-404.   [39] *Opp.*, 55, 501-16.

on Relics[40] and the first of his writings against the Nicodemites,[41] not to mention several works of lesser importance. And all these were only the firstfruits of the intense literary activity carried on by Calvin right to the end, with tireless and truly astonishing industry.

So many and such various works required the presence of a whole staff of collaborators capable of assisting Calvin intelligently and at the same time with the spirit of submissiveness demanded by his authoritarian character. Few such were to be found by the reformer in Genevan circles. In compensation for this, however, the refugees flowing more and more numerously into the town included some minds of the first quality. Doubtless he had his disappointments with several of these; but on the whole they belonged to an élite who wanted nothing better than to put themselves at the service of the ideas for which they had already sacrificed so much. If conflicts broke out nevertheless, these were often due to faults or misunderstandings by Calvin's adversaries; but also because the reformer himself, increasingly convinced that he was acting solely by virtue of a divine mission, did not admit discussion of his ideas—especially not about dogmatic principles, but not even about matters of personal opinion, sometimes of only the smallest importance.

One of the first conflicts of this kind was that which set Calvin and Castellion in opposition. In 1543 Castellion had asked to be entrusted with a post as preacher. In accordance with the rules then in force, he presented himself for the preliminary examination required in such a case: and in the course of interrogation he happened to speak against the canonical status of the Song of Songs, and against the particular interpretation that Calvin put upon the article of the Credo about the descent into hell.[42] For Calvin, the affirmation that the Christ had really gone down into hell after his death belonged to the domain of fables;[43] the descent into hell ought to be regarded simply as an

[40] *Opp.*, 6, 405, 452; see the introduction by A. AUTIN to the republication that appeared in the *Collection des Chefs-d'oeuvres méconnus*, Paris, 1921.
[41] *Opp.*, 6, 537-8.
[42] BUISSON, op. cit., vol. I, pp. 195 ff.; DOUMERGUE, op. cit., vol. VI, pp. 9-15; H. M. STUCKELBERGER, 'Calvin und Castellio', in *Zwingliana*, vol. VII, pp. 94 ff. [43] *Inst.*, II, 16, 9.

image for the sufferings endured by Christ on the cross and of his death in the flesh. Castellion, on the other hand, stuck to the literal interpretation as the only one that corresponded to the thought of the Biblical author. They might well have considered that these were points of secondary importance; but Calvin, taking his stand primarily upon the canonicity of the Song of Solomon, made the whole problem of the authority of the Scriptures depend upon it. He insisted that Castellion should not be admitted to the pastoral ministry, without, however, demanding his dismissal from the school. In the certificate that he handed to Castellion in the name of his colleagues, which reads like a sort of official report upon the incident, he even added this conciliatory sentence: 'Though he has not been admitted, it is not because of any blemish whatever in his life, nor of any impious doctrine upon a capital point of the faith or in contradiction to it, the cause is only that which we have just explained.'[44] But the antagonism between the two men was too profound for the matter to rest there. In May 1544, in the course of the fraternal censure of the ministers by the Congregation, Castellion launched a vehement criticism of the Genevan pastors. Calvin at once lodged a complaint against him with the Magistracy, which began by admonishing the 'school master' and then, a year after, obliged him to leave the town. This was only a first incident: it was the precursor of others much more serious. The immediate consequence of Castellion's departure was the rapid deterioration of the school, which could not be reorganized until ten years later, and then upon new principles.

During all this earlier period, the disciplinary activity of the Consistory was limited to matters of public morality, in which its intervention was fully justified in the eyes of the public. In 1545, the Magistracy, perhaps of its own initiative, increased the statutory punishments for deeds of moral delinquency;[45] a little later, at Calvin's demand, it was ruled that offenders should be brought before the Consistory after being sentenced by the secular tribunal. Though this was a complication of the procedure, naturally it could only heighten the importance of the Consistory. About the same time, the latter began to display

---

[44] *Opp.*, 11, 676.
[45] LANG, *Johannes Calvin*, p. 119; KOEHLER, op. cit., vol. 11, p. 591.

a hitherto unexampled zeal, with rather a pronounced taste for intrigue, and even for informers. It summoned before it the most diverse and sometimes the oddest of cases. On this point we may quote what the historian Walker, who could hardly be suspected of prejudice against Calvin's Church organization, wrote about this side of the Consistory's work:

> No age or distinction exempted one from its censures. Men and women were examined as to their religious knowledge, their criticisms of ministers, their absences from sermons, their use of charms, their family quarrels, as well as to more serious offences. Other examples, from the later activity of the Consistory in Calvin's time, show disciplinary procedure against a widow who prayed a 'requiescat in pace' on her husband's grave; for having fortunes told by gipsies; against a goldsmith for making a chalice; for saying that the incoming of French refugees had raised the cost of living and that a minister had declared that all those who had died earlier (i.e., before the Reformation) were damned; for dancing; for possessing a copy of the *Golden Legend;* against a woman of seventy who was about to marry a man of twenty-five; against a barber for tonsuring a priest; for declaring the Pope to be a good man; making a noise during a sermon, laughing during preaching; criticizing Geneva for putting men to death on account of differences in religion; having a copy of *Amadis de Gaules;* or singing a song defamatory of Calvin.[46]

These, as the author himself observes, are chosen from among the most curious cases. They must not make us forget that the ordinary activity of the Consistory was directed to very numerous cases of a gravity that justified intervention. On the other hand, it is certain that responsibility for the prosecutions, far from being always incumbent upon Calvin, rested mainly upon colleagues of his who exercised it with less discretion. Lastly it must be remembered, if we are to do justice to the Consistory's work, that the Magistracy's jurisdiction was no less prone to inquisitorial animus, and that in spite of frequent wrangles about com-

[46] WALKER, op. cit., pp. 304 ff. KOEHLER, op. cit., vol. II, pp. 580-8, gives numerous supplementary details with precise references.

petence, it generally helped in the work of the Consistory by confirming the measures taken by the latter and referring more cases to it.[47]

However, Calvin was clearly the moving spirit of the Consistory. To study the official documents is to find traces of his initiative almost everywhere. Everything had to contribute to making a saintly city of Geneva. The inns were forbidden to the citizens; they were replaced by five 'abbeys', where the guests were placed under supervision, and where they found a French version of the Bible for their distraction: this innovation lasted hardly more than a month.[48] The profane theatre was of course prohibited. But the presentation of sacred pieces was authorized, though certain zealots immediately found these too licentious, in spite of Calvin's opinion in their favour.[49] Towards the end of 1546, there was an attack upon the personal names that were most common in Geneva, on the pretext that they were not Biblical. This measure too proved to be so unpopular that it had to be postponed till some years later.[50] It would almost seem that the Devil himself took a hand, to assist the Consistory in its moralizing activities: for in October 1546 he bore away through the air (so Calvin himself testifies) a man who was ill with the plague, and who was known for his misconduct and impiety.[51]

The first effect of setting up this system of ecclesiastical police was to exasperate a great part of the population. Although he was not the originator of all the measures that were taken, Calvin at once became the target for the popular indignation. About

[47] See the examples cited by KOEHLER, op. cit., pp. 588 ff.
[48] Ibid., pp. 593 ff.
[49] Ibid., p. 602. Cf. the letter to Farel of 3rd June 1546, *Opp.*, 12, 347.
[50] KOEHLER, op. cit., p. 596.
[51] Calvin took part in the inquest; he mentioned the event in a sermon and in a letter to Viret of 14th Nov. 1546, *Opp.*, 12, 413 ff. One may compare with this incident Calvin's attitude to sorcery and his intervention in the affair of the sorcerers and sorceresses of Peney in 1545. Cf. O. PFISTER, *Calvins Eingreifen in die Hexer- und Hexenprozesse von Peney*, Zurich, 1947. The author of this study rightly rejects the traditional Calvinist apologetics, but is himself ruled by preoccupations foreign to the rules of historical criticism. The whole question deserves re-examination in the light of the jurisprudence of the epoch.

the month of January 1546, a member of the Little Council, Pierre Ameaux, asserted that Calvin was nothing but a wicked man, a Picard who was preaching false doctrine.[52] This attack might well have been treated with contempt, but Calvin felt that his authority as an interpreter of the Word of God was being attacked: he so completely identified his own ministry with the will of God that he considered Ameaux's words as an insult to the honour of Christ aimed at the person of one of his ministers. The Magistrates offered to make the culprit beg Calvin's pardon on bended knees before the Council of the Two Hundred, but Calvin found this an insufficient reparation, and declared that he would not go up into a pulpit again until they had given him satisfaction. The case was then heard over again, and on April 8th Ameaux was sentenced to walk all round the town, dressed only in his shirt, bareheaded and carrying a lighted torch in his hand, and after that to present himself before the tribunal and cry to God for mercy. One can imagine the impression this made upon the inhabitants, when they saw a member of the Magistracy hustled through the town in such pitiful apparel for having insulted the pastor of St Peter's. A pastor of the country-side dared to criticize Calvin's attitude in this affair: he was immediately unfrocked.

But even all this was of small importance compared with the emotions aroused in Geneva and the surrounding cantons when the Consistory came into opposition with two of the most respected families of Genevan patricians, the Perrins and the Favres. It must indeed be acknowledged that the members of the Consistory proved their courage and independence, by attacking the most highly placed and the lowest indifferently. But this particular case was aggravated by the fact that the two families in question were among the firmest supporters that Calvin and Farel had had since the beginning of their Genevan activities. Ami Perrin was the uncontested leader of the Guillermins, who had brought Calvin back to the town. But neither Perrin nor his father-in-law François Favre were in favour of the inquisitorial methods of the Consistory. And the private conduct of both these men caused them to be summoned several times before the ecclesiastical jurisdiction. They resisted this for some

[52] DOUMERGUE, op. cit., vol. VI, pp. 83 ff.

time, refusing to present themselves, or replying with insolence to the reprimands addressed to them. When at last the Consistory wanted to compel François Favre to submit, his son-in-law Ami Perrin publicly raised before the Council the question of the competence of the Consistory. This was highly alarming, but Calvin managed to win the Councillors to his point of view, and Perrin went away for some time on a diplomatic mission to the Court of France.[53]

In June 1547, further trouble: a member of an old Genevan family, Jacques Gruet, was found to be in possession of compromising papers.[54] Among these was the draft of a petition to the Council aimed against the activity of the Consistory; another of a letter to the King of France asking him to intervene and re-establish order in Geneva; and lastly several writings judged to be blasphemous. Calvin and some of the Magistrates thought there was a plot; Gruet was put to the torture, but they did not succeed in making him reveal any accomplices; finally, he was beheaded.[55] This affair was not brought before the Consistory, but Calvin played a part in it, and had no difficulty in persuading the Council to adopt his view of it. In September the situation suddenly darkened. Ami Perrin had just returned to Geneva, and was now in the pay of the King of France. Appearances notwithstanding, Perrin's intentions seem to have been praiseworthy. Charles V had just won his first success against the German Protestants in the war of Schmalkalden, and people were anxious, almost all over the Protestant cantons of Switzerland, to strengthen their means of defence in case the Emperor might be thinking of attacking the towns that had gone over to the Reform. In these conditions it was natural to think first of all of ensuring aid from

[53] Ibid., vol. vi, pp. 91 ff. We must remember not to confuse the party of the 'libertines', of which Perrin, Vandel and Favre were leaders, with the sect of 'spiritual libertines' against which Calvin launched his treatise *Against the fantastic sect of the libertines* (1545), which, incidentally, embroiled him with Marguerite of Navarre. These spiritual libertines were mystics, more or less connected with the Reform, whose aspirations must have pleased the sister of Francis I. Cf. w. NIESEL, 'Calvin und die Libertiner' in the *Zeitschr. für Kirchengeschichte*, 1929, pp. 58-74.

[54] DOUMERGUE, op. cit., vol. vi, pp. 120 ff.

[55] Cf. the texts published by H. FAZY, 'Procès de Gruet' in the *Memoires de l'Institut national genevois*, 1886.

the King of France, who for many years had been the traditional ally of the Protestants outside his kingdom. At Geneva itself, a French refugee named Laurence Maigret had been for some time, and with Calvin's agreement, in communication with the Court of France with a view to eventual aid. The negotiations of Perrin and Maigret had been kept secret with the greatest care; and, divulged at the same moment, they excited lively emotions. The affair was complicated by the return of the Favres, who had taken flight to escape from the grip of the Consistory. François Favre and Perrin were both arrested.

Bernese intervention soon enabled Favre to obtain release. The Bernese, who regarded a possible alliance between France and Geneva with a suspicious eye, did their best to provoke the arrest of Maigret while they were intervening in favour of Perrin, whom they could count upon. Calvin, for his part, put forth efforts to save his friend Maigret. The old antagonism between Calvin and Bern was thus revived in an unexpected fashion. Towards the 'libertine' Perrin, Calvin's attitude was frankly hostile from the beginning.[56] As one would expect, stormy debates took place in the Council of the Two Hundred. The affair ended in a sort of compromise: the two accused were acquitted, and Perrin was reinstated in his functions. The general opinion was that he had become the spokesman for the old Genevans, against whom Calvin was accused of making common cause with the French refugees. Political passions became so heated that the populace attacked refugees openly in the streets, and Calvin himself was exposed to the gibes and insults of the mob whenever he left his house.[57]

At the elections of 1548 the two parties were in complete opposition: on one side were the partisans of Calvin, the majority of them French or Italian refugees, and on the other side the old Genevans under the leadership of Perrin. The latter were victorious; and for six years Calvin had to labour against the new majority in the Councils, which strove by every means to regain for the Magistracy that authority which in its

[56] But there is no justification for the categorical assertion of LANG, op. cit., p. 127, that Calvin 'worked with all his might to save Maigret and to destroy Perrin'.

[57] *Opp.*, 9, 892; F. W. KAMPSCHULTE, *Joh. Calvin*, vol. II, pp. 93 ff.

view had been usurped by the Church and especially by the Consistory.

To discredit their adversaries, the 'Calvinists' called them libertines, alleging that they did not want discipline, and that this could only mean that they knew it would show them up for what they were. It has been proved that these supposed libertines were neither more nor less attached to the Reform and to religion than were Calvin's supporters; but they had another conception of ecclesiastical authority.[58]

Meanwhile, intrigues and quarrels continued on both sides. To the preachers' denunciations of the attitude of Perrin's friends, the Council replied by enjoining the former not to mention their grievances in the pulpit without having first referred them to the Magistracy.[59] In September 1548 there came to the knowledge of the public a letter which Calvin had written to Viret three years before, criticizing the attitude of the Magistracy in no uncertain terms. Calvin was summoned and required to justify himself: the situation was such that at one moment he thought he would have to leave Geneva.[60] But the Council did no more than call upon him 'to do his duty better another time'.

In fact, the new Magistracy was not so systematically hostile as the Calvinists supposed. It came to the assistance of pastors and even of the Consistory whenever it thought its own authority was not in question. For instance, in 1550 the Council approved the rule that pastors should make one visit each year to the houses of all their parishioners to see for themselves whether the ecclesiastical regulations were being observed.[61] New ordinances were also enacted against blasphemers. Despite the political opposition of the 'libertines', Calvin's situation continued to improve. The more and more violent persecutions that were taking place in France produced a continual influx of new refugees, which naturally reinforced his party. The number of

[58] For a somewhat different explanation, cf. DOUMERGUE, op. cit., vol. VI, pp. 119 ff.; see also LANG, op. cit., p. 128.
[59] Cf. *Opp.*, 21, 429 ff. [60] *Opp.*, 21, 434-41.
[61] See the text of the *Ordinance* of 1561. *Opp.*, 10a, 116; for the date, cf. CHOISY, *La Théocratie à Genève*, p. 108.

refugees admitted to citizenship increased from year to year.[62] But it was not so much by their number, which was small enough, as by their social status and intellectual level that they provided valuable recruits. In this little crowd of nobles, intellectuals and ex-priests, Calvin found his ablest collaborators. In May 1549 Théodore de Bèze himself arrived in Geneva, and this future successor of Calvin was appointed professor of Greek at Lausanne, which was politically dependent upon Bern but which the Genevans regarded as a sort of annex to their own Church. At the same time as Bèze, came Laurent of Normandy (who became Calvin's intimate friend), the children of Guillaume Budé, then Guillaume de Trie (who was to play a part in the Servetus case), and yet others, all soliciting the right of domicile in this civic haven.[63]

Calvin had nothing to fear from the newcomers from the point of view of Genevan politics—quite the reverse. On the other hand, it was from among them that the first really serious attacks were made upon his teaching. The first trouble of this kind that presents some interest to us was aroused by an ex-Carmelite, Jérôme Bolsec, who established himself as a doctor in the outskirts of Geneva.[64] He was a fervent advocate of Calvinist doctrine, except in respect of dual predestination. Several times before this he had given vent to doubts on the subject, but in October 1551 he developed his arguments at a full session of the Congregation, asserting that Calvin was making God the author of sin, and rendering him guilty of the condemnation of the wicked: that 'this was to make a tyrant or a Jupiter of him; *item*, that one was being led to believe that St Augustine had been of that opinion; but neither he nor any of the ancient doctors held it.'[65] Calvin made a spirited reply 'adducing,

[62] Not all the new citizens, however, were French. From 1541 to 1554, only 310 in all were registered in the book of the citizens, 128 of these during 1547—probably for financial reasons. Cf. E. PFISTERER, *Calvins Wirken in Genf*, Essen, 1940, p. 13.

[63] *Opp.*, 21, 451 ff.; DOUMERGUE, vol. VI, p. 140.

[64] H. FAZY, 'Procès de Bolsec' in the *Mémoires de L'Institut national genevois*, 1866. Upon the theological aspect of the dispute, see A. SCHWEIZER, *Die protestantischen Centraldogmen*, vol. I, Zurich, 1854, pp. 205 ff.

[65] NIC. COLLADON, *Vie de Calvin*, *Opp.*, 21, 73.

besides numerous evidences from the Scriptures, endless quotations from St Augustine so exactly that it seemed as if he had
read and studied them that very day'. One of the 'seigneurs of
justice' who were present at this session immediately had Bolsec
arrested. The prosecution lasted a long while, the formal interrogations being interspersed with personal discussions between
Calvin and the accused. The Magistrates wavered, the more so
because some personal friends of Calvin, such as the seigneur of
Falais, interceded for Bolsec. The Magistracy finally asked the
opinion of the other Swiss Churches, and then political rivalry
became mixed up with it. The ministers of Geneva had already
sent a letter to their colleagues of Switzerland in which they had
expressed, as lucidly as could be desired, their anxiety to be rid
of such a pest as Bolsec and, in case he should be banished, to
preserve the other Churches from him.[66] This was a hardly-
disguised prayer for his capital condemnation: Calvin, however, had no desire for his adversary's death. But the replies
from the Churches of Basle, Zurich and Bern were a disappoint-
ment to him; Farel alone had made the ministers of Neuchâtel
draw up a virulent attack upon Bolsec; the others advised moderation and only alluded to the central issue with great reserve.
Calvin complained, in a letter to Farel, of the 'barbarity' shown
him by the men of Zurich.[67] At one of the next sessions of the
Congregation of pastors he solemnly formulated his teaching,
and obliged all the pastors of the town and district to give it
their explicit adherence.[68] As for Bolsec, he was condemned to
banishment for life.

Whatever Calvin may have thought about it at the time, this
result was a victory for him. But it was a double-edged one, for
by referring the judgment of this case to the temporal power he
had involuntarily made the Magistracy the court of appeal
in a question of dogma. Bolsec was ultimately to take an
ignoble revenge: in 1577 he published a biography of Calvin in
which he recounted all the calumnies he had been able to
collect, a book which continued for more than two centuries
to be the arsenal from which anti-Calvinist polemics were
supplied.

[66] *Opp.*, 8, 207.   [67] *Opp.*, 14, 218.
[68] *Congregation upon the eternal election, Opp.*, 8, 85-138.

Meanwhile, the ill-treatment to which Bolsec had been subjected during his captivity, and his own hostility to Calvin, had won him the sympathies of the majority of the reformer's enemies. There were renewed disorders. Henceforward the Council abstained from lending support to the Consistory, and the leaders of the opposition began publicly to dispute its right to excommunicate. The Council maintained or dismissed ministers against the formal advice of their colleagues. Furthermore, the notary Trolliet, whom Calvin had removed from the ministry and who was a friend of Perrin, also began to raise difficulties on the subject of predestination. In the month of August, Calvin, outraged by the opposition he was encountering, declared to the Council that 'he would rather be discharged from his office than suffer so much in it.'[69] Trolliet, like Bolsec before him, attacked Calvin's doctrine of predestination for having, in effect, rendered sin necessary and ascribed the origin of it to God. In his reply to the Magistracy of Geneva, Calvin maintained the human responsibility, and concluded his indictment of Trolliet with the words: 'As for myself, noble seigneurs, being assured in my conscience that what I have taught and written did not grow in my brain, but that I hold it from God, I must maintain the same, if I do not wish to be a traitor to the truth, for which I think I have already answered enough.'[70] That final sentence put the problem in its true light: it was not so much a question of predestination as of Calvin's authority as an interpreter of the Scriptures— which meant, in fact, of the legitimacy of his whole work. The Genevan ministers, with the support of Viret and Farel, came out in favour of the Calvinist teaching; and once again, the Council had to give way in self-defence. On November 9th, 1552, the special commission set up to compose the difference reported 'that all things being rightly heard and understood, they pronounce and declare the said book of the *Institutes* to be well and saintly made, and its teaching to be the holy doctrine of God, and that they regard it as good and true ministry for this city; and that, now and in the future, no one may dare to speak against the said book, nor against the said doctrine.'[71] However, Trolliet had the benefit of a non-suit, and the certificate of orthodoxy

[69] *Opp.*, 21, 516. [70] *Opp.*, 14, 382. [71] *Opp.*, 21, 525.

The Organization of the Church in Geneva

that the political authority had thus given to Calvin did nothing
to strengthen Calvin's position.

The situation became further inflamed by the elections of
1553, which were a triumph for the anti-Calvinist parties. Ami
Perrin became first Syndic of Geneva. All kinds of new vexations
followed for Calvin and his friends. The pastors were excluded
from the General Council; refugees who had not yet acquired
the rights of citizenship were forbidden to walk abroad wearing
arms according to custom. In his correspondence, the reformer
complained bitterly that he was encountering ill-will and contradiction on every side. 'They suspect everything we say,' he
wrote to Bullinger. 'If I simply said it was daytime at high
noon, they would begin to doubt it.'[72]

It was into this situation, already critical enough, that there
suddenly irrupted the case of Servetus, by far the most important
if all those in which Calvin was involved during his ministry in
Geneva.[73]

Michael Servetus, born about 1511 at Villanueva in Aragon,
has left hardly a trace of his earliest days. In 1531, he suddenly
appeared at Strasbourg and at Basle, where he entered into violent
controversy with the Reformers about the relations between the
divine Word and the man Jesus, as well as about the legitimacy
of persecuting heretics.[74] At the same time he published, at
Haguenau, two works on the Trinity in which, contrary to the

[72] *Opp.*, 14, 611.

[73] All the biographers of Calvin dwell at length upon the trial of Servetus,
which has been the subject of innumerable special studies: the chief of them
are mentioned in DOUMERGUE, op. cit., vol. VI, pp. 173-372. It is also still
necessary to refer to the article by N. WEISS, 'Calvin, Servet, G. de Trie et le
tribunal de Vienne' in the *Bulln. de la Soc. de l'Hist. du Protest. français*, 1908,
vol. LVII, pp. 387-404. The recent articles of H. M. STUCKELBERGER, 'Calvin
und Servet' in *Zwingliana*, vol. VI, 1934, pp. 98-119; and of A. HOLLARD,
'Michel Servet et Jean Calvin' in the *Bibliothèque d'Humanisme et Renaissance*,
vol. VI, 1945, pp. 171-209, the former favourable, the latter very hostile, to
Calvin, contribute hardly anything new to the debate. The best general
work on Servetus is, at present, that of R. H. BAINTON, *Hunted Heretic*; *the Life
and Death of Servetus*, Boston, 1953. Upon the trial at Vienne, cf. also P.
CAVARD, *Le Procès de Michel Servet à Vienne*, Vienne, 1953.

[74] H. EELLS, *Martin Bucer*, pp. 132 ff.; C. GERBERT, *Geschichte der Stras-
burger Sectenbewegung*, Strasbourg, 1889, pp. 114 ff.; E. STAEHELIN, *Das theologische Lebenswerk Oekolampads*, Leipzig, 1939, pp. 535 ff.

traditional definitions, he defended theses very similar to the ancient monarchianism. These two treatises, the *De Trinitatis Erroribus* and the *Dialogi de Trinitate*, aroused the most vigorous protests, and the sale of them was forbidden at Strasbourg by the Magistracy. Servetus afterwards went to Paris, where he studied medicine and attracted the attention of Calvin; then he spent some time as a reader in a printing works at Lyon. In 1540 he turns up again at Vienne in the Dauphiny, employed as physician to the archbishop, whose grace and favour he had managed to obtain. It may have been there that he discovered the circulation of the blood and made himself famous in the history of medicine. But medical and anatomical research did not cause him to renounce theology. He was then reading the neo-Platonic writings with passionate interest, and spending his leisure in the secret preparation of a vast work in which he advocated the restoration of Christianity to its primitive integrity, the *Christianismi Restitutio*. According to Servetus, Christian teaching had been falsified successively by the early Fathers, by the Roman Church and finally by the Reformers. In this book Servetus taught that the Word is the ideal reason, the primordial idea which comprehends and sums up the essences of all things. The creatures appeared to him to be successive degradations of the divinity, from which they proceed by emanation. He rejected original sin, admitting only the existence of actual, conscious sins which, if we are to believe him, do not put in an appearance until after the age of twenty. To wash them away, the Christian has at his disposal a whole series of convergent means: adult baptism, the Lord's Supper, good works, and lastly the purifying fire after death. The author's peculiar views about the Trinity were of course restated in this volume. It might have been dangerous to entrust the manuscript to a printer at Vienne. Servetus therefore addressed himself to a printer at Lyons, a Protestant who, feeling mistrustful of the strangeness of his client's ideas, asked to be shown Calvin's approval of them. Servetus then sent some portions of his work to Geneva: Calvin briefly refuted the errors he found in them, and for good measure referred Servetus to the study of his *Institutes* of 1546. Servetus, however, full of his newly-acquired knowledge, was in no mood to be given lessons. He replied in an insulting tone, and sent

Calvin a copy of the *Institutes* which he had covered with annotations.[75]

Several years after this, the affair seemed finally to have been buried. But in 1553 Servetus managed at last to get his work printed, in the greatest secrecy, at Vienne. A copy of it reached Geneva and fell into the hands of Calvin and his intimates. One of these, Guillaume de Trie, smarting under the reproaches of his parents at Lyons, who deplored his going over to the Reform, replied to them that people were in no position to accuse him of heresy while they themselves were tolerating a heretic of Servetus's calibre in France. De Trie's correspondents at Lyons made inquiries about this, and ended by discovering that the man in question was the physician to the Archbishop of Vienne. Servetus was denounced, arrested and committed for trial by the authorities at Vienne. But there was a lack of incriminating evidence. De Trie, at the request of his parents, then supplied several manuscripts.

Now, among these were some letters from Servetus addressed to Calvin. Calvin let de Trie have them only after much hesitation; still, he did in the end let go of these compromising documents, and he could not have been unaware of the use that would be made of them. However, Servetus managed to escape, and at Vienne they had to be content with a public burning of him in effigy together with his books.

Servetus intended to seek asylum in Naples. But in order to reach Italy he very imprudently travelled through Geneva. He had hardly arrived there when he was arrested upon Calvin's demand, on August 13th, 1553.[76] The Genevan law prescribed that every accuser must yield himself prisoner for the duration of the proceedings he was initiating, so that he himself should suffer an appropriate penalty if the accused were judged innocent. It was therefore no very light undertaking to bring a public action of this kind. Calvin, however, had no hesitation: he charged one of his disciples to lodge the complaint of heresy and blasphemy, and to allow himself to be imprisoned as the law required. Contrary to all expectation, the Magistracy immedi-

[75] Some important fragments of this correspondence have survived: see *Opp.*, 8, 482-500 and 649-720.

[76] The acts for the trial of Servetus figure in *Opp.*, 8, 725-872.

ately took up the cudgels against Servetus: Calvin's pupil was released after a few days and dismissed without even the customary warning. Moreover, the first interrogations to which Servetus was subjected made a very bad impression on the judges. The Council decided to prosecute the case in its own name. As in the Bolsec affair, advice was solicited from the other Protestant cantons: but even before they had replied, the act of accusation had been drawn up, and it was an adversary of Calvin who wrote it. Soon the political partisans and enemies of Calvin were outbidding one another at the expense of Servetus. In the meanwhile, the ecclesiastical tribune at Vienne demanded the extradition of of the heretic, which the Magistracy refused categorically, eager to prove to the world that there were judges in Geneva who knew as well as anyone how to condemn heresy.[77]

Servetus in his prison cell does not appear to have realized the gravity of his situation. No doubt he was hoping to find some supporters in one party at least of the opposition: several members of it did indeed intervene to have his conditions of captivity improved; but their relations with the accused went no further than that.[78] As for Calvin, he did not conceal his hope that Servetus would be put to death, but otherwise than by fire, the usual punishment for blasphemers.[79] Servetus, by his own attitude especially in the course of his disputes with Calvin, seemed purposely to stir up the animosity of his accusers, as though for pleasure. If we can believe the official report, his behaviour was in the last degree arrogant and unmannerly. On September 22nd he went to the length of demanding action against Calvin, whom he in turn accused of manifest heresy, even demanding that the reformer should be expelled from Geneva and his goods awarded to him, Servetus, in compensation for his wrongs.[80] This gesture naturally made the worst possibly impression. Everyone was already convinced of the necessity of getting rid of this heretic,

[77] It is curious to note that the Genevans, on their own account, thought fit to report the arrest of Servetus to the tribunal at Vienne, and to ask it for 'duplicates of the evidence, information and writ of arrest'; *Opp.*, 8, 761, 783 and 790.

[78] See R. BAINTON, 'Servet et les Libertins de Genève' in the *Bulln. de la Soc. de l'Hist. du Protest. français*, 1938, vol. LXXXVII, pp. 261-9.

[79] Letter to Farel of 20th August, 1553, *Opp.*, 14, 590.

[80] *Opp.*, 8, 804 ff.

when the replies came from Basle, Bern, Schaffhausen and Zurich.[81] The Swiss Churches showed themselves unanimous in denouncing Servetus, in congratulating the Genevans upon their zeal, and in urging the Magistracy to prevent the accused from doing further mischief. To annoy Calvin, rather than from conviction, Ami Perrin demanded at the last moment that the Two Hundred should be consulted before judgment was pronounced. But this was ignored, and on October 26th Servetus was condemned to punishment by fire, and burnt alive on the day after, in spite of the intervention of Calvin and some pastors who pleaded for a less barbarous method of execution.[82]

The death of Servetus, for which Calvin bears a large share of the responsibility, has given rise to an abundant literature ever since the day after his execution. Most of the historians, even of those most favourable to Calvin, have bitterly reproached him for having tarnished his renown by such unconsidered action. But this is to forget two things: first, that Servetus suffered the fate that hundreds of heretics and Anabaptists suffered at the hands of Protestant authorities of all shades of opinion, as well as of Catholic authorities; and secondly, that it is contrary to a sound conception of history to try to apply our ways of judging and our moral criteria to the past. Calvin was convinced, and all the reformers shared this conviction, that it was the duty of a Christian magistrate to put to death blasphemers who kill the soul, just as they punished murderers who kill the body. Melanchthon was expressing the general opinion when he wrote to Calvin, on October 14th, 1554:

I have read the writing in which you have refuted the detestable blasphemies of Servetus, and I return thanks to the Son of God who was the arbiter of your combat. To you also, the Church owes, and will in the future owe, gratitude. I am in entire agreement with your judgment. I affirm also that your Magistracy has acted justly in putting this blasphemer to death after a regular trial.[83]

The principal charge against Servetus was not that of holding a

[81] *Opp.*, 8, 808-23.
[82] Letter to Farel of 26th October 1553, *Opp.*, 14, 656.
[83] *Opp.*, 15, 268.

merely heretical opinion such as Bolsec or Trolliet had professed, but that he had denied the Trinity, and thereby, according to contemporary opinion, had made himself guilty of an indubitable blasphemy; he had also, by having his book printed, tried to contaminate his contemporaries and the Church. Besides these, Calvin had two particular reasons for showing special intransigence in this affair. Servetus's theses were diametrically opposed to what was most fundamental in Calvinist theology and piety, namely the exaltation of the divinity of Christ. His contention with Caroli, moreover, had made him more sensitive to anything that touched upon Trinitarian dogma. Also, when Sebastian Castellion published, some months after Servetus's death, a collection of impressive testimonies against the employment of violence in matters of faith, it aroused only a feeble echo.[84] He had touched upon only one aspect of the question, and not the most important in the eyes of his contemporaries. For the rest, Calvin had replied in advance to most of the attacks of Castellion. In his *Defence of the orthodox faith concerning the Holy Trinity* he had defended not only his own attitude at the trial of Servetus but, more generally, the ancient Augustinian principle of repressing heresy by the secular sword.[85] Tolerance, in the sixteenth century, was not, and could not be, anything but a sign of religious opposition or apathy.

Calvin had received the fullest support from the Magistracy throughout this painful affair. Furthermore, it was the political power which had taken over the conduct of the prosecution, in which the reformer figured as hardly more than a technical adviser. His authority as a theologian came out of it enhanced: by the testimonies from the Protestant cantons, he had now been recognized as the authoritative defender of the true faith. But it would be a mistake to conclude from this that he had the upper hand thenceforth in his conflicts with the Magistracy about the discipline and the rights of the Consistory. In fact, the legitimacy of its excommunication had again been rendered doubtful while

[84] BUISSON, op. cit., vol. I, pp. 335 ff., where we find the opinions that were hostile to Calvin collected with great care; cf. STUCKELBERGER, 'Calvin und Castellio' in *Zwingliana*, vol. VII, pp. 102 ff.

[85] *Opp.*, 8, 475-644; *Opusc.*, 1505-1692. Cf. DOUMERGUE, op. cit., vol. VI, pp. 409 ff.

the trial of Servetus was proceeding. Until then, all attacks upon the competence of the Consistory had failed before Calvin's intractable firmness. But now a new offensive, much more formidable than these, was threatening to annihilate all that he had won. A year previously, the Consistory had excommunicated a citizen of the name of Berthelier, one of the moving spirits of the anti-Calvinist opposition. On September 1st, 1553, Berthelier petitioned the Council, and not the Consistory, for authorization to present himself at Holy Communion—an application which naturally implied that the right to pronounce and to remit excommunication belonged to the Magistracy.[86] The request was granted in spite of Calvin's protests. The latter then declared from the height of the pulpit that he would allow no one who had been excommunicated by the Consistory to approach the holy table. After this determined outburst he so fully expected to be obliged to leave the town, that he preached a farewell sermon the same afternoon.[87] In the event, nothing happened; for Berthelier, yielding to the recommendations of the Magistracy itself, did not present himself for Communion.

Tranquillity had hardly been restored, when in November the quarrel revived with renewed vigour as a result of a sermon by Farel on the unruliness of the young. The preacher had no difficulty in justifying himself, especially as a number of young people took up the cudgels on his behalf. But the Little Council took advantage of the occasion to resume the debate about excommunication. The ministers and the Consistory protested and appealed to the text of the Ordinances, upon which it was decided to bring the question before the Two Hundred.[88] There, it was ruled that the Consistory should not go further than simple admonitions, and, with regard to the Communion, 'that it had no power to forbid it to anyone without command from the Council.' The ministers refused, once again, to submit to this. To get out of the deadlock, a majority of the Two Hundred finally appealed to the Protestant cantons for advice; and while waiting for their replies no change was to be made. At the elections of 1554, the supporters of Calvin got possession of three

[86] *Opp.*, 21, 551; WALKER, op. cit., pp. 365 ff.   [87] *Opp.*, 21, 552.
[88] *Opp.*, 21, 559 ff.; 605-14. Cf. CHOISY, op. cit., pp. 157 ff.; KOEHLER, op. cit., vol. II, pp. 607 ff.

syndical posts out of four, and the following year they regained an absolute majority in the Councils. But still no solution had been found for the problem of excommunication. At last, on January 22nd and 24th, 1555, the various Councils put the question to debate, and came uniformly to the decision that they must stand by the edicts, which meant the existing state of things. Thus rebuffed, the opposition tried to put up a show of force; and on May 16th there was a riot, which was fairly harmless but was taken very seriously indeed. The libertine leaders fled to Bern, and were sentenced to death in their absence. A member of the family of Berthelier was put to the question, and beheaded.[89]

Fortified by these rapid successes, the Calvinist party made haste to consolidate its position by obtaining admission to citizenship for a larger and larger number of refugees, thus strengthening its electoral clientele. Little by little the external situation also improved. Under the influence of the 'libertines' who had taken refuge in Bern, the Bernese had at first refused to renew their alliance with Geneva; and at the same time they allowed freedom of action to Calvin's enemies, in particular those who were opposed to his doctrine of predestination. All discussion of this subject was forbidden to Bernese subjects in the Vaud, and so was partaking of the Lord's Supper 'according to the Calvinist ceremonies'.[90] But in 1558, when there was a more definite menace from Savoy both to Geneva and to the Bernese possessions, Bern was at last obliged reluctantly to sign a new political accord with the Genevans. In revenge, however, the Calvinist pastors and professors of Lausanne were expelled from their homes; and the controversies between the Bernese and the Genevan theologians went on without restraint.

In Geneva itself, in the same year, another attack was launched upon the trinitarian doctrine by some Italian refugees.[91] A confession of faith was imposed upon the members of the Italian

[89] *Opp.*, 21, 593; 605-14; CHOISY, op. cit., pp. 169 ff.; DOUMERGUE, op. cit., vol. VII, pp. 25-49.

[90] *Opp.*, 15, 405.

[91] DOUMERGUE, op. cit., vol. VI, pp. 489-502; to be corrected by the indications in W. NIESEL, 'Zum Genfer Prozess gegen Valentin Gentilis' in *Archiv für Reformationsgeschichte*, vol. XXVI, pp. 270 ff.

Church, but one of the most influential of these, Valentin Gentilis, refused to subscribe to it. He was arrested, confronted by Calvin and, if not convinced, was at least induced to retract his opinions. But a commission of jurists regarded this as no more than a pretence, and concluded by condemning him to death as a blasphemer. A further act of submission saved his life, and he was sentenced to make honourable amends and throw his books into the fire with his own hands.[92]

The defence of orthodoxy did not, however, exclude certain concessions in the interests of unity and good understanding between the Churches produced by the Reformation. That Calvin, throughout his life, should have shown himself so preoccupied with the problem of an understanding with the Lutheran, the Zwinglian and even the Anglican Churches, as to regard himself as the successor to Bucer in that domain, may be explained in part by the ecclesiastical situation and the need for a common defence against Rome. But the true reason for his eirenic efforts lay deeper, and was rooted in his very conception of the Church. From the moment when the latter became the body of Christ, and the different Protestant communities acknowledged the same Lord, nothing ought to prevent their union, provided the scriptural doctrine was safeguarded. It was in that spirit that Calvin negotiated with Bullinger of Zurich and tried to come to terms of agreement with the Lutherans of Germany. If he did not always understand the latter or was not understood by them, the purity of his intentions remains beyond doubt. To arrive at an understanding with the Zwinglians was not easy either, and at first it appeared even more hazardous. Nearly ten years were taken up by negotiations, exchanges of documents and proposals of all kinds before the conclusion of the famous *Consensus Tigurinus* of 1549, which established in twenty-six articles a basis of agree-

---

[92] After fleeing from Geneva, he resumed his anti-trinitarian polemics, was imprisoned at Gex and at Lyons, expelled from Poland, and ended his days in 1566 on the scaffold at Bern. For his ideas, one may consult the refutation of them published by Calvin, *Opp.*, 9, 361-420; *Opusc.*, 2239-88 and D. CANTIMORI, *Italienische Haeretiker der Spätrenaissance*, Basle, 1949, pp. 216 ff. and p. 472.

ment upon the sacramental problem.[93] The text of this, which was not published until two years later,[94] did not succeed in dispelling all the divergences, in spite of its limited scope. Its careful drafting, and the reciprocal concessions that the two parties had to make, prevent one, moreover, from finding in this a complete and authentic expression of their thought. Nevertheless, their union has stood the test of time, and outlasted all the efforts made to destroy it.

Almost as soon as the *Consensus* was published, Calvin had to encounter criticisms from the Lutherans. Certainly it is an exaggeration to make out that this agreement between Calvin and the men of Zurich was the deeper cause of the attack from Westphal: it remains true, however, that the ebullient pastor of Hamburg found in the *Consensus* additional reasons for denouncing Calvinist propaganda in the countries of the North, which he regarded as a menace.[95] Westphal had studied under Luther and Melanchthon at Wittenberg, and had a perfect right to pride himself upon his fidelity to the pure Lutheran doctrine. He thought he had given no uncertain proof of this by coming violently to the defence of Flavius Illyricus against Melanchthon in the conflict aroused by the Interim of Leipzig. In 1552, he published his first polemical work, on the subject of the Eucharist, under the provocative title of a *Compilation of confused and divergent opinions concerning the Lord's Supper, taken from the books of the sacramentarians*. This was a real declaration of war addressed to the Calvinists, as well as the Zwinglians, whom he denounced as a danger to Christianity now that they were systematically spreading their teaching in France, the Low Countries, England and even Germany. A year later Westphal returned to the charge by publishing an exegetical and dogmatic study of the words of institution of the Supper. The first reactions came from the com-

[93] In his fine book on *Bullinger*, pp. 125-49, A. BOUVIER has described the whole history of these negotiations in a remarkable way. See also E. BIZER, *Studien zur Geschichte des Abendmahlsstreites im 16 Jahrhundert*, Gütersloh, 1940, pp. 243-74.

[94] *Opp.*, 7, 689-748.

[95] *Opp.*, 9, pp. ix-xxiv. Cf. G. KAWERAU, art. 'Westphal' in *Realencyclopädie für protest. Theol. und Kirche*, 3rd edn vol. XXI, pp. 185 ff.; P. TSCHACKERT, *Die Entstehung der lutherischen und reformierten Kirchenlehre*, Göttingen, 1910, pp. 531 ff.; E. BIZER, op. cit., pp. 275 ff.; BOUVIER, op. cit., pp. 150 ff.

munities of refugees of the Reform who had established themselves in Denmark and North Germany. After hesitating whether or not to reply, Calvin did so, on the advice of Bullinger. He had hoped that the Swiss Churches would have come to agreement to issue a statement in common, but he had to be content to publish his *Defence of the sound and orthodox doctrine of the Sacraments*[96] under his own name, in 1555. In this he refuted Westphal's theses in somewhat contemptuous terms, and without even doing Westphal the honour of mentioning his name. In the same year, and before he had had sight of Calvin's treatise, Westphal produced two complementary writings to demonstrate the patristic foundations of his position, and then a few months later he answered Calvin's pamphlet with a *Just defence against the false accusation of a certain sacramentarian*. In each renewal of the altercation the tone rose into a higher key—which to anyone who knows the controversial manners of that time is saying more than a little. In the writing last named, Westphal defended himself in the most violent terms against Calvin's reproof that he was a troubler of the peace of the Church, and insistently retorted with the accusation he had made in his *Compilation*, namely, that his contradictors managed to agree with one another only when it was a question of denying the real presence in the Eucharist.

In 1556, Calvin replied in turn, by a *Second defence of the holy and right faith in the matter of the Sacraments*,[97] which he dedicated 'to all those good ministers of Christ and true servants of God who love, hold and follow the pure teaching of the Gospel in Churches of the lands of Saxony and Low Germany'. This was manifestly an appeal to Melanchthon and his supporters. Westphal then wrote three more pamphlets one after another, all published during 1557, in the first of which he assembled all the declarations of Melanchthon which he thought favourable to his own argument. In the same year the presses turned out Calvin's rejoinder entitled *Last warning from John Calvin to Joachim Westphal*.[98] Still during 1557, Westphal published his *Refutation of some enormous falsehoods of J. Calvin*, and then in the following year a *Confession touching the Lord's Supper* and an *Apology* for that confession.

[96] *Opp.*, 9, 1-40.
[97] *Opp.*, 9, 41-120; *Opusc.*, 1725-1818. [98] *Opp.*, 9, 137-252; *Opusc.*, 1817-52.

As in the case of the first dispute over the sacraments between Luther and Zwingli, the conflict rapidly spread more widely. In Germany, it grafted itself on to the issue that kept the supporters and the detractors of Melanchthon at loggerheads. In Switzerland, it reawakened the prejudices of the Zwinglians against the Lutherans. From both sides there poured forth innumerable writings meant to aid and abet the two protagonists and support their assertions. And just as in the days preceding the Colloquy of Marburg, it was these enthusiastic and often blundering allies who gave the lamentable quarrel its vast extension and its irresolvable character. It is true that Calvin and Westphal helped to envenom the controversy by the way they conducted it; the insults they hurled at one another's heads like a couple of Homeric heroes would of themselves have been enough to worsen the situation. Their partisans carefully memorized these personal insults and bandied them about in their circles with evident relish. In this way they aroused an infinity of local quarrels on the margins of the main conflict, which completed the rupture between the two parties. It should be added that neither side took much account of its adversary's real positions and that both persisted in attacking opinions that their opponents, in most cases, had never meant to defend.

After his *Last Warning*, Calvin refused to go on with this tiring and sterile debate: he was undermined by ill-health, and preoccupied by the reshaping of his *Institutes* and by the organizing of the Churches in France. Théodore de Bèze was deputed to reply to Westphal's last writing. However, Calvin defined his standpoint for the last time in the *Institutes* themselves, by devoting a great part of the seventeenth chapter of Book IV to the problems raised by Westphal: in this he inserted some important fragments of his first *Defence* of 1555 and of his *Last Warning* of 1557. Yet the demon of controversy seized him once more in 1561, when he published, in reply to a diatribe from Tileman Hesshusius of Heidelberg, *A clear exposition of the wholesome doctrine of the true partaking of the flesh and the blood of Jesus Christ.*[99] But the outcome

[99] *Opp.*, 9, 457-524; *Opusc.*, 1951-2018. This Hesshusius was the very type of that small-mindedness which can only conceive of theology under the aspect of disputations as gross as they are inopportune. DOUMERGUE, op. cit., vol. VI, p. 517, has every right to call him the 'perfect fanatic'.

of all these efforts was hardly encouraging; the war of pamphlets was only widening and deepening the gulf between Lutherans and Calvinists.

In Geneva itself, Calvin was concentrating his efforts during this period upon an enterprise destined to have very different consequences—the creation of the Academy, which can be said without the least exaggeration to have been his crowning work.[100] Humanists and reformers, divided as they were upon so many things, were in agreement upon one point at least: the necessity, in the training of a man and a Christian, of an education as complete and extensive as possible, founded upon the study of the ancients. Luther, Melanchthon, Zwingli, Bucer and Calvin insisted, each one of them, upon the value of such an education, which was to terminate in a deeper study of the various theological disciplines. And it must be said to the credit of Protestantism of all shades, that one of its chief titles to renown has always been, up to very recent times, that of having formed a body of pastors provided with a high degree of intellectual culture.

When at last his hands were freed and he had the indispensable men, Calvin applied himself to this task with extraordinary ardour, in addition to all his other work. His task was facilitated by the arrival in Geneva of the professors expelled from Lausanne with Théodore de Bèze at their head. To find the necessary funds he organized collections, and on June 5th, 1559, he was able to preside over the inaugural session of the new Academy. In the 'laws' that he drew up for this institution, he emphasized the respective parts played in education by discipline, by religious exercises, the study of the ancients and of theology.[101] The organization itself comprised a series of classes ranging from secondary studies to the teaching of theology. Here the High School of Jean Sturm had served as a model. The Genevan Academy, in its turn, inspired the Protestant Academies which

[100] WALKER, op. cit., pp. 386 ff. The most comprehensive study of this aspect of Calvin's work is that of CH. BORGEAUD, *L'Académie de Calvin*, Geneva, 1900. See also DOUMERGUE, op. cit., vol. VII, pp. 141 ff.

[101] *Opp.*, 10a, 65-90.

were founded in France in the seventeenth century and also, very probably, the schools created by the Jesuit order.

In November 1561, the Ecclesiastical Ordinances were subjected to a revision, but without Calvin's having been able, for all the prestige that he then enjoyed, to obtain the insertion in them of all his ideas.[102] Nevertheless the new text was, on the whole, of authentically Calvinist inspiration, even in the passages dealing with 'the distinction shown to us in the Holy Scripture between the sword and authority of the Magistrate, and the superintendence that the Church should exercise, to bring all Christians to the obedience and true service to God, and to prevent and correct scandals'.[103] The authority of the Consistory was also clearly accentuated. And in practice, its zeal was rivalled by that of the Magistracy: the ever-growing number of excommunications[104] corresponded with the promulgations of new sumptuary laws. All serious resistance had disappeared. As though to give outward proof of its complete reconciliation with the reformer, on Christmas Day 1559 the Magistracy offered him the freedom of the city.[105]

In the moments of respite that his illness allowed him, Calvin was now able to devote himself wholly to the perfecting of his work and to the recommendations intended for his disciples, among whom he had already chosen Théodore de Bèze to succeed him. On February 6th, 1564, he preached for the last time. In March, the Council announced public prayers on his behalf, which had never been done for one particular person. On April 27th, the various Councils went in procession to visit him and receive his farewells, and on the next day he took leave of the pastors of the neighbourhood. For the last time, Farel sped from Neuchâtel to see his friend. Calvin died on May 27th, 1564.

The work he left at Geneva was of modest appearance: a Church and a school of his own creation, a town that he had completely transformed. But in fact his work was already spreading throughout Europe, even into England and Scotland. And yet it was neither Geneva nor the far-distant Churches now acknowledging his name, which had been at the centre of his

---

[102] *Opp.*, 10a, 91-124. KOEHLER, op. cit., vol. II, pp. 616 ff.
[103] *Opp.*, 10a, 121. [104] Cf. KOEHLER, op. cit. vol. II, p. 614, n. 544.
[105] *Opp.*, 21, 725.

preoccupations: in reality it was France. He had left France in order to evangelize it from without, to organize his new communities from afar. All his life he had striven to attain this goal glimpsed in his youth.[106] He had succeeded in grouping the Reformed communities into a confederacy of coherent Churches unified under the same doctrine and the same discipline. But he died too soon to be able to advise and guide them during the terrible crisis of the religious wars—that is, at the very moment when they were to have the greatest need of him.

[106] It lies outside the scope of this summary account to retrace the stages and the details of Calvin's activities outside Geneva. See IMBART DE LA TOUR, op. cit., p. 423.

PART TWO

The Theological Doctrine

CHAPTER ONE

'The Institutes of the Christian Religion'

'The whole of Calvinism is in the *Institutes*—a work of capital importance, the work most valued by Calvin, who spent all his life revising and reshaping as well as enriching it. All his other works—commentaries, controversies, smaller dogmatic or moral treatises—are related to it like advanced redoubts meant to defend the heart of the place against the enemy.'[1] Not only do the *Institutes* occupy the central place in Calvin's literary production, so abundant in other directions; this is also a work in which, during his whole career as a reformer, he methodically set down all the problems that were presented to his reflection, or that a deepening of his own thought led him to examine more closely. Whatever interest and value may attach to his other theological writings, the *Institutes* are the faithful summary of the ideas he expounded in them. Moreover, the *Institutes*—at least in their final form—purport to give a complete account of Christian teaching. They therefore present a synthesis of Calvinist thought, and one that is sufficient in itself; whereas to define the positions of a Luther or a Zwingli, one must have recourse to writings very different from one another.[2]

[1] IMBART DE LA TOUR, *Calvin et l'Institution chretiénne*, p. 55.
[2] We shall quote the *Institutes* from the French version of the edition of 1559; the choice imposes itself if one is taking the theological point of view, for this version comprises the whole of Calvinist thought and is the most accomplished expression of it. But whenever the need makes itself felt, we will indicate the different stages of this thought as they are marked in the successive editions.

I. THE SUCCESSIVE EDITIONS OF THE 'INSTITUTES'

The first edition of the *Institutes of the Christian Religion* was published in March 1536 by the Basle printers Thomas Platter and Balthasar Lasius.[3] This was in one volume of 516 pages of small format, such as could readily be slipped into the vast pockets of the clothes then worn. The work at that time consisted of six chapters: the first four were devoted to the Law, the Creed, the Lord's Prayer, and the sacraments of Baptism and the Lord's Supper—which was the classic order of Luther's *Catechisms*. And the work was, in fact, conceived as a catechism; that is what the publishers and Calvin himself called it.[4] A fifth and a sixth chapter, one dealing with false sacraments and the other with the liberty of the Christian, were inspired by the special reasons which had also given birth to the 'Epistle to the King' printed at the head of the work. The tone of these two chapters, which is polemical, is in sharp contrast with the calm and objective exposition of the first four chapters—that is, of the catechism properly so called. In the fifth chapter, Calvin combats the sacramental nature of penitence, of orders, of confirmation, extreme unction and marriage. In the sixth, he expounds not only his conception of Christian freedom, but also his ideas upon what the relation between Church and State would be in a society inspired by the Gospel. This is at once a reply to the official condemnation of the famous Placards of 1534 and a protest against the attitude of the Crown of France with regard to the Reform. Here Calvin strongly affirms that it is necessary for the prince to respect the faith of his subjects, so long as it is in conformity with the Gospel. The doctrine that he expounds here, in all its generality, he also shows, in practical application to the situation then obtaining in France, in his 'Epistle to the King'—an item of a purely apologetic character intended to clear the reformed in France from the accusation of rebellion which had been laid against them, and which Guillaume du Bellay had

---

[3] Cf. *Opp.*, xxiii-xxxii. DOUMERGUE, op. cit., vol. I, pp. 592 ff.; A. AUTIN, *L'Institution chrétienne de Calvin*, Paris, 1929, pp. 47 ff., 75 ff.; O.S. vol. III, p. vi. Only the most important editions will be mentioned here.

[4] AUTIN, op. cit., p. 37.

developed in a memorandum addressed to the Protestants of Germany, in which he tried to justify the persecutions that followed the affair of the Placards.[5]

The success of this first publication of the *Institutes* must have been considerable, for we learn that the edition was completely exhausted less than a year after it had appeared.[6] This is all the more worthy of remark since the work was in Latin, and its appeal therefore limited to a relatively small cultured public. Was there also, as was long supposed, a French version of this first edition? The learned editors of the *Opera Calvini* had no difficulty in rejecting the hypothesis of a French edition prior to the Latin edition of 1536,[7] on the basis of Calvin's own formal declaration in the preface to his edition of 1541. They therefore denied the existence of a translation of the edition of 1536. But it has been possible to demonstrate that in the French text of 1541 Calvin reproduced passages borrowed from the edition of 1536, taking no account of the modifications of detail which had been made to them in the Latin edition of 1539: the translation of 1541 reposed, then, so far as these passages are concerned, upon the text of 1536, of which, consequently, a French translation must have been in existence. All the same, it does not seem possible to affirm that this first translation had been published.[8]

Calvin's activities in Geneva and the setbacks he encountered there prevented him from perfecting the new edition as quickly as he wished: it did not appear until 1539.[9] The manuscript seems to have been completed about the end of the previous year—that is, during the first months of Calvin's period at Strasbourg. A printer of Basle had made him some offers with a view to printing the work, but the author's slow progress obliged him to postpone publication, and finally to entrust it to the Strasbourg printer Wendelin Rihel, who had published most of the works of Bucer. This second edition, of 1539, is again in Latin. To facili-

---

[5] Cf. PANNIER, the Introduction to his edition of *l'Epître au Roi*, Paris, 1927, pp. 9 ff.

[6] *Opp.*, 10b, 91.   [7] *Opp.*, 3, pp. xiv ff.

[8] PANNIER, 'Une Première *Institution* française dès 1537' in the *Revue d'Hist. et de Philos. relig.*, 1928, pp. 513-34; O.S. vol. III, pp. vii ff and 518 ff.; W. NIESEL and P. BARTH, 'Eine französische Ausgabe der ersten *Institutio* Calvins' in *Theologische Blätter*, Leipzig, 1928, pp. 2-10.

[9] *Opp.*, 1, xxxvii ff.; AUTIN, op. cit., 85-92; O.S., vol. III, pp. ix-xv.

tate its diffusion in France, a part of this edition circulated under the name of Alcuin, a transparent anagram for that of Calvin. The *Institutes* of 1539, however, was no longer the little volume of modest format that had come to light three years earlier; it now presented itself as a respectable in-folio containing nearly three times as much matter as the first edition: Calvin had indeed added eleven more chapters to his work.

The text of 1539 begins with two new chapters—on the knowledge of God and on the knowledge of man, problems that Calvin had no more than outlined in rather summary fashion in 1536, in the chapter upon the Law. In consequence of the recent discussions he had had with the Anabaptists, and of his painful controversies with Caroli, perhaps also under the impression left upon him by the reading of Servetus's writings, Calvin considerably enlarged his exposition of the Trinity. With the intention of further refuting the Anabaptists, he added a whole chapter on the relations between the Old and the New Testaments. The same motives led him to insert a formal defence of infant baptism, and several passages upon the value of the Scriptures, upon sanctification and against millenarianism. Two chapters, also new, deal with penitence and with justification by faith, questions which had hitherto received only a limited development. Under the influence of the works of Bucer, and of conversations he had had with the Strasbourg reformer, Calvin was led to insert in his *Institutes* another chapter in which, for the first time, he systematized his ideas upon predestination and divine Providence. This chapter, which moreover showed long familiarity with the works of St Augustine, had a polemical intention which was scarcely disguised. In it, Calvin emphasized the part that should be played by the exposition of predestination in Christian dogmatics; whereas Melanchthon had again, only recently (in the 1535 edition of his *Loci Communes*), dismissed all speculation on this subject as useless and confusing.[10] A last chapter, devoted to the Christian life, brought this second edition to an end; and here Calvin was able to make use of his pastoral experience and of the reflections suggested to him by reading Bucer's treatise *On the Cure of Souls*, which had appeared the year before.

[10] Cf. J. KOESTLIN, 'Calvins *Institutio* nach Form und Inhalt', in the *Theologische Studien und Kritiken*, vol. 41, 1868, pp. 40 ff.

Passing on from examination of the external form of the 1539 edition to its contents, we have to acknowledge a palpable improvement upon the *Institutes* of 1536. 'Although the edition of 1536 is merged into it, it is distinguished from all the others by a peculiar liveliness and freshness in the management of the thought. Together with the commentary upon the Epistle to the Romans this is the mature result of Calvin's labours upon the principal epistle of St Paul the Apostle. It proceeds upon the fundamental theological lines which were to be followed in all subsequent editions of the *Institutes*.'[11] In the first place, Calvin has succeeded in giving his exposition a more coherent and systematic character. It is easy to see that he has a better mastery of his material and that his theological culture has become sensibly enriched in the course of the three preceding years. One has only to note the sources of all his quotations to realize the extent and the depth of the reading that they reflect. To the Latin Fathers to whom he referred in 1536 are now added several of the Greek Fathers, notably Origen. Theologians of the Middle Ages also take a more considerable place; though in respect of these the quotations are still almost limited to Peter Lombard and his *Sentences*. However, it would be a mistake to imagine that Calvin's reading was limited to theologians; he had not ceased to steep his mind in the thought of antiquity even after his conversion. Plato, whom he seems hardly to have known before, now becomes one of the writers to whom he most often refers, although he generally avoids doing so by name. Lastly, ecclesiastical history now occupies more of his attention, to judge by his frequent references to it, and these were to become increasingly numerous in succeeding editions.

But although, upon a whole series of points, the edition of 1539 was thus notably an advance upon its predecessor, it was still far from satisfying all that was required. More systematic and more logical though it was, it left no little to be desired precisely in the domain of which Calvin is commonly acclaimed a master. Its planning, in particular, still presented rather grave defects. Even in later years the author appears always to have found trouble in inserting additions to his work in the places

[11] P. BARTH, 'Fünfundzwanzig Jahre Calvinforschung' in the *Theologische undschau*, 1934, p. 164.

naturally appropriate to them. Thus, in the 1539 edition, the passages about the knowledge of God were not all brought together in the first chapter, as they should have been, and the exposition of Providence was manifestly not in the right place, as Calvin himself indicated it later.

A little while after publishing his second *Institutes*, he set to work translating it into French. Perhaps it was because of the changes he had intended to introduce into the work that he had refrained from publishing a translation of the text of 1536; and so he was resuming that project at Strasbourg—doubtless as early as 1539. The French version of the *Institutes* was not published, however, until 1541, and then at Geneva by the printer Jean Girard, a few weeks after Calvin's return to that town.[12] From the literary point of view this edition of 1541 is indeed a masterpiece. For the first time, an original theological work came out in French, in a French style that was both elegant and highly personal, a style which was to play a part in the fashioning of the language well into the seventeenth century. And yet it could be said that Calvin's translation remains true to the Latin of the original, so much so that sometimes it seems to have been modelled upon it.[13] This strong imprint from the Latin periods and constructions persisted, as we know, in the classic French of St Francis de Sales and of Bossuet, who owe as much of their style to Calvin as to Montaigne, or to other authors of the end of the sixteenth century.

Naturally, the French edition of the *Institutes* was meant for the reformed of France who could not read the Latin of the original work. It had an abundant circulation in France, and such a success that it established itself at once as the basic manual of dogmatic in the reformed Churches. It can be affirmed without fear of error that when these Churches became Calvinist they owed it to the various French editions of the *Institutes*. The Latin editions remained, in the nature of things, the preserve of theologians and the learned, through whom as intermediaries

[12] *Opp.*, 3, pp. xxviii ff.; *O.S.*, vol. III, pp. xv-xviii; AUTIN, op. cit., pp. 92-7. Cf. J. W. MARMELSTEIN, *Etude comparative des textes latins et français de l'Institution*, Groningen, 1923.

[13] LEFRANC, Introduction to the edition of *l'Institution chrétienne*, *texte original de 1541*, Paris, 1911, vol. I, p. 18.

they had their effect. But the French editions had an influence far more extensive and direct, comparable only to that of the German Bible of Luther and the reformist works that he wrote in the vernacular. We also have proof that Calvin's contemporaries immediately perceived the importance of his publication. The *Institutes*, both in Latin and in French, was the only work expressly mentioned in the act of the Parliament of Paris of July 1st, 1542, decreeing the suppression of heretical books.[14]

In 1543 Calvin produced a new Latin edition of his work, and this too was followed by a translation in 1545.[15] The alterations and additions in this new edition are of much less importance than those in the edition of 1539. The new volume began—and this is a reminder of the sojourn in Strasbourg—with a eulogy of Calvin written by Jean Sturm. The number of chapters was increased by four, which brought the total up to twenty-one. Two of these new chapters dealt with vows and with human traditions, while the old chapter on the Symbol of the Apostles was now distributed among four chapters. The last of these incorporated the old chapter on the ecclesiastical power, and also contained a somewhat detailed exposition of Calvin's ideas about ecclesiastical organization. We should note at once that the four chapters of 1543 upon the Credo were to serve as a more or less rigid framework for the whole of the work, when it came to be re-cast in 1559.

The edition of 1550, followed by the translation of 1551,[16] contained the first apparent novelty: the chapters are subdivided into paragraphs in order to help the reader to find his way through such a voluminous text. The continual growth of the work is shown by several additions upon Holy Scripture and its authority, upon the worship of saints and of images, and lastly by an original exposition on the human conscience. The French version marks a further progress; it contains as many as three supplementary sections upon the resurrection of the body, which

[14] N. WEISS, 'Arrêt inédit du Parlement de Paris contre *l'Institution*', in the *Bulln de la Soc. de l'Hist. du Protest. français*, 1884, vol. XXXIII, pp. 15 ff.

[15] *Opp.*, 1, pp. xxxiv ff.; 3, pp. xxx-xxxiv; O.S., vol. III, pp. xviii-xxii and xxiv-xxvi; AUTIN, op. cit., pp. 103 ff.

[16] *Opp.*, 1, pp. xxxvi ff.; 3, p. xxxiv; O.S., vol. III, pp. xxvi-xxix and xxxiii ff.

Calvin did not incorporate in the Latin editions until 1559, although that of 1550 had been several times reprinted in the interval.

Thus we arrive at the Latin edition of 1559 and the French of 1560, which represent the culminating point in this work of a whole lifetime.[17] By that time Calvin was already suffering severely, and in fear of his approaching end he had determined to produce a new and definitive version of his book.[18] With the aid of his brother Antoine and some friends he set to work, and, in spite of atrocious pain, he delved into the previous editions, adding a little here and a new development there, suppressing passages which seemed to him ill-expressed or unclear. Théodore de Bèze, in his first *Life of Calvin*, wrote: 'He built his last *Institutes of the Christian Religion* under the worst stress of that illness and, what is more, translated it into French from beginning to end.'[19]

In spite of that formal testimony, the authors of the *Opera Calvini* felt able to affirm, after comparing the Latin and French editions side by side, that 'the French translation of the *Institutes*, in its definitive and received form, excepting the portions retained from the old edition, was written with a certain carelessness, by less expert hands, and without the author's supervision.'[20] Some twenty years later, G. Lanson took up the problem of the authenticity of the translation of 1560 and, after a fresh examination, came finally to the conclusion that 'Calvin himself prepared the French text of 1560; that he did not write, but dictated his additions; that he did not prepare the last state of the manuscript and did not correct the proofs.'[21] While attributing a larger part to Calvin than the Strasbourg editors did, Lanson therefore admitted as a certainty that alien interventions had taken place,

[17] *Opp.*, 1, pp. xxxix-xlii; 3, pp. xxxvii ff.; *O.S.*, vol. III, pp. xxxvi-xliii and xlv-xlviii; AUTIN, op. cit., pp. 115-26. Cf. KOESTLIN, op. cit., pp. 50 ff.

[18] TH. DE BÈZE, *Vie de Calvin*; *Opp.*, 21, 41. The same author's *Vita Calvini*, *Opp.*, 21, 156; COLLADON, *Vie de Calvin*, *Opp.*, 21, 87.

[19] *Opp.*, 21, 33.   [20] *Opp.*, 3, p. xxvii.

[21] G. LANSON, '*L'Institution chrétienne* de Calvin' in the *Revue historique*, 1894, p. 66. Cf. also A. LEFRANC, *Grands Ecrivains de la Renaissance*, p. 375 ff.; and J. DEMEURE, '*L'Institution chrétienne* de Calvin: examen de l'authenticité de la traduction française' in the *Revue d'Histoire littéraire de la France*, 1915, vol. 22, pp. 402 ff.

which might, at the last moment, have modified Calvin's text. One of the reasons on which he relied, and to which the editors of the *Opera Calvini* had given weight, was 'the great number of inaccuracies, omissions, of otiose and embarrassing additions' encountered in the French edition, which furthermore contained 'passages in which it is obvious that the translator has not even understood the Latin text'.[22] But it has since been demonstrated that the French editions prior to that of 1560 also contained errors, and even misconceptions, analogous to those relied upon to deny Calvin's paternity of the French text of 1560. It is the merit of J. W. Marmelstein especially, to have supplied proof that this text is perfectly authentic and may therefore be taken as the legitimate basis for study of Calvinist thought.[23] He established, in particular, that 'among the thirteen misconceptions or meaningless passages enumerated by the editors of the *Opera* there are readings that present perfectly correct translations, and others which are simply inadvertences, either of the author or of the printer'; and that, contrary to the opinion that had prevailed, '1560, in many places, respects the original better than 1541, more nearly approaches the literal sense of the Latin text, and repairs many faults and omissions that the previous editions had allowed to remain.'[24] It is true, as we have already noted, that from a purely literary point of view, the French edition of 1560 cannot compare with that of 1541, with its inimitable spontaneity and its surprising unity of style. In 1560 Calvin, prematurely aged, paid no great attention to form, although this remains very fine. What mattered to him above all in his last editions was to give strict precision and as logical a structure as possible to his thought.

The new text presents an appearance that the earlier editions would not lead one to expect. Instead of the twenty-one chapters of 1543, the reader is confronted by four large sections comprising eighty chapters in all. The bulk of the *Institutes* is once more increased, now by nearly a quarter compared with the preceding edition. It has indeed become, as its sub-title announces, 'almost a new book'. The additions made by the author are explicable, at least partly, by recollection of the controversy in which he had

[22] *Opp.*, 3, p. xxvi.   [23] MARMELSTEIN, op. cit., pp. 5-24 and 60-6.
[24] Ibid., pp. 113 and 115.

been engaged during the previous few years. An important place is given to the quarrel with the Lutherans, with Westphal in particular, on the subject of the Eucharist. On the other hand, the doctrines of Osiander touching the image of God in man, the work of Christ and justification, are subjected to formal refutation. Other passages recall the struggles against the 'spiritual libertines'. The portions which had already, before this, been written against the errors of Servetus are copiously developed. Lastly, the author takes up a position against the teaching of Lelius Socinus upon the merits of the Christ and the resurrection of the body. But there are still other additions which were made with no polemical intention. Calvin himself had realized that there were still lacunae in his work. He did his best to fill them, for instance by completing what he had said about the forces of nature in man, or about the work of Christ. Apart from these various additions, it must be said that he modified his text very little. The principal changes are due to the new arrangement of the material, according to a more systematic plan and a stricter internal logic.

The four books of the *Institutes* of 1559 deal, in succession, with the knowledge of God 'in his titles and qualities as Creator and sovereign governor of the world'; 'of the knowledge of God the Redeemer as he has shown himself in Jesus Christ, which was first known by the Fathers under the Law, and has since been manifested to us in the Gospel'; 'of the manner of participation in the grace of Jesus Christ, of the fruits which come to us therefrom and of the effects which ensue'; 'of the external means or aids which God uses to bring us to Jesus Christ his Son and to keep us in him'. It would be a study of great interest to find out, in detail, just how Calvin has redistributed throughout these four books the material of which the earlier editions were composed, what motives could have persuaded him to transfer this or that development to a certain place in the text rather than leave it where it was before. All we will say here is that the plan of a catechism, which had hitherto prevailed, was now definitely abandoned in favour of an exposition which, in its general arrangement, is modelled upon the quadripartite division of the Apostles' Creed which Calvin had adopted in his edition of 1543. There are also some rather important divergencies. The third section, which for consistency's sake ought to have been devoted to the Holy Spirit, actually deals only with his activity within man. On the other hand, Calvin speaks of the Resurrection before entering upon the subject of the Church, and this, too, is out of step with the sequence of ideas presented by the Creed. Appearances notwithstanding, the relations between the last edition of the *Institutes* and the traditional plan of the Apostle's Creed remains rather external and formal.

In fact, the dogmatic exposition in its new aspect consists of two main parts. The first is constituted by Book I, and is concerned with the doctrine of God (Trinity, Creator, Providence), the scriptural revelation and man (independently of sin and of the need for salvation). The second part extends over the other three books, and deals with the historic revelation and the plan of salvation. This in its turn is subdivided into two parts: firstly, preparation for the work of salvation, under the old covenant, and its accomplishment in the incarnation of the Son of God (Book II); and secondly, the attribution and application of salvation by the Holy Spirit, (a) by the intimate operation of the Holy Spirit within the believer, even to its completion in the future life (Book III); and (b) by the external means that the Holy Spirit employs to complete this operation and bring it to its right end (Book IV).

What we know, from the accounts of Théodore de Bèze and other friends of Calvin, of the way in which he composed his last edition might lead one to think that the labour of continual juxtaposition and addition must have damaged the unity of the exposition. On the contrary, this edition of 1559 stands out among its predecessors by its greater coherence. Never did the author succeed so well in mastering the enormous material that he had to organize; nor did he ever constrain himself to such objectivity. With regard to the general tone of the work and its style, the results are less satisfactory. Passages of a polemical nature are still very numerous, and they reflect the irritability and the vehemence that Calvin found so hard to restrain. Much more than in the earlier editions he subjects his adversaries to the most varied and unseemly abuse, which detracts from the rest of an exposition that is so judicious and intended to be scientific.

Yet whatever its defects, this edition of 1559-60 remains monumental work; truly a theological *summa* of Reformed Protestantism. Even in Calvin's lifetime its success was immense, and it was never discredited afterwards. It was indubitably one of the causes of the very rapid rise of a Calvinist orthodoxy, strictly adherent to the formulas of the *Institutes*, which even the later controversies have only with difficulty managed to modify.

II. THE SOURCES OF THE 'INSTITUTES'

If meditation upon the Scriptures was the origin of the ideas that Calvin expressed in his theological writings, as it was also the foundation upon which Luther and Zwingli had built, it is no less true that neither Calvin nor the reformers who went before him could have spun their works out of their personal reflections alone. For all the power and originality of his mind, Calvin could not but draw largely upon previous theologians. The history of philosophical, moral and theological doctrines demonstrates that what appear to have been the most novel and even revolutionary ideas owe their originality much more to the new arrangement of conceptions known long ago, than to the creative power of those who are regarded as their inventors. Calvin is no exception to that general rule, all the less so because, although rightly counted among the reformers, he was a whole generation younger than Luther, Zwingli, Melanchthon and Bucer, and could not have done what he did without reference to the writings and the deeds of those forerunners. If there is a problem about the sources of Luther's thought, still more is there a problem about those of Calvin's, were it only that of determining what rightly belongs to him.

But this problem is far from having found a solution in every respect. For a long while now the attention of historians has been arrested by the peculiar bent of Calvin's mind, a mind more constructive than imaginative, interested in humanist erudition rather than in making original discoveries. This has induced them to look for the origins of Calvin's thinking, but they are far from having reached agreement about them. For some, Calvin was the most faithful disciple of Luther; others have seen him as a renegade from Lutheran thought; others again have derived his doctrine, wholly or in part, either from St Augustine or from Bucer, to say nothing of those disciples who, out of respect for their master, think they ought to reject influences of any kind. To meet the question with an answer which, if not definitive, would at least be precise enough in detail, clearly demands a meticulous comparison of all Calvin's writings with all the other works that might, directly or distantly, have determined his way of seeing things—a gigantic labour, not impossible in itself, but one that no one has yet had the courage and patience to undertake.[25] For the present, therefore, we must be content with the few partial results that seem to have been gained in this domain.

It is doubtless unnecessary to repeat that Calvin made the closest study of the Bible—the whole of it—and that he had a more remarkable knowledge than any other reformer of the Old Testament. One need only recall the position he ascribed to the Scriptures as the basis of his teaching, and the importance of exegetical works in his whole literary output.[26] It is to his assiduous reading of the Bible, and especially of the Prophets and of St Paul, that we must look for the source of many a subtle shade of meaning in his theology and, more generally, for light upon his religious mentality. Again, we must never lose sight of the fact that he did not study Scripture or interpret it as a disinterested scientist but as a theologian who was a reader of St Augustine and of Luther, ever preoccupied to find confirmation of his own dogmatic positions.

Secondly, he read with close attention a great many works of the Fathers of the Church. If his commentary on the *De Clementia* already revealed a recent initiation into St Augustine's *City of God*, the works he composed after his conversion show that until the end of his life he never ceased to deepen his thinking about the ancient Greek and Latin authors. As early as the *Institutes*

[25] The references collected by P. BARTH and W. NIESEL in their edition of the Latin *Institutes* of 1559, *O.S.*, vols. III-IV, are still only a beginning, which may at most serve as a point of departure for further research.

[26] Cf. the testimonies collected by GOUMAZ, *La Doctrine du salut*, pp. 27 ff. and 31-62; see also H. CLAVIER, *Etudes sur le calvinisme*, Paris, 1936, pp. 115-39.

of 1536, in what he writes about the faculties of the human soul, he quotes Plato, Aristotle, Themistius, Cicero, as well as John Chrysostom, Origen and St Augustine. 'Such a collection of quotations, of such richness and conciseness, could not easily be found in the writings of the other reformers. Moreover, these quotations are inserted into the context where they belong, without research or learned ostentation; and one can see that the author has not merely picked them up here and there, but has been drawing upon a treasury at his free disposal.'[27]

Among the Greek Fathers he would seem, at the outset of his career, to have had a predilection for St John Chrysostom, whose *Homilies* he had once intended to publish in a French translation: in the preface that he wrote for this project, he did not hesitate to declare that in matters of scriptural interpretation Chrysostom surpassed all the ancient writers whose works have come down to us.[28] However, the influence of St Augustine upon the reformer is more important and may even be said to be unique of its kind. He makes St Augustine his constant reading, and feels on an equal footing with him, quotes him at every opportunity, appropriates his expressions and regards him as one of the most valuable of allies in his controversies.[29] If he sometimes regrets the allegorism and the 'quibbles' used by St Augustine in his exegesis, he nevertheless sees him as a faithful interpreter of the Scriptures.[30] Upon points of doctrine he borrows from St Augustine with both hands: he draws inspiration from his doctrines of free will[31] and of the sacraments,[32] and in the chapters on grace and on pre-

---

[27] KOESTLIN, op. cit., p. 35.   [28] *Opp.*, 9, 834.

[29] Cf. P. POLMAN, *L'Elément historique dans la controverse religieuse du XVIe siècle*, Gembloux, 1832, pp. 65 and 90-4; J. KOOPMANS, *Het oudkerkelijk dogma in de reformatie bepaaldelijk bij Calvijn*, Wageningen, 1938, pp. 32 ff. One may profitably consult the monumental work of L. SMITS, *Saint Augustin dans l'œuvre de Calvin*, Assen, 1957, which is very accurate and almost exhaustive.

[30] *Opp.*, 9, 835; *Inst.*, III, 2, 35.

[31] BARNIKOL, *Die Lehre Calvins vom unfreien Willen und ihr Verhältnis zur Lehre der übrigen Reformatoren und Augustins*, Neuwied, 1927, pp. 99 ff.

[32] P. POLMAN, op. cit., p. 91; J. BECKMANN, *Vom Sakrament bei Calvin*, Tubingen, 1926, pp. 163 ff. However, the last-named author has manifestly exaggerated the Augustinian element in Calvin's teaching upon the sacraments. Cf. W. F. DANKBAAR, *De sacramentsleer van Calvijn*, Amsterdam, 1941, pp. 225-40.

destination he employs all the Augustinian arguments to his purpose.[33] Did he not go so far as to say, in his *Treatise on Predestination*, 'As for St Augustine, he agrees so well with us in everything and everywhere, that if I had to write a confession upon this matter it would be enough for me to compose it from evidences drawn from his books.'[34] Such profound agreement can be explained only by a common conception of the nature of theological problems.

However, agreement upon a certain number of points of doctrine does not signify a return to the traditional notion of patristic authority. The Scriptures alone have a normative value for faith, which cannot be claimed for the Fathers of the Church. Besides, Calvin does not hesitate to part company with them whenever they seem to him to deviate from the straight path of Scripture. Bucer, who made use of their writings, but without always drawing the distinctions that Calvin thought indispensable, incurred reproach from the latter for having attributed too much authority to the Fathers' views of the invocation of the saints.[35] In the *Treatise on Scandals* he attacks their teaching upon free will and their complaisant attitude towards the philosophers.[36] Frequently, too, he rejects their exegeses, accusing them of neglecting the obvious meaning of the sacred text.[37] With regard to the Councils he takes up a similar attitude: their decisions are to to be examined in the light of the historical circumstances in which they were held, and evaluated by the Biblical criterion which alone remains valid. Upon that condition, 'we willingly receive the ancient Councils, those of Nicaea, of Constantinople,

[33] See, for example, *Inst.*, III, 22, 8 and 10; 24, 1.

[34] *Opp.*, 8, 266; *Opusc.*, 1404.

[35] *Opp.*, 10b, 142; cf. STROHL, *Bucer, humaniste chrétien*, p. 28.

[36] *Opp.*, 8, 19; *Opusc.*, 1321: 'Certainly, Origen, Tertullian, Basil, Chrysostom and others like them would never have spoken as they do, if they had followed what judgment God had given them. But from desire to please the wise of the world, or at least from fear of annoying them, they mixed the earthly with the heavenly. That was a hateful thing, totally to cast man down, and repugnant to the common judgment of the flesh. These good persons seek a means more in conformity with human understanding: that is to concede I know not what to free will, and allow some natural virtue to man; but meanwhile the purity of the doctrine is profaned.'

[37] *Opp.*, 9, 834.

of the first of Ephesus, of Chalcedon and the like which were
held to condemn the wicked errors and opinions of the heretics:
we pay them honour and reverence, I say, so far as belongs to
the articles that were there defined. For the Councils contain
nothing but a pure and natural interpretation of the Scripture'.[38]
That in certain cases Calvin could be an energetic defender of
the theology of the ancient Councils is proved by his attitude
with regard to the traditional trinitarian and Christological
doctrines, especially in his controversies with Servetus, Gentilis
and Socinus.

Certain authors have tried to demonstrate that even Roman
Law was not without influence on Calvin's theology. They have
derived from this, in particular, his conception of the majesty of
God, which might have been developed from the political concept of majesty according to the Roman jurists,[39] and his conception that God is above the law which might be a theological
transposition of the *princeps legibus solutus*.[40] Although the former
hypothesis does not seem to be tenable, the latter is based upon
what is, at the very least, a somewhat disconcerting terminological
identity, especially if we take account of the importance of the
Roman adage in Calvin's political teaching.[41] We shall presently
show, however, that the Calvinist notion of the sovereignty of
God is related far more closely to certain medieval conceptions.

As for scholastic authors in particular, we must begin by
emphasising that Calvin knew them much better than he is
commonly said to have done. First of all, the instruction he had
received at Montaigu left direct traces in the vocabulary of
Calvin, who readily employs the terminology in use in the schools.[42]
This influence also appears in his persistent taste for dialectical
definitions. Does this mean that, with regard to the scholastic
definitions themselves, Calvin's attitude was other than purely
negative? It has been proved that he studied the works of St
Anselm, of Peter the Lombard, and of Thomas Aquinas, whom he

[38] *Inst.*, IV, 9, 8. Cf. P. POLMAN, op. cit., pp. 76 ff.; KOOPMANS, op. cit.,
pp. 34 ff.

[39] NOESGEN, 'Calvins Lehre von Gott' in the *Neue kirkliche Zeitschrift*,
Erlangen, 1912, pp. 694 ff.

[40] BEYERHAUS, op. cit., p. 83.

[41] BOHATEC, 'Calvins Lehre von Staat und Kirche', pp. 36 ff.

[42] See the examples brought together by GOUMAZ, op. cit., pp. 92 ff.

quotes word for word. Similarly, he knew and made much use of St Bernard.[43] But the instruction at Montaigu was on strictly nominalist lines, and by force of circumstances Calvin was introduced to the leading representatives of the Franciscan school and in particular to Duns Scotus and Ockham, or at least to their disciples.[44]

Now, the idea of God that we find in Calvin has led to comparisons with the theology of Scotus. A. Ritschl was one of the first to come to this conclusion—that the idea of God which dominates the doctrine of double predestination implies the *potentia absoluta* of the nominalists.[45] He was followed by a whole succession of theologians and historians who traced the Calvinist conception of God to Duns Scotus.[46] Others, however, rebelled against their opinion, either because they would not admit that Calvin had borrowed anything from scholasticism, or because they regarded it as a distortion of the real thought of the reformer. They took their stand mainly upon a passage in the *Institutes* in which Calvin says: 'We do not approve of the dream of the Papist theologians touching the absolute power of God; for their ramblings about it are profane, and as such must be held by us in detestation. Nor do we imagine a God without any law, seeing that he is law to himself.'[47] That seems to be as clear a refutation as one could wish of the hypothesis that Calvin was dependent upon Duns Scotus. Following E. Doumergue and H. Bois, A. Lecerf has relied upon this text for his denial of all Scotist influence.[48] In a very thorough analysis of Calvin's notions this writer declares: 'The Calvinism of Calvin and . . . the Calvinism

[43] He is mentioned no less than twenty-one times in the *Institutes* of 1559 alone.

[44] Cf. also P. BARTH, 'Fünfundzwanzig Jahre Calvinforschung', p. 168.

[45] A. RITSCHL, 'Geschichtliche Studien zur christlichen Lehre von Gott' in the *Jahrbücher für deutsche Theologie*, vol. 13, Gotha, 1868, p. 107.

[46] We may cite as examples H. Bois, Walker and Seeberg.

[47] *Inst.*, III, 23, 2.

[48] Cf. DOUMERGUE, op. cit., vol. IV, p. 119; H. BOIS, *La Philosophie de Calvin*, Paris, 1919, pp. 18 ff. The latter, reconsidering his previous interpretation, writes (p. 21): 'Calvin is no disciple of Duns Scotus. His God is not one of lawless caprice; therefore it must not be said that for Calvin, as for Duns Scotus, everything that God does is just for the sole reason that he does it.'

of the confessions are fundamentally opposed to the lucubrations of Scotus and Occam which are unjustly imputed to him . . . the power of God is not the *potentia absoluta* of Duns Scotus and Occam. God cannot perform actions unworthy of his Majesty, nor lie, nor command what is wrong or contradictory; not because he lacks the power, but because his power is not a blind force of nature.'[49]

Impartial examination of this question compels one to recognize that the debate rests upon a misunderstanding of what Duns Scotus really thought. The works of Seeberg and of Minges have led, in effect, to the conclusion that the absolute power of God is limited in Duns Scotus by the principle of non-contradiction, which excludes any decision of God that is contradictory to his previous decrees, and also by the very nature of God—that is, by his goodness.[50] It cannot be claimed, then, that Duns Scotus identifies absolute power with the purely arbitrary. On the other hand, the resemblance to Calvin's doctrine becomes all the stronger. In the *Institutes*, he tells us that 'the will of God is so much the supreme and sovereign rule of justice that whatever he wills must be held to be just in so far as he wills it. So that when one asks, Why did God do this? we must reply, Because he willed it. If one goes further and says, Why did he will this?, that is asking for something greater and higher than the will of God, which there cannot be.'[51] The echo of Scotus in this passage can hardly be contested. Similarly, Calvin asserts in the commentary upon Exodus that God 'is independent of all law in this sense, that he is his own law and is the norm of all things',[52] and again that 'it is not permissible for any mortal to attack or find fault with the least of the commandments of God, not only because his government is above all laws, but because his will is

[49] Cf. A. LECERF, 'La Souveraineté de Dieu d'après le calvinisme', International Calvinist Congress, Amsterdam 1934, s' Gravenhage, 1935, pp. 26 and 29. In the same sense, ST. LEIGH HUNT, 'Predestination in the Institutes' in *De l'élection éternelle de Dieu*, Geneva, 1936, p. 134.

[50] R. SEEBERG, *Die Theologie des Joh. Duns Scotus*, Leipzig, 1900, pp. 163 ff. and *Lehrbuch der Dogmengeschichte*, vol. III, 4th edn, Leipzig, 1930, p. 654; P. MINGES, 'Der Gottesbegriff des Duns Scotus', 1906.

[51] *Inst.*, III, 23, 2. Cf. SEEBERG, *Lehrbuch der Dogmengeschichte*, vol. IV, 2, p. 576, n. 1.

[52] *Opp.*, 24, 49.

the most perfect norm of all the laws.'[53] Now, if God is his own
law, that means that he is bound by what he has decided, that
his will is immutable but not subject to any external causality;
and that is exactly what Duns Scotus meant to convey by his
teaching. Then how are we to explain the passage, quoted above,
in which Calvin expresses disapproval of 'the dreams of Papist
theologians touching the absolute power of God'. This was
doubtless meant to apply only to the arbitrary speculations and
the exaggerations of certain nominalists of the late Middle Ages,
or to express hostility to the distinction that Scotus himself had
introduced between the absolute power and the ordered power
of God, a distinction that must have seemed a mere subtlety to
Calvin.

The doctrine of God is, however, not the only one that reveals
traces of nominalism. In his great commentary upon the
Sentences of Peter Lombard, Duns Scotus had declared that the
passion of Christ was, in itself, of no particular value or special
efficacy; that value and efficacy had been conferred upon it by
the Divine will, which had deigned to accept the passion of
Christ as sufficient, and had destined it to the work of redemption.[54] This is also Calvin's point of view as it appears in the
reply to Socinus of 1555, and in Book II of the *Institutes*.[55] The
same agreement can be established with regard to the relations
between predestination and redemption, the latter being logically
subordinated to the former.[56] It would not perhaps be altogether
arbitrary, after all, to look for possible points of contact between
the Scotist theory of the concomitancy of the action of the Holy
Spirit and of the reception of the Eucharistic elements, and
Calvin's enlargements upon the same subject—provided, of
course, one left out of account that notion of a Divine covenant
with the Church which Duns Scotus introduced here.[57]

Among the more contemporary sources we must naturally give

[53] *Opp.*, 24, 131.
[54] Commentary on Book III, dist. 19, notes 4-7; Cf. SEEBERG, *J. Duns
Scotus*, pp. 275 ff.
[55] *Opp.*, 10a, 160 ff.; *Inst.*, II, 17, 1.
[56] Comm. on Book III, dist. 19, n. 11; SEEBERG, op. cit., p. 281; *Inst.*,
II, 16, 4.
[57] SEEBERG, *Dogmengeschichte*, vol. III, p. 511.

a special place to the humanists and the reformers. Of the degree to which Calvin retained the imprint of humanism after his conversion we have said enough and need not enlarge further, except to recall that his exegesis continued to be based upon the method devised by Valla and by Erasmus. The interpretations of the latter more than once determined those that Calvin thought he had to adopt. Was there a still deeper Erasmian influence, extending for example even to theological concepts? Only a profounder comparison would enable one to answer that question, but certainly one is often reminded, when reading Calvin's expositions, of formulas or expressions invented by Erasmus. Although Erasmus's name nowhere appears in the *Institutes*, it has been possible to show that numerous passages on the contempt of the world, the longing for death, earthly duties, even upon the notion of faith and upon eschatology, present striking analogies with parallel texts from the great humanist. Similarly, Calvin's work has retained many important traces of Budé, which have been pointed out, with meticulous care, by Bohatec.[58] Of Lefèvre d'Etaples, on the contrary, it cannot be said that any of his theology has survived in that of Calvin or even left evident traces. Indeed, there was never any common measure between Lefèvre's religious aspirations and the dogmatics of the Reform. H. Dörries, in a remarkable article, has supplied proof which in my opinion is decisive, that Calvin owed very little to Lefèvre, who had not fully embraced the principles of the Reform upon any important point, and whose mystical tendencies, if not vocabulary, Calvin seems always to have rejected with the utmost energy.[59]

[58] M. SCHULZE, *Calvins Jenseitschristentum*, *passim*; POTGIETER, *De Verhouding tussen die teologie . . . by Calvijn*, pp. 44 ff. and 256, had argued against any dependence of Calvin upon Erasmus. J. BOHATEC, *Budé und Calvin*, pp. 242 ff.; 406, 417, 427 ff., etc., has taken up the question with his habitual accuracy and recognized an Erasmian influence upon Calvin that is fairly extensive, but limited by the fundamental requirements of his theology. See also A. M. HUGO, *Calvijn en Seneca*. For what concerns Budé, the work of BOHATEC provides all the useful information.

[59] Cf. H. DOERRIES, 'Calvin und Lefèvre' in the *Zeitschr. für Kirchengeschichte*, 1925. Already before this H. STRATHMANN, 'Die Entstehung der Lehre Calvins von der Busse' in *Calvinstudien*, p. 218, n. 1, had pointed out the divergencies separating Calvin from Lefèvre upon the idea of faith, upon justification and

But what of the reformers properly so called? Calvin always professed the liveliest admiration for Luther, of whose works he had read a whole series quite early in life—that is, of those accessible to him, for, having no knowledge of German,[60] he had to be content with those written or translated in Latin.[61] The fact of the Lutheran influence is in itself beyond any serious question.[62] It is true that one would have to take some trouble to find in Calvin's writings any complete arguments or even phrases borrowed literally from Luther: but the influence that one author receives from another is not necessarily expressed in quotations or plagiarisms. It may be of a more subtle nature, and exist none the less undeniably. In this case it has long been recognized by most of the authors who have dealt with the question.[63] Besides, contemporaries were aware of it, and as late as 1554 Haller of Bern was reproaching Calvin for being too definitely a partisan of Luther.[64]

---

morals: for the contrary view, see L. VON MURALT, 'Uber den Ursprung der Reformation in Frankreich' in *Festschrift Hans Nabholz*, Zurich, 1934, p. 149; followed by A. BOUVIER, *Henri Bullinger*, p. 118.

[60] See W. NIESEL, 'Verstand Calvin Deutsch?' in the *Zeitschr. für Kirchengeschichte*, Gotha, 1930, vol. 49, pp. 343 ff.

[61] In his long letter to Calvin of 24th Oct. 1554 Bullinger could still write: 'Neque enim libros ejus [Lutheri] vel legere, vel intelligere potuisti', quum hujus generis pleraque germanice scripserit.'

[62] It is nevertheless questioned by A. D. R. POLMAN, *De Praedestinatieleer van Augustinus, Thomas van Aquino en Calvijn*, Franeker, 1936, p. 323, when he writes: 'No influence of Luther on Calvin has been established with certainty.'

[63] Cf. among others, F. W. KAMPSCHULTE, *Joh. Calvin*, vol. I, p. 257; DOUMERGUE, op. cit., vol. II, pp. 569 ff.; W. DIEHL, 'Calvins Auslegung des Dekalogs in der ersten Ausgabe seiner *Institutio* und Luthers Katechismen' in *Theol. Studien und Kritiken*, Gotha, 1898, pp. 141-62; K. BETH, 'J. Calvin als reformatorischer Systematiker' in the *Zeitschr. für Theologie und Kirche*, Tubingen, 1909, vol. XIX, 336; K. HOLL, *J. Calvin, Gesammelte Aufsätze*, vol. III, p. 262; P. WERNLE, *Calvin*, Tubingen, 1919, pp. 2 ff., 85 ff., 115 ff., etc.; SEEBERG, *Dogmengeschichte*, vol. IV, 2, pp. 556 ff.; O. RITSCHL, *Dogmengeschichte*, vol. III, Göttingen, 1926, pp. 165 and 199 ff.; A. LANG, 'The Sources of Calvin's *Institutes*' in the *Evangelical Quarterly*, London, 1936, pp. 130-41.

[64] Letter to Bullinger of 28th December 1554, *Opp.*, 15, 362: 'Vestram libertatem ergo Calvinum valde probo; videtur enim nimium semper Lutherum et Bucerum defendere.'

The Lutheran influence is already externally evident in the planning of the *Institutes* of 1536, which reproduces the order of the contents of Luther's *Little Catechism*.[65] But fundamentally also the *Institutes* are often indebted to Luther's thought, above all in the exposition of the Decalogue and of the first (perhaps also the third) article of the Creed. Calvin begins his chapter on the Law by showing that sacred knowledge consists entirely of the knowledge of God and the knowledge of ourselves. (As we know, in the second edition he was to detach this fragment and use it as material for two new chapters.) But, Calvin proceeds, Adam, by reason of the Fall, lost the gifts of grace and of his initial communion with God; man has become the child of wrath. Thenceforth self-love blinds him so that he is not aware of the misery of his condition. The Law itself was given to man to show him how far he is from the right path. In the Law we see, as in a mirror, our sins and our condemnation. Thus it is the consciousness of sin that leads us back towards God, who grants us his grace anew in Jesus Christ, provided we receive it with faith. This knowledge of our sin, and the faith which enables us to benefit by the mercy of God, are free gifts.[66] Throughout this exposition we have no difficulty in recognizing some of the fundamental ideas of Luther, those that dominate the whole of his *Catechism*. Similarly in accord with Luther Calvin defines faith, not as a mere belief, but as a complete trust in Christ and in the goodness of God. And still further comparisons of the same nature could be established.

It is naturally a very delicate matter, where nothing is borrowed textually, to decide exactly which of the Lutheran writings Calvin had actually read. No doubt he knew the *Little Catechism* in a Latin version of the *Betbüchlein*, which had appeared in several editions under the title of *Enchiridion piarum precationum*.[67] But it is probable that he also had knowledge of the *Greater Catechism*, at least from 1539. Moreover he made use of the *Treatise on*

---

[65] See the study by w. DIEHL mentioned above.

[66] *Opp.*, I, 27-31; O.S., vol. I, 37-41. We are only summing-up the thought of Calvin in our exposition.

[67] LANG, op. cit., p. 135; MOORE, *La Réforme allemande et la littérature française*, Strasbourg, 1930, pp. 321 ff.

Christian Liberty, of the *De Captivitate Babylonica* (especially of the chapter on the false sacraments), the *De Servo arbitrio*, the *Sermon on the body and the blood of the Christ against the Enthusiasts*, which had existed in a Latin translation since 1527, the *Sermon on the venerable sacrament of the body of Christ*, published in 1519 and translated in 1524, and, finally and above all, the *Postille* translated by Bucer.[68]

Calvin's dependence upon the reformer of Wittenberg is to be understood through the 'intimate relatedness' which has been demonstrated by Lang, who also points out that 'in the first edition of the *Institutes* he seems almost to be a Lutheran of southern Germany. But afterwards too, Calvin was entirely in agreement with Luther with regard to all the fundamental doctrines bearing upon justification, upon the total perversion of sinful man, upon sinning and original sin, upon Christ the unique Saviour and mediator, upon the appropriation of salvation through the Holy Spirit, the Word and the sacraments. We even have authority to claim that the central teaching of Luther on the justification of faith and regeneration by faith was preserved more faithfully and expressed more forcibly by Calvin than by any other dogmatician of the Reform.'[69]

These comparisons are confirmed and legitimized by the homage that Calvin himself never ceased to render to Luther and to his work. The general tone of this is shown in the following passage from the *Treatise on Free Will against Pighius* (1543): 'Now again, as before, we expressly declare that we hold him to be an excellent apostle of Christ, by the labour and ministry of

---

[68] Upon this last work, cf. MOORE, op. cit., p. 97.

[69] A. LANG, 'Zwingli und Calvin', Bielefeld, 1913, p. 106. These remarks are based upon numerous critical works undertaken since the end of the last century. They do but confirm the judgment at which J. KOESTLIN, with a sure intuition, had arrived forty-five years earlier. After emphasizing the 'Lutheran' character of the *Institutes* of 1536, he wrote: 'In the developments concerning the Christ who made himself wholly one of us, who overcame death, who interceded for us with his whole person and his entire work, by his obedience and by the fact that he took his sins upon himself, one perceives an intimate relatedness to Luther, precisely in what differentiates him from Melanchthon. Upon the subject of predestination, one would discover nothing that Luther might not have written at that epoch.' KOESTLIN, 'Calvins *Institutio* nach Form und Inhalt', p. 428.

whom, above all others, the purity of the Gospel has been restored in our times.'[70] Nevertheless, though he was always ready to acknowledge what he owed to Luther, Calvin had too strong a personality to profess himself of Luther's school without criticism or reservations. 'I would wish,' he said in his *Last Warning to Westphal*, 'that whatever faults may have been mingled among the great virtues of Luther might rather have remained buried; and in truth there is nothing to keep me from touching upon them, more than the great honour and reverence I bear towards the many excellent gifts with which he was endowed. But to wish to embrace the vices for the virtues, that would indeed be contrary to all good.'[71] After 1536 he parted with Luther over the question of the Lord's Supper; and later on, the differences tended rather to sharpen, whether it was a question of the Canon of Scripture, of predestination, of the doctrine of the Church, of Christology or the sacraments. But what divided them still more than the finer points of doctrine were the differences of their early training and their religious mentality. We must beware, however, of reducing this opposition to that which might exist between an individualistic or perhaps even mystical piety, and a religion of intellectualist tendency. The one no more defines Luther than the other does justice to Calvin. Still less is it appropriate to bring into account—or only in a very slight degree—the traditionally-invoked opposition between the Germanic and the Latin mind. Nor would it be right to look for an explanation of the problem in an alleged contrast between the Christo-centric theology of Luther and Calvin's theocentric position, for we shall have occasion to point out that the thought of the latter, just like that of Luther, is entirely dominated by the person of Jesus Christ. The profound reason for their divergence resides rather, it would seem, in their different conceptions of the relation between Christ and the believer.

From 1536 Melanchthon, with whom he was afterwards linked in friendship, must be considered one of the sources of Calvin's thought, through his *Loci Communes*. This was known to the author of the *Institutes*, perhaps in the edition of 1521 and cer-

[70] *Opp.*, 6, 250; *Opusc.*, 311. Cf. *Opp.*, 6, 459 and 473; 11, 705; 12, 325, etc.

[71] *Opp.*, 9, 238; *Opusc.*, 1936.

134

tainly in that of 1535 which had just appeared, and of which he was to write the preface to the French translation published in Geneva in 1546. The expositions upon the tables of the Law, upon faith, hope and charity, upon repentance and upon Christian liberty include characteristic reminiscences of Melanchthon's famous work of dogmatic. The same is true in what bears upon the general doctrine of the sacraments and baptism. Lastly, points of contact have been demonstrated between Melanchthon's Christology and that of Calvin.[72] Furthermore Calvin did not hesitate, while he was at Ratisbon, to put his signature to the *Confession* of Augsburg, which its author, Melanchthon, regarded as a faithful summary of his theology. Some fifteen years later the French reformer also declared: 'There is nothing in the Confession of Augsburg which is not in accord with our teaching';[73] and, in 1557: 'I do not repudiate the Confession of Augsburg, to which I subscribed willingly and with full agreement as its author interpreted it.'[74] And nevertheless, upon two points of capital importance he was obliged to state that deep disagreement separated him from Melanchthon; namely, upon free-will and predestination.[75]

If, in spite of all the divergences which in certain respects opposed them to him, Calvin could still feel he was a fellow-worker with Luther and Melanchthon, the same could not be said with regard to Zwingli: and it was precisely his reading of Luther that made Calvin turn away from the reformer of Zurich and even refuse for a long time to read his writings.[76] However, he must have had knowledge of the *De vera et falsa religione* even before he had completed the *Institutes* of 1536, for he makes several allusions to it, notably concerning the sacraments.[77] Later on, he read more of him, but even when, under the influence of

[72] A. LANG, 'Melanchthon und Calvin' in the *Reformierte Kirchenzeitung*, 1897, p. 58; and the same author's *The Sources of Calvin's Institutes*, p. 135; H. STRATHMANN, 'Die Entstehung der Lehre Calvins von der Busse' in *Calvin-studien*, 1909, pp. 219-28.

[73] *Opp.*, 16, 263. [74] *Opp.*, 16, 430.

[75] For what he says about this, see his preface to the French translation of the *Loci Communes*, 1546, *Opp.*, 9, 848.

[76] Cf. the passage already quoted from the *Second defence against Westphal*, *Opp.*, 9, 51; see also p. 20 above.

[77] *O.S.*, vol. 1, pp. 120, 122, 137.

Bucer, he took a more equitable line in his judgments of Zwingli, Calvin continued to look upon him as only a second-rate theologian.[78] In 1540, in a letter to Farel, Calvin ridiculed the prestige accorded to Zwingli at Zurich: 'These good people burn with indignation when anyone has the audacity to prefer Luther to Zwingli; as though the Gospel would go to ruin if one took away anything from Zwingli. And yet one is not thereby doing any injury to Zwingli; for if one compares them side by side, you yourself know how far Luther excels him.'[79] The actual personality of Zwingli must have remained completely foreign to Calvin; he could not understand that confusion of a preaching of the Gospel with preoccupations inspired by a strictly local patriotism, which was exemplified in the reformer of Zurich. But he must have been even more repelled by his theological attitude, and not only towards the question of the sacraments. Zwingli appeared to him too contaminated by the 'philosophers', too 'profane', and also too fond of paradoxes.[80] That one cannot under these conditions speak of any dependency of Calvin upon Zwingli is clear enough.[81] It is indeed quite incomprehensible how certain contemporaries such as Bolsec and Westphal could have been so blinded by partisanship as to present Calvin as a

[78] Cf. the letter to Viret of 12th September 1542, *Opp.*, 11, 438; and the letter to Bullinger of January 1552. *Opp.*, 14, 253.

[79] *Opp.*, 11, 24.

[80] Cf. the appraisal by VON SOOS in his interesting parallel between Zwingli and Calvin, *Zwingliana*, vol. VI, p. 315; 'While, for Zwingli, God is the first cause, therefore a philosophical concept which also dominates his theodicy and imparts an *a priori* character to his theology, to Calvin God is object of religious adoration, therefore a religious concept and, as such, the basis of a system *a posteriori*.'

[81] VON SOOS himself, who insists upon the analogies between the thought of the two reformers, is obliged to say: 'The question is not how far and in what way Calvin was dependent upon Zwingli, but how far and in what they are in accord' (ibid., p. 310). One cannot subscribe to the opinion of LANG, 'Zwingli und Calvin', pp .106 ff., according to which Calvin and Zwingli shared in the same type of piety. The same author affirms that the most important conceptions in Zwingli reappear in Calvin but in more elevated form, purified and more vital: cf. his 'The Sources of Calvin's *Institutes*' in the *Evangelical Quarterly*, 1936 ; F. BLANKE, *Calvins Urteile über Zwingli aus der Welt der Reformation*, Zurich, 1960, pp. 18 ff., also seems to allow too much to the Zwinglian influence.

successor of Zwingli, especially in what had to do with the doctrines of predestination and the Eucharist. At the very most, we might admit some similarity in the radicalism with which they both rejected everything that either nearly or distantly recalled Roman ideas or usages. Similarly, at a pinch one might concede an indirect influence transmitted to Calvin by Farel or by some Strasbourg theologians.[82]

In his article of 1868, J. Koestlin pointed out that in those parts of the *Institutes* which are devoted to the Eucharist, Calvin 'aligns himself with the theologians who drew up the *Tetrapolitan Confession* in 1530'.[83] Some years later J. M. Usteri showed that these connections could be extended to the doctrine of Baptism.[84] But the problem of the influence of the Strasbourg reformers was not even satisfactorily stated with regard to Bucer, until Lang took it up in 1900.[85] Since then, further contacts have been discovered, and the thesis of Calvin's dependence on Bucer has found a number of defenders.[86] It must be admitted that some of them, in the enthusiasm of their discoveries, yielded to a temptation to ascribe too much to Bucer, and tried to find the germ of most of Calvin's teachings in him. Also, this very soon provoked a reaction, and not only among the few who, in order

---

[82] The first phrase of the *Institutes*, in which some have tried to find an echo from the *De vera et falsa religione* (chap. II: 'fieri nequit, ut rite de religione tractetur, nisi ante omnia deum agnoveris, hominem vero cognoveris,' *Corp. Reform.*, vol. XC, p. 640) comes in reality from Budé, as we have been shown by BOHATEC, *Budé und Calvin*, p. 31 and pp. 241 ff.

[83] KOESTLIN, op. cit., p. 429.

[84] J. M. USTERI, 'Calvins Sakraments—und Tauflehre' in *Theol. Studien und Kritiken*, 1884, pp. 417 ff.; and the same author's 'Die Stellung der Strassburger Reformatoren Bucer und Capito zur Tauffrage', ibid., pp. 456 ff.

[85] A. LANG, *Der Evangelien kommentar Martin Butzers und die Grundzüge seiner Theologie*, Leipzig, 1900, pp. 9 ff., 158, 164, 185 f., 198, 365 f., 370 ff.

[86] F. LOOFS, *Leitfaden zym Studium der Dogmengeschichte*, Halle, 1906, pp. 878 ff.; WERNLE, op. cit., pp. 55, 81, 149, 357; O. RITSCHL, op. cit., p. 158; PANNIER, *Formation intellectuelle*, pp. 66 ff.; H. STROHL, 'Bucer et Calvin' in the *Bulletin de la Soc. de l'Hist. du Protest. français*, 1938, vol. LXXXVII, p. 354 ff. J. COURVOISIER, *La Notion d'Eglise chez Bucer*, Paris, 1933, pp. 135 ff. and the same author's 'Bucer et l'œuvre de Calvin' in the *Revue de Théol. et de Philos.*, Lausanne, 1933, pp. 66 ff.; W. PAUCK, 'Calvin and Butzer' in the *Journal of Religion*, Chicago 1929, pp. 237 ff.

not to have to tackle the problem, tried to deny its existence.[87] In fact, a marked prudence is now the fashion among researchers into Calvin's sources. We know that from the fact of two authors having known one another and given expression to similar ideas, it does not automatically follow that one owed them to the other. And in the present case, and on several of the points which have been adduced to indicate a dependence of Calvin upon Bucer, it turns out that the same doctrine had been taught by St Augustine, whose work was equally well known to both. The whole question ought to be subjected to a fresh examination, taking account of the precise dates of appearance of the respective doctrines of Bucer and Calvin, and also of such eventual divergences as there may be.

But with all these reservations, of which more systematic study might lengthen the list, it is now well established that the part played by Bucer in the formation of Calvinist theology remains extremely important. Even before he made personal acquaintance with Bucer in 1537, Calvin had been in correspondence with him, and had read at least his commentary on the Gospels of Matthew and John. At the Synod of Bern in 1537, to which Bucer and Capiton had come in order to vindicate the approach to Luther which the signing of the Concord of Wittenberg had implied, Calvin submitted to the two Strasbourg reformers a confession of faith in the Eucharist which reproduced Bucer's point of view.[88] In this he affirmed communion in the body and the blood of Christ as well as in his spirit, and the reality of this communion, while rejecting the local presence of the body of the Christ in the

[87] It was thus that K. HOLL, *Gesammelte Aufsätze*, vol. III, n. 2, was already trying to dispose of the Bucerian element. He was followed by NOESGEN, 'Calvins Lehre von Gott' in the *Neue kirkliche Zeitschrift*, 1912, pp. 587 and, more recently, by P. BARTH, who wrote: 'The alleged theological influence of Bucer upon Calvin seems to me very doubtful in spite of all that has been advanced in favour of it. Calvin's formulas are everywhere too plainly distinct from the theology of compromise of the Strasbourgers' ('Fünfundzwanzig Jahre Calvinforschung', p. 168). A. D. R. POLMAN, *Die Praedestinatieleer*, pp. 325 ff., states that, for his part, he has found nothing in the first edition of the *Institutes* of Bucer's characteristic teachings, and that Calvin did not take up any position towards them until after his sojourn at Strasbourg.

[88] *Opp.*, 9, 711 f.; cf. the preface by P. Barth, *O.S.*, vol. I, p. 433.

Eucharistic elements. We may take this document, which was countersigned by Bucer and Capiton, as the true point of departure for the Calvinist doctrine of the Lord's Supper, even more so than the corresponding passages in the *Institutes* of 1536. Upon this question of the Eucharist, then, we may affirm with Lang that Calvin adopted, anyway at the outset, an attitude identical with that of Bucer with regard to Luther.[89] But it is incorrect to add, as this author does, that Calvin would not have allowed himself to be drawn, as Bucer was at the Concord of Wittenberg, into concessions incompatible with his fundamental principles. There was not in fact any divergence at all, on this particular point, between Bucer and Calvin at that time. During his sojourn at Strasbourg Calvin could not have obtained the post he did at the High School without subscribing to both the Tetrapolitan Confession and the Concord of Wittenberg. And, in the *Exemplar Excusiationis quae praefationi inseretur*[90] he himself declared that he did not wish to question the Concord of Wittenberg, but on the contrary to strengthen it, by his Eucharistic doctrine. He even thought that he had found in this an effectual means of overcoming the opposition between Wittenberg and Zurich. And that, moreover, was an illusion he shared with Bucer.

As early as the Institutes of 1536 it is possible to pick up certain traces of his attentive reading of Bucer's commentary. Thus Calvin has made use of the second edition of this commentary in his third chapter, devoted to prayer. He reproduces the whole sequence of ideas expressed by Bucer concerning Matthew 6.5-13.[91] Instead of the seven petitions traditionally distinguished in the Lord's prayer, Bucer had seen only six; Calvin does the same, adducing, it is true, somewhat different reasons for it and classifying the petitions in another way. If he is under Bucer's influence, that does not mean that he is giving up all personal initiative. But comparisons can also be drawn between their ways of interpreting the different petitions. For instance, Calvin and Bucer are in accord in depriving the clause 'as we forgive

[89] LANG, *Joh. Calvin*, p. 78.

[90] HERMINJARD, *Correspondence*, vol. VI, pp. 132 ff.

[91] We borrow these examples from LANG, 'The Sources of Calvin's *Institutes*', p. 138.

them who trespass against us' of its conditional character, and regarding it only as a 'simile' or a 'sign'.

Whatever analogies may be discernible between the *Institutes* of 1536 and Bucer's thinking, the influence of the latter becomes definitely more recognizable when we open the *Institutes* of 1539. During the interval, Bucer had published, in 1536, a third edition of his commentary on the Gospels and, in the same year, his great *Commentary on the Epistle to the Romans*. Now, traces of both these works reappear very plainly in the 1539 and 1541 editions of the *Institutes*. The new chapter on predestination betrays, this time without any possible doubt, an attentive reading of the Strasbourg reformer. Yet as soon as we try to define the extent of this influence, we again find ourselves up against very great difficulties. Bucer and Calvin start from the practical observation that there are two distinct categories of men, the elect and the reprobate. This is a statement that Calvin had already made in 1536, and he could have found it fully developed in St Augustine's *City of God*, whence Bucer for his part had certainly lifted it. But at that time Calvin had not deduced from those premisses any doctrine of predestination of the least degree of completeness. Following St Augustine, he had asked himself who were the true members of the Church and had identified them with the elect alone, with those whose salvation is definitive and unlosable. However, in practice, one had to beware of distinguishing the elect from the reprobate, which God alone could do. By virtue of 'a certain judgment in charity' Christians therefore have to ascribe election and membership of the Church to all those who confess faith in God and in Christ, separating themselves only from those who are excommunicated as heretics and from notorious evil livers.[92] Practical considerations were therefore not absent from the Calvinist notion: it may have been intended to give them enough weight to preserve, in principle, a multitudinous Church, in contrast to the Anabaptists and the spiritualists who had tried to incorporate none but proven Christians in the Church. This way of looking at things is already met with in St Augustine, who developed his teaching, partly at

[92] *Opp.*, 1, 72-5; *O.S.* vol. 1, pp. 86-9. AUGUSTINE, *De praedestinatione sanctorum*, chaps. 34-8, M.L. vol. XLIV; VAN DEN BOSCH, *De outwikkeling van Bucers praedestinatie-gedachten*, Amsterdam, 1922.

least, in the course of his struggles with the Donatists. It turns
up again in Bucer, and he too found himself time and again in
conflict with the Anabaptists and their ideal of a church of
'the perfect'. But we cannot infer from this that Calvin was
dependent upon Bucer; it remains much more likely that both
of them, each in his own way, were making use of Augustinian
writings.

In the *Institutes* of 1539-41, however, doubt is no longer possible.
This time Calvin is expounding a complete system of predestination. He now makes the election or reprobation of each individual
dependent upon the Divine predetermination, and the reason he
gives for both is the manifestation of the glory of God. He avails
himself of the special developments given in Bucer's *Commentary
upon the Epistle to the Romans*, and adopts the Bucerian point of
view upon the theoretical and not only the practical importance
of predestination, upon its definitive and ineluctable character
and upon the part played in this, according to Romans 8.30, by
vocation, justification and glorification.[93]

No doubt we might be able to discover similar considerations
in St Augustine, but Calvin is not now limiting himself to the
reproduction of the Augustinian ideas that Bucer had also
accepted. Of these he has preserved the peculiar tone and the
arrangement that they assumed under the pen of his Strasbourg
colleague. But there are still notable differences between them.
We know that Calvin insists upon the distinction between predestination and foreknowledge and denies emphatically the
existence of any casual relation between them.[94] In Bucer, on
the contrary, foreknowledge and predestination are fused together.[95] On the other hand it seems evident that in Bucer,
reprobation shades off into the background, whereas in Calvin
election and reprobation balance one another.[96]

[93] BUCER, *Metaphrases et ennarrationes perpetuae epistolarum D. Pauli Apostoli*,
Strasbourg, 1536, pp. 358-60.

[94] *Inst.*, III, 21, 5.

[95] BUCER, op. cit., p. 355; Luther writes similarly of 'praedestinatio sive
praescientia' in his commentary upon Genesis 26. 9, and brings the two
notions into close connection, to the point of confusing them, in the treatise
De Servo Arbitrio, W. A. 18, 615 ff. We may note also that Calvin rejects the
'seed of election' which was said by Bucer to exist among the elect.

[96] Cf. M. SCHEIBE, *Calvins Prädestinationslehre*, Halle 1897, p. 72 f.

Still further borrowings from Bucer's writings could be pointed out in this edition of 1539, notably on the question of the permanent validity of the Law,[97] and of the equality of the two Testaments as expressions of the Divine Will.[98] In the same order of ideas, Bucer had affirmed, several years before Calvin, the identity of the sacraments of the Old and New Testaments.[99] Upon another point too, that of repentance, certain turns of Calvin's thought are due, it appears, to Bucer—more especially that which re-attaches repentance to the life of regenerated man, a conception which also goes back to Luther.[100] The whole of the chapter upon the Christian life unfolds in an unmistakable Bucerian atmosphere, in which one has no difficulty in recognizing influences from the exchanges of thought that had taken place between the two men.

But it is above all in regard to the idea of the Church that the points of comparison become palpable. It could be said that all Calvin's ideas on this subject are already to be found in Bucer's *Commentary* of 1530. But, here again, this does not necessarily mean that they have been directly borrowed from him. For in itself, this notion of the Church unified under its two aspects, visible and invisible, is one that Calvin might just as well have found in St Augustine as in Bucer.[101] However, the emphasis placed upon the visible Church in 1539, and even more in the edition of 1543, is so Bucerian in tone that one can hardly be in doubt about its origin. Furthermore, throughout the beginning of the eighth chapter of 1543 we can rediscover, developed and systematized, the leading elements of the definition of the Church

[97] LANG, *Der Evangelienkommentar M. Butzers*, p. 144 f., 329 ff.; *Inst.*, II, 7, 14.

[98] BUCER, *Enarrationes perpetuae in sacra quatuor Evangelia*, Marburg, 1530. *In Evangelium Matthaei*, fo. 57a; 3rd edn, Basle, 1536, p. 142; cf. *Opp.*, 49, 271.

[99] See, at least so far as Baptism is concerned, BUCER, op. cit., *In Evangelium Johannis*, fo. 16a; edn of 1536, p. 601.

[100] H. STRATHMANN, op. cit., pp. 230-9.

[101] Cf. AUGUSTINE, *De Baptismo*, 1, 26; 5, 26 and 38, M. L. XLIII; *De Doctrina Christiana*, 3, 45, M. L. XXXIV. Upon Luther's conception, J. KOESTLIN, *Luthers Theologie*, Stuttgart, 1901, vol. II, pp. 267 ff. Upon Bucer, J. COURVOISIER, *La Notion d'Eglise chez Bucer*, pp. 69 ff., 81 ff. The best general study in French is that of H. STROHL, 'La Notion d'Eglise chez les Réformateurs' in the *Revue d'Hist. et de Philos. religieuses*, 1936, pp. 265-319.

that Bucer had included in his *Treatise on the Cure of Souls* in 1538.[102]
But Bucer's most important contribution to the progressive
elaboration of Calvinist ecclesiology is not there; it must be
looked for rather in the domain of church organization. In the
first place, Calvin adopted Bucer's declaration that ecclesiastical
organizations are not subject to human arbitrament, that they
are of Divine right because they are dictated by the Holy Spirit.[103]
And then, he took over the theory of the four ministries which,
as we saw, were incorporated in the *Ecclesiastical Ordinances* of
1541 and of which, two years later, Calvin inserted the doctrinal
justification in the *Institutes*.[104] As for the church discipline,
Calvin had adopted this in principle before he presented himself
at Strasbourg. He had also been able to see it functioning, in a
very imperfect manner, at Basle, but no doubt the successors of
Oecolampadius had given him knowledge of their wishes in this
respect, and of the ecclesiastical conceptions which the latter had
been developing. The practice of the discipline was hardly any
more satisfactory at Strasbourg, but in that city Bucer had made
himself the more and more exigent champion of ecclesiastical
jurisdiction, which he conceived, moreover, as a part of the cure
of souls.[105] Calvin turned to his own purpose the whole of Bucer's
argumentation upon this question, including the incorporation
of discipline in the cure of souls.[106] With regard to the justification

[102] One can find this definition, among others, in COURVOISIER, op. cit., p. 98.

[103] G. ANRICH, *Strassburg und die calvinische Kirchenverfassung*. Bucer had
elaborated his theory when in contact with Oecolampadius, and had defined
it on the occasion of the Strasbourg Synod of 1533. Cf. STROHL, op. cit., pp.
309 ff., where numerous comparisons with Bucer's ideas and terminology are
indicated.

[104] See the bibliography indicated above, Book I, chap. III, n. 19. Add
LANG, *Der Evangelienkommentar*, pp. 370 ff. J. COURVOISIER, op. cit., pp. 146 f.,
rightly observes that: 'Bucer gave to Calvinist theology the theory of the
visible Church considered as a Divine institution, and the theory of the
ministries exercised in this Church, in which, fundamentally, lies what is
generally considered the Reformed idea of the Church.'

[105] Upon the position of Oecolampadius and the Basle regime, cf. E.
STAEHELIN, *Das theologische Lebenswerk Joh. Oekolampads*, pp. 506 ff. For Bucer,
consult LANG, *Der Evangelienkommentar*, pp. 185 ff. and STROHL, op. cit., pp.
310 ff.

[106] BOHATEC, 'Calvins Lehre von Staat und Kirche', p. 551; in the opposite
sense, LANG, op. cit., p. 312.

of discipline, the *Treatise on Holy Communion* that Calvin wrote
during his period at Strasbourg summarizes the ideas outlined
by Bucer in the *Catechism* of 1534 and in other contemporary
writings.[107]

Let us restrict ourselves to these few indications. They are
sufficient to show that even if the influence of Bucer on Calvin
was less extensive than has sometimes been said, it was at least
considerable, provided, of course, that we do not confuse influence
with servile imitation, and that we respect the ever-predominant
factor of Calvin's personality. 'Bucer,' he wrote, 'is too long to
be read in haste by those who are distracted by other occupation,
and too high to be easily understood by those who do not consider things so closely. For so incontinently does he set about
treating of a subject, whatever it may be, that his mind, which
is of such an incredible fertility, furnishes him with so much in
hand that he cannot restrain himself and come to an end.'[108] In
1553, two years after Bucer's death, Robert Estienne published
in Geneva a magnificent reprint of the *Commentary* on the Gospels
and, a year later, a second volume which contained the *Commentaries* on the Psalms and on the Book of Judges. Calvin was
perhaps not unconcerned in this posthumous homage. He also
encouraged the publication of French translations of his old
friend's leading works. In this way, and better still by the use
he made of some of Bucer's ideas, he largely repaid whatever
debt of gratitude he owed to the reformer of Strasbourg.

III. THE PURPOSE OF THE INSTITUTES

Before entering upon our exposition of the theology of Calvin,
we must endeavour to answer one last question: what precisely
was the aim that the author set before himself when he was

[107] *Opp.*, 5, 443: 'It is not meet that we should presume to be of the body
of Christ, giving ourselves up to all licentiousness and leading a dissolute life.
Since in Christ there is only chastity, benignity, sobriety, truth, humility
and all such virtues, if we would be his members, all lewdness, vanity, intemperance, falsehood, pride and similar vices must be far from us. For we cannot
mingle these things with him without doing him great dishonour and shame.'

[108] *Opp.*, 10b, 404. Cf. *Opp.*, 46, p. vii (*Argument upon the Gospel of our Lord
Jesus Christ according to S. Matthew, Mark and Luke*) where Calvin said he had
imitated Bucer.

publishing and endlessly remodelling the *Christian Institutes*?[109]
Calvin himself took care to enlighten us upon this point with a
wealth of detail not usually to be expected from him. In the
'Epistle to the King' that prefaces the edition of 1536, he indeed
declares:

> When I first set myself to the writing of the present book,
> nothing was less in my thought, most noble king, than to
> write things that would be presented to your Majesty. My
> intention was only to teach some rudiments whereby those
> who were touched with any good affection to God might be
> instructed in true piety. And chiefly I desired by this labour
> of mine to serve our people of France, among whom I saw
> several who had hunger and thirst for Jesus Christ and few
> indeed who had received a right knowledge of him. Which
> consideration of mine can be easily perceived in the book,
> inasmuch as I have accommodated it to the simplest form of
> teaching that was possible to me. But seeing that the fury of
> some iniquitous persons had risen so high in your kingdom
> that it had left no room for any sound doctrine, it seemed to
> me expedient to make this present book serve as much for
> the instruction of those whom I had at first meant to teach,
> as also for a confession of faith before you; from which you
> might know what this doctrine is, against which those who
> now trouble your kingdom with sword and with blood are so
> inflamed with rage.[110]

At first, then, Calvin's intention was to write an exposition,
as simple as possible, of Christian doctrine as a whole, a sort
of *Catechism*, as he afterwards called it. But when, in consequence
of the persecutions that steeped the country in blood at the
beginning of 1535, and above all, as Calvin expressly says in
his preface to his *Commentary on the Psalms*,[111] when he learned
that people were trying to justify these persecutions by alleging
that they were directed only against 'the Anabaptists and seditious

---

[109] AUTIN, op. cit., pp. 29 ff.; H. OBENDIEK, 'Die *Institutio* Calvins als
"Confessio" und "Apologie" ' in the *Theologische Aufsätze Karl Barth zum 50
Geburtstag*, Munich, 1936, pp. 417-32.
[110] *Opp.*, 3, 9.   [111] *Opp.*, 31, 24.

persons', he decided to make his book useful for apologetic purposes as well. It was then, no doubt, that he added the two last chapters.

Historically, these two different and simultaneous aims may be of equal interest; but from the theological point of view the former is obviously by far the more important. Calvin himself must have thought so; for while he left the apologetic sections and especially the 'Epistle to the King' very nearly unchanged in subsequent editions, he subjected the theological exposition to the profound modifications we know, which he regarded as so many improvements.

The edition of 1536 was, therefore, to have been an elementary manual, designed to make 'a few rudiments' known to newly-converted readers. This practical and, in the highest meaning of the term, even edifying aim was predominant. Nevertheless this edition was printed in Latin, which rendered it accessible only to a small minority. If the author did make a French version of it, it is more than probable that the public never had the benefit of it. But the 'Notice to the Reader' in the second Latin edition, that of 1539, shows us that Calvin was defining and modifying his former intention. He is not now concerned to give the learned a succinct exposition of the reformed doctrine, but a properly dogmatic introduction to the reading of Holy Scripture.[112] Calvin no longer seems to have in view the general mass of the partisans of the Reform or of the merely curious: he is directing his work more especially to students of theology. Like Melanchthon when he was publishing his *Loci Communes* of 1521, Calvin is now seeking above all to provide for the needs of theological instruction by producing a manual of dogmatics, which could serve as a guide for students.

> My purpose [he writes at the beginning of the Latin edition of 1539] has been so to prepare and instruct those who wish to give themselves to the study of theology that they may have easy access to the reading of the Holy Scriptures, make good progress in the understanding of it, and keep to the good and straight path without stumbling. For I think I have so understood the whole of the Christian

[112] *Opp.*, 1, 256 f.

religion in all its parts, and have summarized it in such order, that whoever has rightly understood the form of instruction that I have followed will easily be able to judge and resolve for himself what he should seek in the Scriptures and to what end he must relate the purpose of the same. And yet in sooth there is no need that, in my *Commentaries*, where I expound the books of Holy Scripture, I should enter into long disputations upon the matters dealt with there, seeing that the present book is a general address in guidance of those who wish to be helped; and in fact it can be seen that I have no love at all for excessive talk, nor any use for long prolixity.[113]

Calvin now conceives his *Institutes* as complementary to his courses in exegesis, as a manual in which he will have developed his dogmatic convictions once for all, and which is to dispense him from having to restate them when dealing with the various passages of Scripture that he may have occasion to explain to his hearers or readers.

But that was not the only aim of the *Institutes*. The author did not lose sight of the great mass of readers who, without giving themselves up to the special study of theology, wished none the less to come to some clearness on the subject. It was for their sake that he published French translations of his book, without, however, modifying the didactic aim he had assigned to it. The argument of the French edition of 1541 is explicit:

In order that readers may be better able to profit by this

[113] The Latin in the edition of 1560 is more exact, and bears more of the mark of the period in which it was written: 'Hoc mihi in isto labore propositum fuit: sacrae theologiae candidatos ad divini verbi lectionem ita praeparare et instruere ut et facilem ad eam aditum habere, et inoffenso in ea gradu pergere queant. Siquidem religionis summam omnibus partibus sic mihi complexus esse videor, et eo quoque ordine digessisse, ut si quis eam recte tenuerit ei non sit difficile statuere, et quid potissimum quaerere in scriptura, et quem in scopum quidquid in ea continetur referre debeat. Itaque hac veluti strata via, si quas posthac scripturae enerrationes edidero, quia non necesse habebo de dogmatibus longas disputationes instituere, et in locos communes evagari, eas compendio semper astringam. Ea ratione, magna molestia et fastidio pius lector sublevabitur; modo praesentis operis cognitione, quasi necessario instrumento, praemunitus accedat.'

present book, I wish especially to show them, in brief, the use they are to make of it. For in doing this, I shall be showing them the end towards which they ought to aim and direct their attention in reading it. Although indeed the Holy Scripture contains a perfect doctrine to which one can add nothing, since therein our Saviour has willed to display the infinite treasures of his wisdom, nevertheless any person who is not well practised in it can make good use of some guidance and direction, to know what he is to look for if he is not to stray hither and thither but to keep to a sure path, tending ever towards the end to which Holy Scripture calls him. Wherefore, the duty of those who have received from God a more ample enlightenment than others is to come to the aid of the simpler in this respect, to lend them, as it were, a guiding hand and help them to find all that God has willed to teach us by his word.[114]

And, a little further on: 'I dare not give too great a testimony (to this book) and declare how much the reading of it may be profitable, for fear lest I seem to think too highly of my own work; yet this I may well promise, that it could be as a key and an entrance, and give access to all children of God, well and truly to understand Holy Scripture.'

Let us pass over what may, indeed, seem a little strange to our eyes, in the way that Calvin praises his book and the qualities he claims for it. The fact remains that, for Calvin, the Holy Spirit calls upon men, or at least upon those who have received the faith, to imbue themselves with the Divine revelation by the reading of Holy Scripture. But this reading is not as easy as people suppose, and Calvin thinks that one is all too likely to fall into error; that is, to misinterpret the Scriptures, if one is not provided with a reliable guide, able to show the reader what he ought to be seeking therein and how to find it. That is true in the first place of the theologians, who have to be more especially instructed, and who will find this guide in the Latin versions of the *Institutes*. But it is also true for the whole body of the faithful; and that is why Calvin afterwards undertook the labour of translating each of his new editions into French.

[114] *Opp.*, 3, p. xxxiii.

In 1560 for the first time he inserted his Latin preface, intended for students and for the learned, in the French edition of his work. In doing so Calvin made the fundamental aim of his work yet more clearly apparent, while at the same time he was under-lining, for the benefit of all readers, the function that, in his view, had to be fulfilled by dogmatics.

CHAPTER TWO

God, Creator and Sovereign Ruler of the World

In the present exposition of the theology of Calvin, I propose to indicate some of the most original aspects of Calvinist thinking, the choice of which is bound to be partly arbitrary. On the other hand, we need hardly recall the fact that each one of the subjects we shall be entering upon could be and has been the subject of numerous special works of research, and of controversies which it would be impossible for us to review in detail. In order that this book may preserve its character as an introduction, as simple as possible, to the theology of Calvin, I have thought it best to rely upon the words of the author of the *Institutes* rather than those of his commentators, however perspicacious and ingenious they have been. This does not mean that we shall deprive ourselves of the help of their works whenever we find them of some service to us.[1]

[1] It is advisable, before proceeding, to mention here the most important works that have been written in exposition of Calvin's theology as a whole. Besides some chapters devoted to Calvin by some of the historians of dogmatics (F. LOOFS, *Leitfaden zum Studium der Dogmengeschichte*, 4th edn, Halle, 1906, pp. 875 ff.; R. SEEBERG, *Lehrbuch der Dogmengeschichte*, vol. IV, 2, pp. 551-663; O. RITSCHL, *Dogmengeschichte der Protestantismus*, vol. I, Leipzig, 1908, pp. 62 ff., vol. III, Göttingen, 1926, pp. 156-242), the list must include vol. IV of E. DOUMERGUE's *Jean Calvin*, the book by L. GOUMAZ, *La Doctrine du salut d'aprés les commentaires de Jean Calvin sur le Nouveau Testament*, which constitutes a fairly complete exposition of Calvin's theology, and above all P. WERNLE, *Calvin*, Leipzig, 1919. Among yet more recently published studies, we must retain that of H. BAUKE, *Die Probleme der Theologie Calvins*, Leipzig, 1922, which endeavours to explain Calvin's originality by the form in which he knew how to clothe his ideas; the small, very condensed book by A. DE QUERVAIN,

The Knowledge of God and of Revelation

I. THE KNOWLEDGE OF GOD AND OF REVELATION

The *Institutes of the Christian Religion* begins with this affirmation: 'The entire sum of our wisdom, of that which deserves to be called true and certain wisdom, may be said to consist of two parts: namely, the knowledge of God, and of ourselves.'[2] From the beginning of his work, Calvin places all his theology under the sign of what was one of the essential principles of the Reform: the absolute transcendence of God and his total 'otherness' in relation to man. No theology is Christian and in conformity with the Scriptures but in the degree to which it respects the infinite distance separating God from his creature and gives up all confusion, all 'mixing', that might tend to efface the radical distinction between the Divine and the human. Above all, God and man must again be seen in their rightful places. That is the idea that dominates the whole of Calvin's theological exposition, and underlies the majority of his controversies.

But what does he mean by the knowledge of God?[3] Is it the

Calvin, sein Lehren und Kämpfen, Berlin, 1926, which is mainly concerned with Calvin's significance today; and lastly the remarkable synthesis by w. NIESEL, *Die Theologie Calvins*, Munich, 1938, which gives a good account of a project rather similar to our own, and from which I have often derived inspiration. Naturally, the biographers of Calvin have also given space to his theology. The summary accounts of it that they have given are of very unequal value: let us cite, among the most successful, those of A. LANG, *Joh. Calvin*, pp. 61-93; IMBART DE LA TOUR, *Calvin et l'Institution chrétienne*, pp. 55-115, and J. D. BENOIT, *Jean Calvin*, pp. 223 ff.

[2] *Inst.*, I, 1, 1. Instead of 'the sum of our wisdom', the edition of 1536 had said 'the sum of the holy doctrine'. Calvin therefore enlarged the scope of this affirmation in and after 1539, by making all true wisdom dependent upon the dual knowledge of God and of ourselves.

[3] Cf. DOUMERGUE, op. cit'. vol. IV, pp. 41 ff.; WERNLE, op. cit., pp. 167-86; NIESEL, op. cit., pp. 19-49; P. LOBSTEIN, *La Conaissance religieuse d'après Calvin*, Paris 1909; P. J. MULLER, *De Godleer van Calvijn*, Gröningen, 1881, pp. 12 ff.; B. B. WARFIELD, 'Calvin's Doctrine of God' in the *Princeton Theol. Review*, 1909; NOESGEN, 'Calvins Lehre von Gott und ihr Verhältnis zur Gotteslehre andere Reformatoren' in the *Neue kirkliche Zeitschr*, 1912; H. ENGELLAND, *Gott und Mensch bei Calvin*, Munich, 1934. One should also take account of the often pertinent remarks of E. A. DOWEY, *The Knowledge of God in Calvin's Theology*, New York, 1952.

natural knowledge that we might have of him, upon which the ancient philosophers founded their affirmations about divinity? To ask that question is to have answered it, however little enlightened one may be as to Calvin's meaning. We are not here concerned with rational speculations about the existence or the nature of God, for, as Calvin writes: 'what we think about him of ourselves is but foolishness and all we can say about him is without savour.'[4] Besides, we cannot know God in his essence; it is in vain to ask *Quis est Deus*. 'His essence is so incomprehensible that his majesty is hidden, remote from all our senses.'[5] Here Calvin is only following an opinion very widely held among the Fathers of the Church; and it is with a quotation from Hilary of Poitiers that he introduces his theme: 'Leave to God the privilege of knowing himself; for it is he only who is able to bear witness of himself who knows himself by himself alone. And we shall be leaving him what belongs to him if we understand him as he declares himself, and ask nothing at all concerning him except through his word.'[6] We are failing to recognize the incomprehensibility of God if we try to bring him closer to us by sensible representations, or by invoking theophanies which are intended precisely to remind us that we are unable to grasp God in his essence.[7]

'We know God, not when we merely understand that there is a God, but when we understand what it is right for us to understand of him, what is conducive to his glory—in short, what is expedient. For, correctly speaking, we cannot say that God is known where there is no religion nor piety. . . . For of what profit would it be to confess with the epicureans that there is some God who, being free from the care of governing the world, takes pleasure in idleness? Rather should the knowledge we have of him teach us to fear and revere him, and then teach and

[4] *Inst.*, I, 13, 3.

[5] *Inst.*, I, 5, 1. Similarly, in the Catechism of 1542: 'For our understanding is not capable of understanding his essence.'

[6] *Inst.*, I, 13, 21.

[7] *Inst.*, II, 8, 17; I, 11, 3: 'Every sign that he has ever chosen for his appearances to men has been such as would instruct and warn them that his essence is incomprehensible.' Cf. P. BRUNNER, *Vom Glauben bei Calvin*, Tubingen, 1925, p. 45.

induce us to look to him for all good and return praise to him.'[8]
What interests Calvin is not an abstract knowledge of God such as
we might deduce from philosophy; on the contrary, it is a
knowledge of what he is in relation to ourselves, the knowledge
which, as Luther also taught, brings us to love and fear God and
render him thanks for his benefits.[9]

But how does one attain this knowledge of God? 'No one,'
says Calvin, 'can have even the least taste of sound doctrine and
know that it is of God, unless he has been to this school, to be
taught by the Holy Scripture.'[10] The Scripture reveals to us, in
fact, what we ought to and can know about God.[11] But it is
not enough of itself. To find God, one must not limit oneself to
reading or studying the Bible as one would any other book. Such
a study may very well make us fall back upon purely human
doctrines, and then we shall have done no more than return, by
a roundabout way, to the speculations that Calvin rejects, and
of which he finds striking examples in the 'profane philosophers'.
To read the Scriptures, under the conditions requisite for finding
the revelation that God brings to us in them, one has to approach
them with a new heart. In other words, one must have the
faith. And that is as much as to say, with Calvin, that 'the
mysteries of God are understood only by those to whom it is
given.'[12]

What should we really be looking for in the Scriptures? It was
to give an answer to that question, as we know, that Calvin wrote
his *Institutes*. He was not so much concerned to present his
readers with a summary of the Scriptures, or even with the
teaching that they contain, as to point out what they should
search for, and to what end they should relate what the Scriptures
gave them. In a passage we have already quoted from the
'Epistle to the King', he had announced his intention of 'teaching
a few rudiments, whereby those who are touched by any good
affection to God would receive instruction in true piety'.[13] Now,

[8] *Inst.*, I, 2, I and 2.
[9] See, for example, the explanations of the first Commandment and of the
first article of the Creed in the *Greater Catechism* of Luther.
[10] *Inst.*, I, 6, 2.
[11] *Inst.*, I, 6, entitled 'To attain unto God the creator, the Scripture must
be our guide and mistress.'
[12] *Inst.*, I, 7, 5.   [13] *Opp.*, 3, 9.

by this true piety, he doubtless means 'a reverence and love towards God conjoined together, to which we are attracted, knowing the good that it does us':[14] but by that he also, and more especially, means the knowledge of Christ, and that is what he sees as the true end of the Scriptures. In the preface that he wrote for the Genevan editions of the Bible he again insisted upon this idea: 'The Scripture,' we read there, 'is not given us to satisfy our foolish curiosity or to serve our ambition. But it is useful St Paul tells us; and why? To teach us good doctrine, to console us, exhort us and render us perfect in every good work. So to that use let us put it. If we are asked: what is all this edification that we ought to receive from it, the answer, in a word, is that we learn thereby to put our trust in God and to walk in fear of him. And, inasmuch as Jesus Christ is the fulfilment of the Law and the Prophets and is the substance of the Gospel, that we incline towards no other end but to know him.'[15] Fruitfully to read the Scriptures, thereby to find the divine revelation, they must be approached with the firm intention of finding Jesus Christ in them. All else is but human wisdom or mere fantasy.[16] And the reason for this is that Christ is the one and only mediator through whom God makes himself known to us. We therefore cannot know God as we ought and as he wishes to be known, unless we seek him in Christ: that is why the aim of all study of the Scriptures must be the Christ. Calvin assures us moreover that this has been so ever since the ancient Covenant: 'The saints of the past have never known God otherwise than by looking to him in his Son, as in a mirror. When I say this I mean that God has never manifested himself to men except by his Son; that is, by his unique truth, wisdom and light. From that fount, Adam, Noah, Abraham, Isaac and Jacob drew all that they had of spiritual knowledge. From that same source the Prophets derived all the teaching that they gave or have left to us in writing.'[17] And how much more was this the case with the

[14] *Inst.*, I, 2, 1.   [15] *Opp.*, 9, 825.

[16] Commentary upon John 5.39, *Opp.*, 47, 125: 'The Scriptures must be read with this intention, that in them we find Christ. Whoever turns aside from this purpose, even though he torment himself with learning all his life long, will never attain to the knowledge of the truth. For what sagacity or intelligence can we have without the Wisdom of God?'

[17] *Inst.*, IV, 8, 5.

Apostles! In short, Jesus Christ is at the centre of the whole of the Bible, of which he is the vivifying spirit, since God, hidden from sinful man, has been revealed only in Jesus Christ, and it is the Bible that bears witness to that revelation.

This is so exclusively true in Calvin's eyes, that although the pagans too profess to worship a Creator god, they are in reality worshipping only an idol. As soon as he departs from the one firm foundation of the revelation in Christ, man is bound to follow his natural tendency to make himself gods in his own image. Commenting upon Romans 1.22, Calvin writes: 'It is a vice that has been by no means peculiar to philosophers to think oneself wise in the knowledge of God, but one that is common to all nations and all states. For there is not one of them who has not wanted to confine the majesty of God within the conception of his own understanding and make a God such as he could grasp with his senses.'[18] And in the commentary on Hebrews 11.6: 'Men labour in vain to serve God, if they do not know the right way, and that the religions that have nothing of the true and certain knowledge of God, all added together, are not only vain but harmful, for all those who do not distinguish God from idols are unable to have access to him.'[19] Consequently, what differentiates Christianity from other religions, even if they be monotheistic, is that it knows God only in Jesus Christ. And even as God has willed to reveal himself in the incarnate Christ, so also does Christ make himself known in his living word: 'But because God does not speak to us every day from the heavens, and there

[18] *Opp.*, 49, 25.

[19] *Opp.*, 55, 148. Cf. 55th Sermon on Deuteronomy, *Opp.*, 26, 427: 'The pagans were talking nonsense when one of them said: "I worship God." For what did he mean by that? Dreams, fantasies. For when men profess to worship God without having known him, there is no doubt that they are worshipping idols. The Turks themselves will say today that they worship God the creator of heaven and earth, but it is only an idol that they worship.' Similarly Luther, in his *Greater Catechism*, says: 'The pagans too had the idea that to have a God meant really to trust in him and believe; but their trust was false and misplaced, for they put it not in the one and only God, beside whom there is no true God either in heaven or on earth. The pagans, with their false gods, were worshipping creations of their own imagination and dreams, and entrusting themselves to mere nothingness.'

are only the Scriptures alone, in which he has willed that his truth should be published and made known unto even the end, they can be fully certified to the faithful by no other warrant than this: that we hold it to be decreed and concluded that they came down from heaven, as though we heard God speaking from his own mouth.'[20]

Thus we come to the problem of the authority of the Scriptures and their inspiration.[21] Whence do the Scriptures derive their authority over men, and within what limits are they authoritative? What grounds have we for affirming that they 'came down from heaven' or that we hear God speaking in them 'from his own mouth'? What is the warrant for that submission to the Scriptures which Calvin is demanding of every believer when he writes: 'Our knowing should be nothing else than the receiving, in a spirit of meekness and docility, of all that we are taught by the Scriptures, without any exception.' Of itself Scripture is nothing but the dead letter, like any other historical document. Before we can find the living word of God in it, and have assurance that this word is personally addressed to each one of us, there must be an intervention of the Holy Spirit. It is the Holy Spirit who makes use of the Biblical writings to put us in contact with the word of God, and who at the same time works within us so that we may discover this word in the Scripture and accept it as coming from God. In a celebrated passage, Calvin has defined what he meant by this operation of the Holy Spirit, its bearing witness in the soul of every believer to the truth and authenticity of the Scripture: 'Though indeed God alone is sufficient witness to himself in his word, nevertheless that word will obtain no credence in the heart of man if it be not sealed by the interior witness of the Spirit. . . . Wherefore it is necessary that the same Spirit who spoke by the mouth of the Prophets must enter into

[20] *Inst.*, I, 7, I.

[21] DOUMERGUE, op. cit., vol. IV, pp. 70 ff.; O. RITSCHL, *Dogmengeschichte*, vol. I, pp. 63-4; R. SEEBERG, *Dogmengeschichte*, vol. IV, 2, pp. 566 ff.; DE GROOT, *Calvijns opvatting over de inspiratie der Heilige Schrift*, Zutphen, 1931; J. A. CRAMER, *Calvijn en de Heilige Schrift*, Wageningen, 1932; P. BRUNNER, *Vom Glauben bei Calvin*, pp. 92 ff.; THOS. C. JOHNSON, 'J. Calvin and the Bible' in the *Evangelical Quarterly*, London, 1932, pp. 257-66; H. CLAVIER, *Etudes sur le Calvinisme*, pp. 25 ff.; NIESEL, op. cit., pp. 27 ff.

our own hearts and touch them to the quick, in order to persuade them that the Prophets have faithfully set forth that which was commanded them from on high.'[22]

There is one necessary and indissoluble bond between the Scripture and the Holy Spirit: the Spirit inspired the authors of the books of Scripture, and it is he also who inspires us when we read their writings so that we may have tangible proof of the identity of that inspiration. The Spirit is immutable: he does not bear witness within us of anything other than in the writings of the Prophets and Apostles, which he uses to enable us to know God through Jesus Christ. For Calvin, the interior witness of the Holy Spirit is the supreme criterion upon which the authority of the Scriptures is founded. Also, he rejects the external authority founded upon the authority and tradition of the Church, as these are claimed by the Roman Church.[23] With at least equal vigour, he opposes the spiritualists who regarded the Scriptures as obsolete, or allowed them only a secondary importance, upon the pretext that the Spirit was continuing his revelations outside the text of the Bible.[24] And he rejects the identification of the Spirit and the word of God; the Spirit does nothing other than certify the Word contained in the Scriptures. The witness of the Holy Spirit adds nothing to the Scripture; he tells us nothing about it that it does not already contain; in a word, that witness is no new revelation disclosed in addition to the scriptural texts. The Holy Spirit acts here in the same manner as when he gives to a

[22] *Inst.*, I, 7, 4. Cf. DOUMERGUE, op. cit., vol. IV, pp. 59 ff. For comparison, BUCER, *Enarrationes in sacra quatuor Evangelia*, 1536, p. 520: 'Proinde ei qui syncere scripturas intelligere volet, pieque illis uti in primis orabit Christum, ut ipse mentem sibi aperiat, coelestique luce perfundat. Haec enim ubi abfuerit, pernicies e scripturis referri poterit, fructus non poterit.'

[23] *Inst.*, I, 7, 1.

[24] *Inst.*, I, 9, 1. *Opusc.*, 756. See also the commentary on Acts 16.14, *Opp.*, 48, 378: 'Then let a crowd of day-dreaming and fantastic minds hold their peace, those who under cover of the Holy Spirit reject and hold in disdain all external doctrine. For we must keep to that moderation which St Luke observes here: that we can obtain nothing by only hearing the word of God, without the grace of his Holy Spirit, and that the Spirit who is given to us is not at all a spirit who engenders contempt or disdain of the word, but rather one who gives faith in the same to our understanding, and writes it in our hearts.'

believer the certainty of his adoption, or brings him into contact with the Christ in the sacraments.[25]

As for the other criteria that might be adduced in support of the authority of the Scriptures, such as their contents, their style, their originality, the predictions and miracles that they record—to these Calvin ascribes only a very secondary importance. The Spirit alone can certify that one is finding the word of God in Scripture, and he does so only to the elect.

This formal principle of the interior witness of the Holy Spirit is affirmed by Calvin with growing conviction in the successive editions of his work. He insists more and more strongly upon the Spirit's assurance to us that God is speaking in the Scripture. Its contents are divine because the authors of the various Biblical texts were only instruments employed by God to put his revelation into writing.[26] 'The apostles were only the sworn notaries of the Holy Spirit, so that their Scriptures might be held authentic; the successors have no other commission than to teach what they find contained in the Holy Scriptures.'[27] That inspiration extends to the whole of their contents. Calvin cannot allow anyone to draw distinctions between the different books of the Bible, of the kind that Luther had introduced by retaining only those writings which refer to Christ. All are on the same level and all are inspired. Historical criticism like that of Valla and Erasmus, which Luther had admitted to some degree, could never, according to Calvin, end in a diminution of the importance of this or that book, and still less in justifying its exclusion from the canon. When Sebastian Castellion began to express doubts about the inspiration of the Song of Songs, Calvin took it for an offence against the majesty of the divine Book. It was not, of course, because the Church had adopted and guaranteed the scriptural canon that Calvin also imposed acceptance of it. It was because the canon rested upon the witness of the Holy Spirit. But Luther also thought he was guided by the Holy Spirit to rediscover the word of God in the Bible, and he had no more found it everywhere than Castellion had. Whether he wished it or not, Calvin

---

[25] W. KOLFHAUS, *Christusgemeinschaft bei J. Calvin*, Neukirchen, 1939, p. 146.

[26] Cf. BUCER, op. cit., pp. 3 and 21, where the apostles are regarded as organs of the Holy Spirit. Calvin uses the same term.

[27] *Inst.*, IV, 8, 9.

allowed himself to be guided in this matter by ecclesiastical tradition much more than by his own principles.

But if all the books of the Bible are equally inspired, it necessarily follows that the Old Testament has as much value as the New Testament; and that is indeed the conclusion that Calvin came to, not only in theory but also in the use he was led to make of the books of the old Covenant. The will of God is immutable. He cannot therefore have willed or said anything in the Old Testament other than what is in the New. The two parts of the Bible can claim with equal right to be regarded as the word of God.[28] On this point Calvin is often accused of having fallen into an excessive legalism. What might be said with more justice is that he drew his own inspiration as much from the Old as from the New Testament, but did so by making every effort to find in the one as much as in the other, what he regarded as the end and aim of the Scriptures, namely Jesus Christ. This attitude was perfectly consistent with his notion of Scriptural revelation and of the books of the Bible.

The writings in the Bible, then, are the word of God, and the Holy Spirit which inspired their writers bears witness in us to the faithfulness with which they accomplished their task. From this it has generally been concluded that Calvin professed the doctrine of the literal inspiration of the sacred Books, and the majority of historians have found no difficulty in considering him, if not the inventor of that doctrine, at least one of its most notorious representatives.[29] They could, it is true, try to justify this by the attitude adopted by a number of the reformer's disciples. But in fact Calvin himself never affirmed literal inspiration.[30] The expressions that he uses show, on the contrary, that

[28] Commentary upon Romans 15.4, *Opp.*, 49, 271: 'If the spirit of Christ is in all things and everywhere like unto itself, there can be no doubt at all that today, by the Apostles, he has dispensed his teaching to the edification of his own, as he did of old time by the Prophets.'

[29] See, for example, R. SEEBERG, op. cit., vol. IV, 2, p. 567.

[30] H. HEPPE, *Die Dogmatik der evangelisch-reformierten Kirche*, Neukirchen, 1935, pp. 16-17; DOUMERGUE, op. cit., vol. IV, pp. 73-4; NIESEL, op. cit., pp. 28 ff. One cannot but agree with the affirmation of H. CLAVIER, *Etudes*, p. 27: 'Contrary to first appearances, extreme literalism is not implied in those passages that deal with inspired doctrine. Though the letter does not escape from the control of the Spirit, it is for its content alone,

he did not draw this conclusion from his theory of the inspiration of the Bible. Although it is true to say that he thought one could find the word of God in the Bible, he nevertheless said that the word we possess in the Scriptures is a mirror which reflects something, but does not impart to us the thing itself.[31] The Scripture itself is 'an instrument by which the Lord dispenses the illumination of the Spirit to the faithful',[32] but it is not to be identified with the Lord himself. Though the content of the Scripture is divine, inasmuch as it is the word of God, the form in which that content is clothed is not therefore divine. The authors of the books of the Bible wrote under the inspiration of the Holy Spirit; they were none the less liable to introduce human errors into it upon points of detail which do not affect the doctrine.[33]

After this necessary digression upon the authority of the Scriptures, we must now return to the question of the means available, according to Calvin, for attaining to the knowledge of God. What we have stated thus far is that even when deprived of faith, men are led to believe in a God, but that in such a case they cannot have true knowledge of him, and therefore are led to fabricate idols. True knowledge of God can be acquired only by means of the Scriptures.

Yet in the *Institutes* Calvin devotes a whole chapter to the knowledge of God that is naturally rooted in the minds of men.[34] 'We think it beyond doubt,' he writes there, 'that men have a sense of divinity in them, nay even of a natural movement [thereto]. For so that none should take refuge in the plea of

for its spiritual content, that divine infallibility is claimed.' Cf. also pp. 81 ff.

[31] *Inst.*, III, 2, 6.   [32] *Inst.*, I, 9, 3.

[33] Cf. Commentary on Matthew 27.9, *Opp.*, 45, 749, and on Hebrews 11.21, *Opp.*, 55, 159.

[34] *Inst.*, I, 3. DOUMERGUE, op. cit., vol. IV, pp. 41 ff.; WERNLE, op. cit., pp. 170 ff.; W. LUETGERT, 'Calvins Lehre vom Schöpfer' in the *Zeitschrift für systemat. Theologie*, Gütersloh 1932, pp. 421 ff.; P. BARTH, 'Das Problem der natürlichen Theologie bei Calvin', Munich, 1935; G. GLOEDE, 'Theologia naturalis bei Calvin', Stuttgart, 1953; P. MAURY, 'La Théologie naturelle d'après Calvin' in the *Bulletin de la Soc. de l'Hist. du Protest. français*, 1935, vol. LXXXIV, pp. 267-79; T. F. TORRANCE, *Calvin's Doctrine of Man*, London, 1949, pp. 128 ff.

ignorance, God has imprinted in everyone a knowledge of himself, the recollection of which he renews in us, distilling it as it were drop by drop, so that, seeing that we know from first to last that there is a God and that he made us, we should be condemned by our own knowledge that we had not honoured him and had not dedicated our lives in obedience to him.'[35] God has made himself known to men 'everywhere, in all places and in all things', and that in so clear and evident a manner that no man can plead his ignorance. He has made himself known directly by 'a seed of religion planted in each one by secret inspiration' and indirectly by all the works of his creation. In a passage in his preface to the Bible of Olivétan, Calvin rises almost to lyrical heights, paraphrasing the *Coeli enarrant gloriam Dei*:

> In every part of the world, in heaven and on earth, he has written and as it were engraven the glory of his power, goodness, wisdom and eternity. Truly indeed, then, has St Paul said that the Lord never left himself without a witness, even to those to whom he has sent no knowledge of his word. For all creatures, from the firmament even to the centre of the earth, could be witnesses and messengers of his glory to all men, drawing them on to seek him and, having found him, to do him service and honour according to the dignity of a Lord so good, so potent, wise and everlasting; they were even helping each one in his place upon that quest. For the little singing birds sang of God, the animals acclaimed him, the elements feared and the mountains resounded with him, the rivers and springs threw glances toward him, the grasses and the flowers smiled. So that in truth there was no need to seek him afar, seeing that everyone could find him within himself, inasmuch as we are all sustained and preserved by his virtue abiding in us.[36]

Moreover, Calvin believes he can discern three modes of natural revelation: God shows himself first of all in nature,

---

[35] *Inst.*, I, 3, I.

[36] *Opp.*, 9, 793 and 795. Cf. *Inst.*, I, 5, I: 'God has so manifested himself (to men), in such a beautiful and exquisite edifice of heaven and earth, showing and presenting himself there every day, that they cannot open their eyes without being obliged to perceive him.'

161

especially in the nature of man himself; then he manifests himself in the natural evolution of things, and lastly in the history of mankind. But a thing that must be insisted upon is that the knowledge thus gained is but imperfect and incomplete; and moreover men do not make the use of it that they should. 'Hardly will one find one in a hundred who nurses it in his heart until it germinates, but not even one in whom it ripens, still less does it bear fruit in due season. For some fall away into their foolish superstitions, and others maliciously and of deliberate purpose turn away from God, so far are they all from the true knowledge of him; whence it comes that no well-ordered piety remains in the world.'[37] Besides the Scriptures, which are the sole instrument employed by the Spirit to make us know God in Jesus Christ, we have, then, a natural knowledge of God which is innate, as it were, in all men, and yet which can lead them only to their condemnation, seeing that this knowledge does not pass through Christ the only mediator between God and men, and true piety is thus necessarily absent from it.

The natural knowledge of God has therefore only a negative value in the first place: it deprives men of all excuse before God; legitimizes their condemnation. But has not this natural knowledge of God also a positive function? In other words, has not Calvin admitted a second revelation besides that of the Bible, perhaps inferior to it, but one which none the less imparts a genuine knowledge of God? Several of Calvin's assertions seem indeed to justify that question. In the *Institutes* itself we read: 'The right way to seek God, and the best rule we can follow, is not to force ourselves with too bold a curiosity to inquire into his majesty, which we ought rather to worship than investigate too curiously, but to contemplate him in his works, by which he renders himself near and familiar to us and, we might say, communicates himself.'[38] Before this, Calvin had gone so far as to say: 'Inasmuch as God is known in the first place simply as the Creator, no less by this beautiful masterpiece the world than by the general teaching of the Scriptures, and then afterwards appears as our redeemer in the face and person of Jesus Christ, thence is engendered and brought forth a double knowledge.'[39] Is that not in contradiction with those passages where the

[37] *Inst.*, I, 4, I. [38] *Inst.*, I, 5. 9. [39] *Inst.*, I, 2, I.

author has said that God cannot be truly known except by the Scriptures?[40] It would be so, if humanity had remained still in its original condition—that is to say, but for the Fall. After that event as before it, God continuously manifests himself in his creation. But in consequence of the Fall, we will not and can not know God in his external works. God still shows himself in them, but to derive a true knowledge through them, man would have to be still in the same state of integrity as he was before the Fall. 'Since we fell from life into death,' wrote Calvin in 1559, 'all that we are able to know of God inasmuch as he is our Creator is of no avail, unless it be conjoined with the faith that offers us God as our Father and as our Saviour in Jesus Christ. That indeed was the natural order, that the building of the world was to be the school for our instruction in piety, the means which was to lead us into eternal life, the perfect felicity for which we were created: but since the Fall and the rebellion of Adam, whithersoever we turn our eyes, nothing appears to us above or below but malediction'.[41] And it is not only in the creation outside us that God still reveals himself. The 'seed of religion', which consists in the recognition that 'there is a divinity'[42] persists within man, but it is 'so corrupted that it produces only harmful fruits'. The elect themselves have no more than this to incline them towards piety so long as the Lord has not 'taken them out of this pit of perdition'.[43] 'There is such a perversity mixed with the ignorance of men and with their stupidity that, destitute of right judgment, they let pass by without any true feeling all the signs of the true glory of God, as shiningly manifest in heaven as upon earth. Seeing indeed that the true knowledge of God is a singular gift of his goodness, seeing also that the faith by which alone it is rightly known proceeds only from illumination by the Holy Spirit, it follows that our minds cannot enter into it by the guidance of nature alone.'[44]

The categorical refusal to admit any positive knowledge of a

[40] Cf. the commentary on Acts 14.17, *Opp.*, 48, 327; 'Faith is not conceived solely from the sight of heaven and earth and their adornment, but by the hearing of the word. From which it follows that men cannot be brought to a saving knowledge of God except by the guidance of the word.'

[41] *Inst.*, II, 6, 1.   [42] *Inst.*, I, 4, 4.   [43] *Inst.*, III, 24, 11.

[44] *Opp.*, 48, 416 (commentary on Acts 17.27).

God in fallen man set Calvin in contradiction with the humanists, and with a good many Christian theologians who attributed at least a commencement of that knowledge to a few privileged men, philosophers in particular. This was notably the point of view of Zwingli and his disciples. To the objections that might be raised from that quarter Calvin replied: 'I do not deny that here and there we can see in the books of the philosophers some sentences said to be of God, well written; but in these there is always an appearance of such inconsistency that one can clearly see that they had only confused imaginings of him. It is true enough that God gave them some small savour of his divinity, so that they could not claim ignorance in excuse of their impiety, and without moving them to speak one of those sentences by which they might have been convinced; but what they did see they saw in such a light that it could not have addressed them to the truth. They are far from having attained it.'[45] True it is, and Calvin does not hesitate to admit it, that the philosophers did receive some special enlightenment concerning God; but far from weakening his argument, this only makes it the more convincing to him. The gifts they received did not enable the philosophers to acquire more of the knowledge of God than other men have. Those gifts only served in the end to render them yet more inexcusable.

The Fall deprived all men of the will to know God, and of the possibility of knowing him as their Father in Jesus Christ, which is the only saving knowledge one can have of him. Therefore God cannot but condemn them, and that condemnation is perfectly just, seeing that man, incapable even of an approach to God after the Fall, remains none the less responsible for his fault. Also, there remain no other means of knowing God for fallen humanity but to embrace the revelation that has been given of him in Jesus Christ. 'After the ruin of Adam, no knowledge of God could be profitable to salvation without a mediator.'[46] And that mediator we know only through the Scriptures, upon the further condition that we read them under the inspiration of the Holy Spirit. In this inspiration resides the only revelation that can make us know God not only as he exists, or in the works of

[45] *Inst.*, II, 2, 18.
[46] *Inst.*, II, 6, 1. Cf. P. BARTH, 'Die Fünf Einleitungs kapitel von Calvins *Institutio*' in the *Kirchenblatt für die reformierte Schweiz*, 1925, No. 11.

his Creation, but such as he is in relation to us (qualis est). Then
alone is the veil that hid the natural revelation from us torn away,
and man regenerated finds again, as man had seen them before
the Fall, the traces of God in nature.

II. THE TRINITY

If it is only in the Scriptures that God reveals himself for our
salvation, it follows that we can know no more of him than he has
chosen to impart to us. Now, if we search the Scriptures, what
do we find about God? 'He reveals himself as the one God in
such a manner,' replies Calvin, 'that he offers himself to our
contemplation in three distinct persons.'[47] We remember that
the inadequacies of the first edition of the *Institutes* made it
possible for Caroli to bring the accusation of 'Arianism' against
Calvin, and that the latter could not help displaying a somewhat
curious attitude on that occasion. Nevertheless, there is no doubt
whatever that he always thought the trinitarian dogma must be
maintained in its integrity. In this he was following Luther's
policy; and it was also in conformity with Luther that he took
up the defence of traditional trinitarian terminology, which
some people deprecated as non-Biblical. 'True it is, that we must
take from the Scriptures the rules for our thinking as much as for
our words, and refer to it both all the cogitations in our minds
and all the words of our mouth. But who is to prevent us from
expounding in clearer words those things that are obscurely
shown in the Scriptures, if that is done without too much licence
and upon good occasion?'[48] Bucer had been having greater

[47] *Inst.*, I, 13, 2. Cf. DOUMERGUE, op. cit., vol. IV, pp. 92 ff.; WERNLE,
op. cit., pp. 34 ff.; NIESEL, op. cit., pp. 50 ff.; J. KOOPMANS, op. cit., pp.
56-66. Apart from the *Institutes*, Calvin's most complete treatises are his
*Declaration for the maintenance of true faith held by all Christians, of the Trinity of
Persons in one God, against the detestable errors of Michael Servetus*, *Opp.*, 8, 453-644;
Opusc., 1505-1692; and *The Impiety of Valentin Gentilis openly discovered and
decried*, *Opp.*, 9, 361-420; *Opusc.*, 2239-88.
[48] *Inst.*, 13, 3. Cf. LUTHER, *Von Concilien und Kirchen* W. A. 50, p. 572;
'Without doubt, one ought to teach nothing touching upon divine things
which is not in the Scripture, as St Hilary says in his *De Trinitate*. But this
does not mean that one must not use any terms other than those in the

difficulty in admitting the terminology sanctified by tradition, until the day when, for reasons analogous to those advanced by Luther and Calvin, he also was led to adopt it without reservation.[49] For Calvin, indeed, 'this novelty of terms is then principally necessary when the truth has to be maintained against calumniators, who invert it by their tergiversations.'[50] The allusion to Servetus is transparent. Servetus had figured since about 1530 as the typical adversary of trinitarianism as it had been admitted by the great Councils of the fourth century. It was against Servetus that Bucer had already developed his conception of the Trinity; and it was also during his own controversy with the famous Spanish physician that Calvin came to give more and more importance to trinitarian doctrine. And yet with regard to this conflict, where Calvin so unhesitatingly threw all his authority and reputation as a reformer into the balance, we may wonder whether it was the trinitarian question in itself that was his dominant interest.

In the edition of 1536, Calvin limited himself to a very brief exposition of the traditional doctrine of the Trinity. Here he adduced the unity of baptism and faith according to Ephesians 4.5 in support of the unity of God, emphasizing at the same time the duty of administering baptism in the name of the three Persons of the Holy Trinity, and that these three Persons simultaneously were the object of the faith.[51] But obviously that was not going very far. In 1539, the disputes aroused by Caroli obliged Calvin to be more emphatic. He multiplied the Biblical quotations in support of the divinity of the Son and of the Holy Spirit, and of the distinction between the three divine Persons. Above all he underlined the importance of the divinity of Christ for the faith, and of the divinity of the Holy Spirit for communication with God the Creator and God the Redeemer. But, in this second edition, he treated the terminology with greater breadth of view; the reading of the Fathers of the Church had

---

Scriptures, especially in discussions, and when the heretics try blindly to travesty those things and alter the meaning of Scripture.' See KOOPMANS, op. cit., pp. 40 ff.

[49] Cf. for instance, the *Apologie de la Tétrapolitaine*, Strasbourg, 1531, fo.ĸ. 4b.

[50] *Inst.*, I, 13, 1.   [51] *Opp.*, I, 58 ff.; *O.S.*, I, pp. 71 ff.

shown him many an example of great freedom in this respect.
In 1559, on the contrary, he went back to a more rigorous treatment; the controversy with Servetus had shown him the indis-
pensability of keeping within the usual terms if one wanted to
avoid all suspicion of heresy.

When Calvin, in 1559, developed the theme that the divinity
of the Son is a necessary foundation of the faith, he was showing
us, without doubt, why he had the maintenance of the trinitarian
dogma so much at heart, even to the point of making common
cause with the Genevan judges in their condemnation of Servetus.[52] To deny the divinity of the three Persons was tantamount
to ruining the divinity of the Christ and, at the same stroke,
removing the keystone not only of Christian theology, but of all
saving faith.[53] Just as Luther revolted so violently against the
antinomians, so did Calvin, whose religion was quite as Christo-
centric as Luther's, refuse to tolerate any detraction from the
honour of Christ or from the value of his work of salvation.

But in Calvin's eyes, to admit the unity at the same time as
the trinity of God involved important consequences for the
Person of Christ as well as for the faith of his followers. The
essence of God is one; and since this essence has been revealed in
the flesh, it is therefore the entire divinity who gave himself to
us in the person of the Christ. 'We must conclude, then, that the
essence of God is common to the Son and the Spirit in its entirety.
But if that be true one cannot, in regard to the same, distinguish
the Father from the Son, seeing that they are but one.'[54] On the

[52] About 1938, in the preface to the Latin edition of the *Catechism* and the
Confession of Faith of 1537, Calvin had somewhat loftily affirmed his orthodoxy
on this point. Cf. *Opp.*, 5, 318.

[53] This has been very well shown by NIESEL, op. cit., p. 52 f.

[54] *Inst.*, I, 13, 23. Calvin declares it impossible that each one of the three
Persons could have 'a portion of the divine essence', and teaches, in accordance
with Peter Lombard (*Sent.* I, dist.), and with the Fourth Lateran Council of
1215 (DENZINGER, *Enchiridion symbolorum* No. 431 f.), that the divine essence
is absolutely one and unbegotten in all three Persons. Luther, on the
other hand, had adopted the criticism of Joachim de Flora, accusing Peter Lombard
of having replaced the Trinity by a divine quaternity of Father, Son, Holy
Spirit and common essence (W. A. 39, 2, 287 f.). 'It appears to them,' writes
Calvin in *Inst.*, I, 13, 25, 'that we are setting up a quaternity . . . as though we
were saying that the three Persons flowed in and out of one essence like three
rivulets. But on the contrary, it is plain from our whole teaching that we do

other hand, seeing that this divinity is identical with the God of the Old Testament, we can apply the name of Yahveh to the Christ, and attribute to him all that is said about Yahveh in the books of the Old Covenant.[55] And as for the believers, it follows from the unity of the divine essence and its indivisibility that they, being now one with Christ, receive the divinity in his plenitude, so that 'the believing soul recognizes the presence of God indubitably and, as one may say, touches him with his hand.'[56]

The unity of the divine essence so strongly insisted upon by Calvin does not, however, in the least detract from the real distinction that must be made between the three Persons of the Trinity. Carefully avoiding anything that could have been considered an innovation, Calvin formulates his thought as follows: 'These vocables, Father, Son and Holy Spirit, denote to us a real distinction, so that none may think they are different titles attributed to God simply to signify him in several manners. But we have to observe that it is a distinction, not a division. The passages that we have adduced show well enough that the Son has his attributes distinct from the Father; for he could not have been the word in God unless he were other than the Father, and would not have had his glory with the Father if he were not distinguished from him. . . . The distinction of the Holy Spirit from the Father is shown to us when it is said that he proceeds from

---

not treat of the Persons of the essence in separation from it . . . If the Persons were separated from the essence, this argument would be of some weight; but in that case it would be a Trinity of Gods, not of the Persons whom, we say, a single God contains in himself.'

[55] *Inst.*, I, 13, 23: 'The God who appeared to Isaiah was the true and only God, and nevertheless St John affirms that he was Jesus Christ. He who, by the same Prophet, warned the Jews that he would be a stumbling-block to them, was the one true God; yet St Paul states that this is Jesus Christ. He who, from the very beginning, speaks loudly and clearly saying that every knee shall bend before him, is the one living God; and St Paul interprets this as Jesus Christ. When we add to this the evidences that the Apostle adduces: Thou, O God, hast founded the heavens, and the earth is the work of thy hands. *Item.* All the angels of God worship thee; we cannot say that all this is not cognizable as one single, true God. And nevertheless the Apostle tells us that these are the proper titles of Jesus Christ.'

[56] *Inst.*, I, 13, 13.

the Father; [his distinction] from the Son when he is named as another; as when Jesus Christ announced that another Comforter would come, and in several other passages.'[57] Throughout this exposition Calvin employs to his own purposes the arguments that were traditionally put forward to explain, or at least to define, the unity of the essence at the same time as the distinction between the Persons. He is closely following St Augustine and perhaps also remembering the writings of certain Greek Fathers.[58] And it is again tradition to which he is appealing when he defines the attributes of the three Persons of the Trinity: 'To the Father, the commencement of every action and the source and origin of all things are attributed; to the Son, the wisdom, the counsel and the order in which all things are disposed; to the Holy Spirit, the virtue and efficacy of all action.'[59] But although devoid of originality, this trinitarian doctrine constitutes an essential part of the theology of Calvin. It enabled him, notably, to lay the emphasis that he did upon the divinity of Christ.

III. THE CREATION

When we are seeking God in the Scriptures, as we must, he appears to us first of all as the Creator of all things.[60] That, indeed, is the general teaching of the Scriptures, a teaching which must be carefully distinguished, according to Calvin, from the doctrine of the Redemption. 'For although no one, in that ruin and desolation of the human race, ever thought that God was Father to him, or even saviour or propitiator, until Christ came in the midst to pacify him towards us; nevertheless, it is one thing to be informed that God, since he is our creator, not only sustains us by his virtue, governs us by his providence, maintains and nourishes us by his bounty and continues all kinds of blessings towards us; and another thing, in face of this, to receive and

---

[57] *Inst.*, I, 13, 17.

[58] Besides the *De Trinitate* of St Augustine he quotes at the very least the *De Trinitate* of Cyril of Alexandria, of whom he made use in other writings.

[59] *Inst.*, I, 13, 18. Cf. AUGUSTINE, *De Trinitate*, VII, 1-4, XV, 27-37, M. L. XLII, 931 ff., 1079 ff.

[60] P. J. MULLER, *De Godsleer van Calvijn*, pp. 47 ff.; NIESEL, op. cit., pp. 57-66.

embrace the grace of reconciliation as he offers it to us in Christ.'[61]
The divine Creation and Providence belong, then, to this general
knowledge of God given us by the Scriptures, which is to be distinguished from the special knowledge of God considered as the
Father who has been reconciled with us by Jesus Christ. But
that does not mean that we can acquire the knowledge of God, as
the Creator and as Providence, apart from Jesus Christ. Whatever aspect of God we may be seeking to know, it is in Christ
alone that we can find it. It is only through his mediation
that we attain to the knowledge, at least since the Fall, of
God the Creator, as well as of God the Redeemer. Much
more, it is by Christ, the Word of God, that all things were
created.[62]

More generally, Calvin affirms that the world and man were
created by the entire Trinity. And this act of creation brings
before us certain attributes of God. By the fact that he made the
world out of nothing, he reveals himself alone as eternal, as the
being-in-itself who alone can communicate to the creatures such
being as they possess. Indeed, in the act of creation no external
means intervened: the Word of God was sufficient to call forth
all things out of nothingness: it is therefore creative and acts by
itself. But it does not do so at hazard: Calvin assigns to the
Creation an end, a purpose, which is no other than man—at
least, in the immediate sense. 'God has ordained all things to
our profit and salvation, and in order to contemplate his power
and his grace in ourselves and in the benefits he has conferred
upon us, thereby to incite us to trust in him, to call upon him,
to praise and love him. And that he created all things for man
this he has shown by the order that he has kept. . . . For it was
by no means without cause that he divided the creation of the
world between six days, when he could as easily have completed

[61] *Inst.*, I, 2, I.

[62] Commentary on Psalm 33.6, *Opp.*, 31, 327, and on Philipp. 3.21, *Opp.*,
52, 57: 'It is also highly expedient to note that the authority and power to
raise the dead, even to do all things at his good pleasure, is attributed to the
person of Christ, which is a glory by which his divine majesty is excellently
adorned. What is more, we gather therefrom that the world was created by
him, for it belongs to the Creator alone to subject all things to himself.' Add
to these the *Congrégation de la divinité de Christ*, *Opp.*, 47, 477; and Commentary
on John 1.5, *Opp.*, 47, 7.

the whole in one minute of time as he wrought it little by little. But in this he wished to show us his providence and his fatherly care for us, that before having created man, he made ready for him everything which, as he foresaw, would be useful or beneficial to him.'[63]

The teleology expressed in this passage, and which sometimes assumes a rather naïve aspect—especially in Calvin's sermons—corresponded no doubt to a tendency in his personal faith, but it also went with a pedagogical motive: the more one insisted upon the human orientation of the Creation, the more enormous and unpardonable the sin of Adam must appear to be, and the more wonderful the goodness of God who had nevertheless found a way to redeem man. However, if man is the present purpose of the Creation, the true final cause of it, as of every manifestation of the divine will, is summed up in the glorification of God. The divine glory thus appears as an ultimate goal which superposes itself upon the immediate aim of human finality. All men, good or bad, must contribute to the heightening of his splendour. Calvin often emphasized this, for example in his *Treatise on Predestination*, where we read:

> Although indeed God could well do without all his creatures, nevertheless it is arguing foolishly to deduce from this that he had no regard to his own glory in creating man. . . . Although God lacks nothing, still the principal aim he had in creating men was that his name might be glorified in them. . . . The wicked are created for the day of their perdition: for that does not happen save in so far as God wills to reveal his glory by them; even as he has said in another place, that he raised up Pharoah in order that his name should be manifest among the peoples. And were this not so, what would become of so many evidences of Scripture which tells us that the sovereign aim of our salvation is the glory of God.[64]

On the other hand, in several places Calvin lays emphasis on the fact that the Creation does not consist only of the world that

[63] *Inst.*, I, 14, 22; cf. 14, 2.
[64] *Opp.*, 8, 293 f; *Opusc.*, 1431; *Opp.*, 31, 194 f.; 33, 481.

is visible and perceptible to the senses, but also of the spiritual and invisible world peopled by the angels as well as by human souls.[65]

Although he says in advance that in speaking of angels he will study 'to observe such moderation as God commands us; that is, not to speculate more highly than is expedient, for fear lest readers be led away from the simplicity of the faith',[66] the length of his exposition does not fail to surprise us. He begins by establishing that the angels are really creatures, but that it would be a vain curiosity to try to determine when they were created. The angels, celestial spirits, are the ministers of God, who 'makes them his messengers to men, to manifest himself to them'. The titles attributed to them in the Scriptures serve 'to magnify the dignity of their ministry'. Then Calvin adopts for his own purpose the classical notion of tutelary angels commissioned to protect humanity. 'They are always watchful for our salvation, they are always ready to defend us, they straighten our ways and have care for us in all things to guard us from any evil encounter.' But Calvin dare not go so far as to put each man under the protection of one particular angel; besides, that is of little importance; 'for if anyone is not content with this, that all the police of heaven are watching over our salvation and ready to help us, I do not see how it will profit him any more to say that he has one special angel as his guardian.'[67] Nor does he commit himself further concerning the hierarchies of angels and their external appearance. They have no more right to our worship than have any other creatures, 'seeing that they have no sufficiency in themselves, but draw from the same fount as we do'.[68] They are, as it were, the hands of God 'which never move to do anything but by his will and disposition'.[69] As for the multitude of devils who ceaselessly assail us, the Scripture teaches us 'to be on the watch to resist their temptings and not to be taken by surprise in their ambushes'. Calvin sees them as 'spirits having intelligence', and he adds, in order to underline the reality of their existence, 'It would be using quite improper forms of speech to say that the judgment of God will come upon the devils, that

[65] *Inst.*, I, 14, 3 ff. Commentators usually pass over this very rapidly. . . .
[66] *Inst.*, I, 14, 3.   [67] *Inst.*, I, 14, 5-7.
[68] *Inst.*, I, 14, 10.   [69] *Inst.*, I, 14, 12.

the eternal fire is prepared for them, that they are already in prison awaiting their last sentence, and that Jesus Christ tormented them at his coming, if there were not any devils after all.'[70]

Besides the angels—and the demons—human souls are to be ranked among the created spiritual beings. Man, therefore, in himself alone, is like an epitome of God's creative work, since he participates in both the sensible and the spiritual worlds by his body and by his soul. 'As to man's having two parts, namely body and soul, we ought to make no difficulty about it. By the word "soul" I mean the immortal spirit, nevertheless created, which is the nobler part.'[71] Calvin affirms, then, three distinct things about the human soul: first that it is immortal, second, that it is created, and lastly that it is the nobler of the two parts of man. Although the whole of this section of the *Institutes* underwent profound revision in 1559, one would have no trouble in finding these same affirmations in the earlier editions and in other writings of Calvin. At the most, one could say that his doctrine of the immortality of the soul may have been influenced a little, at first, by Hellenic elements which afterwards faded more and more into the background. Excepting the allusion to Plato that we shall find again presently, they indeed became negligible.[72] The thesis of the immortality of the soul is supported, in 1559, by a whole series of psychological arguments and scriptural texts. With the aid of these, Calvin sets himself to demonstrate that the soul has an essence of its own and cannot be reduced to a 'breath' or to 'some strength breathed into the body'.[73] Even when men are immersed in their darkness they are 'always touched with some sense of their immortality'. The consciousness they have of good and evil is an evidence that the soul is immortal. So is their knowledge of God, which makes them 'surpass the world', and distinguishes them from animals; 'for such awareness as the

[70] *Inst.*, I, 14, 19.   [71] *Inst.*, I, 15, 2.

[72] Compare, upon this point, H. QUISTORP, *Die letzten Dinge im Zeugnis Calvins*, Gütersloh, 1941, which seems, however, to give too much importance to these survivals of a humanist metaphysic. Our knowledge of this work has been limited to detailed reviews of it. One may consult the introduction by W. ZIMMERLI to his edition of the *Psychopannychia*, Leipzig, 1932.

[73] *Inst.*, I, 15, 2.

brute beasts have does not go beyond their bodies, or in any case extends no further than to what is present to their sensuality, whereas the agility of the human mind, ranging in discourse over heaven and earth and the secrets of nature, storing so many things in its memory, digesting them and drawing the consequences from time past into the future, shows that there is some part of man which is separate from the body.' And lastly, sleep, or more correctly dreams, give evidence of immortality. 'For not only does sleep suggest to them thoughts and apprehensions of what has never happened, it also gives warnings of things to come, which are called presentiments.' On the other hand numerous passages in Scripture 'not only distinguish the soul from the body but, attributing to it the name of the whole man, declare that it is the principal part of us'. To this Calvin attaches a long development upon man considered as the image of God, in which he finds further confirmation of the soul's immortality, since this latter alone can be the seat of the glory of God.[74] It was precisely because Plato saw the image of God in the soul that he was excepted from the generality of philosophers, to whom, in Calvin's view, it would be folly to look for a right definition of the soul.[75]

The immortality of the soul has survived the Fall. The Anabaptists contested this, and in support of their opinion invoked Romans 6.23: 'the wages of sin is death', and Ezekiel 18.4, 'the soul that sins shall die': but to this Calvin had already replied in his *Psychopannychia*, 'The soul, even when it is dead, has its immortality, the which we affirm, and say that it has its feelings of good and of evil, and that this death is something other than that which they would like to obtain, namely, that it should be reduced to nothing.'[76] But we must not, for all that, make Calvin an advocate of the soul's eternity, nor even of its purely natural immortality. In an important passage in his *Treatise on Free Will against Pighius* he wrote: 'From what origin did it come except from nothing? If he (Pighius) said that that perfection

---

[74] *Inst.*, I, 15, 2 and 3. Cf. T. F. TORRANCE, op. cit., pp. 35 ff.

[75] *Inst.*, I, 15, 6.

[76] *Opp.*, 5, 203 f.; *Opusc.*, 36 f. For Calvin, the death of the soul is 'the formidable judgment of God, the weight of which the poor soul cannot bear without being altogether confounded, cast down and lost'.

which God had given man in the beginning was not of such a
nature as to exist by itself and of itself, in that I would willingly
be of his opinion. For likewise we do not agree that the soul is
immortal of itself. What is more, that is the teaching of St Paul,
who ascribes immortality to God alone. We do not therefore
believe, however, that the soul is mortal by its nature, for we do
not estimate the nature of the same by the primary faculty of the
essence, but by the perpetual state, that God has put into his
creatures.'[77] What Calvin means by this cumbersome formula
amounts to this: that God drew out of nothing the substance of
the soul, which is created just like every other creature, and that
its qualities are products of the divine will. In his conflict with
Servetus, he was led to insist upon this created character of the
soul, in opposition to the 'Manichaean dreamings' that his
adversary was seeking to rehabilitate, according to which 'the
soul was an offshoot of the substance of God, as though some
divinity had flowed into man'. Certainly, Calvin goes on, 'what
St Paul alleges from a pagan poet is very true—that we are the
issue of God; but that means in quality, not in substance;
namely, inasmuch as he has endowed us with divine faculties
and virtues. Nevertheless, it were too monstrous a folly to divide
up the essence of the Creator so that each one might possess a
portion of it. . . . The Creation is not a transfusion, as though one
were drawing wine from a cask into a bottle; it is the origination
of an essence which did not exist at all.'[78]

Not only is the soul created, but its immortality is a gift of God
which he could withdraw from the soul if he wished; and the
soul deprived of the divine support would perish just like the
body and return to nothing. This is no more than a particular
case of the constant intervention of God in his creation, of his
'panergism', and of the relation of close dependency upon their
creator in which the creatures always find themselves. In this

[77] *Opp.*, 6, 360 f.; *Opusc.*, 441 f. Cf. sermon on I Timothy, 1.17-19, *Opp.*,
53, 92.
[78] *Inst.*, I, 15, 5. We may note incidentally the interest of this passage; it
contains an implicit refutation of the doctrine of the soul according to the
mystics. Calvin, moreover, alludes shortly afterwards to the ideas of Osiander,
who upon this point was inspired by that doctrine.

there may be some recollection of the Scotist teaching that Calvin had received at the College of Montaigu, much as one can trace analogous affirmations of Luther to the Occamist conception of God.[79]

Man, the immediate object of the Creation, has received from God a special, privileged place in the bosom of that creation. God has made him, not simply a dweller upon earth like the animals, but has also granted him life to come, after the death of the body and until the last judgment. And besides this, God has favoured man with special gifts, among them one to which Calvin attaches especial importance; namely, that God created man in his own image and likeness. What does that mean? After having rejected the distinction between image and likeness which was classic among the scholastics, he offers the following explanation of this gift, which has been the object of so much theological speculation:

> Seeing that the soul is not the whole of man, are we not bound to find it absurd that, in view of this, man should be named the image of God? Nevertheless I hold to the principle I adduced just now: that is, that the image of God extends to all the dignity by which man is raised above every species of animal. In which, under this word, is included the whole integrity with which Adam was endowed when he enjoyed a right mind, had his affections well regulated, his senses well tempered and everything in him well ordered to represent by such adornments the glory of his Creator. And though the sovereign seat of this image of God was placed in the mind and in the heart, or in the soul and its faculties, yet there was no part, even until the body itself, which did not reflect some glint of him.[80]

Only angels are also participants in this divine resemblance, 'seeing that our sovereign perfection, as Christ testifies, will be to resemble them'. The image of God imprinted on man consists, then, of the integrity and righteousness which were the attributes of Adam when he came fresh from his Creator's hands, the

[79] R. SEEBERG, *Joh. Duns Scotus*, pp. 212 f.
[80] *Inst.*, I, 15, 3.

perfect example of which has been shown in Christ the second Adam.[81]

IV. PROVIDENCE

Calvin seems rather soon to have become aware that in his edition of 1539 he had not put his exposition of divine Providence in the place appropriate to it: but it was not until the edition of 1559 that he placed this immediately after his full discussion of the Creation.[82] For indeed, he explains, 'to make a creator God temporal and of brief duration, who had accomplished his work in only one operation, would be a cold and meagre thing: and it is chiefly in this that we must differ from the pagans and all profane people, that for us, the virtue of God shines in the present, as much in the enduring state of the world as in its first beginning.'[83] God is the Creator of the world: but having once created it he remains its absolute master, takes interest in it, intervenes in it at every moment, and abandons none of his power to the blind play of natural laws, still less to chance. Here we find again the notion common to Luther and Zwingli, and upon which Bucer was so insistent, of a continuous action of God in the midst of his Creation.[84]

But it is not without interest to see how Calvin in his turn insists upon this notion. It occupies a prominent place in his commentaries and sermons, and in the definitive edition of the *Institutes* there are two whole chapters upon it. Moreover, im-

[81] Cf. *Inst.*, 15, 4: 'We see that Christ is the most perfect image of God, being more comfortable with which we are so much restored that we resemble God in true piety, justice, purity and intelligence.'

[82] See, upon the question as a whole, H. STROHL, 'La pensée de Calvin sur la Providence divine au temps ou il était réfugié à Strasbourg' in the *Revue d'Hist. et de Philos. religieuses*, 1042, vol. XXII, pp. 154-69; J. BOHATEC, Calvins Vorsehungslehre in *Calvinstudien*, pp. 339-441; E. DE PEYER, 'Calvin's Doctrine of Divine Providence' in the *Evangelical Quarterly*, London, 1938, vol. X, pp. 30-44; WERNLE, op. cit., pp. 305-22; NIESEL, op. cit., pp. 66-74.

[83] *Inst.*, I, 16, I.

[84] Cf. Luther's explanation of the first article of the Creed in the 'Little' and the 'Greater' Catechisms. ZWINGLI, *De vera et falsa religione* in the *Corp. Reform.*, vol. XC, pp. 645 ff., and above all his sermon at Marburg, *De Providentia Dei*, edit. Schuler & Schulthess, vol. IV, pp. 79 ff., which Calvin perhaps knew. For Bucer, cf. LANG, *Der Evangelienkommentar*, pp. 117 ff.

portant portions of his treatise *Against the Libertines* (1545) are devoted to it, and so is the whole of an appendix to what has been called the *Consensus Genevensis*; that is, the *Treatise on Predestination* (1552). Indeed, even when he had perceived that for systematic reasons it would be better to deal separately with Providence and predestination, the parallelism between the two notions was too close for him to be able to lose sight of it for a moment.[85] Predestination can in fact be regarded as in some respects a particular application of the more general notion of Providence. After 1539, the point of view which related Providence to the Creation had not, however, escaped him. 'The human mind,' he wrote, 'having once realized the virtue of God in the Creation, stops there . . . but faith must indeed go farther; it must recognize him as perpetual governor and guardian, whom it has known to be the Creator. And that he not only drives the machinery of the world and all its parts in a universal motion, but sustains, nourishes and cares for every creature, even for the little birds.'[86]

The notion of Providence implies that of God's permanent and universal activity in the world. Also, as Calvin wrote in 1559, 'When we speak of the providence of God, this word does not signify that he, remaining idle in the heavens, watches over what is happening on earth: rather is he like the captain of a ship, holding the helm in order to cope with every event.'[87] The errors into which the pagans fell prove that man, if left without any light but his own, cannot understand what this Providence is.

---

[85] STROHL, op. cit., pp. 163 ff.

[86] *Inst.*, I, 16, 1. In 1543 he added the following passage to his development of the theme of the Creation: 'Whenever we call God the Creator of heaven and earth, let it also come into our minds that it lies in his hand and in his power to dispose of everything he has made, and that we are his children, whom he has taken into his charge to feed and to govern; so that we may await every good thing from him, and have a sure hope that he will never allow us to lack those things that are necessary to our salvation, and that our hope may depend upon nothing else; and that whatever we desire, we ask it of him; and that, whatever good things we have, we ascribe them to him with thanksgiving; that, being moved by such great liberality as he shows us, we may be brought to love and honour him with all our hearts.' All this, which was repeated in the definitive version (I, 14, 22), might have come straight from the *Greater Catechism* of Luther.

[87] *Inst.*, I, 16, 4. Cf. K. HOLL, *Was verstand Luther unter religion, Gesammelte Aufsätze*, vol. I, pp. 45 ff.

For that, he needs help from the revelation of God that we have in Jesus Christ: 'All those who have been taught from the mouth of Christ that the very hairs of our head are all numbered will look further for the cause, and will hold themselves well assured that all events, whatever they be, are governed by the secret counsels of God.'[88] Faith is therefore indispensable to anyone who wishes to grasp what the Providence of God is, and how far it extends. Where unbelievers can see only the play of natural forces or the effect of chance, believers will perceive the hand of God.

In 1545, in his treatise *Against the Libertines*, Calvin distinguished three aspects of Providence which he does not seem to have separated with such care afterwards, at least not in the *Institutes*. He mentions first of all 'the order of nature', in which God 'leads all creatures according to the condition and property that he gave to each one when they were formed'. While he still remains the first and the direct cause of all being and all activity, God acts here by conforming himself to the laws that he himself has imposed upon his creation. To this 'universal operation' Calvin opposes the 'special providence' through which 'God works in his creatures and makes them of service to his goodness, justice and judgment, according as he wills either to help his servants or to punish the wicked; either to try the patience of the faithful or to administer fatherly chastisement.' Consequently, the special Providence is concerned more particularly with man, and with the constant intervention of God in the life of man. No doubt he brings secondary causes into play, including among his instruments even Satan and the wicked, but these are only 'means that he employs to accomplish his will'. But this again is not simply a matter of the external action of God upon man. On the contrary, the third aspect of Providence consists in this: that God 'governs his believers, living and reigning within them by his Holy Spirit', which means that he is practically indistinguishable from the interior witness of the Holy Spirit.[89] We have a good right, then, to see this as saving grace. It is by this that he transforms and regenerates the elect, making them, in some sort, the beneficiaries of a new creation. Thus placed, under the

---

[88] *Inst.*, I, 16, 2.
[89] *Opp.*, 7, 186-90; *Opusc.*, 765-9; cf. *Opp.*, 8, 347 ff.; *Opusc.*, 1438 ff.

control of the order of nature, of special Providence and of the interior operation of the Holy Spirit, the believer finds himself in a complete and absolute dependence upon God, which, however, he does not feel as a restraint, but as the means to his fulfilment.

The passages quoted indicate that Calvin not only admitted the intervention of a universal Providence, but providence of such a kind that absolutely nothing that happens in the world can escape from its direct causation. This causation was reaffirmed in a passage that he inserted into the *Institutes* in 1559: 'Events, whatsoever they may be, are governed by the secret counsel of God. In respect of the things that have no souls, we must maintain this point as settled; although God has assigned its own property to each one of them, yet they cannot put these into effect except in so far as they are directed by the hand of God.'[90] But it is not enough to see God as the prime mover or even as the preserver of his Creation. That would be to ignore the function of special Providence which intervenes at every moment of the lives of individuals and nations. 'I do not blame at all,' he writes, still in 1559, 'what is said about the universal providence of God, provided that this is granted me on the other hand—that the world is governed by God, not only in that he maintains the course of the world in being such as he established it all at once; but in that he has a particular care for each creature. True it is, that all species have some secret guidance according as their natures require it, as though they were obeying a perpetual law to which God constrained them; and thereby what God has once decreed flows on and goes its way as if by voluntary inclination.' But that is only the external side of things, which is seen by philosophers and unbelievers. The reality is rich in other ways than they think, and the interplay of natural laws does not at all exclude the constant intervention of God. 'It is a perversity to want to hide and obscure, under such colours, the special providence of God, which is so well and plainly shown to us by clear and certain testimonies of Scripture that it is a wonder how anyone can doubt it.'[91] Thus every creature is directly subject

[90] *Inst.*, I, 16, 2. See also the beautiful passage to which he was inspired by Daniel 2.20 and 21, *Opp.*, 40, 575 ff.

[91] *Inst.*, I, 16, 4.

to God and to his will. Repeating what he had said in his treatise *Against the Libertines* and in many other places, Calvin affirms that this is particularly true of man both in isolation and in society.

Human societies, whether consciously or not, are directed by God, who at every moment determines their history and their vicissitudes. History, and especially sudden revolutions, are regarded by Calvin as particularly eloquent testimonies of the power of God, which 'indicate plainly that human things are directed by him'.[92] That, under these conditions, Calvin should have seen the society above all others, which is the Church, as the object of the special care of divine Providence is not at all surprising. In chapter 17 of Book I, he again enumerates the various aspects under which Providence can be envisaged:

> In the first place, it is noteworthy that the Providence of God must be referred as much to the past as to the future; secondly, that it so moderates and guides all things that it works sometimes by the interposition of means, sometimes without means, and sometimes against all means; and finally, that it tends towards this end: that we may know what care God has for the human race; above all how carefully he watches over his Church, for which he has the closest regard.[93]

This special solicitude of God for his Church must not, however, give us to think that the Church is the purpose of Providence. That purpose is no other than God himself, to whom the faith in Providence should orientate us. 'When the providence of God shines in the heart of the faithful, not only will it be delivered from the fear and distress which formerly oppressed it, but it will be relieved of all doubt.'[94]

But divine Providence is not concerned only with believers and the elect; it is exercised equally over the reprobate; furthermore, it makes use of them, as we have already said. To this point Calvin devotes a whole chapter, which is headed: 'That

[92] *Opp.*, 40, 577.
[93] *Inst.*, I, 17, 1; cf. 17, 6: 'Because God has chosen his Church for his dwelling, there is no doubt but that he wishes to show by singular examples the fatherly care he has of it.'
[94] *Inst.*, I, 17, 11.

God makes such use of the wicked, and so inclines their heart to execute his judgments that nevertheless he remains pure from all stain or defilement.'[95] From the moment that every creature is seen as an instrument in the hands of God, it is clear that he must make use of the wicked themselves as means to his Providence. 'We know, by the first chapter of Job, that Satan as well as the angels presents himself before God to hear what will be commanded him. This is indeed in a different manner and to quite another end; but be that as it may, it shows that he can attempt nothing but by the will of God.'[96] So indeed it is by virtue of a decree of the divine will that the devil and the wicked have the power to operate. Far from thinking that diabolic intervention as an instrument of God's designs might raise doubts of his goodness in the faithful, Calvin sees the strict dependence in which the powers of evil are held by God as a source of consolation for the believer:

> When he recognizes that the devil and all the company of the wicked are held firmly in the hands of God as by a bridle, so that they can neither conceive any evil, nor, when they have conceived it, contrive to do it, nor having contrived it lift even a little finger to execute it, save in so far as God commands them; nay, even that they are not only held in his leashes and controls but constrained by the bit of his bridle to obey him: in that, he [the believer] has enough for his consolation.[97]

If the wicked, and Satan himself, are thus employed in the service of God, must we not conclude on the one hand that God is the author of evil, and on the other that the wicked are not responsible for acts performed at the command of God? Calvin's reply, as is to be expected, is not very original. He energetically denies any participation by God in the origination of evil and lays the entire responsibility upon the evil-doers. That Satan and the wicked are bent upon evil is not at all because God has implanted it in them or suggested it to them, but because they themselves are turned away from God and perverted.[98] Calvin examines

---

[95] *Inst.*, I, 18.   [96] *Inst.*, I, 18, 1.   [97] *Inst.*, I, 17, 11.

[98] Cf. *Inst.*, I, 14, 16: 'Everything that is damnable (in the devil) he acquired by his turning away from God.'

the question at full length in the chapter in which he inquires 'how God works in the hearts of men'. He comments upon Job 1.17, and distinguishes, in the evil action of the Chaldeans who robbed Job of his cattle, the triple intervention of God, of the devil and of men; and he comes to this unexpected conclusion:

> The Chaldeans, abandoning themselves to evil-doing, contaminate their souls and their bodies. It is therefore correct to say that Satan works in the reprobate, within whom he exercises his rule; that is, the rule of perversity. One can indeed say also that God does not work in them at all, inasmuch as Satan, who is the instrument of his wrath according to his will and ordination, drives them hither and thither to execute his judgments. . . . I am speaking of the particular action of God which shows itself in each of his works. By which we see that there is no objection to one and the same work being attributed to God and to the devil and to man. But the difference in the intention and the means makes the judgment of God appear everywhere above reproach, while the malice of the devil and of man shows itself in all its disorder.[99]

The justice of God being beyond all question, the wicked remain wholly responsible; for while they are carrying out the designs of providence, they are violating, in what concerns them personally, the commandments of God. 'When God accomplishes, through the wicked, that which he has decreed in his secret counsels, they are not therefore excusable as though they had been obeying his command, which they violate and traverse so far as it is in them to do, and by their evil covetousness.'[100] All this elaboration is directly inspired by St Augustine. Like him, Calvin declares that the wicked are condemned on account of the evil intention which animates them, and which is their own; the fact that God makes use of their evil actions to a good end does not in the least diminish the perversity of their will.[101]

---

[99] *Inst.*, II, 4, 2. [100] *Inst.*, I, 18, 4.

[101] AUGUSTINE, *Enchiridion ad Laurentium*, XXVI, M. L. XL, 279: 'Haec sunt magna opera domini . . . et tam sapienter exquisita, ut cum angelica et humana creatura peccasset, id est, non quod ille, sed quod voluit ipsa fecisset, etiam per eandem creaturae voluntatem, qua factum est quod creator noluit,

And, like St Augustine, the author of the *Institutes* cites the case of Judas:

> Indeed, for the betrayal wrought by Judas, it would be no more reasonable to attribute any blame to God because he willed to deliver his Son to death, and did so deliver him in fact, than to give Judas the praise for our redemption and salvation, inasmuch as he was the minister and instrument of them.

---

impleret ipse quod voluit, bene utens ad malis, tamquam summe bonus, ad eorum damnationem, quos iuste praedestinavit ad poenam et ad eorum salutem, quos benigne praedestinavit ad gratiam . . . Hoc quippe ipso quod contra voluntatem fecerunt eius, de ipsis facta est voluntas eius. . . . Nam deus quasdam voluntates suas, utique bonas, implet per malorum hominum voluntates malas, sicut per Iudaeos malevolos bona voluntate patris pro nobis Christus occisus est.'

CHAPTER THREE

God, the Redeemer in Jesus Christ

I. THE KNOWLEDGE OF MAN AND OF SIN

One can know God only by Jesus Christ, who himself can be found only through the Scriptures. Similarly, man can have a true knowledge of himself and of his situation only by contemplating himself in the mirror that the Scripture presents to him. This it is, as we have seen, that enlightens us about the original state of integrity and likeness to God in which Adam was created. Now, we are obliged to admit that this first state of mankind was very different from our present situation. But left to our intellectual faculties alone, we could never discover the causes of that difference, nor even grasp the full extent of it. And it is the Scriptures, once more, that give us the reason for this, in the story of the Fall, and that enable us to measure the effects that the fault of Adam has had upon the whole of humanity and each one of its members. The testimony of Scripture obliges us to acknowledge that our reason is disabled, and that our heart is so evil that we cannot do anything else but sin. By the fact of the Fall we have lost the special prerogative that attached to our having been the immediate purpose of the Creation: the image of God that we bore upon us was destroyed, effaced, or to use Calvin's own more discreet formula, 'it was so deeply corrupted that all that remains of it is a horrible deformity.'[1]

---

[1] *Inst.*, I, 15, 4. It is hardly necessary to say how closely Calvin keeps to the general line of Luther's thought on this point. Upon the question as a whole, cf. DOUMERGUE, op. cit., vol IV, pp. 137 ff.; A. LECERF, *Le Déterminisme et la responsabilité dans le système de Calvin*, Paris, 1895, pp. 35 ff.; WERNLE, op. cit., pp. 189 ff.; NIESEL, opp, cit,. pp. 75-85; W. A. HAUCK, *Sünde und Erbsünde nach Calvin*, Heidelberg, 1939.

Here again, Calvin found himself confronting the problem of
the origin of evil. From the moment when all creatures are seen
as so dependent upon God that they would return to nothingness
if he did not endow them with continuing being, it does indeed
seem that the fall of man must logically be referred to a decision
of the divine will. On the other hand, Calvin's view accords with
St Augustine's in ascribing goodness to the creature as it came
from the hands of the Creator. If it has fallen, God must, therefore, have meant it to do so. Calvin does not attempt to deny
that. But at the same time he is bound to affirm the entire responsibility of man. In effect, man in his state of integrity 'had free
choice, by which if he had wished he would have obtained eternal
life. . . . Thus Adam could have kept his status if he had wished,
seeing that he stumbled only by his own will; but because his
will was pliable to good or to evil and the constancy to persevere
had not been given him, that is why he so soon and so easily
fell.'[2] As for our knowing why God did not endow Adam with
the gift of perseverance, 'that is hidden in his closest counsel, and
it is our duty to know nothing but in moderation.' It would seem
to follow from this that God left Adam free to choose, and limited
himself by tolerating Adam's fall.[3]   Elsewhere, Calvin 'keeps
more logically to his usual teaching, which ascribes all things to
the express will of God. Thus in his *Treatise on Predestination* he
writes:

> The faithful indeed make these two things agree with one
> another; that the state of man was so constituted at his
> creation that in stumbling and falling of his own will he was
> the cause of his ruin; and that nevertheless he was thus
> determined by the admirable wisdom of God, to the end
> that the voluntary ruin of Adam should be a reason for
> humility to all his race. For although God knew that this
> was expedient, it does not follow that man was not ruined
> by his own fault, who had otherwise been endowed with a

[2] *Inst.*, 1, 15, 8. Cf. NOESGEN, 'Calvins Lehre von Gott', pp. 706 ff.
[3] Cf. LUTHER, *De servo arbitrio*, W. A. 18, p. 708: 'Sed mox sequitur,
quomodo sit homo factus malus, desertus a Deo ac sibi relictus. . . .' p. 712:
'[Deus] permisit Adam ruere . . . Deus est, cujus voluntatis nulla est causa nec
ratio.'

good nature and formed in the image of God. I say once again, that I know well enough what an appearance of absurdity and contradiction this presents to profane people and those who despise God.[4]

As for the profoundest source of sin, this lies in the motive for the sin of Adam. Calvin sees it as pride, or more precisely, as faithlessness conjoined with pride, rather than as the self-love that St Augustine had found in it. Just as humility before God is the sign of a right attitude towards him, sin is characterized by a disobedience inspired by pride. But this pride is all the more misplaced and blameworthy since, even apart from sin, the weakness and misery of man place him in utter dependence upon the power and the mercy of God. Here Calvin is using expressions which remind one anew of the declarations of the nothingness of man that Luther had made in his earliest writings. In appearance, Calvin is placing himself in contradiction with what he had affirmed about the distinctive qualities of man before the Fall, and the privileges that God had granted him. But in fact this is not so. Adam had certainly been created in the image of God, but all the good that he was then capable of doing, he did not do by virtue of his own abilities, but thanks to the gifts and assistance that God bestowed upon him. There was nothing in that for him to be proud of. 'It is noteworthy,' writes Calvin, 'that when he was made out of earth, this was to hold him in leash lest he should puff himself up, for there is nothing more against reason that that we should preen ourselves upon our dignity, when we live in a cabin of filth and mud, and when we are, in part, no more than earth and mire.'[5] And a little further on he says again: 'To man, when he was exalted to the highest possible degree of honour, the Scripture attributes no more than to say that he was created in the image of God; by which it signifies that he was enriched not by his own goodness, but that his blessedness was in his participation in God.'[6] So long as he was adding further touches to his book, and his thought was taking a more rigid turn, Calvin continued to accentuate the passages in which he pointed to the misery of man. The weaker men had been, even before the Fall, the more disastrous was the condition

[4] *Opp.*, 8, 294 f.; *Opusc.*, 1432. [5] *Inst.*, I, 15, 1. [6] *Inst.*, II, 2, 1.

of mankind after having sinned, and the more Calvin could magnify the immensity of the grace which had made their regeneration possible.

He asserts, indeed, and he will declare ever more firmly right up to 1559, that 'what is noblest and most to be valued in our souls is not only broken and wounded, but altogether corrupted, whatever of dignity it may reflect.'[7] And, in terms that might have been taken from Luther, he explains how the consequences of the Fall not only deprived us of the good that was in us, but has made us a source of continual sinning:

> That perversity is never idle within us, but continually engenders new fruits; namely, those workings of the flesh that we have just described; just as a burning furnace ceaselessly throws up flames and sparks, and as a spring spouts its water. Wherefore those who have defined original sin as a lack of the original justice which ought to be in man, although in these words they have comprehended all the substance, still they have not sufficiently expressed the force of it.[8] For our nature is not merely empty and destitute, but it is so fecund of every kind of evil that it cannot be inactive.

Calvin readily identifies this evil tendency with concupiscence, as St Augustine did,[9] but only if we make this addition to it, 'that every part of man, from the understanding to the will, from the soul to the flesh, is defiled and altogether filled with that concupiscence.'[10]

The reason and the will, then, are both tainted by sin. The will, in particular, can no longer strive for anything but evil. And yet, even after the Fall, reason and will subsist to a certain degree, enough at least to distinguish man from the brute beast. Just as Luther, with regard to fallen man, had distinguished between the lower things that are subject to reason, and spiritual things,[11] so Calvin for his part established a distinction between

[7] *Inst.*, II, 1, 9.

[8] The allusion is to the scholastics, more especially to the nominalists.

[9] AUGUSTINE, *Contra duas epistolas Pelagianorum*, I, 13, 27, M. L. XLIV, 563; *Contra Julianum*, I, 72, M. L. XLV, 1097.

[10] *Inst.*, II, 1, 8.

[11] Cf. among other passages in LUTHER, the sermon on Exodus 18, W. A. 16, p. 354, and the commentary on John 1.8, W. A. 46, p. 587.

the 'external things which depend upon nothing in the kingdom of God' and 'the true justice which is reserved to the spiritual grace of God'.[12]   Chapter 2 of Book II, setting out to establish that 'man is now destitute of free will, and miserably subjected to every evil,' contains long developments upon this theme, which prove the great importance that Calvin attached to it.   He endorses 'the well-known sentence of St Augustine' which affirms that 'the natural gifts were corrupted in man by sin, and that the supernatural were altogether abolished.'[13]   What are we to understand by these supernatural gifts?   He tells us that they are 'as much the purity of faith, as the integrity and righteousness that belong to heavenly life and everlasting felicity'.   But, in losing these spiritual gifts, man is by his own act shut out from heavenly things and no longer able even to conceive of them.   Faith, love of God and of the neighbour, and the desire for holiness, have become completely alien to him.   The natural gifts, on the other hand, have not been wholly taken from him; but in these too there is a loss of efficacy.

This is especially clear in the case of the will.   Since the time of the Fall, man 'has not been deprived of will, but of healthy will'.[14]   Care must be taken to distinguish between the will in itself, and a good or a bad will.   In his state of integrity, Adam's will was not only at his own disposal; he could also direct it towards good or towards evil.   But since the Fall, 'it is certain that man has had no free will to do good without the help of the grace of God.'[15]   It is true to say that man was thenceforth 'a slave

[12] *Inst.*, II, 2, 5: 'It is a thing common to the faithful and to unbelievers, to judge of things of here below.' (Sermon on Job 28.1-9, *Opp.*, 34, 504.)

[13] *Inst.*, II, 2, 12. Cf. Commentary on John 1.5, *Opp.*, 47, 6, and PETER LOMBARD, *Sent.* II, dist. 25, 8: 'Naturalia bona in ipso homine corrupta sunt et gratuita detracta. . . . Vulneratus quidem in naturalibus bonis quibus non est privatus, alioquin non posset fieri reparatio; spoliatus vero gratuitis quae per gratiam naturalibus addita fuerunt.'

[14] *Inst.*, II, 3, 5; Cf. H. BARNIKOL, *Die Lehre Calvins vom unfreien Willen.* With regard to this study, particularly interesting for the comparisons that the author makes with Luther, Melanchthon and Bucer, F. KATTENBUSCH has pointed out the importance of the distinction between the will as such and free will, in his article 'Arbitrium und voluntas dasselbe?' in *Theologische Studien und Kritiken*, 1931, pp. 129 ff.

[15] *Inst.*, 2, 6.

to sin, the meaning of which is that his spirit is so wholly alienated from the righteousness of God that he neither knows, desires nor undertakes anything that is not wicked, perverse, iniquitous and defiled'—to quote the terms used by Calvin in his first Genevan *Catechism*.[16] In the *Institutes* of 1539, he appeals to a formula of St Bernard's which seems to him perfectly to sum up his own opinion: 'Simply to will, is human; to will the bad belongs to corrupted nature; to will the good is of grace.'[17]

But might we not say that, from the moment when man in his state of sin cannot do otherwise than tend to evil, it is incorrect as well as unjust to speak of his responsibility? To this Calvin replies that experience tells us that this sin is indeed our own sin. When we sin, we do it not because we are compelled to, but voluntarily, by the force of our perverted and evil will. We are yielding to an interior necessity, not to an external constraint such as might serve to excuse us. That is indeed the argument adduced by the 'sophists'—that is, the scholastics—in order to credit man with free will. But that is a term that Calvin does not like: 'What a mockery is this, to decorate such a petty thing with such a proud title!'[18] But above all this expression seems to him ambiguous and likely to condone error. Also, he prefers to follow Luther in denying free will altogether; and like Luther in the *De servo arbitrio* he defends the distinction between necessity and constraint.[19] 'We must observe this distinction: that man,

[16] *Opp.*, 22, 36.

[17] *Inst.*, II, 3, 5. Cf. ST BERNARD, *Tractatus de gratia et libero arbitrio* VI, 16, M. L. CLXXXII, 1010: 'Velle siquidem inest nobis ex libero arbitrio, non etiam posse quod volumus. Non dico velle bonum, aut velle malum: sed tantum velle. Velle etenim bonum, profectus est; velle malum defectus. Velle verum simpliciter, ipsum est quod vel proficit, vel deficit. Porro ipsum ut esset, creans gratia fecit; ut proficiat, salvans gratia facit; ut deficiat ipsum se deficit.' One can see that some shades of difference remain between this conception and Calvin's.

[18] *Inst.*, II, 2, 7.

[19] LUTHER, *De servo arbitrio*, W. A. 18, 634: 'Nonne clare sequitur, dum Deus opere suo in nobis non adest, omnia esse mala quae facimus, et nos necessario operari quae nihil ad salutem valent? . . . Necessario vero dico, non coacte, sed ut illi dicunt, necessitate immutabilitatis, non coactionis, hoc est, homo cum vacat spiritu Dei, non quidem violentia, velut raptus, obtorto collo, nolens facit malum . . . sed sponte et libente voluntate facit.' Cf. J. VON WALTER, *Die Theologie Luthers*, pp. 160 ff. Bucer maintains the use of the

after having been corrupted by the Fall, sins voluntarily, not against his heart nor by constraint; that he sins, I say, by liking and strong inclination, not by constraint or violence; . . . and nevertheless that his nature is so perverse that he cannot be moved, driven or led except to evil.'[20] The necessity to which our nature subjects us is an absolutely general rule, and it applies to God and the devil no less than to man, which clearly differentiates it from all constraint: 'If this does not in the least prevent the will of God from being free in doing good, that it is necessary for him to do good, and if the devil never leaves off sinning voluntarily, though he cannot do aught but evil, who will argue that sin is not voluntary in man because he is subject to the necessity of sinning?'[21]

It follows from this that the Christ, by bringing salvation to us, does not free us from an external constraint but that he has to renovate us in ourselves by rectifying our deformed will and orientating it towards righteousness. This work of regeneration is directed, of course, only to the elect. But they too, like the reprobate, are entirely subject to sin until their conversion, a term which, as we see, is to be taken in its most literal sense. Conversion is a turning back of the will, which frees us from the grip of original sin, but does so little by little, in such sort that it cannot be regarded as complete so long as our earthly existence endures. The will, as such, is not abolished: 'it is created anew, not in order to become a will, but to be converted from evil to good.'[22] But that is only a beginning of what the Saviour will have to complete 'by confirming us in perseverance'. Even until death, an elect soul to whom it is given by faith to become aware of his election will have to fight hand to hand against sin, and all

---

term 'free will', basing himself upon St Augustine and St Thomas Aquinas; cf. *Metaphrases epistolarum Pauli*, 1536, pp. 400 f. But he also naturally makes the distinction between *necessitas* and *coactio*, ibid, p. 360: 'Libertas siquidem arbitrii est, facultas ex proprio arbitrio, sine ulla coactione agendi quod videtur, sine coactione inquam, non sine necessitate. Deus siquidem necessario vult quae recta sunt, nec potest diversum velle, et tamen libertatem habet arbitrii summam: et nos tum demum plenam libertatem habebimus quando non poterimus velle quae mala sunt, et necessario volemus quae bona unt.'

[20] *Inst.*, II, 3, 5.   [21] Ibid.   [22] *Inst.*, II, 3, 6.

the more so because he knows that this ceaselessly recurring sin is voluntary.

And yet in spite of this fundamental perversity of fallen humanity, Calvin concedes that there are human actions which are not bad in themselves. There are even men who accomplish things that are worthy of praise. This does not mean that the men themselves are good, but only that God grants them special gifts. The explanation given by Calvin is connected with the one we shall find presently dealing with the works of the illustrious pagans. It may be that he is showing greater rigour on the moral than on the intellectual plane, which would not be surprising, since the reason was less impaired by the Fall than was the will. However that may be, he does not hesitate to endorse St Augustine's view that the virtues of the pagans are no better than vices.[23] True, he does not ascribe the same degree of corruption to them all, or more precisely, he makes distinctions of value between their deeds,[24] but they remain none the less corrupt. 'God, being willing to provide for the human race,' we read in the *Institutes*, 'endows with singular virtues those whom he raises to dignities, as it was certainly of his doing that there arose all the heroes and worthies renowned in history. As much must be said concerning those who remain in private life. But as each one, while he rose to excellence, was also impelled by his ambition, a blemish by which all virtues are defiled and lose all their grace before God, whatsoever may appear worthy of praise in profane people ought to be accounted as nothing.'[25] The supernatural value of all those great virtues that we admire in the great men of history is null and void: 'before the throne of God's judgment they will not be worth a straw for obtaining justification.' It is

[23] AUGUSTINE, *Contra Julianum*, IV, 3, 25, 26 and 32, M. L. XLIV, 750 ff.

[24] *Inst.*, II, 3, 4: 'I confess that the virtues which were in Camillus were gifts of God, and that they could be seen as laudable if appraised in themselves, but how are they to signify that there was integrity in his nature?' Cf. AUGUSTINE, op. cit., IV, 3, 25, M. L. XLIV, 751: 'Minus enim Fabricius quam Catalina punietur, non quia iste bonus sed quia ille magis malus.' The difference is not so much between Camillus and Catalina as between their deeds objectively considered.

[25] *Inst.*, II, 3, 4. Cf. LUTHER, Commentary on Genesis 8, W. A. 2, 350: 'Hos divinos motus magnorum hominum corrumpit postea in ethnicis gloriae studium et ambitio.'

hardly necessary to point out how far this is from the humanists or from Zwingli—who also attributed the virtues and the intuitions of the pagans to God, but would willingly have seen these as so many signs of their election.[26]

Though the domain of spiritual things is the Paradise which fallen man is forbidden to enter, he is not so excluded from lower and terrestrial things. 'When the human understanding applies itself to some study, it does not so labour in vain as not to profit at all.'[27] After having depicted the spiritual misery of fallen man in the most sombre colours, Calvin now proceeds to paint a much less pessimistic picture of man dealing with his earthly interests. The humanist who was still sleeping within him suddenly awakens, to our surprise. But then, first of all, what does he understand by these earthly interests? 'I call those things earthly,' writes Calvin, 'which do not touch at all upon God and his kingdom nor upon the true righteousness and immortality of the future life, but belong to the present life and are as though enclosed within the limits of it. . . . In [this] first class are included political doctrine, the right way of managing one's house, the mechanical arts, philosophy and all the disciplines that are called liberal.'[28] And, to show that man has a natural inclination to live in society and accept government by the laws: 'There is in all men some seed of political order, which is a strong argument that no one is destitute of the light of reason concerning the government of the present life.'[29] After having mentioned the mechanical and liberal arts, Calvin concludes: 'These examples, then, show that there is some universal apprehension of reason imprinted naturally in all men.' However, that is another proof of the divine grace which desired not to deprive man of all light. And all the more is this so in the case of the philosophers: 'When we see in pagan writers this admirable light of truth, the which appears in their books, it ought to admonish us that the nature of man, fallen though he be from his integrity and much corrupted, does not cease still to be adorned with many of the gifts of God. If we

[26] ZWINGLI, *De Providentia*, edit. Schuler and Schulthess, vol. IV, p. 123.
[27] *Inst.*, II, 2, 13.
[28] Upon the similar, but more radical, attitude of Luther, cf. KOESTLIN, *Luthers Theologie*, vol. II, pp. 50 f.
[29] *Inst.*, II, 2, 13.

recognize the Spirit of God as the unique fountain of truth, we shall never despise the truth wherever it may appear, unless we wish to do dishonour to the Spirit of God; for the gifts of the Spirit cannot be disparaged without scorn and opprobrium to himself. But can we now deny that the ancient jurists showed a most enlightened prudence in constituting such good order and such an equitable administration? Can we say that the philosophers were blind, either in studying the secrets of nature so diligently or in writing of them with such skill? Shall we say that those who taught us the art of argument, which is the way to speak reasonably, had no understanding? Can we think of the other disciplines that they were follies? On the contrary, we cannot read the books that have been written on all these subjects without wonderment.'[30] Nevertheless, the admiration aroused by these productions of the human mind ought not to be directed to the authors of them but to God who is their initial source. Did not certain pagans themselves acknowledge that philosophy, the laws and medicine were so many gifts from heaven? A Christian has yet greater reason to think so. As he did when dealing with the great deeds of history, here also Calvin dissociates the achievement from the man who is only the instrument of it. By thus ascribing the intelligence and wisdom of the ancients to God, he believed he could reconcile his enduring admiration for their writings with the doctrine of human corruption ensuing from the fall of Adam. Far from minimizing the consequences of original sin, as Zwingli had done, Calvin could insist upon it with extraordinary force and violence, while still showing as much understanding as the reformer of Zurich for pagan antiquity.

Among the classic problems presented by original sin, a place apart is occupied by the question of its mode of transmission. Upon the answer that one gives to this depends, in great part, the importance we can attribute to original sin in each of Adam's individual descendants, and the responsibility we make them bear. For if this sin is transmitted by a kind of natural heredity this responsibility must be much attenuated; one will even tend to assimilate original sin to a sort of inherited malady, as in the teaching of Zwingli. We should guess that Calvin could never

[30] *Inst.*, II, 2, 15.

have adopted such a point of view.[31] Also, he teaches that the
transmission of original sin can be explained only as a judgment
of God, a judgment deliberately passed upon all mankind: 'That
the whole human race has been corrupted in the person of Adam
alone follows not so much from heredity as from the ordinance of
God, who, even as he had richly endowed us all in one man, also
took them all from us in the same man. Wherefore we must be
said to be all corrupted together in one Adam, rather than that
each of us has derived vice and corruption from his fathers and
mothers.'[32] Adam, in fact, represented the whole of the human
race, which was summed up, as it were, in his person, and therefore the whole of mankind was condemned at the same time as
Adam.[33] By putting forward this explanation, Calvin thought
to forestall the objection that fallen man would be suffering
punishment for a sin he had not committed: 'It must not be
said that this obligation is incurred solely by the fault of another,
as though we were answering for the sin of our first father without
having deserved anything. For what has been said, that by Adam
we are made accountable to the judgment of God, does not mean
that we are innocent and that, without having deserved any
punishment, we are bearing the unmerited effect of his sin: but
that since, by his transgression, we are all involved in confusion,

[31] All the same, Calvin sometimes expressed himself in terms which remind
one of the Zwinglian doctrine, for example in *Inst.*, I, 15, 8: 'Adam at his first
creation was very different from all his posterity, who, having their origin in
a corrupted and rotten stock, derived from it a hereditary contagion.' But the
Latin text uses the more neutral term 'Haereditariam labem'. Cf. ZWINGLI,
De vera et falsa religione (Corp. Reform., vol. XCII, pp. 371 ff.): 'Morbi autem
vocabulo hic non utimur ad iuris consultorum normam . . . sed quatenus
cum vitio coniunctus est, eoque perpetuo. . . . Quod malum naturalem defec-
tum solemus Germanice "ein natürlichen pärsten" adpellare, quo nemo vel
peior, vel sceleratior existimatur. Non enim possunt in crimen aut culpam
rapi, quae natura adsunt.'

[32] Commentary upon John 3.6, *Opp.*, 47, 57.

[33] *Inst.*, II, 1, 7: 'We must not rest content knowing that the Lord put
into Adam the graces and gifts that he meant to confer upon human nature,
so that the latter, when he lost them, lost them not only for himself but for
us all. . . . The defilement did not have its cause and basis in the substance
of the flesh or of the soul, but in God's having ordained that the gifts he had
entrusted to the first man were common to him and to his own, to keep or
to lose.'

he is said to have laid us all under obligation.'³⁴ Consequently, no one is without sin, not even little children. Upon this point Calvin is reproducing the reasoning of St Augustine in his anti-Pelagian treatises.³⁵ 'The children themselves are included in this condemnation, not only for the sin of another, but for their own. For although they have not yet produced the fruits of their iniquity, yet they have the seed of it hidden within them: and what is more, their nature is a seed of sin; whence they cannot but be displeasing and abominable to God. Whence it follows quite rightly and properly, that such evil is accounted as sin before God. For [Calvin adds as a good jurist], without guilt we should not have incurred condemnation.'³⁶

II. THE LAW

Fallen man is utterly incapable of any good, since by his fault he has separated himself far from God and become estranged from him. But God did not disinterest himself in men. By revealing his law to them, he re-established contact between himself and them. Historically, the divine mercy was manifested by the adoption of Abraham and his descendants and by the conclusion of a perpetual Covenant with them. But the Law was an integral part of that Covenant, of which it was the seal and warrant that God had not turned away from man.³⁷ 'By that word "Law",' Calvin continues, 'I mean not only the ten precepts which show us the rule of righteous and holy living, but the form of religion as God published it by the hand of Moses.'³⁸ No doubt the Law, in itself, is nothing. Calvin does not hesitate to turn it to derision, and speaks about it with a rationalism which was rather audacious for those times:

³⁴ *Inst.*, II, 1, 8.

³⁵ AUGUSTINE, *De peccatorum meritis et remissione*, I, 25 and 34; III, 7, M. L. XLIV, 123, 128 f., 189 f.; *De anima et eius origine*, IV, 11, 16, M. L. XLIV, 535; *Contra Julianum*, V, 11, 44, M. L. XLIV, 809.

³⁶ *Inst.*, II, 1, 8.

³⁷ DOUMERGUE, op. cit., vol. IV, pp. 181-96; WERNLE, op. cit., pp. 3-32, 126 ff.; NIESEL, op. cit., pp. 86-97. Upon the relation between the Law and the Covenant, cf. *Opp.*, 38, 688, 48, 289.

³⁸ *Inst.*, II, 7, 1.

For there could be nothing more silly and frivolous than to offer the fat and the stinking entrails of beasts in order to reconcile oneself with God, or to take refuge in a few sprinklings of blood or water to cleanse stains upon the soul. In short, if all the service that was rendered under the Law be considered in itself and as though it did not contain any foreshadowings or figures which had their corresponding truths, this would seem but so much child's play.

But clearly it was not without cause that God gave the Law. The Law presents itself to us under a double aspect: on the historical plane, it constitutes the legislation peculiar to the people of Israel, and as such it is adapted to the time and place of that nation. 'For our Lord did not administer it by the hand of Moses in order to publish and impose it over all the earth; but, having taken the Jewish people under his special care, protection, guidance and government, he willed also to be their legislator in particular; and, as befitted a good and wise legislator, in all these laws he had a singular regard to their utility for this people.'[39] But the Law is not this alone; it is precisely in being much more than this that it differs from the civil and religious legislations of other peoples. What makes its value unique is that it is wholly orientated towards the Christ. At the head of chapter 7 of Book II of the *Institutes*, Calvin wrote: 'That the Law was given, not to keep the ancient people to themselves, but to nurture the hope of salvation that they should have in Jesus Christ, until his coming.' Whenever he had an opportunity he returned to this theme, producing endless variations upon it and supporting it with new arguments. Commenting upon Romans 10.5, he enlarges copiously upon the fact that 'Moses had, in general, the duty of instructing the people in the true rule of piety'.[40] The ceremonial law itself, he notes in allusion to Acts 13.39, was to be 'like a pedagogy that would lead [the Jews] to Christ as though by hand'.[41] But, apart from Jesus Christ, 'it is certain that this is no more than minor baggage', 'than a mockery'.[42] Without him, the Law 'is an empty thing and of

[39] *Inst.*, IV, 20, 16.
[40] *Opp.*, 49, 197. [41] *Opp.*, 48, 305; cf. 49, 196.
[42] Sermon on Galatians 4.8-11, *Opp.*, 50, 603 f.

no strength'.[43] The Law considered as a whole is a figure of Jesus Christ, and that is how Calvin wants it to be interpreted.

But this Law, which was valid in its entirety for the people of Israel, is admitted by Calvin to be divisible, since the coming of Christ, into the traditional distinctions between moral, ceremonial and judicial laws.[44] In what more particularly concerns the moral law, as it is set down in the Decalogue and in other passages of the Old Testament, he also accepts its division into three functions or usages, such as those recognized by Melanchthon since 1530[45] and further accentuated by Bucer in his *Commentaries*.[46] Like them, he makes the distinction between the pedagogic function of the Law considered as 'the mirror of sins', its political function in the wider sense, and thirdly, the permanent part it is called upon to play among believers.

> The first [function] is, that in demonstrating the righteousness of God, which means what is pleasing to him, it admonishes each one of his own unrighteousness, and renders him certain of it, even to his conviction and condemnation by it. . . . The Law is like the mirror in which we first contemplate our own weakness, then the iniquity that proceeds from the same, and finally the malediction which comes of both, even as in a mirror we perceive the blemishes upon our face.[47]

This notion of the Law as the mirror of sin had been abundantly exploited by Luther and Melanchthon.[48] Calvin introduces a similar line of argument into the *Institutes* when he writes, for example:

[43] *Opp.*, 47, 124.   [44] *Inst.*, IV, 20, 14.

[45] MELANCHTHON, *Loci communes*, edit. 1535, (*Corp. Reform.* vol. XXI, 405 f.). Cf. HERRLINGER, *Die Theologie Melanchthons*, Gotha, 1879, pp. 214 ff.

[46] BUCER, *Enarrationes*, 1530, fo. 50 a-51 b, 1536, pp. 123-7.

[47] *Inst.*, II, 7, 6 and 7.

[48] We find an example of this in the frequent use that is made of Romans 3.20 in the *De servo arbitrio*; for instance, W. A. 18, 677: 'At totum quod facit lex (teste Paulo) est, ut peccatum cognosci faciat.' Or again, 766: 'Is enim est fructus, id opus, id officium legis, quod ignaris et caecis lux est, sed talis lux, quae ostendat morbum, peccatum, malum, mortem, infernum, iram Dei, Sed non iuvat, nec liberat ab istis, Ostendisse contenta est.' See also MELANCHTHON, *Loci communes*, ed. Plitt-Kolde, pp. 154 ff.

Now, that our iniquity and condemnation is proven and signed by the testimony of the Law, this is not so that we should fall into despair and, having lost courage, should abandon ourselves to ruin; for that will not happen if we turn it to our profit. It is very true that the wicked do discourage themselves in this fashion, but that comes of the obstinacy of their heart. But the children of God must come to another end, which is to listen to what is said by St Paul, who himself confesses that we are all condemned by the law, so that every mouth may be shut and that all may be made beholden to God; and yet in another place he teaches that God has imprisoned all in unbelief, not in order to destroy them or even allow them to perish, but to grant mercy to all; namely, to the end that, putting away all vain thought of their virtue, they may realize that they are upheld only by his hand. Nay more, that, being altogether empty and destitute, they should fall back upon his mercy.[49]

The second function of the Law is to hinder the wicked who will cease to do evil only from fear.[50] Without doubt, 'their heart is not touched' and they obey only by compulsion. By conforming with the Law, therefore, they become 'in no way more righteous or better before God'.

And not only does the heart still remain evil; they also have a mortal hatred of the law of God, and forasmuch as

[49] *Inst.*, II, 7, 8. Cf. the Catechism of 1537, *Opp.*, 22, 45 f.; Sermon on Genesis 15.6, *Opp.*, 23, 701; Sermon on Deuteronomy 5.21, *Opp.*, 26, 382. One will note in particular how near Calvin comes to Luther in his Sermon on Deut. 5.23-7, *Opp.*, 26, 398: 'By the Law God requires of men what is due to him: but now let us consider whether it is possible for us to acquit ourselves. On the contrary, we are like poor debtors who have not a penny to pay. So we are overwhelmed. For whatever it may be, God does not absolve us at all, but shows that we deserve to be accursed and damned by him. . . . But that is not so in the Gospel; for there God bears with us, he not only forgives us our faults, but he writes his will in our hearts.' . . . Similarly, Luther added, at the end of the passage quoted in n. 48 above: 'Tum homo cognito morbo peccati tristatur, affligitur, imo desperat. . . . Alia vero luce est quae ostendat remedium. Haec est vox Evangelii ostendens Christum liberatorem ad istis omnibus.' But there remains none the less a difference of accent that one should take care not to underestimate.

[50] MELANCHTHON, *Loci communes* of 1535 in the *Corp. Reform.*, vol. XXI, 405.

God is its author they hold him in execration. . . . This feeling
shows itself more openly in some, in others it is more hidden,
nevertheless it is in all those who are not regenerate. . . .
This constrained and forced righteousness is necessary to the
community of men, for the tranquillity which our Saviour
provides by preventing all things from being overturned in
confusion—which is what would happen if everything were
permitted to everyone.[51]

Lastly, Calvin comes to speak of the third use of the Law,
which, according to him, is its principal use, and concerns none
but the faithful. It is here that the author of the *Institutes* has
laid himself the most widely open to the reproach of legalism
so often laid against him. Nevertheless, it is a point upon which
he could invoke illustrious sponsors. As early as 1521, Melanchthon had written in his *Loci communes*: 'The laws are prescribed
to the faithful so that thereby the Spirit should mortify the flesh.
For liberty is not yet made perfect in us, but we lay claim to it
while the Spirit is growing and the flesh is being mortified. The
Decalogue serves to mortify the flesh; the same cannot be said of
the ceremonial or judicial laws. It follows that the Decalogue is
necessary for the faithful, but not the other laws.'[52] Later on,
Melanchthon laid more emphasis on this enduring value of the
Law, in which he was followed by Bucer on his own account,
probably under the influence of Zwingli.[53] And in the *Institutes*
of 1536 Calvin in his turn was already attributing normative
value to the Law in the Christian life. In 1539 he did no more
than complete and clarify this:

> Although the faithful have the Law written in their hearts
> by the finger of God, that is to say, though they may have
> that affection by the leading of the Holy Spirit, that they
> desire to give way to God, still they have a double profit

[51] *Inst.*, II, 7, 10.   [52] *Loci communes*, edit. Plitt-Kolde, pp. 220 f.
[53] BUCER, *Metaphrases epistolarum Pauli*, 1536, pp. 310 f.: 'Caeterum quia
in nobis adhuc caro superest, et carne legi peccati servimus, utcunque mente
legi Dei consentimus; nam reliquum semper est malum concupiscentiae;
hactenus est nobis adhuc usus legis admonentis et condemnantis, hoc quicquid
est carnis, quod in nobis etiamnum viget, quo sentientes mortem in quam nati
sumus, hoc magis Christo nos addicere et ab ipso plenius a corpore mortis
hujus liberari studeamus.'

from the Law; for this is a very good means for them, to
make them hear better and more certainly from day to day
what is the will of God to which they aspire, and to confirm
them in knowledge of the same. . . . Furthermore, because we
have need not only of doctrine but also of exhortation, the
servant of God will make such use of this law that by frequent
meditation upon it he will be quickened in obedience to God,
and confirmed in it and restrained from his faults.

In conclusion, Calvin declares: 'Since the spiritual man is not
yet relieved from the burden of his flesh the Law will be a
perpetual spur to keep him from sleeping or sloth.'[54] Much
more: by the illumination that is given them, Christians alone
are able rightly to understand and to apply the Law and the
Prophets.[55]

But this Law, upon which Christians are to meditate in order
to find in it the 'principles and conditions' of their master, and
which is to be a perpetual spur to them, how far is it valid?
Was it not, after all, abrogated by the coming of Christ? Calvin
admits this without difficulty, as far as the political and ceremonial laws of the Old Testament are concerned: still, he is of
the opinion that these may serve as examples, and that 'the
ceremonies were not abolished in respect of their effect, but only
of their use.' With them too, it is the Christ who gave them
their true meaning and who—as Calvin rather paradoxically
affirms—enables us to understand it by the very fact that he has
abolished them. 'For as these would have been nothing in
ancient days but juggling or fools' play, as they say, had not the
death and resurrection of Jesus Christ been shown in them, so,
on the other hand, had they not come to an end, one would be
unable today to say why they were ever instituted.'[56] In the

[54] *Inst.*, II, 7, 12.
[55] Sermon on Ephesians 2.19-22, *Opp.*, 51, 427: 'In Jesus Christ we have
so great a brightness that things which were then obscure are now all patent
and manifest to us. Wherefore let us apply our study to the law and the
Prophets, well knowing that they lead us to our Lord Jesus Christ, for he is
the end proposed to us . . . as it is said that Jesus Christ is the fulfilment of
the Law.' Calvin returns to the question of the positive function of the Law
when he comes to speak of sanctification, *Inst.*, III, 6 and 7, 1.
[56] *Inst.*, II, 7, 16.

ceremonial laws, there were no more than the first indications and foreshadowing of that which Christ came to make fully manifest.[57] They are therefore obsolete today, since the revelation of the Christ has replaced them and brought about their fulfilment. The same is true of the political and juridical laws which were given to the Jews to instruct them in 'certain rules of justice and equity for living peaceably together, without being a nuisance to one another',[58] rules which have now been absorbed into the law of the charity of Christ. 'So just as, the ceremonies having been abrogated, true religion and piety survive in their entirety, so also the said judicial laws can be broken and abolished, without any violation of the duty of charity.'[59] And indeed, though the contingent provisions of the political laws concerned only the people of Israel, the substance of them—that is, 'equity and righteousness'—is not affected by their abrogation.[60]

The situation is quite different with regard to the moral law: to just the degree that this is integral with the substance of the Law, it is maintained as it was. But while it is relatively easy to distinguish between the substance and the accidental prescriptions in ceremonial and judicial law, here there can be no such discrimination. 'When the Lord Jesus said that he had come not to destroy the Law but to fulfil it . . . he showed by this that the reverence and obedience due to the Law were in no way diminished by his coming. And that with good reason, seeing that he came to bring a remedy for transgressions of the same. The teaching of the Law, then, is in no way violated by Jesus Christ, as our training in all good works, instructing, admonishing,

---

[57] Note, by the way, that Calvin is introducing here, above all in IV, 20, 15, and rather unexpectedly, something that strongly resembles the notion of a progressive revelation in the course of the history of Israel. Cf. the commentary on Galatians 3.23, *Opp.*, 50, 220.

[58] *Inst.*, IV, 20, 15.

[59] Let us recall that BUCER used to defend a conception much more favourable to the utilization of the political laws of the Old Covenant. Cf. *Epistola d. Pauli ad Ephesios*, 1527, fo. 57b; *Enarrationes in Evangelia*, 1536, pp. 122 and 141: 'Cumque melior institutio Reipublicae ea quam Dominus dedit per Moschen a nemine inveniri possit, et illa puniri et tolli sontes praecipiat: verae ac germanae charitatis opus erit, secundum illas Dei leges in sceleratos animadvertere.'

[60] Cf. Sermon on Deuteronomy 23. 18-20, *Opp.*, 28, 115.

reproving and chastising us.'[61]   Nevertheless, St Paul declares
that Christ redeemed us from the curse of the Law (Gal. 3.13).
To reconcile this declaration with that of the Law's fulfilment in
Jesus Christ, Calvin has recourse to a new distinction between
the two functions of the Law, that of instruction and that of sub-
jugating the conscience.   The former alone is integrally maintained, even in respect of believers; the latter has been abolished
by the coming of Christ, which has delivered us from 'that
rigorous exaction with which the Law pursued us unremittingly,
without leaving a single fault unpunished'.[62]

Here we find ourselves deep in the problem of Christian liberty
which had been given so much prominence by Luther, and
which Calvin had touched upon even in the first edition of 1536,
though he never gave it the doctrinal importance that the
German reformer had attached to it.   In the *Institutes* of 1559,
however, Christian liberty forms the subject of a special chapter,
which he placed after his refutation of justification by works and
before the exposition on prayer.   To avoid having to return to
this point, we will indicate here the main line of the conception
that Calvin developed.

As we have seen, the Law was not in itself abrogated by the
Christ, but only the slavery and malediction attaching to it
under the ancient Covenant.   Christians therefore remain subject
to the Law, but not in the same way as the Jews used to be.   And
it is in this modification of the function of the Law that, as Calvin
conceives it, Christian liberty consists.   Clearly to grasp his
thought, we must envisage, one after another, the three aspects or
'parts' he believes he can distinguish in this notion.

'The consciences of the faithful, when it is a question of seeking
assurance of their justification, arise and stand above the law, and
forget the righteousness of the same.'[63]   This is a logical conse-

[61] *Inst.*, II, ö, 14. Cf. the sermon on Deut. 4.32-5, *Opp.*, 26, 209: 'Is the
Law of God diminished, I mean as to the substance of it? It is true that the
ceremonies are no more in use . . . but the doctrine of the Law, containing
the promises of salvation, the Covenant whereby God chooses those whom he
wills to have in his Church, the evidences of the remission of our sins and
then his willingness to show us the right rule for good living, all this remains
and must be perpetual even unto the end of the world.'

[62] *Inst.*, II, 7, 15.

[63] *Inst.*, III, 19, 2. Melanchthon had adopted, since 1522, an analogous

quence of the fact so powerfully emphasized by Calvin, that the
Law enables no man to justify himself before God. Under that
condition we are presented with but one alternative: 'we must
either be excluded from the hope of being justified, or we must
be delivered (from the Law); and so delivered that we have no
regard to our works.' In other words, legal justification is identified, by Calvin as by the other reformers, with justification by
works: the latter being excluded, because impossible, there is no
longer any reason for bringing the Law into our justification.
'When it is a question of our justification, we have to put away all
thinking about the Law and our works, to embrace the mercy
of God alone, and to turn our eyes away from ourselves and
upon Jesus Christ alone.'

The first aspect of Christian freedom then, is the liberation of
the Christian from any care about the Law so far as his justification is concerned. And here is the second aspect, expressing one
of the fundamental themes that Luther had developed in his
treatise *On Christian Freedom* of 1520: 'The other part of Christian
freedom, which depends upon the foregoing, is this: it inclines
the conscience to observe the Law, not at all as constrained by
the necessity of the Law, but that, being delivered from the Law,
they are freely obedient[64] to the will of God. . . . Never will
they be firmly determined to obey the will of God voluntarily
and with an open heart unless they have first obtained that
deliverance.'[65]   But, although now under grace and no longer
under the rigour of the Law, it is in that Law that the believer
will continue to know the will of God, at the same time as in
the Gospel. To be in conformity with it, then, one has only to
contemplate it in the Law, where God has made it explicit. We

---

division: 'Primum in eo est, quod damnare lex non possit, quamquam
habentes peccatum, modo credamus legis maledictionem a Christo sublatam
esse. . . . Postea vero quam cor hoc libertatis genere, hoc est, remissione
peccatorum pacatum est, quia spiritus in tale cor effunditur, iam lex dei fit,
cognoscitur deus, fiditur deo, timetur deus ac diligitur. Diligitur et proximus
. . . Ideo liberi sumus ab omnibus externis observationibus et ceremoniis.'
(Edit. Plitt-Kolde, p. 218.)

[64] This means: of their own choice. The Latin text has: 'voluntati Dei
ultro obediant.'

[65] *Inst.*, III, 19, 4.

can hardly deny that there is a certain' legalism about this, tending to efface the antinomy between the Law and the Gospel upon which Luther had been so insistent. But in reality, this is only so from an external point of view, from the standpoint of the unbeliever. To the believer, on the contrary, the situation is reversed as soon as he has become a member of Christ. For, as far as he is concerned, the Gospel, far from being in any sense reduced to the Law, assimilates the latter to itself. Bucer had already made this distinction in his famous Introduction to his commentary on the Epistle to the Romans, where he wrote: 'Even as the Law, to those who are deprived of the renovating Spirit, brings condemnation and death, so does it give salvation and life to those who are endowed with that Spirit; that is why it is in no sense abolished, but is so much the more potent in each one as he is more richly endowed with the Spirit of Christ.'[65] Conversely, the Gospel itself, in the unbeliever, becomes the letter that kills and the means to his condemnation. Upon this point Calvin conforms himself to the Bucerian thesis, as we shall have occasion to notice when he is dealing with the relations between the Old and the New Covenants. What we find, in fact, is a spiritualization of the Law in its relation to all those who have received the gift of the Law and have been received into Christ.[67]

'The third part of Christian freedom,' continues Calvin, closely following Melanchthon, 'teaches us not to treat as matters of conscience before God, those things that are indifferent in themselves, and tells us that we may do them or not, indifferently. And the knowledge of that liberty is also very necessary to us. For in default of it our consciences would never be at rest, and would entertain superstitions without end.'[68] And, like the author of the *Loci communes*, he underscores the doctrinal and practical importance of this point. But while Melanchthon confined him-

[66] BUCER, *Metaphrases epistolarum* Pauli, 1536, p. 28.

[67] Cf. KOLFHAUS, *Christusgemeinschaft bei Calvin*, p. 79: 'It is as member of Christ that we hear the imperatives of the Law of God; Calvin everywhere understands the Law and the Gospel as the indivisible Word of God, as the doctrine of God.' See also w. HOLSTEIN, 'Christentum und nichtchristliche Religion nach der Auffassung Bucers' in the *Theologische Studien und Kritiken*, Gotha, 1936, pp. 107-41, the conclusions of which, however, seem to us unacceptable.

[68] *Inst.*, III, 19, 7.

self to generalities and Biblical examples, Calvin appeals to immediate experience, with that sense of the picturesque that never deserts him: 'There is more importance in these things than people commonly suppose. For as soon as ever consciences are harnessed and put in bonds, they enter into an endless labyrinth and a bottomless pit which it is not easy for them to get out of. If anyone begins to doubt whether it is allowable for him to use linen for sheets, shirts, handkerchiefs or napkins, he will soon be no more confident that it is legitimate to use hemp: in the end he begins to vacillate as to whether he may even use sackcloth.' The same applies to food and all those unimportant things with which consciences ought not to be preoccupied. The only exceptions that he recognizes are the 'carnal cupidities' which would cause us to misuse the gifts of God, or to disregard what we owe to our 'weaker brethren', whom we may scandalize by an inopportune use of our freedom. From this he comes to the conclusion that the end to which Christian freedom serves is 'that without scruple of conscience or trouble of mind we may apply the gifts of God to the uses for which they have been granted us'.[69] This shows how far he was from the narrow puritanism which has been so unjustly fathered upon him.

To conclude what is said about the Law and its uses, it remains only to say a word about the natural law.[70] Like the Decalogue itself, the natural law is of the authorship of God, who has inscribed it in the conscience of every man. One can even say that, for Calvin, the Decalogue is only a special application of the natural law which God came to attest and confirm. The Fall having entirely vitiated human reason and volition, from that same moment it also obscured the faculty of discernment of good and evil implanted in us by the law of nature. The latter retains all the same a real importance, even in fallen humanity. 'If the Gentiles,' writes Calvin, 'have the righteousness of God naturally imprinted upon their minds, we certainly will not call them blind, in the matter of knowing how to live. And in fact it is common

[69] *Inst.*, iii, 19, 8.

[70] BEYERHAUS, *Calvins Staatsanschauung*, pp. 66 ff.; A. GROBMANN, *Das Naturrecht bei Luther und Calvin*, Hamburg, 1935; J. BOHATEC, *Calvin und das Recht*, Feudingen, 1934, pp. 1-93; M. E. CHENEVIÈRE, *La Pensée politique de Calvin*, Geneva, 1937, pp. 61-77.

knowledge that man is well enough instructed in the right rule of good living by this natural law of which the Apostle speaks.'[71] With regard to the first tablet of the Law, that which proclaims our duties towards God, Calvin affirms that all men are brought to realize the existence of God, and that they have an obligation to worship him. But this is where original sin comes in, and vitiates human faculties. Egotism shackles the moral judgment and paralyses effort. Calvin can also legitimately claim that the natural law 'knows nothing of what is paramount on the first tablet, that we put our trust in God and render him the praise of virtue and justice, invoke his name and observe his day of rest. What human understanding has ever, I do not say known, but imagined or dreamed that the true honour and service of God, lay in those things?' On the other hand, the Fall has had rather less effect in respect of the second tablet of the Law, which concerns our duties towards our neighbours. 'As for the precepts of the second tablet, these are,' he concedes, 'somewhat the more intelligible the nearer they come to human and civil life, although [the human understanding] is sometimes in default even in this part.'[72] There remains nevertheless a natural solidarity between men, despite their egotism. The pagans themselves have the notions of equity and rights, and we have seen that Calvin does not hesitate to put political doctrine on a level with those lower things which the reason, even when vitiated by sin, is still in a position to conceive and to administer. In this, we cannot doubt, there was a very clear recollection of the Stoic idea of an organic unity in human society.[73] And perhaps, in certain passages at least, the logic of the jurist has overborne that of the theologian. But the latter soon takes his revenge. Calvin shows us, indeed, that man under the tyranny of sin no longer conforms spontaneously to the dictates of the natural law. He has to be obliged and constrained from without to do so, by regulations and laws meant to compel him to respect them, laws which, for that reason, must themselves necessarily be inspired by this natural law.[74] Not that we can ever manage to make the requirements of natural law coincide exactly with positive law. There remains a hiatus,

[71] *Inst.*, ti, 2, 22.   [72] *Inst.*, II, 2, 24.

[73] Cf. *Opp.*, 27, 329; 26, 9 f.; BOHATEC, op. cit., pp. 45 ff.

[74] *Inst.*, IV, 20, 16.

which is precisely the fact of sin. Neither are the true end and
permanent demands of the natural law to be found here. No
doubt sinful man retains the 'judgment of good and evil',[75] but
that is to make him inexcusable before God. The aim of the
natural law is thus combined, upon the religious plane, with the
purpose of the Law in the Old Testament. It deprives man of
any excuse founded upon ignorance, for in doing evil he is condemned by his own conscience. 'It is enough that they know so
much of it as not to be able to reject it without being convicted
by the evidence of their own conscience, and beginning already
to be terrified of the throne of God.'

Calvin expended a great deal of skill in presenting a coherent
doctrine of natural law, which was an attempt to reconcile the
Pauline texts with the definitions of the Roman jurists. And he
did, no doubt, partly succeed in this by distinguishing between
the application of the natural law in the political life and its
function in the human conscience. Yet one cannot help feeling
that this element in his theology is somewhat of a foreign body,
assimilable to it only with difficulty; and that its existence
alongside the divine Law that is expressed in the Decalogue is
hardly justifiable. So it seems, at least, to those who have received
some knowledge of the revealed Law.

III. THE OLD AND THE NEW TESTAMENTS

By deducing, from the immutability of the divine will, that it
could not express itself otherwise in the New Testament than in
the Old, Calvin exposed himself to the reproach of having blurred
the clear distinction that the reformers had established between
the Law and the Gospel, or, if one prefers, of having placed the
Old and the New Testaments on exactly the same level. By also
insisting as he did upon the part played by the Law, and attributing an active function to it in the Christian life, he gave
further cause for the complaints that were addressed to him on
this subject, not only from the ranks of the antinomians properly
so called, but also from many of the anabaptists and spiritualists.
It was both in order to reply to his adversaries and to define his
point of view that he inserted in the *Institutes* of 1539 a chapter

[75] *Inst.*, II, 2, 24.

'On the similarity and the difference between the Old and the New Testaments', which he developed in 1559 into three distinct chapters. For analogous reasons, Melanchthon had added to his *Loci communes*, from 1535, a chapter on the distinction between the Old and the New Testaments.

The comparison that Calvin draws between the two Testaments leads him, in effect, to differentiate them by their chronological position in the plan of salvation, rather than by their content. The Old Testament holds out in the form of a promise what the New Testament offers us as a present reality. The new Covenant is none other than the re-establishment of the old Covenant which had been broken by the chosen people.[76] Nay, further—the Christ, who is the foundation of all true religion, could not, for that reason, be absent from the covenant made with Abraham, and therefore it is he who dominates both of the Testaments. 'Malachi, after exhorting the Jews to listen to the Law of Moses and to follow it with constancy, says that if they do not fall away, the sun of righteousness will soon arise upon them; by which he signified that the use of the Law was to keep them in expectation of the Christ whose coming was near, and that meanwhile they must hope for more of his light.'[77] It was as sacrificing priest and as king that Christ was foretold in the Old Testament, according to the two lines, royal and sacerdotal, of his human ancestry, so that Calvin finds himself able to write: 'No less in the line of Levi than among the successors of David, Jesus Christ was presented to Jewish eyes as in a double mirror.'[78] And even as he dominates the whole of the Old Testament, so also it is he alone who can give its promises their true meaning.

There is, however, one capital difference which Calvin cannot fail to underline. A whole chapter is devoted to showing how

[76] BUCER had said the same when he wrote, in the *Enarrationes in Evangelia*, 1536 ?. 142: 'Idem noster Deus est, qui Iudaeorum fuit, idem est foedus ac testamentum, quod cum illis atque nobiscum percussit, nisi quod illis et ceremonias ritusque externos varios adiunxit, quare et vetus foedus vel testamentum vocatur, nobis non item, sed voluit ab elementis mundi nos esse liberiores.'

[77] *Inst.*, II, 9, 1. Cf. DOUMERGUE, op. cit., vol. IV, pp. 197 ff.; WERNLE, op. cit., pp. 266 ff.; NIESEL, op. cit., pp. 98 ff.

[78] *Inst.*, II, 7, 2.

Christ was known to the Jews under the Law, but was fully revealed only by the Gospel.

> Although, then, this only Son, who to us this day is the splendour of the glory, and the living image of the hypostasis of the Father, was known of old by the Jews who were his people . . ., as we have quoted elsewhere from St Paul, he was the leader of the people in the redemption from Egypt: yet what the same apostle said is also very true; which is that God, who commanded light to come out of darkness, enlightens us by the Gospel in our hearts, to make us contemplate his glory in the face of Jesus Christ.[79]

But if the Old Testament was able to show Jesus Christ only 'from afar and darkly', if we had to wait for the incarnation for him to appear in full light, and if, in particular, it was indispensable for anyone who wished to possess him to 'receive and embrace him after re-clothing himself with the promises of the Gospel', it is no less true that the resemblance between the two Testaments extends very far indeed. 'Who then will dare to take Christ away from the Jews, for whom we believe the Covenant of the Gospel to have been made, the one foundation of which is Christ? . . . If God, in the manifestation of his Christ, has fulfilled the oath he swore of old, one cannot say that the purpose of the Old Testament was not in Christ and in the life eternal.'[80] Bucer had similarly affirmed that so far as the substance is concerned there is no difference between the two Testaments, for both are founded upon the Christ and rest upon the same faith; that moreover the writings of the New Testament attest 'how great the knowledge of Christ was among the ancient people'.[81] But Calvin returns to the charge:

[79] *Inst.*, II, 9, 1.   [80] *Inst.*, II, 10, 4.

[81] BUCER, *Enarrationes in Evangelia*, 1536, pp. 120: 'Collatio novi et veteris Testamenti . . . non est proprie novi Testamenti, quod per Christum constat, et veteris, quod pepigit Deus cum patribus. Nam omnino in substantia utrunque idem est. Sunt enim et ipsi per Christum servati.' *Metaphrases epistolarum Pauli*, 1536, p. 26: 'Dominus nihil . . . vel per Abraham, vel per Mosen, qui duo primi sequestri fuere foederis prisci, istituere voluit, sed ut haberent suis promissis fidem, et fidem eiusmodi, qualis de huius temporis sanctis Epistola ad Ebraeos praedicat. Hanc ante omnia in quovis foedere, quod cum hominibus unquam percussit, requisivit'; p. 159: 'Quantam

The Apostle not only makes the people of Israel like and
equal to us by the grace of the Covenant but also in the
meaning of the sacraments. . . . Not only has our Lord conferred the same blessings upon them as upon us, he has also
declared his grace among them by the same signs and sacraments, as though he were saying: 'It seems to you that you
are out of danger because the baptism by which you were
signed and the Supper of the Lord bear singular promises.
You must bethink yourselves that the Jews were not un-
provided with the same sacraments, yet the Lord did not
therefore refrain from exercising his judgment with rigour.
They were baptized at the passage of the Red Sea . . . ; they
ate the same spiritual meat and drank the same spiritual drink
as are given to us,' [the Apostle] explaining that this is Jesus
Christ.[82]

Bucer had doubtless treated this with less precision, but at
bottom he was undeniably in agreement with Calvin. Did not
Bucer also say that, as to their substance, the sacraments of the
Old and the New Covenants were identical?[83] We may add,
moreover, that Calvin was no more than Bucer the author of
these comparisons which may seem so strange to us; for, as they
both tell us, they took them from St Augustine's treatise against
the Manichaean Faustus.[84] In the *Institutes*, Calvin also foresees
the objections that could be made to this, and in a special chapter

---

Christi cognitionem fuisse in populo veteri Evangelicae et Apostolicae literae
clare admodum indicant'; p. 189: 'De Christo, Mose et prophetae scripserunt:
huius spiritu freti et veteres, quae Deus ipsis promisit ac praecepit, rite in-
tellexerunt, et pronis animis amplexi sunt.' In Luther, too, one could find
numerous passages affirming the Christian witness to the Old Testament; for
examples, the Sermons on Genesis 3, 15, W. A. 24, 99 and on Romans 13.11,
W. A. 10, 1, 2nd part, 4. But it is doubtful whether Calvin knew these.

[82] *Inst.*, II, 10, 5.

[83] BUCER, *Metaphrases epistolarum Pauli*, 1536, p. 158: 'Quis non videat
multo clarissime, rationem sacramentorum, utriusque populi, quantum ad
substantiam, eandem esse, nec differre, nisi quod nunc sunt omnia et evi-
dentiora ac inde efficatiora, tum patent latius.'

[84] AUGUSTINE, *Contra Faustum*, XV, 11; XIX, 13; XIX, 16, M. L., vol. XLII
314, 355, 356 f.

he returns to the differences between the Old and the New Testaments.

'Of these differences,' he writes, 'I take good care to say that they all belong, and ought to be referred, to the difference of manner which God has observed in dispensing his teaching, rather than to the substance of it.'[85] Thus the substance or the ground of the two Testaments is identical; the differences are in the methods employed by the Holy Spirit in imparting the knowledge of that substance, first to the Jews and then to the Christians. Calvin deals with five of these differences of method.

The first is seen in the greater clarity of the New Testament in the sphere of things invisible. The hope of Israel was directed above all to earthly happiness; hence the high value they attached to the present life and its blessings. Thence also the belief in recompenses meted out now and here below, to the virtues and the vices of men. This, it must be emphasized, does not mean at all that heavenly blessedness was not the true end and aim proposed to Israel, but that 'by all the promises he made to them, God willed to lead the Jews as though by hand, and in the hope of his heavenly grace.'[86] Here Calvin is manifestly taking up Bucer's point of view upon the pedagogical side of the Old Testament promises.[87]

'The second difference between the Old and the New Testaments,' Calvin tells us, 'lies in their images.'[88] And, again like Bucer, he appeals especially to the Epistle to the Hebrews to demonstrate that 'at the time when the truth was still absent, the Old Testament represented it by images, thus having the shadow instead of the substance.' The priesthood in particular and the worship under the old Covenant are figurative of the Christ and his redemptive work. The new Covenant is new only in the measure that it 'has been consecrated and ratified by the blood of Christ', 'then the truth of it is fulfilled, and thus the new and eternal Covenant is made.' It is no exaggeration, then, to say with Wernle that 'the novelty of Christianity can be no more

[85] *Inst.*, II, 11, 1.   [86] Ibid.
[87] BUCER, *Metaphrases epistolarum Pauli*, 1536, p. 189: 'Ad hunc [Christum] omnis legis institutio, et ceremoniarum disciplina paedagogia quaedam fuit; per hunc omnia erant illis perficiendâ.'
[88] *Inst.*, II, 11, 4.

than relative if we place ourselves at Calvin's point of view.'[89]

Calvin perceives a third difference between the two Testaments in the opposition adduced by St Paul (in Corinthians 3.6) between the Law and the Gospel. Throughout the passage devoted to this third difference, Calvin reverts to distinctively Lutheran ideas. The mission of the Law is 'to command all things that are good and just, to forbid all wickedness, to promise reward to all who observe righteousness, to threaten sinners with the vengeance of God, without its being able to change or correct the perversity which exists in all men by nature'.[90] But too much accentuation of the divergences between the Law and the Gospel would not, as we have seen, be in harmony with Calvin's conception as a whole. So he hastens to return to the defence of the Law: 'The difference which is made between the letter and the spirit must not be understood as though, in ancient times, the Lord had thrown his Law to the Jews fruitlessly and uselessly, converting no one to himself, but is stated by comparison, in order to magnify the abundance of grace with which the same legislator, as though he were assuming a new personality, has been pleased to adorn the preaching of the Gospel in order to honour the kingdom of his Christ.'[91] Indeed, if we compare the number of those who have been won by the preaching of the Gospel with the number 'of those who have received the teaching of the Law in true affection of heart', the former seem to be much the more numerous. But Calvin adds—from which one gathers that the comparison strikes him as unfair—that 'if we consider the people of Israel apart from the Church, there were then many true believers.' He would doubtless have endorsed Bucer's affirmation that 'the true religion of the heart existed no less among the ancients than in our own days.'[92]

The fourth difference between the Old and the New Testaments follows from the one last mentioned: they are opposed to one another as servitude is opposed to liberty. 'It all comes to this, that the Old Testament was given to alarm consciences;

[89] WERNLE, op. cit., p. 273.
[90] *Inst.*, II, 2, 7. [91] *Inst.*, II, 11, 8.
[92] BUCER, *Enarrationes in Evangelia*, 1536, p. 429: 'Nec enim minus apud priscos vera religio cordis fuit atque hodie, et aeque tum atque modo opus spiritus sancti illa extitit.'

and that by the New, joy and lightness was given to them; that the former held consciences fettered and harnessed to the yoke of servitude, while the latter unloosed and set them at liberty.'[93] One could, no doubt, object that the Fathers of the Old Testament too partook of that liberty, since they 'had the same spirit of faith as we': but it was not the Law that gave them that liberty. They found it in advance, as it were, of the letter of the New Testament, or, if one prefers, of the Gospel. Besides, the freedom they had was not such as to exclude all fear and slavery to the Law, seeing that they were still subject to the ceremonial law. The knowledge they were able to have of the Gospel was thus only partial, whereas ours is complete.

The fifth and last difference resides in the fact that 'until the coming of Christ, God had, as it were, singled out one people to whom he committed the Covenant of his grace.'[94] All the other nations were given over to error. 'But when the fullness of time had come, which had been ordained for the reparation of all things, when, I say, the Mediator between God and men had been made manifest, breaking down the partition which had long held the mercy of God enclosed within one people, he caused peace to be announced to those who were afar off as well as to those who were near, to the end that, all being together reconciled to God, they should be united in one body.'

One could not, then, strictly speaking, claim that Calvin remained insensitive to what separates the Old Testament from the New. But whatever differences between them he was concerned to discover, they did not, to his eyes, in any way affect the substance itself of the divine revelation or of the Covenant that God had willed to make with men. This remained the same in both Testaments. If it is none the less justifiable to speak of a New Testament and an Old Testament, that is because the Christ came to renew and confirm the Covenant that the Jews had broken, and to extend it to all peoples, rather than to bring another Covenant new in itself.

[93] *Inst.*, II, II, 9.   [94] *Inst.*, II, II, II.

IV. CHRIST AND HIS WORK OF REDEMPTION

From this fundamental and substantial unity of the Old and New Testaments, one might have drawn the conclusion that the work of Christ is not of such fundamental importance as theological tradition has attributed to it. It is the diametrically opposite conclusion at which Calvin arrives, precisely because he does not confine the work and the action of Christ within the New Testament, but sees their intervention quite as much in the Old Covenant. The Biblical witness as a whole is to be regarded as witness to Jesus Christ, and theology has no other purpose than the guidance of believers in this quest of the Christ through all the Biblical writings. Calvin's Christocentrism, it cannot be said too often, is as definite and as clearly expressed as that of Luther. But naturally, this is more evident in the chapters of the *Institutes* which are specially devoted to Christ and his redemptive work than it is elsewhere.

Calvin had made the traditional trinitarian teaching his own, without the slightest reservation. The same attachment to the dogmatic tradition is prominent in his Christology. What is original in his contribution to this never touches the fundamental affirmations of the Councils of the ancient Church. He adopts in full the dogma of the two natures of Christ and the current explanations of the relation between the two natures.[95] 'So much and more was it necessary,' he writes, 'that he who was to be our Mediator should be true God and man.'[96] Indeed, for any contact to be established between the most holy God and sinful man, it was necessary for God to come right down to man, since man would never, of his own strength, have been able to raise himself up to God. 'The majesty of God is too high,' said Calvin, 'for us to say that mortal men could attain to it, seeing that they

---

[95] DOUMERGUE, op. cit., vol. IV, pp. 207-24; WERNLE, op. cit., pp. 39-47; NIESEL, op. cit., pp. 104-13; M. DOMINICE, *L'Humanité de Jesus d'après Calvin*, Paris, 1933, pp. 37-51; E. EMMEN, *De Christologie van Calvijn*, Amsterdam, 1935, pp. 31-46, 89-109; J. KOOPMANS, *Het outkerkerkelijk dogma in de Reformatie*, pp. 77 ff.

[96] *Inst.*, II, 12, 1.

can do no more than crawl over the earth like little worms.'[97] That, of course, is the state of man since the Fall. But Calvin had no very high opinion of humanity even before the original sin. It is not so surprising therefore, that he could write: 'Even if man had remained in his integrity, still his condition was too base for him to attain to God. How much less could he have raised himself so far, after having been plunged by his ruin into death and hell, after staining himself with so many defilements—nay, even stinking in his corruption and all overwhelmed with misery?'[98] Even before the Fall, contact with God could be made only so far as God's goodness willed to lower itself so far as man. All the more certainly, since then, has man been incapable of reaching up to God, and this is confirmed, in Calvin's eyes, seeing that the angels themselves, though they have preserved the image of God in them, have need 'of a leader, through their relation to whom they were given strength to adhere to God for ever'.[99]

Sin has, indeed, a double consequence: man becomes an object of horror to God and, conversely, man acquires a horror of God and hates him, for the divine righteousness fills him with fear. Thus the man enslaved to sin cannot take up any other attitude towards God but that of escape from him, be it only by denying him, which is also a manner of hiding from him. But Christian doctrine tells us that to re-establish contact with God, and for men to become his children again, there is need of a mediator and that this mediator is Christ. It is just this, according to Calvin, which distinguishes Christianity from the other religions —its having affirmed the necessity of an 'intermediary'.[100] But

[97] *Inst.*, II, 6, 4. Cf. Among numerous similar passages, the Course upon Hosea, *Opp.*, 42, 264: 'Deum a nobis quaeri non posse, nisi in mediatore Christo. . . . Nisi Christus se medium nobis offerat qua via possemus ad Deum accedere?' or again, the sermon on I Ephesians 1.1-3: 'Without this Mediator, it is certain that we are all foreclosed [by God] and the majesty of God ought to make the hairs of our head stand on end.' *Opp.*, 51, 256.

[98] *Inst.*, II, 12, 1.

[99] Ibid., cf. Commentary on Colossians 1.20, *Opp.*, 52, 89, and the *Reply to the Brothers of Cologne*, *Opp.*, 9, 338; *Opusc.*, 2023 f.

[100] Commentary upon Acts 17.8: 'Here are the principal marks by which our faith is distinguished from that of the pagans; namely, that it holds up

of what nature could such a mediator be? We read in the *Institutes*:

> Not without reason did St Paul, when pointing to Jesus Christ as Mediator, expressly refer to him as man. . . . He could quite well have named him God, or indeed have omitted the name of either man or God: but because the Holy Spirit speaking through his mouth knew our infirmity, he used this remedy to show the way; that is, to put the Son of God upon our level, so as to make us familiar with him. . . . By calling him man, he showed that he was near to us—nay, more, so close that nothing could come closer, being of our own flesh. In short, he means what is explained at greater length elsewhere: namely, that we have a high priest who is not unable to have compassion upon our weaknesses, seeing that he was in all points tempted in the same manner as men, save that he was without the slightest sin.[101]

In other words, Jesus Christ was fully man, and nothing human was unknown to him excepting sin. Commenting upon Hebrews 4.15, which he had reproduced in the passage just quoted, Calvin tells us exactly what is meant by the infirmities mentioned in this text: 'The best opinion is from those who, besides external poverty and miseries, understand also the affections of the mind, such as fear, sadness, the horror of death and other such things.'[102] For, he observes elsewhere, 'Jesus Christ was not only man as to his body but as to his soul also. He was subject to passions, fears and sorrows, as we see him to have been. And since he thus willed to take a human soul, why should he not have had the qualities that pertain to the nature of souls?'[103] Only it must be added that though Christ knew these infirmities, it was because he was fully willing to know them, and could have been exempt from them. His voluntary abasement was for no other purpose than to give us greater access to him, 'so that we might communicate his benefits to all'. That Christ was truly man was moreover

---

Christ alone as mediator, that it teaches that men must look to him alone for their salvation.' *Opp.*, 48, 406.

[101] *Inst.*, II, 12, 1. [102] *Opp.*, 55, 54.
[103] Sermon on Luke 2.50-2, *Opp.*, 46, 487 f.

an indispensable condition of our salvation. Never should we
have been able to contemplate the glory of God face to face had
it not been hidden under the veil of humanity. By consenting
to the incarnation of his Son, God meant to show us his com-
passion. Besides, this incarnation humiliates our pride by showing
us that God had to lower himself so far to us. But it is something
more also: to us it has the value of a pledge, a guarantee of
reconciliation: 'Having then this surety, that the Son of God
took a body in common with ourselves, and was made flesh of
our flesh and bone of our bone, we have a sure confidence that
we are children of God his Father, seeing that he did not disdain
to take on what is ours, to be made one with us and to make us
companions with him in what is his; and, by that means, to be
equally with us Son of God and Son of Man.'[104] His character as
Mediator introduces even into his humanity an irreducible
duality, but that is the condition of his saving work. On the one
hand, he was 'the spotless lamb of God', and on the other he was
'a sinner, guilty and accursed' in order to substitute himself for
us in the reconciliation with God.[105] It was only by fulfilling that
double condition that he was 'able to make satisfaction for all
our debts . . . to deliver us from the condemnation of death under
which we stood . . .' and to be 'our advocate who pleads in our
name', 'the bond of peace between God and us'.[106]

However, reconciliation with God presupposes that the disobedience which was the origin of sin has been replaced by
obedience—such an obedience as could satisfy the judgment of
God. For it was necessary—to use the terms employed by Calvin
—to pay what was owing for sin. Here, then, according to the
formula that had become traditional, sin appears as a debt that
must be paid if we are to be redeemed before God. But no man,
reduced to his own resources, could have discharged such a debt
—Jesus no more than any other if he had been no more than a
man. God himself had to intervene. 'Our Saviour Jesus appeared,
having clothed himself in the person of Adam and taken his name
and put himself in his place, in order to obey the Father and
present his body before the righteous judgment of the latter; to

[104] *Inst.*, II, 12, 2.
[105] Commentary on Galatians 3.13, *Opp.*, 50, 210.
[106] Sermon on Timothy 1.9-10, *Opp.*, 54-60.

suffer the punishment that we had deserved, in that flesh wherein the fault had been committed. To sum it up: inasmuch as God alone could not feel death, and man alone could not overcome it, he conjoined human nature to his own, in order to subject the weakness of the former to death, thus purging and acquitting us of our debts, and to win victory for us in virtue of the latter, by waging the combat with death on our behalf.'[107] We have good right to regard this last passage as a classic expression of the doctrine of satisfaction as it had been current ever since St Anselm. Everything in it is exactly in balance and harmony. Man had rendered himself guilty of sin and had offended God in such a manner that he was doomed to death. So that justice should be done, man had to expiate his sin. But man was incapable, by his own strength, of overcoming death: God alone could do so, but he had to take on human nature, so that it should indeed be man who expiated sin. It is by a kind of necessity of justice, then, that the Redeemer of mankind had to be both man and God.[108]

Whenever Calvin comes to speak of the person of the Christ, he takes care to place emphasis simultaneously upon the unity of the God-man and upon the distinction between the two natures. In the measure that he insists upon their unity, we might once again make an easy comparison with Luther, but if so, we just as quickly perceive that in Luther's case the tendency to underline the unity of the Christ is far more pronounced than in Calvin's, so much so that Luther has sometimes been accused of monophysitism. For Calvin, as for him, it is a necessity of the faith never in the least degree to separate God from Christ. And yet Calvin affirms equally and more clearly still, that the distinction between the two natures is indispensable if we do not want to end by admitting a change in the divinity itself, brought about by the fact of the incarnation and necessarily equivalent to a diminution of it. This is a very important aspect of Calvin's theological thought, and perhaps what is most original in it.[109]

[107] *Inst.*, II, 12, 3.

[108] See, for example, *Inst.*, II, 12, 2.

[109] K. BARTH, *Die Kirchliche Dogmatik*, 3rd edn, Zollikon, 1945, vol. I, 2, p. 27, views the opposition between the Christological conceptions of Luther and Calvin as a reflection of a dual tradition going back to the New Testament:

He had no difficulty in finding passages of Scripture which seem to him to confirm both the unity of the two natures and the distinction between them. In support of the former he believes he can adduce the phrase ascribed to Elizabeth in Luke 1.43: 'And why is this granted me, that the mother of my Lord should come to me?' 'As for what Elizabeth said, "the mother of my Lord",' he comments in a sermon, 'this is to show us that in the Son of God the two natures were so united, that is to say, he had so conjoined the human nature he took from us with his divine essence, that these were but a single person.'[110] He rejects, equally, the error that would attribute two persons to Christ, and that which would mix all together and 'make the divine essence into humanity'. Other Scriptural passages show us, indeed, 'how these two natures should be distinguished, as when it is said that his body was the temple "in whom dwelleth all the fullness of the Godhead bodily" (Colossians 2.9). Similarly, when he is explaining I Timothy 3.16, 'God was manifest in the flesh,' he sees the word 'manifest' as an indication 'that we must know Jesus Christ in no way as dual, but one and single although he has two natures'.[111] And the illustration he uses here is significant. He compares the two natures of the Christ to the two eyes of man: 'Each eye can have its vision separately; but when we are looking at anything . . . our vision, which in itself is divided, joins up and unites in order to give itself as a whole to the object that is put before it.'

What mattered above all to Calvin was to avoid anything that might be interpreted as a confusion of the divinity with the humanity, even at the centre of the personality of Christ. From the very beginnings of his theological reflections he had felt the necessity of safeguarding the divinity of Christ from any contamination by humanity. Certainly Christ was both true God and true man and he conjoined the two natures in a single person, but that was not an exception, not even a unique exception, to the absolute transcendence of the divinity. The *Institutes* of 1536

Luther belonging rather to the Johannine succession and to Eutyches, while Calvin would belong to the line of the Synoptics and of Nestorius.

[110] *Opp.*, 46, 109; cf. Commentary on Luke 1.43, *Opp.*, 45, 35.
[111] *Opp.*, 53, 326.

were already concerned to show, by the simile of man as a com-
position of body and soul, that the two parts of a whole could
perfectly well preserve the properties peculiar to each of them.
Calvin made his terminology more precise in the *Confession of the
Trinity* of 1537, which was written during the controversies with
Caroli.[112] Two years later the second edition of the *Institutes*
provided the definitive text:

> But this which is said, that the Word was made flesh, ought
> not to be understood as though it were converted into flesh
> or confusedly mingled therewith; but only that it took from
> the womb of the Virgin a human body, to be a temple in
> which he dwelt. And he who was the Son of God was made
> the Son of Man, not by confusion of substance but by unity
> of person: that is, he so joined and united his divinity with
> the humanity that he had taken, that each of the two natures
> retained its properties; and nevertheless Jesus Christ has
> not two distinct persons, but only one.[113]

Thus far, Calvin had confined himself to a correct exposition
of the traditional teaching about the two natures of the Christ
and the unity of his person, such as Luther also had admitted.
But a difficulty was not long in presenting itself with regard to
the consequences one could draw from this double affirmation.
In the course of his controversy with Zwingli over the Eucharist,
Luther had been led to ascribe a considerable importance to the
'communication of idioms' or properties. Let us remember that
by this he meant the attribution to Christ's humanity of certain
properties of his divine nature and, conversely, the attribution
of certain properties of his human nature to his divine nature.
In the *Greater Confession of the Eucharist* of 1528 he wrote: 'Because
the divinity and the humanity form in Christ one single person,
the Scripture attributes to the divinity, on account of this personal
unity, everything that concerns humanity, and conversely.'[114]
Zwingli, on the other hand, claims that what the Scripture affirms

[112] *Opp.*, 9, 703-10; see, in particular, 706: 'Sic autem coniunctam humani-
tati divinitatem asserrimus, ut sua utrique naturae solida proprietas maneat;
et tamen ex illis duabus unus Christus constituartur.'
[113] *Inst.*, II, 14, 1 and commentary on Matthew 24, *Opp.*, 45, 672.
[114] LUTHER, *Vom Abendmahl Christi, Bekenntnis*, W. A. 26, 321.

of the Christ according to his humanity and which belongs only
to his divinity, is told in but an inadequate manner and that
consequently there could not be, properly speaking, any communication of the *idiomata*. Calvin's constant care to make a
difference, as clearly as possible, between the divinity and the
humanity ought to have led him to similar conclusions. Yet he
does not reject the communication of the idioms as such. 'The
Scripture,' he says in a passage of 1536 which was maintained
in all the subsequent editions, 'speaks according to this form of
Jesus Christ; for sometimes it attributes to him that which can
refer only to the humanity, sometimes that which belongs particularly to the divinity; sometimes that which is appropriate to
the two natures together and not to one alone. Finally, and by
the communication of idioms, it assigns to the divinity that which
is proper to the humanity, and to the humanity that which concerns the divinity.'[115] But in 1543 he introduced, a little further
on, a passage which reveals his real tendencies, in the course of a
polemic against heresy: 'We must beware of the raging madness
of Eutyches, who, in trying to demonstrate the unity of the
persons[116] in Jesus Christ, destroyed both natures. For we have
already adduced so many evidences where the divine nature is
distinguished from the human, and there are so many throughout
the Scriptures, that they ought to shut the mouths of even the
most contentious.'[117] And, a few pages later on, he declares
again: 'Jesus Christ then was adorned with this excellence
according to the flesh . . . of being the Son of God: but we must
not, however, imagine the unity of his person as a confused
mixture which robs the deity of what belongs to it.'[118] Yet while
he emphatically affirms the unity of Christ's divinity with his
humanity, Calvin cannot go further into the question of the communication of the idioms without much hesitation, and whenever
he thinks he can concede something on this point, he automatically attaches the reservation that, in the person of Christ,
divinity and humanity keep their own characteristics without
reacting upon one another any more than is required for the
existence of this union *sui generis*, and for the mediation of which

[115] *Opp.*, 1, 66; cf. *Inst.*, 11, 14, 1.
[116] The Latin text has, more correctly, 'unitatem personae'.
[117] *Inst.*, 11, 14, 4.   [118] *Inst.*, 11, 14, 7.

Christam and his Work of Redemption

it is the bearer. 'Although in unity of person he was God and
man together,' . . . we read in the commentary on Luke 2.40,
'it does not therefore follow that all that belonged to the divinity
was communicated to the human nature, but that so far as was
needed for our salvation the Son of God kept his divine power as
though hidden.'[119] This was the case, according to Calvin (who
is here following Irenaeus), with respect to the passion and the
death of Jesus. And he explains by this same distinction the
Scriptural passages which raise the question of progress in the
knowledge of Jesus, or of his ignorance: 'That though Christ as
man did not know the last day, that derogates no more from
his divine nature than does his having been mortal.'[120]

Similarly the divine nature preserves its properties, and more
especially its ubiquity, in which Calvin, contrary to Luther,
denies that the human nature participated. Here again we find
Calvin's constant preoccupation that nothing should be allowed
to diminish the divinity or divest it of any of its privileges. The
divinity of the Christ fills all things; it is not bound to his
humanity, although it dwells in that humanity. In other terms,
the divinity is not dependent on the humanity even in the smallest
degree. It is true that the Christ came down to our level by
assuming human nature, but he 'put off none of his majesty,
neither lessened nor diminished himself in his eternal glory'.[121]
Here we must quote the famous passage in the *Institutes* of 1559
in which Calvin summed up, in paradoxical form, the whole of
his thought on this subject: 'Although he united his infinite
essence with our nature, nevertheless that was without being
enclosed or imprisoned; for he came down from heaven miraculously, in such sort that he still dwelt there; and he was also
carried miraculously in the womb of the Virgin, and conversed,
and was crucified in such a manner that at the same time,
according to his divinity, he was still filling all the world as
before.'[122] But even in 1536 Calvin had expressed the same opinion
with a singular clarity, this time in respect of the Lord's Supper,
which had been the occasion of controversies about the ubiquity.

[119] *Opp.*, 45, 104.
[120] Commentary on Matthew 24.36, *Opp.*, 45, 672.
[121] Sermon on Ephesians 1.15-18, *Opp.*, 51, 318.
[122] *Inst.*, II, 13, 4.

223

'When it is said (I Corinthians 2.8) that "they crucified the Lord of glory", this does not mean that he suffered anything of his divinity, but that Jesus Christ, who suffered that ignominious death in the flesh, was himself the Lord of glory. For the like reason, the Son of Man was in heaven and on earth, because Jesus Christ, according to the flesh, conversed here below during his mortal life and yet never ceased to dwell in heaven as God. Following upon that, in the same passage, it is said that he came down from heaven: not that his divinity went out of heaven to enclose itself within the flesh as in a cell, but because he who filled everything nevertheless dwelt bodily and in an indescribable fashion in his humanity.'[123] These are the clearest formulations of what has since been called the *extra calvinisticum*: they vividly define the very basis of Calvinist thinking concerning the essential separateness of the two natures and the maintenance of their respective characteristics. While Luther had taken the unity of the person of Christ as his point of departure and, by extending the traditional notions of communication of the idioms and of the ubiquity, finished by admitting the ubiquity not only of the divine, but also of the human nature of the Christ, Calvin took his stand upon the immutability and incommunicability of the divinity, and thence arrived logically—or at least apparently so —at very different conclusions. He retained the ubiquity of the single divine nature, which he even accentuated to some degree. But he categorically rejected the ubiquity of the body of the Christ, for the same reasons that made him dismiss anything tending towards the deification of man, even in the person of Jesus Christ. Great as is the importance he attributes to the humanity of Christ and to its necessity for the work of salvation, we can say with M. Dominicé that 'this humanity of the Christ has value for him only by its union with the divine nature.'[124] but upon condition that we keep in mind the distinction between the two natures and Calvin's unilateral interest in the divine nature and its exaltation. We know, and we shall have occasion to return to it at greater length, how much he relied upon this

---

[123] *Inst.*, IV, 17, 30. Calvin had, moreover, some sponsors in the traditional theology. Without going as far back as the Cappadocians, we can cite THOMAS AQUINAS, *Summa Theologica*, III, q. 5, art. 2 and q. 10, art. 1.

[124] DOMINICE, *L'Humanité de Jesus*, p. 48.

attitude in his belated polemic against the Lutheran advocates of the bodily presence of Christ in the Eucharistic elements. If we place ourselves at the point of view of Christological doctrine we may, however, wonder whether, by thus accentuating the distinction between the two natures, he did not endanger the fundamental unity of the person of Christ, and whether some of the affirmations he made would not tend towards somewhat unorthodox conclusions.

Returning to what is properly called the work of Christ, Calvin sought to sum up the different aspects of this in his doctrine of the three offices or ministries of Christ, as prophet, as king and as sacrificial priest. This systematization does not appear in the first edition of the *Institutes*. Calvin developed it only gradually, beginning in 1539: twenty years later he came to devote a whole chapter to it. It is possible that he derived this idea first from Bucer, who had alluded to it in his *Evangelical Commentary*. [125] The importance that Calvin, for his part, attached to this triple mission of the Christ is shown by the place he assigned to it, between the exposition of the Incarnation and that of Christ's work of salvation. He defines the three functions of Christ and their meaning in a few sentences: 'That prophetic dignity with which we say that Jesus Christ was invested means this: we know that every part of perfect wisdom is contained in the sum of the doctrine that he taught.'[126] The kingdom of Christ is neither earthly nor carnal, but spiritual. It is expressed by the action of the Holy Spirit leading believers to the life ever-lasting, enabling them to bear the miseries of existence here below, in the assurance that they have a king who provides for their necessities.[127] But the rulership of Christ extends not only over the good, it includes also the wicked and is charged with

[125] BUCER, *Enarrationes in Evangelia*, 1536, p. 606: 'Rex regum Christus est, summus sacerdos, et prophetarum caput.' We can trace this back to EUSEBIUS, *Hist. Eccles.*, I, 3, 9, the first allusion to the triple function of the Christ. Upon the attitude of Luther, cf. J. V. WALTER, *Die Theologie Luthers*, pp. 235 ff. J. F. JANSEN, *Calvin's Doctrine of the Work of Christ*, London, 1956, tries to minimize the part played by the three offices in Calvin's theology.

[126] *Inst.*, II, 15, 2.

[127] *Inst.*, II, 15, 4. Cf. BUCER, loc. cit.: 'Non imperis externo modo regis . . . sed spiritu sancto mentes, sed spontaneas regit ad salutem sempiternam.'

the breaking of their rebellion: 'As he assumes the office of king
and shepherd to the gentle . . ., the opposite is also said, that
he bears a sceptre of iron to break and splinter all the proud and
rebellious like earthen pots. . . . One can indeed see several
examples of this already, but the full effect of it will appear at
the last day; and this same will be the last act of the reign of
Christ.'[128] Lastly, here is the reason that Calvin advances to
justify the sacerdotal office of the Christ: 'As for the sacrifice,
we have briefly to note that the purpose and use of this is that
Jesus Christ wins favour for us and renders us acceptable to God
by his holiness, inasmuch as he is a spotless mediator. But because
the curse from the time of Adam has justly closed the entrance
to heaven, and that God, inasmuch as he is judge, is against us,
it was necessary that the sacrificer, in order to open the way to
grace and to appease the wrath of God, should intervene with
satisfaction; and therefore Jesus Christ, to acquit himself of this
office, had to go before with sacrifice.'[129] But this sacrifice of
Christ consists in his passion and his death, voluntarily assumed
in a spirit of obedience, instead and in place of sinful humanity.
'Jesus Christ intervened, and by taking on himself the punishment
prepared for every sinner by the just judgment of God, he effaced
and abolished by his blood the iniquities which had caused
enmity between God and men, and by that payment God was
satisfied.'[130] However, this is not a sort of settlement of accounts
in the juridical sense. What matters to Calvin, and what he,
like Luther sees as the deepest reason for the reconciliation with
God, is that the Christ 'did and accomplished this by the whole
course of his obedience . . . and indeed, for the death of Jesus
to be valid for our salvation, his voluntary subjection is of the first
importance, for the sacrifice would have been of no avail in
justice, had it not been offered in frank affection.'[131] Although,
properly speaking, there can be no question of any obedience
by Christ, except according to his human nature, it was the
whole of Jesus Christ, in his capacity of mediator, who submitted
himself to the Father and who, by his obedience, obtained for us
the divine reconciliation.[132] But then a question presents itself:

[128] *Inst.*, II, 15, 5.   [129] *Inst.*, II, 15, 6.   [130] *Inst.*, II, 16, 2.
[131] *Inst.*, II, 16, 5. Cf. LUTHER, *Postilla*, W. A. 10, 1, I, p. 365 f.
[132] Commentary upon Micah 5.4, *Opp.*, 43, 371.

How could the obedience and the suffering of Christ be of such value that they could bring about the salvation of all the elect? Luther too had asked himself this question, and thought he had answered it satisfactorily on the basis of the union of the two natures: he explained, in effect, that the divine nature of the Christ was so united to his human nature that it participated in the activity and in the sufferings of the latter, although in an inconceivable and inexplicable manner. It was from this fact that the satisfaction offered by the Christ acquired its inexpressible and unique value. On the other hand, man was relieved of the accusation under which he laboured, of having failed to fulfil the Law, since Christ, who was the master of the Law, had fulfilled it by his obedience.[133] Calvin takes up this same question in a new section of the *Institutes* of 1559. The arguments adduced by Lutheran theology may well have seemed to him to rest upon the doctrine of the communication of idioms, though that was not expressly mentioned. Calvin's interest in this question was awakened rather late, hardly before the controversy with Lelius Socinius in 1555. Socinius asked Calvin to explain how God could have been determined by the merits of Christ, when he had decided to save men by an act of his free and sovereign will. There was a double difficulty in that. On the one hand, if the divine will was free and sovereign it was in no need of any outside intervention to realize its decisions. On the other hand, if it was free and sovereign it could not be determined by such intervention, not even by the merits of the Christ. Calvin answered this in a special memorandum, and it was this reply that he afterwards inserted in the *Institutes*[134] in the form of extracts from it, and preceded by an important introduction in which he said:

> Some flighty minds losing their way among their own subtleties, although they confess that we obtain salvation by Jesus Christ, nevertheless cannot bear the name of merit because they think the grace of God is thereby obscured. By this they

[133] LUTHER, Sermon on I Peter 1.18, W.A. 12, 291; Sermons on John 14 and 15, W. A. 45, 559; Sermons on John 3 and 4, W. A. 47, 87.

[134] *Responsio ad aliquot L. Socini senensis quaestiones, Opp.*, 10a, 160-5; *Inst.*, II, 17, 1-5.

mean that Jesus Christ was the instrument or the minister of
our salvation, not its author, chief and captain as he is called
by St Peter. Now, I confess indeed that if anyone supposed him
simply or of himself to oppose the judgment of God there
would be no room for any merit, because no worthiness is
to be found in man which could oblige God or deserve anything of him. . . . In speaking of the merits of Jesus Christ
we are not ascribing the origin of them to him, but referring
back to the decree and ordinance of God which is the cause
of them, inasmuch as he made him mediator, out of pure
graciousness, to obtain salvation for us. And thus it is a rash
act to oppose the merit of Jesus Christ to the mercy of God.
. . . For Jesus Christ was unable to merit anything but by
God's good pleasure; but [only] because he was destined
and ordained to that, to pacify the wrath of God by his
sacrifice and to wipe out our transgressions by his
obedience.[135]

This amounts to saying that the Christ was able to deserve our
salvation only because God would have it so. We have already
pointed out the identity between this point of view and that of
Duns Scotus.[136] Here again we may wonder whether, by thus
depriving the obedience and the passion of Christ of any value
independent of the divine will, Calvin did not too much diminish
the humanity of the Christ to the advantage of the divinity. Was
he not yielding, perhaps unconsciously, to the tendency which
had led him to exalt the divine nature one-sidedly, even in the
person of Christ? Be that as it may, his thought on this point is
closely correlated to the position he had taken up in regard to
the distinction between the two natures. We should note, however, that upon occasion Calvin knew how to attribute a certain
autonomy to Christ, as in the following passage: 'Our Lord
Jesus Christ did not have the office of enlightening us in the faith
and of reforming our hearts today, only inasmuch as he is our
mediator and inasmuch as he is a minister of God, but because
he has that also of himself.'[137]

[135] *Inst.*, II, 17, 1.   [136] Cf. above, p. 129.
[137] Sermon on Ephesians 6.19-24, *Opp.*, 51, 859.

An analogous attitude predominates also in Calvin's explanations of the relation between the redemptive work of Christ and predestination. The question arises, in fact, and Calvin faced it, whether the simultaneous affirmation of predestination and of redemption by means of the incarnation and death of the Son of God does not contain an internal contradiction. From the moment that God has predetermined some men to salvation and others to reprobation for all eternity, where is the need for any intervention by the Christ, either to communicate their salvation, or still less to obtain it for them? It looks at first sight as though the decree of election must exclude any need for redemption. That, of course, could no more be the opinion of Calvin than of the theologians before him who had bent their backs over the same problem. On the contrary, it proved possible and quite legitimate to resume the position he had taken up in the *Institutes* of 1543 and that he had developed afterwards, by saying that 'the work of salvation is as unthinkable, apart from its relations with election, as would be an election eternal in itself; the history of salvation unfolds itself in relation with election, and completes the latter.'[138]

'The Holy Spirit,' Calvin affirms in the passage in question, 'usually employs this manner of speaking in Scripture; that God was at enmity with men until they were brought back into grace by the death of Christ; that they were under a curse until, by his sacrifice, their iniquity was blotted out. Similarly that they were separated from God until they were re-joined with him in the body of Christ. Now, such ways of speaking are accommodated to our minds, in order to make us better able to understand how wretched the condition of man is without Christ.'[139] What we have here, then, is a pedagogic adaptation to human capacities. Nevertheless it is not that alone: the remission of sins and the reconciliation of men to God by the sacrifice of Christ correspond effectively with the reality of things, but represent only one aspect of it.

Although God, in using such a style [of speaking], is accom-

[138] P. JACOBS, *Prädestination und Verantwortlichkeit bei Calvin*, Neukirchen, 1937, p. 78 f.; E. EMMEN, *De Christologie van Calvijn*, pp. 57 ff.
[139] *Inst.*, II, 16, 2.

modating himself to the scope of our crudity, all the same it is true: for he who is sovereign justice itself cannot love the iniquity he sees in all of us: we have things enough in us to be hated by God. Therefore, in respect of our corrupt nature, and then of our evil life, we are all under the hatred of God, guilty before his judgment and born in damnation; but because God does not wish to lose in us what is his own, he still, by his goodness, finds something to love in us; for although we are sinners by our own fault, we nevertheless remain always his creatures: although we have deserted death, still he did create us for life.[140]

We must therefore consider two aspects of the question separately: on the one hand, the fact that God loved us before the creation of the world, and that despite the Fall he still loves us because we continue to be his creatures; and, on the other, the fact that our iniquity is hated by God and separates us from him, until the sacrifice of Christ dispels that hatred, and Christ, in uniting us with himself, reunites us with God. Thus Calvin is able to write, in his commentary upon II Corinthians 5.19, 'As for God, his love was first in time and in order; but with regard to us, the beginning of the love of God towards us is at the sacrifice of Christ.'[141] It is the same reality, but seen from the standpoints of God and of man, turn by turn. The love of God cannot be known and apprehended by man except through the intermediation of Jesus Christ. 'If we want to have assurance that God loves us and is for us, we had best turn our eyes upon Jesus Christ and fix our minds upon him: as in truth it is through him alone that we obtain that our sins are not imputed to us, the imputation of which arouses the wrath of God.'[142] It is by Christ, then, and by him alone that we can enter anew into contact with God, and benefit by the love that he has kept for us in spite of our sin. It is he who 'lifts us up even to heaven', who 'leads us so graciously and as it were takes us by the hand', who is 'the key that opens the door of the kingdom of heaven to us'.[143] In other terms, he is the indispensable instrument that God uses to attract his elect to him. His office as Mediator is

---

[140] *Inst.*, II, 16, 2.   [141] *Opp.*, 50, 71.   [142] *Inst.*, II, 16, 3.
[143] Commentary on I Timothy 2.5, *Opp.*, 52, 270; cf. 53, 161.

closely connected with the Incarnation; yet, in order to call the elect under the old Covenant, he was Mediator even before his manifestation in the flesh,[144] and he remains so after his death,[145] 'inasmuch as he appears today before the face and the majesty of God so that we may be heard in his name'. Calvin also adds, in conclusion: 'For this reason St Paul says that the love with which God loved us before the creation of the world[146] had always been founded in Christ (Ephesians 1.4). That doctrine is clear and in conformity with the Scripture, and it brings into harmony those passages in which it is said that God showed us his love by delivering his only Son to death, and that nevertheless he was our enemy until Jesus Christ, by dying, had discharged the debt.'[147]

The sacrifice offered in time by the Christ modifies, at least considered from the human point of view, the attitude of God himself towards men. In reality, that attitude is unchanged and immutable; it cannot therefore be influenced *a posteriori* by the work of Christ. That work is limited to the removal of the obstacle that prevents the divine love from making its way to men. The initiative remains moreover with God, and it is his love for men which has removed the barrier constituted by sin, and the divine wrath that was the consequence of it, by deciding to accept the satisfaction to be offered by Jesus Christ.[148]

Christ's work of salvation thus appears as the necessary consequence of the eternal decree of election. Redemption is included in predestination and founded upon it, as Duns Scotus had taught before. It is the means or instrument chosen from all eternity. This does not mean, however, that in Calvin's view Christ the Mediator was reduced to the fulfilment of a merely instrumental part. The Christ took part in the election, because he is one of the three Persons of the Holy Trinity. Election, then, is in this sense also founded upon Christ. Being the Mediator, he has rendered election effectual, for by his sacrifice he has

---

[144] Sermon on Daniel 8.16-27 and 9.17-18, *Opp.*, 41, 504 and 557 ff.

[145] Sermon on I Timothy 2.5-6, *Opp.*, 53, 167.

[146] That is, at the time when election was decreed.

[147] *Inst.*, II, 16, 4.

[148] Cf. Sermon on Galatians 1.3-5, *Opp.*, 50, 292 f.

appeased the wrath of God and has restored to its efficacy
the love that God had dedicated to the elect of all eternity. In
doing this he conformed himself to the divine will, which had
freely chosen this means of salvation, but was his will, equally
with that of the Father and that of the Holy Spirit.

CHAPTER FOUR

The Hidden Work of the Holy Spirit

The order of the subjects expounded in the third Book of the *Institutes* is rather surprising at first sight. Having indicated that 'the things which have been said above concerning Jesus Christ are of profit to us through the hidden operation of the Holy Spirit,' the author speaks of faith and of regeneration by faith: to this he adds chapters on penitence and on 'the life of the Christian man'. It is only then that he comes to deal with justification by faith and the emptiness of works, and then with Christian freedom, prayer, predestination, and finally with the resurrection. The majority of commentators have been struck by this somewhat unaccustomed order and have tried to give reasons for it, especially to explain why Calvin placed his developments upon justification after the exposition of regeneration. It is possible, as some argue,[1] that a polemical animus against the Roman doctrines played some part: by beginning with regeneration and the Christian life, Calvin may have wished to show that justification by faith was not, as the adversaries of the Reform alleged, a pretext for a passive attitude. But we must not forget that Calvin regarded his *Institutes* as a manual, and that didactic preoccupations also played their part in the arrangement of his subjects. When, after having discussed faith, he comes to penitence, he indeed tells us the reason which led him to adopt this plan: it was 'because, having rightly grasped this point, we shall easily be able to see how man is justified.' He is therefore following a logical order, or at least endeavouring to do so. In any case, the plan he decided upon does not signify that he attributed a greater importance to regeneration than to justification or that

[1] For example, WERNLE, op. cit., p. 402 f.; NIESEL, op. cit., p. 124.

he ever thought of introducing a causal link between them: as we shall see, he placed them side by side upon the same level.

I. THE MANNER OF PARTICIPATION IN THE GRACE OF JESUS CHRIST

The question to which Calvin is seeking an answer at the beginning of his third Book is this: The Christ having made satisfaction for our sins, and having by his merits won salvation for us, how can we appropriate this salvation and receive the grace that accompanies it? 'We now have to see,' he writes at the head of the opening chapter, 'how the blessings that God the Father has committed to his Son are to reach us, seeing that the Son did not receive them for his own use, but to bring them to the poor and the indigent. Firstly, it must be noted that so long as we are apart from Christ and separated from him, all that he has done and suffered for the salvation of the human race is useless and of no importance.'[2] No doubt Christ, by his death, has obtained for us the possibility of effectually receiving the benefits that God intended for us, but this, according to Calvin, is as yet no more than a kind of potential grace, which man, while he is a sinner and therefore separated from Christ and a stranger to him, cannot receive automatically. The benefits that the Christ won on our account do not remain abstractions. Contact with God can be established only on the personal plane and by the intermediation of Christ. It is therefore indispensable for us to begin by entering into relations with Christ, and these relations can only be those of person to person. All the more is this so, because the Christ has won the gifts that were destined to us in such sort that they are embodied in him. If we want to benefit by them, we have therefore to unite ourselves as closely as possible with the Christ, 'he must become ours and dwell in us.'[3]

'For that reason,' Calvin goes on in this same section, '(Christ) is named our leader, and the first-born among many brothers;

[2] *Inst.*, III, I, I.

[3] A. GOEHLER, *Calvins Lehre von der Heiligung*, Munich, 1934, pp. 24 ff.; W. KOLFHAUS, *Christusgemeinschaft bei Joh. Calvin;* NIESEL, op. cit., pp. 114 ff. J.-D. BENOIT, *Calvin directeur d'âmes*, pp. 76 ff.

and it is also said, on the other hand, that we are grafted into him, and that we are clothed with him, because nothing that he possesses belongs to us . . . until we have been made one with him.' Communion with Christ, the *insitio in Christum*, is the indispensable condition for receiving the grace that the Redemption has gained for us. There is no question, when Calvin is speaking about union or communion with Christ, of any absorption into Christ, or any mystical identification that would diminish human personality in the slightest degree, or draw Christ down to us. The author of the *Institutes* had already shown himself too hostile to any glorification or deification of man, and of earthly and sinful man above all, to be suspected of trying to revert to this by a roundabout way. But the relationship with Christ is none the less of the closest, while allowing of the integral subsistence of the properties of man and those of the Christ. 'In this sense, then,' declares Calvin in his Ninth Sermon on the Passion, 'let us know the unity that we have with our Lord Jesus Christ; to wit, that he wills to have a common life with us, and that what he has should be ours: nay, that he even wishes to dwell in us, not in imagination, but in effect; not in earthly fashion but spiritually; and that whatever may befall, he so labours by the virtue of his Holy Spirit that we are united with him more closely than are the limbs with the body.'[4] This spiritual union extends to the whole man, body and soul. 'The spiritual union that we have with Christ belongs not only to the soul, but also to the body, so much so that we are flesh of his flesh and bone of his bone (Ephesians 5.30). Otherwise the hope of the resurrection would be faint indeed, were not our union what it is; namely, complete and entire.'[5]

Calvin was led to define his thought on this point in the course of his polemic against the mystical speculations of André Osiander. The latter, who in the early days of the Reform had played a major part in the introduction of Lutheran ideas at Nuremberg, had become, after the Interim, a professor at Königsberg. Of a disposition easily carried away to extremes, he had always professed doctrines of a marked originality.[6] Towards the end of

[4] *Opp.*, 46, 953.
[5] Commentary on 1 Corinthians 6.15, *Opp.*, 49, 398.
[6] E. HIRSCH, *Die Theologie des Andreas Osiander*, Göttingen, 1919.

his life, he set himself to work out a peculiar theory of justification which exposed him to the definite hostility of the
Lutherans as well as of Calvin.[7] He abandoned the thesis upheld
by both Luther and Melanchthon, according to which the
righteousness conferred upon us by justification is of a purely
formal and imputed character. Osiander held that the righteousness of Christ justifies us so fully that we become really righteous,
not merely so by imputation, and this by grace of the action
upon us of the interior Word; that is, of the Christ dwelling in
us by faith and according to his divine nature. 'What he maintains so definitely and with such importunity,' Calvin afterwards
said, very correctly, in his *Institutes*, 'that the righteousness we
have in Jesus Christ is essential and dwells in us essentially,
tends . . . to this end: that God mingles himself with us with
such a mixture as do the foods we eat.'[8] Everything in Calvin's
theology was bound to revolt against such a conception. He
could no more admit the mystical side of it than the affirmation
that by the essential indwelling of Christ in man the latter became
really righteous. But above all, he was obliged forcibly to reject
this attempt to mingle the divinity of the Christ with our humanity,
and so far to abase it. However, although he in fact always
avoided any confusion of that kind, Calvin himself uses no less
remarkably emphatic terms when he is trying to describe our
union with Christ by faith. It seems, however, that he did not
perceive the danger, or at least imprudence, of certain formulations until he had read some of Osiander's writings which appeared
in 1550 or 1551. Before that he had not hesitated to employ
such expressions himself, while attaching a different meaning to
them. In 1545 he had gone so far as to write in the *Institutes* that
'(the Apostle) adduces this reason, that Jesus Christ dwells in us,
not only adhering to us by an indissoluble bond, but, by a
wonderful union that surpasses our understanding, he daily
unites himself with us more and more in one same substance.'[9]

[7] W. NIESEL, 'Calvin wider Osianders Rechtfertigungslehre' in the *Zeitschr.
für Kirchengeschichte*, vol. 46, Gotha, 1928, pp. 410-30.

[8] *Inst.*, III, 11, 10.

[9] *Inst.*, III, 2, 24. The Latin text did not go so far as this; there, Calvin
avoided the expression 'one same substance', and simply wrote: *donec unum
penitus nobiscum fiat.*

The maintenance of this passage in the edition of 1560 must be ascribed to inadvertence. We find, moreover, a similar idea in the commentary on Ephesians 5.29 (which is from 1548), where we read this: 'As Eve was formed of the substance of Adam her husband, so that she was like unto a part of him, (so) in order to be true members of Christ we communicate in his substance, and by that communication are assembled into one and the same body.'[10] An even more peculiar text occurs in a homily on I Samuel 2.27-30 pronounced by Calvin near the end of his life: there it is said that by communion with Christ we are inserted into his body, that we become his members, that we have life in common with him and that 'even as he is one with regard to the Father, we become one in regard to him.'[11] One could easily read this sentence as the expression of an essential unity of Christ with his believers. But that would be in contradiction with the whole position taken up by Calvin in the course of his polemic against Osiander; and on the other hand, the tradition concerning the text of these homilies is too uncertain to base oneself on them.[12] Generally speaking, Calvin showed great circumspection in his writings after 1550, as one may judge from the following passage which we quote from the additions of 1559: 'I exalt to the sovereign degree the conjunction that we have with our leader, his dwelling in our hearts by faith, the sacred union in which we enjoy him, so that, being ours, he distributes to us the blessings wherein he abounds to perfection. I do not say, then, that we ought to consider Jesus Christ from afar or outside us in order that his righteousness should be attributed to us, but because we are apparelled with him and grafted into his body; in brief, that he has truly deigned to make us one with him.'[13]

It remains true that, close as that union may be, man and the Christ are not confused together, but on the contrary keep their own characteristics. Although Calvin calls it so, it is not, in the technical sense of the term, a mystical union.[14] No doubt it

---

[10] *Opp.*, 51, 225.   [11] *Opp.*, 29, 353.   [12] Cf. *Opp.*, 29, 237 f.

[13] *Inst.*, III, 11, 10. Cf. Commentary on Romans 6.5: 'We pass from our nature into his.' *Opp.*, 49, 107.

[14] Ibid. ,The French version, moreover, translates *unio mystica* by *union sacrée*.

becomes closer every day, but it does not attain its culminating point until the life to come; all we can know about it on earth is only a commencement. Finally, this is a purely spiritual union. Calvin says so with a clarity that leaves nothing to be desired in the *Institutes* and in his other writings. We can cite, for example, his commentary on John 17.21: 'So that the unity of the Son with the Father be not vain and useless, it is necessary that the virtue of the same should spread throughout the body of the faithful. Whence we also gather that we are one with the Son of God, not to say that he transmutes his substance into us, but because by virtue of his Spirit, he communicates to us his life, and all the benefits he has received from the Father.'[15]

This union with Christ is, then, the indispensable condition for our access to the spiritual life. 'Neither justification nor sanctification, nor perseverance nor the final perfection is possible without that insertion into Christ that the Holy Spirit effects through faith.'[16] It renders us pleasing to God: 'He begins to love us when we are united with the body of his well-beloved Son. . . . We are not otherwise included in that love, except that Jesus Christ is dwelling in us.'[17] Union with Christ makes us participants in the life and spirit of the Lord, until even the angels themselves 'wonder at the riches that God has displayed in uniting us with the body of his Son'.[18] This it is, lastly, that gives us the divine affiliation and the celestial inheritance. 'Those whom God now calls by the Gospel into the hope of salvation, those whom he inserts into the body of Christ', are the very same 'that he makes heirs of the life eternal, and that he has adopted in his eternal and secret counsel'.[19]

But that union itself can be obtained only by faith. This is as much as to say that human initiative does nothing towards it. Experience proves to us, indeed, 'that all do not equally embrace this communication of Jesus Christ that is offered in the Gospel'.[20] Calvin appeals to the reason, which prompts us 'to inquire into

[15] *Opp.*, 47, 387. Cf. *Inst.*, I, 15, 5; III, 11, 5.
[16] KOLFHAUS, op. cit., p. 85.
[17] Commentary on John 17.26, *Opp.*, 47, 391.
[18] Sermon on Ephesians 3.9-12, *Opp.*, 51, 470.
[19] *De aeterna Dei praedestinatione*, *Opp.*, 8, 271.
[20] *Inst.*, III, 1, 1.

the virtue and the hidden working of the Holy Spirit which is the cause of our enjoyment of Christ and of all his benefits'. Therefore it is not from man that the movement which ends in union with Christ can begin; its initiation goes back to Christ himself who works in us through the Holy Spirit. The parallelism between these developments upon the union with Christ and those devoted to the Lord's Supper become especially striking as soon as we envisage the working of the Holy Spirit. It alone enables us to understand what union with Christ is. 'One cannot know by any idle speculation what it is, that holy and spiritual union that is between him and us, and first of all between him and his father, but here is the sole means to that knowledge, when he infuses his life into us by the hidden virtue of his Spirit.'[21] Calvin never tires of repeating that 'the Holy Spirit is the bond, as it were, by which the Son of God unites us to him effectually.'[22] He insists so strongly on this action of the Holy Spirit that one may justifiably wonder whether the Holy Spirit does not in his view occupy a position, in our relations with the Christ, analogous to that of the Christ himself in his relations with the Father. In a good many passages, indeed, the Holy Spirit plays the part of an obligatory mediator between Christ and man, just as the

---

[21] Commentary upon John 14.20, *Opp.*, 47, 331. Upon the function attributed to the Holy Spirit in Calvin's theology, one may consult s. VAN DER LINDE, *De Leer van de Heiligen Geest bij Calvijn*, Wageningen, 1944, and above all w. KRUSCHE, *Das Wirken des Heiligen Geistes nach Calvin*, Göttingen, 1957, a study in depth which examines, from this particular point of view, the principal themes dealt with by the reformer. M. MAKOTO MORII, in an as yet unpublished study, takes up the problem by setting it in the historical context of the evolution of Calvinist thinking.

[22] *Inst.*, III, 1, 1. Cf. in addition, some passages already quoted: *Inst.*, IV, 17, 31; *Opp.*, 51, 768. In the Greater Confession of 1528, a Latin edition of which had appeared in 1539 and was very likely known to Calvin, LUTHER had expressed the same idea: 'The Son, in his turn, gave himself for us, with all his works, his sufferings, his wisdom and his justice, thus reconciling us with the Father, in order that we might be restored to life, might be justified, that we might know the Father and his gifts, and possess them. As such a grace would not be of use to anyone if it remained thus hidden and out of reach, the Holy Spirit comes and gives himself altogether to us. It is he who teaches us to know this work that the Christ accomplished for us. He enables us to obtain it, to keep it, to employ it usefully, to give it to others and to make it bear fruit.' W. A., 26, 505 f.; cf. also W. A., 30, 1, 192.

Christ is mediator between God and man. And in the same way that Jesus Christ is the necessary instrument of redemption, so is the Holy Spirit the no less necessary instrument by means of which this redemption reaches us, in justification and regeneration.

To orientate ourselves towards Christ and make his benefits accessible to us, the Holy Spirit works within us by giving us faith. By faith 'we are grafted into the body of Christ'; it is by faith, then, that we enter into the indispensable communion with the Son of God.[23]

Although Calvin never ascribed to faith the autonomous value that it had acquired in the thought of Luther, it was none the less from the German reformer that he obtained his notion of faith—at least in the form in which it is presented in the *Institutes* of 1536. Here, like Luther, he distinguishes two aspects of faith. 'The one consists in belief in the existence of God and in the veracity of the narratives concerning the Christ.'[24] This is not the true faith, however, but rather the semblance of it. The devils themselves possess this, to no advantage other than an increase of fear and consternation. 'By virtue of the other form of faith, we not only believe that God and Christ exist, but we also believe in God and in Christ. That means not only holding all that is written or said on the subject of God and of Christ to be true, but putting all our hope and trust in one God and Christ alone, and being so confirmed in that faith that we have no doubt of God's good will towards us, that we have the certitude that everything necessary to our soul and our body will be given us by him, that we confidently expect the fulfilment of all the promises of Scripture concerning him, that we unflinchingly believe that for us Jesus is the Christ—that is, the Saviour, that through him we receive forgiveness of sins and sanctification, and that in this way salvation is given to us, so that we are led at last into the kingdom of God which is to be revealed at the last day.'[25] But from 1539 onwards, Calvin was no longer content

[23] Cf. KOLFHAUS, op. cit., p. 52.   [24] *Opp.*, 1, 56; *O.S.*, 1, 68 f.

[25] It is advisable to notice the relationship between this passage and Article 20 of the *Augsburg Confession*. See also the explanation of the First Commandment in the *Greater Catechism* of Luther, and the definition in BUCER, *Metaphrases epistolarum Pauli*, 1536, p. 6: 'Fides est certa per spiritum

with this definition which identified faith with confidence and hope; he now qualified it as 'a sure and certain knowledge of God's good will towards us which, being founded upon the promise freely given in Jesus Christ, is revealed to our understanding and sealed in our hearts by the Holy Spirit'.[26] Appearances notwithstanding, this did not represent any falling-back upon a more intellectualist position. The knowledge of faith is not directed to any given doctrinal truth, but to God's good will. Nor is this a matter of rationally understanding God's attitude towards us, but of having a full and entire certitude about him. 'The things that we understand by faith are absent and hidden from our view. Wherefore we conclude that the intelligence of faith consists more in certitude than in apprehension.'[27] In modifying his definition of faith, and insisting upon the fact that 'the intelligence is conjoined with the faith,' Calvin was not making a right-about-turn which would have led him to the notion of faith-by-knowledge; he simply meant to disown any complicity with the implicit faith of the scholastics.[28]

Considered in itself, the faith that makes our union with Christ possible is nothing; it is of 'no dignity or value', it is 'only instrumental'.[29] Indeed, the man who has recognized that faith is a gift of God must not presume upon it as though it were something that he possessed of his own. Its value and importance lie in its object or content; that is, in Jesus Christ. By grace of that content, the faith we receive from the Holy Spirit can be the bond that unites us with Christ; and that union itself, let us repeat, is the pre-condition of any enjoyment of the benefits that the Son has acquired on our behalf. But these blessings themselves—in what do they consist, and what effects do they have upon the believer? To this question Calvin unhesitatingly replies: 'We receive and possess by faith, Jesus Christ, as he is

---

sanctum de Dei in nos charitate et paterna benevolentia persuasio, nitens Domino nostro Jesu Christo, qui morte sua peccata nostra expiavit, et vita sua in qua nunc regnat, participes nos suae iustitiae reddit.'

[26] *Inst.*, III, 2, 7.
[27] *Inst.*, III, 2, 14. Cf. KOLFHAUS, op. cit., p. 47.
[28] *Inst.*, III, 2, 3, P. BRUNNER, *Vom Glauben bei Calvin*, pp. 116 ff.
[29] *Inst.*, III., 11, 7.

given to us by the goodness of God, and by participation in him
we have a double grace. The first is, that being reconciled to
God by his innocence, instead of having a judge in heaven to
condemn us, we very clearly have a Father there. The second is,
that we are sanctified by his Spirit, to think upon holiness and
innocence of life.'[30] In other terms, the double grace that the
Christ transmits to us consists in justification and regeneration.

II. REGENERATION AND THE CHRISTIAN LIFE

From the moment when, by faith, we have entered into contact
with the Christ and are grafted into the body of Christ, Christ
lives in us, or, as one may prefer to say, we live by his spirit.
Henceforth there is no longer any question of a life to be spent
apart from God, as ours was spent as long as we were deprived
of faith. Christ dwells in us and takes possession of our whole
being. It is in this that regeneration or sanctification properly
consists.[31] There are two aspects of it which are inseparable
and linked together by penitence: mortification of the old man,
and participation in the new life. The one and the other proceed
directly from union with Christ,[32] and tend towards the final
end of regeneration: that is, to the restoration of the image of
God in its primitive integrity. 'Already in the beginning,' we
read in the commentary on Ephesians 4.24, 'Adam was created
in the image of God, in order that he might present the righteousness of God as in a mirror, but because that image has been
effaced by sin, it must now be restored in Christ. Moreover, in
truth the regeneration of the faithful is no other thing than a

[30] *Inst.*, III, 11, 1.

[31] Calvin makes no special distinction between the two terms; cf. the
Commentary on I Corinthians 1.2: 'The word sanctification signifies choice
and separation, the which is made in us when we are regenerated by the
Holy Spirit in newness of life.' *Opp.*, 49, 308.

[32] R. SEEBERG, *Dogmengeschichte*, vol. IV, 2, p. 595; A. GOEHLER, *Calvins
Lehre von der Heiligung*, pp. 32 ff.; H. STRATHMANN, 'Die Entstehung der Lehre
Calvins von der Busse' in *Calvinstudien*, pp. 191-212; the same author's 'Calvins
Lehre von der Busse in ihrer späteren Gestalt' in *Theol. Studien und Kritiken*,
Gotha, 1909, pp. 402-447; A. LANG, *Zwei Calvinvorträge*, Gütersloh, 1911, p.
20 f.

restoration of the image of God in them.'[33] The double aspect of regeneration itself arises, on the one hand, from the believer's participation in the death of Christ, and on the other from his resurrection. 'If we are truly partakers in his death,' writes Calvin in the *Institutes*, 'by virtue of this our old man is crucified, and the mass of sin remaining in us is mortified until the corruption of our former nature has no more vigour. When we participate in his resurrection, we are thereby revivified in a newness of life which corresponds to the righteousness of God.'[34]

But this does not mean that from being the sinners that we were we now become saints. The death of the old man in us and the new birth are certainly no mere imaginations: on the contrary, they are expressions of a reality. But this reality has its existence solely in Christ—at least as regards its attainment, and so long as we are living on earth. We attain to and participate in it only in the same measure as we are united with Christ. We continue to be sinners even while we are being progressively sanctified. And therefore Calvin can say, in terms that Luther would not have disavowed: 'This restoration is not accomplished either in a minute of time nor in a day, nor in a year; but God abolishes the corruptions of the flesh in his elect in a continuous succession of time, and indeed little by little; and he does not cease to cleanse them of their filth, to dedicate them to himself as temples, to reform their senses to true piety, so that they exercise themselves all their lives in penitence, and know that this war never comes to an end until death.'[35] Sanctification consists partly, then, in recognizing how far we still are in fact from true righteousness. For Calvin, as for Luther, one of the consequences of faith is that it shows the Christian that though he is justified by Christ he remains more or less a sinner all his life, and that this sin has to be combated by penitence. Or, to quote Calvin's own words, 'The children of God are delivered from the slavery of sin by

[33] *Opp.*, 51, 208.   [34] *Inst.*, III, 3, 9.
[35] Cf. Commentary on I Corinthians 1.8, *in fine*, *Opp.*, 49, 312; upon James 1.19, *Opp.* 55, 393. LUTHER, *Sermo de duplici iustitia*, W. A. 2, 146: 'Christus expellit Adam de die in diem magis et magis secundum quod crescit illa fides et cognitio Christi. Non enim tota simul infunditur, sed incipit, proficit et perficitur tandem in fine per mortem.'

regeneration, not at all so that they should have no quarrels with the flesh, as though they were already in full possession of freedom, but rather that this may remain a perpetual field of battle to keep them exercised, and not only to exercise them, but to give them knowledge of their frailty.'[36]   Nor is it only against sin and his ever-reviving concupiscence that the believer will be led to battle, but against the devil himself, against whom he must wage 'open war, endless and unceasing'.[37]

However, the life of the regenerate man is not preoccupied solely by that negative aspect of penitence which is mortification. Though the believer remains a sinner and his sanctification finds its completion only in the beyond, yet the new life is a reality that is not purely eschatological, but expresses itself here and now in definite deeds. 'Although sin is dwelling in us, it is not fitting that it should have strength to impose its rule, inasmuch as the virtue of sanctification ought to predominate and appear above it, so that our life may bear witness that we are truly members of Christ.'[38]   As soon as we are incorporated in Christ, we have the certitude that 'in the end we shall achieve victory in the fight.'[39] The grace given us by the Christ does not have the effect of preventing us from sinning, but it puts an end to 'the reign of sin and death'; that is, to their absolute dominance, which made it impossible for us to struggle effectually against them.[40]

The reality of the new life rests upon the reality of election. None but the elect are called to the enjoyment of it, and the purpose of their election consists precisely in the sanctification initiated during their earthly life.[41] 'As by the Gospel we are called to innocence of life, so must that same be realized in us in fact, in order that our vocation may be effectual.' This is what was perfectly brought to light by P. Lobstein in his classic essay

[36] *Inst.*, III, 3, 10.   A good account of Luther's point of view is given in H. STROHL, *L'Epanouissement de la pensée religieuse de Luther*, Strasbourg, 1924, pp. 41 f., 84 ff.

[37] Second Sermon on the Passion, *Opp.*, 46, 849.

[38] Commentary on Romans 6.12, *Opp.*, 49, 111.

[39] Commentary on Romans 6.6, *Opp.*, 49, 108.

[40] Commentary on Romans 5.21, *Opp.*, 49, 103.

[41] Commentary on I Corinthians 1.2, *Opp.*, 49, 308: 'Our sanctity proceeds and flows from the source of our election by God, and this itself is the purpose of our calling.'

on Calvin's moral teaching: 'We are chosen by God in order
to live a holy and stainless life. The reason for the existence and
the purpose of the gracious election of God is to devote us, who
were servants of Satan and slaves of sin, to the service of the holy
and merciful God. . . . Holiness of life cannot therefore be
separated from the grace of election; the latter is manifested and
attested most of all in this, that a new zeal for sanctification is
awakened in the elect. For those whom God chooses, he renews
and justifies by communicating to them the strength to live a
godly life. The decree of everlasting election does not refer,
then, to an abstract transcendence, or to a rigid objective outside
and above the elect; it is realized in their life and becomes
immanent in it. Where there is no sanctification, the election
which is a prior condition for it must necessarily be absent also.'[42]
The grace that God accords to his elect in Jesus Christ is irresistible, and is accompanied by gifts that enable them to struggle
effectually against sin and to make progress on the path to holiness. 'God by his Spirit trains, persuades, moderates our heart
and governs it as his possession. And by Ezekiel he not only
promises to give a new heart to his elect so that they may walk
according to his precepts, but that they may walk therein in
fact.'[43] For the same reason, too, Calvin affirms with his well-
known vigour that the gift of perseverance is granted to the elect.
From the moment that God chooses and calls them and accords
them the grace to begin their new life, he will assure them of the
possibility of pursuing the struggle throughout their earthly
career. Indeed, 'the Spirit of God, being consistent with himself,
nourishes and confirms in us the love of obedience that he
instilled into us from the beginning.'[44]

No more than Melanchthon or than Bucer could Calvin resist
the temptation to graft a complete practical morality upon this
notion of sanctification. This he expounds in the chapters of the
Institutes which are devoted to 'the life of the Christian man'.[45]

[42] P. LOBSTEIN, *Die Ethik Calvins*, Strasbourg, 1877, p. 22 f.
[43] *Inst.*, II, 3, 10. [44] *Inst.*, II, 3, 11. A. GOEHLER, op. cit., p. 51.
[45] Besides the work of LOBSTEIN, cf. above all DOUMERGUE, op. cit., vol.
IV, pp. 288-317; also his *Le Caractère de Calvin*, Neuilly, 1931, pp. 93-107;
L. GOUMAZ, *La Doctrine du salut*, pp. 279-311; A. GOEHLER, op. cit., pp. 35-43,
71-80; NIESEL, op. cit., pp. 133 ff.; J.-D. BENOIT, *Jn. Calvin*, pp. 268-84 and

In 1539, let us remember, he added a chapter 'On the Christian life' at the end of the work. He reprinted this text with hardly any changes in all the subsequent editions, including the last, where we find it divided up into five new chapters. Still more notably—and this proves the importance that he attached to it— he had a separate reprint made of it in 1550.[46]

It is true that Calvin had already noted, in the previous chapters, a whole series of questions relating to the life of the Christian after his reception of the gift of faith and his incorporation in the Christ. But here he comes back to them at greater length, and with a marked concern for practical necessities. His aim in rewriting this general exposition was to show how the Christian can derive from the Scriptures a rule of conduct for his daily behaviour and his advancement on the path of holiness. 'We have said,' he writes at the head of his exposition, 'that the aim of regeneration is that people may perceive in our lives a melody and harmony between the righteousness of God and our obedience; and that thereby we may ratify the adoption in which God has accepted us as his children. Now, although the law of God contains in itself that newness of life by which his image is restored in us; nevertheless, because our slothfulness has need of much spurring and helping, it will be useful to gather together from various passages of Scripture the ways of rightly regulating our life, so that those who desire to be converted to God may not go astray through ill-considered affection.'[47]

One of the immediate practical consequences of regeneration is that the Christ has liberated us from the ordinances of this world in order that we may serve him better. We no longer belong to ourselves. 'Now, if we are not our own but belong to the Lord, we can see what we have to do, lest we err, and whither we have to direct every part of our life.' And in a tone which is that of the pulpit, Calvin enumerates the consequences that

---

the same author's *Calvin, directeur d'âmes*, pp. 87 ff. and more recently, R. S. WALLACE, *Calvin's Doctrine of the Christian Life*, Edinburgh, 1959.

[46] J. PANNIER, 'Notes historiques et critiques sur un chapitre de *l'Institution* écrit à Strasbourg (1539): De la vie chrétienne', in the *Revue d'Histoire et de Philosophie religieuses*, 1934, pp. 206-29.

[47] *Inst.*, III, 6, 1.

follow from the dominance of Christ within us: that our reason
and our will no longer determine our decisions; let us not seek
what is expedient for us according to the flesh; let us forget ourselves as much as we can, and all that is around us. 'Again,' he
continues in his exhortation, 'we belong to the Lord; let his
will and his wisdom, then, rule over all our actions, so that
every part of our life may be directed to him, as to one single
end.'[48]

The certitude of this permanent presence of God in our life
leads the believer to deny himself, to bear his cross and to direct
his whole attitude towards the life to come. Nor is this, as one
might suppose and as it has sometimes been said,[49] a return to
monastic conceptions with their meticulously graduated exercises
in asceticism. The means indicated by Calvin are concurrent
and simultaneous, and though they may well lead to a relative
asceticism and to contempt for this world in comparison with the
future life, they are not intended to deprive the believer of the
goods of this world, nor indeed to deny all value to them. 'God
is regarded as a king when men, denying themselves and despising
the world and this earthly life, apply themselves to the righteousness of God in aspiration to the life of heaven.'[50] No doubt. But
on the other hand Calvin affirms: 'The use of the gifts of God
is not unruly when it is limited to the purpose for which God
created and designed them, seeing that he created them for our
good. . . . If we consider to what end God created foods, we
shall find that he wished not only to provide for our necessities
but also for our pleasure and recreation. . . . With herbs, trees
and fruits, besides the various uses he gives us of them, it was his
will to rejoice our sight by their beauty, and to give us yet another
pleasure in their odours. . . . Lastly, has he not given us many
things which we ought to hold in esteem without their being
necessary to us?'[51] We know, too, how highly Calvin continued
to value literary beauty and the works of the mind.

[48] *Inst.*, III, 7, 1.
[49] M. SCHULZE, *Meditatio futurae vitae*, Leipzig, 1901, p. 18.
[50] *Inst.*, III, 20, 42.
[51] *Inst.*, III, 10, 2; Sermons on I Samuel 41, c. 12, *Opp.*, 29, 691. P. LOB-
STEIN, op. cit., pp. 108 ff.; DOUMERGUE, *Jean Calvin*, vol. IV, pp. 299-304;
J.-D. BENOIT, *Calvin, directeur d'âmes*, pp. 186 ff.

But all that, of course, was of no account beside the demands of divine righteousness. As Pascal would have said, these are things of another order. 'For whoever beholds God in all his works easily turns his mind away from all vain cogitations. That is the denial of ourselves which Christ so earnestly demands of all his disciples for their first apprenticeship: and by which, when once it occupies the heart of man, first vanity, pride and ostentation are exterminated; and then avarice, intemperance, superfluity and all revelling, with the other vices that are born of love of ourselves.'[52] The denial of ourselves, upon which Calvin based all his ethics, is impossible except by faith in Christ. Luther too, as we know, had insisted upon this action of faith in the beginnings of the Christian life. True penitence proceeded, in his opinion also, from the love of righteousness which itself presupposes grace. Calvin's point of view did not, however, exactly coincide with Luther's. For Luther, the fright felt by the conscience brought face to face with sin must prepare the way for the appearance of faith. For Calvin, on the contrary, one must already have faith in order to become aware of sin and to perceive the necessity of penitence.[53] In the *Institutes* of 1536 he was still sharing the Lutheran conception: 'Penitence,' he said there, 'opens to us the way to knowledge of Christ, which is offered only to miserable and afflicted sinners.'[54] The affliction caused by sin therefore came before the knowledge of Christ. Later on, from 1539, Calvin modified his attitude and would no longer admit any consciousness of sin until after the gift of faith; but, as he maintained the foregoing affirmations in his text, this resulted in a certain inconsistency. By maintaining, with an increasing emphasis, the impossibility of man's knowing anything of his real condition before he had the gift of faith, the author of the *Institutes* remained faithful, however, to his constant preoccupation—to avoid anything that might be interpreted as a means given to man to justify himself.

Since it is by faith that the believer is led to penitence and renunciation, Calvin naturally cannot admit with the philosophers that reason alone could govern human life. Borrowing from the terminology of Erasmus, he opposes to them the

[52] *Inst.*, III, 7, 2.   [53] Cf. J. KOESTLIN, 'Calvins *Institutio*', pp. 461 ff.
[54] *Opp.*, I, 150.

'Christian philosophy' which demands that the reason should 'yield and withdraw, to give place to the Holy Spirit; and to be obedient to his leading, so that man lives no more to himself but has, and suffers in himself, Christ living and reigning.'[55] It follows from this that the renunciation is not simply a negative attitude: self must be renounced, certainly, but this is in order to entrust the conduct of one's life to Christ. Furthermore the self-denial must be accompanied by a positive attitude towards the neighbour, 'not only by fulfilling all the duties that belong to charity, but by fulfilling them with a true affection of love'.[56] Upon this theme Calvin rises to accents of eloquence which are somewhat rare with him and are hardly excelled by certain passages in Luther's *Treatise on Christian Freedom*. 'We ought not,' he writes, 'to dwell upon the vices of men, but rather contemplate in them the image of God, which by his excellence and dignity can and should move us to love them and forget all their vices which might turn us therefrom.'[57]

If the renunciation of self ought to give birth to sentiments of brotherly love towards the neighbour, towards God it finds expression in a complete submission. It is of interest to note here that Calvin emphasizes the love we owe to God less than the trust we must have in him, which is never better shown than by abandoning oneself wholly to his directions. 'No one has duly renounced himself until he is so resigned to God that he willingly suffers his whole life to be governed at God's good pleasure. Whoever has such an affection, whatever may befall him, will never consider himself unfortunate, nor make any complaint about his condition as though taxing [58] God obliquely.'[59] Renunciation, however, is but one of the aspects of the Christian life. Another consists in bearing one's cross. No doubt Calvin sometimes happened to declare that 'patiently to suffer the cross is a part of the renunciation of self.'[60] But this is really an attitude that he takes some care to distinguish from renunciation properly so called—one which constitutes, as it were, a higher degree of it, and that brings us nearer to Christ. 'All those whom the Lord

---

[55] *Inst.*, III, 7, 1. Cf. letter to Mme de Camy of 8th January 1549, *Opp.*, 13, 146.

[56] *Inst.*, III, 7, 7.　[57] *Inst.*, III, 7, 6.　[58] That is, 'blaming'.

[59] *Inst.*, III, 7, 10.　[60] *Inst.*, III, 8, the title.

has adopted and received into the company of his children must prepare themselves for a life that is hard, laborious, full of work and of endless kinds of evils. It is the good pleasure of the heavenly Father thus to exercise his servants in order to prove them. He began that order with Christ his first-born Son, and continues it with all the others. For although Christ was his beloved Son . . . we see nevertheless that he was not treated at all softly and delicately in this world; indeed, one may say that not only was he in unremitting affliction, but his whole life was but a kind of perpetual cross. . . . Whence there comes to us a singular consolation, which is, that by enduring all miseries, all those things that are called adverse and evil, we share in the cross of Christ, to the end that even as he passed through an abyss of every evil to enter into celestial glory, so we also through diverse tribulations may attain thither. . . . The more we are afflicted and endure miseries, so much the more certainly is our association with Christ confirmed.'[61] Here Calvin is pursuing the classic theme of the imitation of Christ, but divesting it of the meritorious character it had assumed in medievalist thinking. The suffering in itself is without value; Calvin said this of the passion of Christ; all the more did he think it about our own sufferings. And indeed, in the case of the natural man, to suffer is no more than to be punished by God. But as soon as we are suffering for Christ and with him, our communion with him is strengthened. To share in the sufferings of Christ is proof that we are united with him.[62]

Calvin certainly does not go so far as to claim that the Christian life should consist only of suffering and tribulation. But these predominate; the combat begins anew every day, and if there are moments of respite we ought to regard them only as intervals of truce that God allows us so that we may take up the struggle

[61] *Inst.*, III, 8, I.

[62] Commentary on Matthew 16.24, *Opp.*, 45, 481. 'No persons ought to be held to be disciples of Christ, unless it be those who are his real imitators and ready to run the course that he did. But he gives us, in brief, the rule for this imitation, so that he may know in what thing he chiefly wishes us to be like him. It consists of two points; namely, the renunciation of ourselves, and the voluntary suffering of the cross'. The whole passage deserves to be quoted. Cf. E. EMMEN, *De Christologie van Calvijn*, pp. 139-47; J.-D. BENOIT, *Calvin, directeur d'âmes*, p. 78.

again with renewed vigour.[63]   In a passage which certainly
reflects his personal experience, Calvin shows, later on, the end
to which our miseries here are directed: 'If, being innocent and
of a good conscience, we are stripped of our goods by the spite of
the iniquitous, we are indeed impoverished before men, but
thereby the true riches accrue to us with God in heaven.   If we
are driven away and banished from our country, we are all the
more readily received into the family of the Lord.   If we are
vexed and molested, we are so much the more reliant upon our
Saviour, to have recourse to him.   If we receive opprobrium and
ignominy, we are so much the more exalted in the Kingdom of
God.   If we die, the way is opened for us into the life of blessedness.'[64]   Nor is this a case of so many rewards being due, or of
merits supposed to have been acquired at the cost of our sufferings.
These are no more than the path prescribed by God for attaining to an ever more intimate union with Christ, and through him
to the life beyond, which remains a free gift, as is also the strength
which enables us to overcome our miseries.

Yet the imitation of Jesus Christ, to which Calvin so willingly
returns in his books and his letters, assumes its true significance
only in relation to the after-life.   To suffer as Jesus suffered would
be nothing, if we were not to share in his glory as well as in his
passion.   And that is why Calvin adds, as a third aspect of Christian
life and of penitence, meditation upon the future life.[65]   At the
beginning of the chapter devoted to this he writes: 'By whatever
kind of tribulation we may be afflicted, we must always look to
this end, to accustom ourselves to despise the present life, so that
we may be incited to meditate upon the future life.   For because
the Lord knows very well how prone we are to a blind and even
brutish love of this world, he makes use of a very proper means to
withdraw us from it, and awaken us from our laziness, that our
heart should not be too much attached to such a foolish love.'[66]
This gives us a clear indication of the place of eschatology in

---

[63] Commentary on Psalm 44.23, *Opp.*, 31, 447.   [64] *Inst.*, III, 8, 7.

[65] See M. SCHULZE, *Meditatio futurae vitae*; the same author's *Calvins Jenseits-
christentum*, Görlitz, 1902, and the criticism (albeit excessive) of these works in
DOUMERGUE, op. cit., vol. IV., pp. 305 ff.; A. GOEHLER, op. cit., pp. 39-43;
NIESEL, op. cit., pp. 142 ff.

[66] *Inst.*, III, 9, 1.

Calvinist theology. It is not an end in itself, as though the reformer were yielding to the attractions of contemplation and ascribing to it a value of its own. Meditation upon the future life is to complete the renunciation of self and perfect the cross that is imposed upon the Christian, by making him feel on his pulses the vanity of earthly things. Thus he will have no hesitation in following Christ and detaching himself from the grip in which even the best are held by this world. 'Never would our heart knowingly school itself to desire and meditate upon the future life, without having first been touched by a contempt for the earthly life. There is no mean between these two extremes: either the earth must be despised by us, or it will hold us bound in an intemperate self-love. Wherefore, if we have any care for immortality we must diligently strive to disentangle ourselves from those sorry bonds.'[67] In this we can succeed by meditating upon death and 'our mortal condition' and also upon the heavenly life and the Last Judgment at which 'the Lord is to gather his faithful into the repose of his kingdom, to wipe away the tears from their eyes, crown them with glory, apparel them with joy, satisfy them with the infinite sweetness of his delights, exalt them to his height and, all in all, make them sharers in his felicity.'[68] But the contempt for the world is clearly justified only in comparison with the future life. The believer is living in this world, from which Calvin has no thought of withdrawing him. So he reminds us, by one of those qualifying passages that are so characteristic of his thought, that 'the faithful must accustom themselves to such a contempt of the present life as nowise engenders any hatred of it, nor any ingratitude to God,' for in spite of its miseries it has a good right to be 'numbered among God's blessings'.[69] For the present, God is thus proving his fatherhood to us, so that it is legitimate to think that he 'is preparing us here for the glory of his kingdom'. In other words, earthly life deserves nothing but contempt when balanced against the future life; but inasmuch as it is the school through which we must pass to attain the life beyond and in which we begin to taste the blessings of God, it reveals itself on the contrary as 'a gift of the divine mercy'.

The trials of all kinds that God sends us have no other purpose but to make us turn our eyes towards him and induce us to

[67] *Inst.*, III, 9, 1 and 2.   [68] *Inst.*, III, 9, 6.   [69] *Inst.*, III, 9, 3.

appeal to him. Prayer, to which Calvin devotes the whole of the
twentieth chapter of Book III, is presented there as the intended
result of the sufferings we undergo, and of repentance.[70] It is
'like a communication of men with God in which, having been
admitted to his real temple which is heaven, they admonish and,
as it were, urgently remind him of his promises, in order that
he may show them by experience, when necessity requires, that
what they have believed to be true simply upon his word was no
lie nor any vain thing'.[71]

Just as Luther had done, Calvin therefore presents prayer as
a sort of verification of the faith.[72] Relying upon the promises
of God and upon Christ's command to address ourselves to the
Father, we have the right to call upon God and ask him for the
fulfilment of these promises. The guarantee of the efficacy of our
prayer is to be found in the Covenant that the Christ has sealed
with his blood, and in the continual intercession that he makes
to the Father on our behalf. Like the whole of the Christian life,
prayer is thus founded upon Jesus Christ and upon him alone.
It can find no support within ourselves, any more than in the
intercession of the saints.[73] 'For since the promise assigns Jesus
Christ to us as mediator, if the hope of obtaining what we ask
does not rest upon him, it deprives us of this boon of prayer. And
in fact, when the horrifying majesty of God comes to mind it
were impossible we should not be terrified, and that the sense of
our unworthiness should not frighten and drive us far away,
unless Jesus Christ had come before and stood between, to
change the terrible throne of glory into the throne of grace.'[74]

But to benefit by this privilege of being able to approach the
divine majesty under the protection of Christ, we must of course
have the faith, and have received grace in consequence of it. And

[70] In the *Institutes* of 1559, Calvin does not discuss prayer until after the
exposition upon justification and upon Christian freedom. For greater clarity
we are applying directly to the Christian life the few indications that we here
borrow from Chap. 20. An analysis of them can be found in DOUMERGUE,
op. cit., vol. IV, pp. 329-41, and in WERNLE, op. cit., pp. 75-85.

[71] *Inst.*, III, 20, 2.

[72] LUTHER, *Concio quo modo sit orandum ad Deum*, W. A. 2, 175. This sermon
had appeared in Latin in the *Enchiridion precationum* by which Calvin's work
is influenced in a good many places.

[73] *Inst.*, III, 20, 8 and 21.   [74] *Inst.*, III, 20, 17.

just as it was the Holy Spirit who communicated that grace to us, so again it is he who will guide us when we desire to address ourselves to God. We cannot, indeed, ask for anything whatever. 'There are some who not only dare to pester God with all their follies, without any reverence or shame, and to lay before his throne anything that they have idly supposed might be good; but they are possessed by such a presumption or stupidity that they do not even scruple to require of God that he should indulge them in cupidities which they would not dare to make known to men.'[75] As soon as prayer relies upon the divine promises, its object must necessarily be the content of those promises. But we do not know by ourselves either what one must ask for nor how to ask for it. It is here that the Spirit comes to our aid. 'As the understanding has to be turned attentively towards God, so is it also required of the heart's affection. But both are wallowing here below, or rather let us say languishing or turning away to perversity. Wherefore God, in order to make up for our weakness, gives us his Spirit for a master, who teaches and tells us what it is legitimate for us to ask, and who also rules our affections. For when we know not how to pray, nor what for, he comes to our aid and intercedes for us "with groanings that cannot be uttered" (Romans 8.26-7). Not that he himself prays or sighs, strictly speaking; but that he uplifts us in faith, and induces us to make good and holy requests, moving us to the sighing that gives value to prayer, for which all the forces of our own nature would not suffice.'[76] Thanks to this intervention by the Holy Spirit we shall be prepared to conform ourselves to the four rules that Calvin lays down for 'well and duly' entering into prayer.

In reality, it is a question of the general attitude required of the faithful rather than of precise and clearly-distinguishable rules. The first condition for praying well is that the mind should be disengaged 'from all carnal solicitudes and cogitations' and its entire attention given to the prayer. The believer must then be penetrated with the feeling that what he is asking for corresponds to a real, definite need, and must infuse 'an ardent affection' into his petitions. 'Moreover, what St Paul says remains equally true, that we must pray at all times.' We have every reason to know that prosperity and happiness, the dangers that

75 *Inst.*, III, 20, 5.   76 Ibid.

threaten us and our spiritual poverties, or again 'the longing to
see the coming of the Kingdom of God and his name glorified'
are all reasons sufficient to justify continual prayers. The third
rule is 'that all those who present themselves before God in
prayer divest themselves of all fantasies about their own glory'.
It is also advisable before praying 'to beg for mercy, with humble
and frank confession of our faults', thus to assure ourselves of the
mercy of God. Lastly, prayer ought to be offered in a spirit of
complete trust in God and in the fulfilment of his promises: 'it
is requisite that the prayer of the faithful should proceed from
that double affection, and contain and represent both of them;
that is, that he is sighing about his present evils, that he is anxious
about those which may come, but that nevertheless he puts his
trust in God, in no doubt but that God is ready to hold out his
hand to save him.' To ask him for what we do not expect he will
wish or be able to give us is to provoke God to anger. Our prayer,
then, as in Matthew 21.22, will have to take faith as its guide.
'For there is no prayer that is pleasing to God but that which
proceeds from such an assumption of faith and is founded upon
such a certitude of hope.'[77] But to speak of faith is to speak of
the inspiration of the Holy Spirit. Calvin, who in his exposition
of the four rules of prayer seemed to be appealing solely to human
initiative, thus returns to the intervention of the Spirit in the
prayer of the believer.

III. JUSTIFICATION BY FAITH

'Now,' writes Calvin after his discussions of regeneration and of
the Christian life, 'we must consider at greater length this point
of justification by faith, and consider it in such a way as to keep
well in mind that this is the principal article of the Christian
religion, in order that every one may take great pains and
diligence to know the resolution of it.'[78] That sentence would

---

[77] *Inst.*, III, 20, 4-12.
[78] *Inst.*, III, 11, 1. DOUMERGUE, op. cit., vol. IV, pp. 263-87; WERNLE,
op. cit., pp. 240-66; NIESEL, op. cit., pp. 123-32. R. SEEBERG, *Dogmengeschichte*,
vol. IV, 2, pp. 598 ff.; W. LUETTGE, *Die Rechtfertigungslehre Calvins und ihre
Bedeutung für seine Frömmigkeit*, Berlin, 1909; A. LANG, *Zwei Calvin vorträge*,
Gütersloh, 1911, pp. 13-20; E. MUELHAUPT, *Die Predigt Calvins*, pp. 112-56;

be sufficient proof, if proof were needed, that his having placed regeneration before justification in the *Institutes* did not imply any judgment of value on Calvin's part. Elsewhere too, he described justification as 'the principle of the whole doctrine of salvation and of the foundation of all religion'.[79] No more to him than to Luther did regeneration appear to be any sort of infused quality that man could present as a value before God. In fact it is not by regeneration at all, but by the forgiveness of sins in Jesus Christ, that God justifies men.

However, we must bear in mind that 'justifying grace is not separate from regeneration although these are distinct things.'[80] Calvin was not content with the mere juxtaposition of justification and regeneration. Not that he placed them in a chronological relation, as one might be led to think by a certain passage in the *Consensus Tigurinus*.[81] Nor was there any causal relation between them. One must also avoid making one the final aim of the other. Sanctification is not the purpose of justification. It proceeds from the same source but remains independent, or, more correctly, is logically distinct from justification. Calvin insisted again and again upon the existence and the nature of the bond that unites these two benefits proceeding from union with Christ. Notably, he showed that this bond consists precisely in the *insitio in Christum*, in the union or the communion with Christ. 'When it is said (I Corinthians 1.30),' we read in the *Institutes*, 'that Christ is made unto us redemption, wisdom and righteousness, it is also added that he is made our sanctification. From this it follows that Christ justifies no one whom he does not sanctify at the same time. For his benefits are joined together as by a perpetual bond, so that when he enlightens us with his wisdom

---

E. EMMEN, op. cit., pp. 110-23; W. A. HAUCK, *Calvin und die Rechtfertigung*, Gütersloh, 1938.

[79] Sermon on Luke 1.5-10, *Opp.*, 46, 23.

[80] *Inst.*, IIII, 11, 11. Cf. GOEHLER, op. cit., pp. 83-8; E. EMMEN, op. cit., p. 123 f.

[81] *Opp.*, 7, 735: 'Dum fide inserti in Christi corpus, idque spiritus sancti virtute, primum iusti censemur gratuitae iustitiae imputatione, de inde regeneramur in novam vitam'. W. KOLFHAUS, *Christusgemeinschaft bei Calvin*, p. 66, has shown that what is intended here is a logical, but not a temporal, sequence.

he redeems us; when he redeems us, he justifies us; when he justifies us, he sanctifies us. . . . Since thus it is, that the Lord Jesus never gives anyone the enjoyment of his benefits save in giving himself, he bestows both together and never the one without the other.'[82] All the benefits of Christ, all the graces that he has acquired for us, are therefore closely locked together by the foundation of them all, which is Jesus Christ.[83] Nevertheless it is important not to confuse them together, 'in order that the variety of the graces of God may so much the better appear to us. . . . [St Paul] shows clearly enough that it is one thing to be justified and another to be made new creatures.'[84] Indeed, sanctification can be no more than begun during this life, where, whatever progress the faithful may make, they remain sinners to their deaths. Justification, on the contrary, is perfect from its first reception, as perfect as the righteousness of the Christ with which it clothes us.[85] For the rest, and from the point of view of the history of theology, it is not this distinction that presents the most interest but the fact that, for Calvin, justification and sanctification are two graces of equal value. The author of the *Institutes* finds himself here in reaction against the unilateral accentuation of justification that one meets with in Luther and his disciples.[86] We may even wonder whether, on this particular point, he had not felt the influence of Erasmus.

In 1536 Calvin did not think it necessary to give an explicit definition of justification, nor to devote a special discussion to it. But it was none the less taken as read throughout the book. In the second edition, on the other hand, we find the following definition: 'He will be said to be justified by faith who, being excluded from the righteousness of works, appropriates by faith

[82] *Inst.*, III, 16, 1.

[83] *Inst.*, III, 11, 6: 'Even as one certainly cannot tear Jesus Christ into pieces, so also these two things are inseparable, since we receive them together, and conjointly in him: namely, righteousness and sanctification.'

[84] Ibid.

[85] *Inst.*, III, 11, 11: 'God commences so to reform his elect in the present life, that he proceeds with this work little by little and does not fully achieve it until death, so that they are still guilty before his judgment. But he does not justify in part, but so that the faithful, being clothed in the purity of Christ, may dare frankly to appear before heaven.'

[86] GOEHLER, op. cit., p. 85.

the righteousness of Christ, being clothed wherewith he appears before the face of God not as a sinner, but as righteous.'[87] In 1543 he completed this explanation with the following particulars: 'Thus we say, in short, that our righteousness before God is an acceptance, whereby, receiving us into his grace, he regards us as righteous. And we say that this same consists in the remission of sins, and in this: that the righteousness of Jesus Christ is imputed to us.'[88] But this imputation is made possible only by our union with the Christ and because we become at that same moment members of his body, although the union with Christ cannot be regarded as the cause of the imputation of righteousness. Imputation and union with Christ are, rather, two inseparable aspects of one and the same divine grace: the one is not possible without the other.

The notion of justification does therefore include (as with Luther and Melanchthon) the idea of a righteousness which is extrinsic and is only imputed to us, without any prejudgment of the real state in which we happen to be. Since 1536 Calvin had affirmed that 'the righteousness of faith is Christ's righteousness, not our own, that it is in him and not in us, but that it becomes ours by imputation' . . . Thus we are not really righteous, except by imputation; and we are unrighteous but held to be righteous by imputation, in so far as we possess the righteousness of Christ by faith.'[89] The same conception is taken up and developed in the successive editions of the *Institutes*: it is re-emphasized after the publication of the writings of Osiander, who supposed that the aim of justification was to render believers really righteous, and who saw the remission of sins as no more than a side-issue; whereas, for Calvin, the remission of sins constituted the very basis of justification. But before this he had already imparted a profound resonance to this doctrine of a righteousness imputed to the sinner, by making it the counterpart of the sin assumed by

[87] *Inst.*, III, 11, 2.

[88] Upon justification considered as imputation and the remission of sins, cf. W. LUETTGE, *Die Rechtfertigungslehre Calvins*, pp. 75-9; NIESEL, 'Calvin wider Osianders Rechtfertigungslehre' in the *Zeitschrift für Kirchengeschichte*, vol. 46, 1928, p. 425 f. On the relations between imputation and union with Christ, see KOLFHAUS, op. cit., p. 60 f.

[89] *Opp.*, 1, 60; *O.S.*, vol. 1, p. 73.

Christ: 'How are we righteous before God?' he asks, in the Commentary upon II Corinthians 5.21 (of 1547-8). 'Certainly in just the same way as Christ was a sinner. For he took on our person to the end that he might be guilty in our name and be judged as a sinner: not for his sins but for the sins of others. . . . Certainly in just the same manner we are now righteous in him, not that we satisfy the judgment of God by our works, but because we are considered according to the righteousness of Christ which we have put on by faith, in order that it might be made ours.'[90] The logical consequence of that doctrine of the imputation of the righteousness of Christ is that never, not even after the remission of our sins, are we really righteous. On the contrary, we have noted that the sanctification which accompanies justification, or at least begins with it, enables us to become more and more precisely aware of our sin.

Calvin's fear of anything that might have led to the admission of any deification of man, even by way of Jesus Christ and even in his person, led him here again, in regard to the righteousness of Christ that is imputed to us, to underline the radical distinction between the two natures of the Christ. Against Osiander, who maintained that it was only the divine nature in Christ that could accomplish the work of our justification, Calvin affirmed:

> Jesus Christ was made our righteousness, taking the form of a servant: secondly, he justifies us because he obeyed God his Father. Thus he does not communicate so great a benefit according to his divine nature, but according to the dispensation entrusted to him.[91] . . . If Osiander answers that to justify us is a work of such dignity that there is no faculty in men that would be equal to it, I grant him that. If he argues from this that no nature except the divine could have had such an effect, I say that he is too grossly mistaken. For although Jesus Christ would not have been able to cleanse our souls by his blood, nor to appease the Father towards us by his sacrifice, nor to absolve us from the condemnation under which we stood, nor, in short, to perform the sacrificial

[90] *Opp.*, 50, 74.
[91] That is to say, because God willed it so, and gave the Christ the power to do it.

office at all, had he not been truly God (since all the abilities
of the flesh were quite unequal to so heavy a burden), yet
nevertheless he did accomplish all those things according to
his human nature.[92]

Calvin goes on to point out that it is by the obedience of the
Christ that we are justified, but that he could not have manifested
that obedience except in his quality as a servant; that is, according to his human nature. He finds another argument in favour
of this thesis in the fact that 'God had prepared as a sacrifice
for sin him who knew not sin.' It would be repellent to the very
notion of divinity if the divine nature of Christ had been the
offering presented for our sins. And since, on the other hand, it
was for humanity that the sacrifice had to be offered, in order to
answer to the notion of satisfaction, it was according to his
human nature only that the Christ could offer himself for us.

We cannot of ourselves, then, acquire the righteousness that
would justify us before God. If nevertheless we are justified,
that is because we have been grafted into him and, in that sense,
have received his righteousness. In short, Christ puts himself in
our place and accomplishes what we ought to have done. And
this is not a single act, a beneficence that comes to an end at our
justification. If it were, the deeds that we did after that justification would have to be taken into account in the judgment
that God pronounces upon us. That judgment, in other words,
would have to be based on the new life that we had acquired.
But to be able to pass that test we should have to be effectually
saintly and definitely freed from all present sin; whereas we
know that the Christian, right up to his death, is battling against
sin, which never ceases to assail him and to which he often happens
to yield. Even after we have received the faith, our works are still
contaminated by sin: nevertheless God does not impute them to
us as sins but holds them acceptable. Calvin is thus led to formu-
late the doctrine of double justification; first, the justification of
the sinner, and then the justification of the justified, or more
correctly of their works.

When God, after having taken man out of such a pit of
perdition, has sanctified him by the grace of adoption,

[92] *Inst.*, III, 11, 8 and 9.

because he has regenerated and reformed him in a new life, he also receives and embraces him as a new creature with the gifts of the Spirit. . . . The faithful, after their calling, are acceptable to God even in regard to their works, for it cannot but be that God loves the good things he has conferred upon them by his Spirit. Nevertheless we must always remember this: that they are not otherwise acceptable to God by reason of their works, except inasmuch as God, for the love he freely bears them and by ever increasing his liberality, accepts those works. . . . But because the faithful, so long as they are encased in their mortal flesh, are still sinners, their good works are only just begun and there is much that is vicious, God cannot be gracious either to his children or to their works unless he is receiving them in Christ rather than in themselves.[93]

The righteousness of the works of the justified therefore depends, like the justification of the sinner, upon the grace of Christ. In his *Sermon on the Double Righteousness* of 1519, Luther also had made the justification of the works of the justified dependent upon the justification of the sinner: 'The second righteousness is proper to ourselves, not that we are the sole authors of it, but because we are co-operating with that first righteousness which is extraneous . . . this righteousness is the work of the former righteousness, and its consequence.'[94] But Calvin places more emphasis upon the parallelism between the two justifications, notably in a passage inserted into the *Institutes* of 1543: 'Just as, then, we appear righteous before God after we have been made members of Christ, inasmuch as our faults are hidden under his innocence,

[93] *Inst.*, III, 17, 5. Cf. GOEHLER, op. cit., pp. 93 ff.; W. A. HAUCK, op. cit., pp. 52-68.

[94] LUTHER, *Sermo de duplici iustitia*, W. A. 2, 146 f. MELANCHTHON, *Loci communes*, edn of 1543 (*Corp. Reform.* vol. XXI, p. 771 f.) : 'Opportere inchoari obedientiam et iustitiam bonae conscientiae, et hanc quanquam procul abest a perfectione legis, tamen in reconciliatis placere Deo propter filium Mediatorem, qui nostram invocationem in nostros cultus perfert ad Patrem, et condonat infirmitatem. Ita propter Christum primum reconciliatur persona, postea et opera recipiuntur, et fides, in utroque luceat.' Cf. R. SEEBERG, *Dogmengeschichte*, vol. IV, 2, p. 472. Upon Bucer's attitude and the Erasmian influence it reveals, see R. STUPPERICH, *Der Humanismus und die Wiedervereinigung der Konfessionen*, Leipzig, 1936, pp. 22-6 and 81.

so are our works held to be righteous, inasmuch as the evil that they contain being covered by the purity of Christ, it is not imputed to us. Wherefore we have a good right to say that by faith alone not only the man is justified, but also his works. But though this righteousness of the works, such as it is, proceeds from faith and gratuitous justification, it must not be supposed to destroy or obscure the grace upon which it depends; but must rather be included in it, and referred back to it, as the fruit to the tree.'[95] That last remark places the whole of the exposition in its true light, by giving prominence to the fact that it is not a question of an objective righteousness of the works nor, consequently, of a return to Roman doctrine. The works of the justified are simply reputed righteous, by virtue of the faith of him who does them, and because they are in some sort covered by the grace of Christ. Imperfect though they are, God can accept them as righteous in the same way that he imputes the righteousness of Christ to sinful man.

It must be noted, on the other hand, that while he affirms that it is by the mediation of faith that we are justified, Calvin does not insist upon this part played by faith. In his view, as we have said, faith is nothing in itself. It acquires its value only by its content; that is, by Jesus Christ. 'We say that faith justifies, not that it is accounted as righteousness to us for its own worth, but because it is an instrument by which we freely obtain the righteousness of Christ.'[96] What matters to Calvin is evidently not that instrument, but the Christ and his work. Furthermore, if we are to believe the *Institutes*, there would be a real danger in overemphasizing the function of faith, for 'if faith in itself justified one by its own virtue, then, seeing that it is always weakly and imperfect, it would be only partly effectual and give us only a part of salvation.'[97] Besides the polemic against Roman teaching upon justification by works, which dominates Calvin's whole development of this idea, there is a point here that is very clearly

---

[95] *Inst.*, III, 17, 10. It is in this sense that Calvin could write, *Inst.*, III, 16, 1: 'We are not justified at all without the works, although not at all by the works, forasmuch as, in the participation in Christ in which our justification resides, sanctification is no less included.' One may observe here again, the tendency to rehabilitate sanctification along with justification.

[96] *Inst.*, III, 18, 8.   [97] *Inst.*, III, 11, 7.

aimed against the Zwinglian conception of the perfection of faith, no less than against the consequences that Osiander had thought himself entitled to draw from 'the fantasy' in which he affirmed 'that man is justified by faith inasmuch as by this same he receives the Spirit of God by which he is made righteous.'[98] Meanwhile Calvin himself has no hesitation, as we have seen, in repeating that faith justifies, but upon condition that we see it as no more than a means by which we are brought into relation with Christ. For definitely, 'it is solely by means of the righteousness of Christ that we are justified before God.' We must, no doubt, attribute all these precautions to Calvin's constant preoccupation not to grant too much to man. Faith may indeed be an absolutely free gift of God; it is no less surely ours, once we have received it; and by too much insistence upon the part it is called upon to play in justification, we might presume upon it and to that extent diminish the work of the Christ and the glory of God.

IV. PREDESTINATION

After Alexandre Schweizer in 1844 and Ferdinand Christian in 1847[99] had claimed that predestination was the central doctrine of Calvin's theology and that all the originality of his teaching proceeded from it, historians and dogmaticians went on for three-quarters of a century repeating that affirmation like an article of faith which did not even need to be verified.[100] It is true

---

[98] *Inst.*, III, 11, 23.

[99] ALEXANDER SCHWEIZER, *Die Glaubenslehre der evangelisch-reformierten Kirche*; F. C. BAUR, *Lehrbuch der christlichen Dogmengeschichte*.

[100] There were, however, a few notable exceptions. Thus RITSCHL, from 1868, contested the unique importance of predestination in Calvinist theology ('Geschichtliche Studien zur Christlichen Lehre von Gott', *Jahrbuch für Deutsche Theologie*, p. 108); so did A. KUYPER, 'Calvinism and confessional Revision' in the *Presbyterian and Reformed Review*, 1891, pp. 379 ff., quoted and in part followed by DOUMERGUE, op. cit., vol. IV, p. 361 f. The last considerable exposition that gives a central place to predestination is that of O. RITSCHL, *Dogmengeschichte des Protestantismus*, vol. III, Göttingen, 1926. The author even goes so far as to reproach Calvin for not having given predestination the place to which it was logically entitled in his system. There is a critical review of the principal works devoted to predestination according to Calvin since the

enough that Calvin attributed great importance to predestination
in both its forms—election and reprobation—and that he never
shared the point of view of Melanchthon, who thought it a subject hardly suitable for discussion.[101] In the different editions of
the *Institutes* Calvin gave it more and more space and, in consequence of attacks that were made upon the doctrine, he was
moved to defend it in several special writings, notably in the
Congrégation sur l'élection éternelle of 1551 (published in 1562)
against Jérôme Bolsec, and in the second work against Pighius
which appeared in 1552 as the treatise *Upon the Eternal Predestination of God*.[102] But to recognize that Calvin taught double predestination, and underlined its dogmatic and practical interest,
is not to say that this must be taken to be the very centre of his
teaching. His earliest writings do not contain any systematic
statement of the problem, and although, later on and under the
influence of St Augustine and of Bucer,[103] he accorded a growing
importance to it, he did so under the sway of ecclesiological and
pastoral preoccupations rather than in order to make it a main
foundation of his theology. While he never ceases, in discussions
of the most various questions, to repeat the great themes of the
freedom of God and his glory and of the divinity of Christ, he

---

middle of the nineteenth century in the important treatise of P. JACOBS,
Prädestination und Verantwortlichkeit bei Calvin, Neukirchen, 1927, pp. 20-40.
Here let it suffice to mention the following works. DOUMERGUE, op. cit., vol.
IV, pp. 351-416; GOUMAZ, op. cit., pp. 261-72; WERNLE, op. cit., pp. 276-
305; R. SEEBERG, op. cit., vol. IV, 2, pp. 578 ff.; O. RITSCHL, op. cit., pp.
167-85; A. LECERF, *Le Déterminisme et la responsabilité dans le système de Calvin*,
Paris, 1895, pp. 49 ff., 108 ff.; M. SCHEIBE, *Calvins Praedestinationslehre*, Halle,
1897; E. EMMEN, *De Christologie van Calvijn*, pp. 67-83; A. D. R. POLMAN,
De Praedestinatieleer, pp. 307-92; 'De l'élection éternelle de Dieu' in the *Actes
du Congrès internationale de Théologie Calviniste*, Geneva, 1936; P. JACOBS, op.
cit., *passim*.; H. OTTEN, *Calvins theologisch Anschauung von der Prädestination*
Munich, 1938; G. DELUZ, *Prédestination et liberté*, Neuchâtel, 1942, pp. 49-61.

[101] Cf. HERRLINGER, *Die Theologie Melanchthons*, Gotha, 1879, pp. 70 f.,
84 f. A very moderate criticism of Melanchthon's point of view is to be found
in the preface by Calvin to the translation of the *Loci communes*, *Opp.*, 9, 848 f.

[102] *Opp.*, 8, 85-138, 249-366; *Opusc.*, 1393-1504.

[103] DOUMERGUE, op. cit., vol. IV, p. 406 f., concerning Bucer's influence
on Calvin in this domain, generalizes too much. The comparisons with St
Augustine, on the other hand, claim our attention almost constantly.

only very rarely speaks of predestination except in the four chapters that are devoted to it in the edition of 1559. As Wernle has said, 'it cannot be over-emphasized: faith in predestination is a long way from being the centre of Calvinism; much rather is it the last consequence of faith in the grace of Christ in the presence of the enigmas of experience.'[104]

In the *Institutes* of 1536, predestination did not yet appear as an independent doctrine. Calvin mentioned it only in two places; in the explanation of the second article of the Creed, and in regard to the definition of the Church. He indicated, without, however, dwelling upon the point, that the descent into hell being inadmissible in the literal sense of the text of I Peter 3.18-19, it must be interpreted as the manifestation of the power of the Redemption to those who had died before the time of Christ. 'The faithful who had always looked to him for their salvation then had clear sight of his presence. The reprobate, on the other hand, realizing too late that he was the one and only salvation from which they would be shut out, now knew perfectly that they had no hope.'[105] Did the opposition here between the faithful and the reprobate already imply the doctrine of predestination that Calvin was afterwards to elaborate? That is debatable. But be that as it may, no further doubt seems permissible when we come to the passage about the Church. Here Calvin mentions, one after another and each in a brief sentence, the union of the faithful in Christ, the community of the elect, the consequences of election—namely the calling, justification and glorification—then the perseverance of the elect and their separation from among the reprobate. He points out the close relation between vocation and justification on the one hand and election on the other: 'No one can enter into the glory of the heavenly kingdom unless he has been in this manner. called and justified; seeing that without any exception the Lord promotes and manifests his election in this way in all the men he has elected.'[106] As he was to do later, he insists most particularly upon the 'unloseableness' of the salvation that is founded upon

[104] WERNLE, op. cit., p. 403. [105] *Opp.*, 1, 70, *O.S.*, vol. 1, p. 83.

[106] *Opp.*, 1, 73; *O.S.*, vol. 1, p. 86 f. Cf. AUGUSTINE, *De praedestinatione sanctorum*, 17, 34, M. L. vol. XLIV, 986. BUCER, *Metaphrases epistolarum Pauli*, 1536, p. 359.

election, and upon the fact that the elect are entrusted to the
keeping of Christ. He observes that the separation of the elect
from the reprobate is effected by God, but that as far as we are
concerned, we cannot clearly distinguish the elect from the
reprobate in spite of some 'sure signs' to that effect given us in
the Scriptures.[107] We must therefore be content to exercise a
'judgment of charity', and count as elect and as members of the
Church all those who by their words and conduct 'profess one
and the same God and Christ with us'. From that moment, then,
Calvin had adopted as his own the doctrine upon election which
was common to the reformers. Had he also adopted the doctrine
of reprobation, considered as the result of a special decree of
God? That is not certain.[108]

The French *Catechism* that Calvin wrote in Geneva in 1537
marks, in this respect, an important and decisive stage. In this
the question of predestination is raised, after the exposition of
the Law and before the articles that deal with the Redemption.
Calvin introduces his material with the following statement:
'The seed of the word of God takes root and grows fruitful only
in those whom the Lord, by his eternal election, has predestined
to be his children and heirs of the heavenly kingdom. To all the
others who, by the same counsel of God before the constitution
of the world, are reprobate, the clear and evident preaching
of the truth can be nothing else but an odour of death in
death.'[109] The point of departure, as in the *Institutes*, is the
fact that the preaching of the word does not equally move all
those that hear it, but bears its fruits only in the elect, whereas
to the reprobate it brings only death. The practical and ecclesio-

[107] *Opp.*, 1, 75; *O.S.*, vol. 1, p. 89: 'Quanquam autem fidei certitudine
agnosci a nobis electi non possunt, quando tamen scriptura certas quasdam
notas nobis describit, ut antea dictum est, quibus electos et filios Dei a reprobis
et extraneis distinguamus, quatenus a nobis vult agnosci, debent quodam
caritatis iudicio pro electis ac ecclesiae membris haberi omnes, qui et fidei
confessione et vitae exemplo et sacramentorum participatione eundem
nobiscum Deum ac Christum profitentur.'

[108] We may wonder, too, whether Calvin did not begin by sharing the
opinion of Luther and Bucer, who made no separation between predestination
and foreknowledge. A sentence like this: 'Solius Dei oculi vident, qui in
finem usque sint perseveraturi' (*Opp.*, 1, 75), might lead one to think so.

[109] 22, 46. Cf. JACOBS, op. cit., pp. 62-71.

logical point of view is evident and clear, as it is also in St Augustine and in Bucer. And this, in spite of the theoretical developments, is what dominates the exposition of predestination to the end. Similarly, we find in this text of 1537 that reprobation is affirmed by the same warrant as election, and this again is both Augustinian and Bucerian, but not Lutheran. Lastly, Calvin tells us (still in his *Catechism*) that the elect and the reprobate have to serve 'as argument and matter to exalt the glory of God', which is also one of the constant themes of the reformer when he is speaking of predestination.[110]

In 1539, predestination became still more closely involved with ecclesiology, and its outward manifestation with the results of preaching. But Calvin placed this further development after the work of salvation and in a chapter also containing an exposition upon providence; and thus it remained up to and in the edition of 1554. But in 1559 Calvin once more revised his plan, by placing the discussion of providence at the end of the doctrine of God, and predestination after the developments upon sanctification and justification. The comparison established between predestination and providence in 1559 may have been based upon the conviction that predestination and providence both proceeded from one decision of the divine will, an eternal decision situated outside time. But it must not be forgotten that St Augustine too, whose influence on Calvin's thought is so strongly apparent at that period, had brought these two concepts into close relation, and that the author of the *Institutes* may have allowed himself to be led by this precedent. In correlation with St Augustine, predestination had been considered by a good many theologians, such as St Thomas Aquinas, as a special application of the divine providence,[111] of which it was a particular case, concerned with each person taken individually. That notion was not unknown to Calvin. However, bearing in mind that for Calvin man was the immediate end of the creation, we can also affirm, conversely, that predestination in a certain sense conditions providence, which is then limited to a preparation of ways and means. That is very likely what Calvin intended

---

[110] *Opp.*, 22, 47.
[111] THOMAS AQUINAS, *Summa Theologica*, 1, q. 23, a. 1 and 3. 'Praedestinatio quantum ad obiecta, est quaedam pars providentiae.'

to convey when he said, in a sermon on Job: 'Let us note that God has decreed for us what he means to make of us in regard to the eternal salvation of our souls, and then he has decreed it also in respect of this present life.'[112] One might therefore have expected him to put predestinati on immediately after the exposition on providence—even, indeed, before the chapters on the creation; and that is in fact what was done by several theologians who claimed Calvin as their authority, beginning with Théodore de Bèze.[113] But in 1559 Calvin said that the question of predestination which might be raised in relation to the doctrine of God was inopportune.[114] On the other hand, he connected predestination with the Christ and his work, in order to show more clearly that it is in Christ that election takes-place.[115] Just as the doctrine of providence, placed at the conclusion of the doctrine of God, might be said to complete the latter as the keystone finishes an arch, so also does the doctrine of predestination complete and illuminate the whole of the account of the Redemption. The link between predestination and providence subsists, then, in the last edition of the *Institutes*, in their two parallel functions.

These questions about the position allotted to predestination in the dogmatic exposition as a whole do not arise, as one can see, from mere erudition: they enable one to see more clearly what importance Calvin meant to give to the problem, and his reasons for doing so. So far as the basis of his teaching was concerned there was, however, hardly any change. As early as the

---

[112] *Opp.*, 34, 363.

[113] See, in this sense, O. RITSCHL, op. cit., vol. III, p. 163: 'He could, in the edition of 1559, have dealt with the doctrine of predestination in relation with that of the divine providence, among the primary aspects of the doctrine of God; and some of the later reformed theologians did so.' Cf. A. RITSCHL, 'Geschichtliche Studien' in the *Jahrbuch für deutsche Theologie*, pp. 95 ff.; NOESGEN, *Calvins Lehre von Gott*, pp. 709 ff.

[114] *Inst.*, I, 15, 8.

[115] It is the merit of P. JACOBS, op. cit., p. 92, to have given prominence to the theological motive which determined Calvin's final choice of his plan: 'That the doctrine of predestination does not appear (which is in conformity with the place of election in the economy of salvation) before the doctrine of creation, this follows from the fact that it cannot be properly considered except from a Christocentric point of view.' Cf. Ibid., p. 147.

edition of 1539 he had expounded it in all essentials, including
those that touch upon reprobation. Calvin had then just completed his *Commentary on the Epistle to the Romans*, and he had also
thoroughly read the work published by Bucer three years earlier
upon this same epistle. The concentration of his reflection upon
the various aspects of the problem of predestination must have
led him very quickly to definitive results. In effect, the additions
that were made to the subsequent editions of the *Institutes*—
additions in which some have tried to see signs of a modification
of Calvin's attitude and a hardening of his doctrine—are in
reality reducible to some new definitions and some more extended
Biblical quotations. As for the passages relating to reprobation,
no doubt they appear in more amplified form, notably so in
1559, as one might have expected in view of the attacks that
had been made upon this point of his teaching, but they contain
no element of doctrine that is really new.

Not enough is ever said about the preoccupations of a practical
kind which were predominant with Calvin, as they had been
with St Augustine and with Bucer, whenever he applied his
mind to the problem of predestination. In his view, this was
never to be discussed as an indulgence in metaphysical speculations, but to throw a fuller light upon the doctrine of justification
by grace alone and give a theological basis for ecclesiology. That
is apparent from the opening of the first chapter upon predestination. 'Now, that the covenant of life is not preached
equally to everyone, and even where it is preached is not equally
received by all—in this diversity there appears a wonderful secret
of the judgment of God. For there is no doubt that this variety
serves to his good pleasure. But, if it is evident that this takes
place by the will of God, that salvation should be offered to
some and the rest be excluded from it, from this there arise great
and high questions which cannot be resolved otherwise than by
instructing the faithful as to what they should hold concerning
election and predestination by God.'[116] Here, Calvin is dissenting
from those who, like Melanchthon, feared that to meditate upon

[116] *Inst.*, III, 21, 1. Cf. AUGUSTINE, *De dono perseverantiae*, 15-17, M. L. vol.
XLV, 1016-20, (quoted by Calvin, *Opp.*, 8, 326 and frequently). BUCER, *Enarrationes in Evangelia*, 1536, p. 672: 'Satis constat illos nescire quid dicant, qui
negant ista palam praedicanda.'

predestination might lead Christians into despair. The questions
raised by divine predestination were inescapable; it was necessary,
then, to show the faithful what they ought to think about them.
Only upon that condition would they be persuaded that they
held all grace from the goodness of God, and thus the glory of
God would be fulfilled. 'Everyone confesses how much the
ignorance of this principle diminishes the glory of God and also
how much it takes away from true humility: it is not placing
the entire cause of our salvation in God alone.' However, we
must also avoid the contrary excess of wishing to enter into the
secrets of God, which would anyhow be impossible for us. It
would also be an act of impiety, for we should be presuming to
do without the means that God puts at our disposal to assure
ourselves of our salvation. 'The election of God is hidden and
secret in itself, but the Lord manifests it by the calling; that is,
when he does this good to us by calling us. Wherefore men are
being fantastic or fanatical if they look for their salvation or for
the salvation of others in the labyrinth of predestination instead
of keeping to the way of faith which is offered them. . . . To each
one, his faith is a sufficient witness of the eternal predestination
of God, so that it would be a horrible sacrilege to seek higher
assurance; for whoever makes difficulties about subscribing to
the simple testimony of the Holy Spirit does him great dishonour.'[117] Under these conditions, one must draw the line
between speculations arising from an impious curiosity and
legitimate knowledge of the doctrine of predestination. The limit
between these two domains is indicated by the Scriptures, which
give us knowledge of what is useful and salutary for us. So Calvin,
for his own explanations, intends to keep to the data of revelation
alone. 'Let us, then, keep this in view above all other things,
that it is no less insane to crave for other knowledge of predestination besides that which is given us in the word of God,

[117] Commentary on John 6.40, *Opp.*, 47, 147; cf. *Inst.*, III, 21, 1, and Sermon on Ephesians 1.3-4: 'St Paul is speaking there of what we know by
experience. . . . We could not understand all that if we were not enlightened
by the Holy Spirit. How, then, should we understand a thing which is far
higher; that is, know whether God, before the creation of the world, elected
us?' AUGUSTINE, op. cit., 11, M. L., vol. XLV, 1007; *Contra duas epistolas
pelagianorum*, IV, 6, 16, M. L. vol. XLIV, 621.

than if one wanted to walk over inaccessible rocks or to see in darkness.'[118]

Seeing that predestination is taught by the Scriptures, it must be admitted, and not only admitted but preached in public. Is it really as scandalous as its adversaries pretend? Or does it not, on the contrary, share with the principal articles of the Christian faith, such as the Trinity, the creation and the divinity of Christ, the privilege of provoking mockery from 'rebellious minds'? To reject the explanations of predestination on the pretext that they may trouble 'weaker souls' is openly to contradict God 'as though he had happened by inadvertence to publish something that could not but be harmful to the Church'.[119] Certain opponents of predestination have taken account of this; they do not deny it, but strive at least to diminish its scope. 'A good many cover it up with diverse cavillings, above all those that seek to base it upon his foreknowledge.' This was no doubt aimed at Pighius and his *Treatise upon Free Will*; but Pighius was no more than the inheritor of a long tradition which had endeavoured to make predestination dependent upon foreknowledge of merits. Others, however, following in this the opinion of St Augustine in his latest writings, affirmed that the eternal decree of God could not be determined by an external cause such as the future behaviour of each individual, but that since God knew in advance what he would bring about in them, predestination and foreknowledge coincided in fact.[120] That indeed

---

[118] *Inst.*, III, 21, 2. The assertion that the Scripture reveals to us all that we ought to know about predestination was often repeated by Calvin. He defines his attitude in his letter to L. Socin of January 1552: 'Ego certe, si quis alius, semper a paradoxis abhorrui et argutiis minime delector. Sed nihil me unquam impediet, quin profitear ingenue quod ex Dei verbo didici.' (*Opp.*, 14, 230.) Bucer says the same, on the subject of predestination: 'Ubique sane induit se Deus homine, agens nobiscum hominibus, proponit nobis sua de nobis consilia ea ratione, qua nos illa ad salutem nostram maxime percipere possumus. Proinde quae praecipit nobis atqua consulit, ea debemus simpliciter amplecti, nusquam inquirere vel caussam eorum quae iubemur, ultra eas quas Deus ipse verbo suo explicat, vel etiam congruentiam eorum cum aliis, eius factis et dictis.' (*Metaphr. epist. Pauli*, 1536, p. 399.)

[119] *Inst.*, III, 21, 4.

[120] AUGUSTINE, *De dono perseverentiae*, 14: 'Haec est praedestinatio sanctorum, nihil aliud: praescientia scilicet, et praeparatio beneficiorum Dei,

271

was the solution at which both Luther and Bucer had arrived.[121] But Calvin gave forcible emphasis to the distinction between predestination and foreknowledge. 'We say rightly that [God] foresees all things, even as he disposes of them; but it is confusing everything to say that God elects and rejects according to his foresight of this or that. When we attribute foreknowledge to God, we mean that all things have always been and eternally remain under his observation, so that nothing is either future or past to his knowledge: he sees and regards them in the truth, as though they were before his face. We say that this foreknowledge extends throughout the circuit of the world and over all his creatures. We call predestination the eternal decree of God by which he decided what he would do with each man. For he does not create them all in like condition, but ordains some to eternal life, the others to eternal damnation.'[122] The distinction was vital to him, for we find him frequently returning to it even in his sermons, in order to throw into relief the absolutely gratuitous nature of election. Election, like reprobation, is an entirely free act of the divine will. 'If we ask why God takes

---

quibus certissime liberantur, quicunque liberantur'; 18: 'Sine dubio enim praescivit si praedestinavit, sed praedestinasse est hoc praescisse, quodfuerat ipse facturus.' M. L. vol. XLV, 1014 and 1023. Cf. THOM. AQUINAS, *Summa Theol.* I, q. 23, a. 5.

[121] LUTHER, *De servo arbitrio*, W. A. 18, 615 ff.; Commentary on Genesis 26.9, W. A. 43, 457; BUCER, *Metaphr. epist. Pauli*, 1536, p. 355: 'Praescire et praenosse . . . nihil aliud est, quam Deum suos iam antequam sint, animo praesumere, et iam tum tanquam essent, inter suos computare. Nam ut si quis ex turba aliqua hominum quosdam animo notet et designet, quos velit sibi ad rem aliquam peculiariter adhibere, ita Deus ex perdita hominum colluvie praevidet ac praenoscit quos vult, eosque iam tum ab aliis apud se seiungit et in sortem sanctorum cooptat, id est, praedestinat'; p. 360, he expressly approves of the attitude of ST TH. AQUINAS.

[122] *Inst.*, III, 21, 5. When Calvin writes, quoting from LAURENT VALLA, *Inst.*, III, 23, 6, *in fine*: 'But since [God] sees things to come for no other reason than that he has determined that they should come, it is folly to dispute and debate what his prescience is doing, when it is apparent that everything occurs by his ordinance and disposition,' he is not denying that distinction, but on the contrary maintaining the difference of nature between foreknowledge and predestination. Foreknowledge has for its object the decisions of the divine will; predestination is identical with that will.

pity on some, and why he lets go of the others and leaves them, there is no other answer but that it pleased him to do so.'[123] To set up a causal relation between foreknowledge and predestination, whether this foreknowledge was of the merits of man or of the graces that God will grant him—this is only another way of placing the will of God in dependence upon a cause external to the act of the will itself, and therefore of limiting it; whereas by definition it allows of no diminution whatever. And this, Calvin thought, would lead one sooner or later to re-admit human freedom in some roundabout way, and so ruin predestination. It is noteworthy that a similar argument is to be found in Duns Scotus, who had strongly affirmed the absolute independence of the divine will and its priority in relation to faith and to human works, and had concluded that whatever foreknowledge God might have of this faith or of those works, it could in no way determine the entirely free and sovereign decree of election.[124]

It is advisable here to recall that this will of God manifested in the calling addressed to the elect can encounter no obstacle on their part, which is to say that grace is irresistible. Just as sinful man necessarily willed and did evil, by reason of the internal necessity of his condition, so does justified man conform himself to the necessity of his new condition by obeying the divine will and necessarily doing what it orders him to do. 'The Apostle teaches not only that grace to will the good is offered us if we will accept it, but that God makes and forms that will within us, which is to say no other thing than that God by his spirit trains, inclines, moderates our heart, and that he rules it as his own possession.'[125] Following St Augustine, Calvin affirms more explicitly: 'Grace is by no means offered by God only to be rejected or accepted as it may seem good to one; it is that same grace alone which inclines our heart to follow its movement, and produces in it the choice as much as the will; so that all the

---

[123] Sermon on Ephesians 1.3-4. *Opp.*, 51, 259; cf. *Opp.*, 26, 520; 47, 297; 51, 149; 55, 353, etc.

[124] Commentary on the *Sentences*, Book I, dist. 41, 10 and 11; cf. R. SEEBERG, *Dogmengeschichte*, vol. III, p. 655, n. 1.

[125] *Inst.*, II, 3, 10. This is what Bucer said when he claimed that: 'nos tum demum plenam libertatem habebimus quando . . . necessario volumus, quae bonae sunt.' (*Metaphr. epist. Pauli*, p. 360.)

'good works that follow after are fruits of the same.'[126] Assuredly, this is so only to the measure of our sanctification, but the elect soul is none the less incapable of resisting God. He is an instrument of the divine will, although this is not to say that his will is annihilated. On the contrary, regeneration liberates his will, but by making him will what God expects of him.[127]

As we have already noted with regard to the relations between redemption and predestination, for Calvin the latter was founded upon Jesus Christ. As it is in him that the promises of salvation find their guarantee, so it is in him that election is sealed. Doubly so, seeing that the Christ took part in the decree of election in his capacity as second Person of the Holy Trinity, and that he is also the artisan of this election in his capacity as Mediator. Whether we place the accent upon predestination itself, logically conceived as the prior condition of salvation, or—where Calvin usually places it—upon the offer of salvation in Christ, we are brought back to Jesus Christ in either case. That Calvin insists so much upon predestination, is precisely for this reason. It is in the fact that election is founded upon Christ that he finds assurance of the certitude of salvation. Communion with Christ ought to relieve us of all doubt on that point: it is the proof of our election. 'Whoever finds himself in Jesus Christ and is a member of his body by faith, he is assured of his salvation; and when we want to know this, we do not need to go up on high to inquire about something that must now be hidden from us. For behold! God himself comes down to us; he shows us enough in his Son; it is as though he were saying: Here I am, contemplate me, and know that I have adopted you as my children. When we receive this message of salvation which is brought to us by the Gospel, from that we know, and are assured, that God has chosen us.'[128] Thus, then, the believer who is united with Christ

[126] *Inst.*, II, 3, 13. AUGUSTINE, *De correptione et gratia*, II, M. L., vol. XLIV, 917 f. BUCER, op. cit , p. 358: '[Praedestinationem] certam esse et immotam hanc Dei voluntatem de nostra salute, quam avertere nulla creatura potest.'

[127] Cf. P. JACOBS, op. cit., p. 136.

[128] *Congrégation sur l'élection éternelle, Opp.*, 8, 114. Cf. BUCER, *Metaphrases epistolarum Pauli*, p. 359: 'Altera pars huius quaestionis erat, ad quid sit praedestinatio consideranda. . . . Ad nihil sane aliud, quam ut de salute tua certior sis et firmior inhaereas promissionibus Dei.'

has no longer any reason for lengthy speculations about his election; it is certified to him. And here, by the way, we can grasp one of the reasons why Calvin gave so much importance to the union with Christ and the function it fulfils in piety. The practical interest he took in the problem of predestination must have brought him back a good many times to this relation between election and union with Christ; and in the *Institutes* he defines something of his thought upon it:

> Of those whom God has chosen as his children it is not said that he elected them in themselves, but in his Christ, because he could not love them except in him, and could not honour them with his heritage without having first made them participants in him. But if we are elected in Christ we shall find no certitude at all of our election in ourselves; nor even in God the Father if we imagine him alone without his Son. Christ, then, is like a mirror in which we have to contemplate our election. . . . For, since it is he in whom the heavenly Father has proposed to incorporate those whom he has willed from all eternity to be his own, to acknowledge as his children all those whom he recognizes as members of the same, we have testimony strong and evident enough that we are written in the book of life if we communicate with Christ.[129]

But there is something more. Election manifests itself, indeed, by clear and positive signs in the lives of the elect, and more particularly by the calling, and the righteousness which expresses it in concrete reality. 'We teach that the calling of the elect is as a sign and testimony of their election. Similarly, that their justification is another mark and evidence of it, until they come into the glory wherein lies its fulfilment.'[130] The preaching of the Gospel is in itself alone a sign that God has taken pity on us: but the sure sign of our adoption is that 'we take to heart, and

---

[129] *Inst.*, III, 25, 5. Cf. Commentary on Matthew 11.27, *Opp.*, 45, 319: 'Although our salvation has always been hidden in God, Jesus Christ is nevertheless the channel through whom this salvation flows down to us; and we receive it by faith so that it may be firm and well ratified in our hearts.' Add also *Opp.*, 8, 321.

[130] *Inst.*, III, 21, 7; cf. III, 24, 4.

with affection, the doctrine that is preached to us.'[131] The signs never deceive, but faith alone is able to recognize them and draw the conclusions that follow, and notably to ascend from the calling to election. However, in the chapter of the *Institutes* where he is counting the blessings of justification, Calvin seems to be speaking another language, and trying to discern the proof of election in the works that proceed from faith. 'If all the gifts that God has bestowed upon us, when we recall them in memory, are as rays of the light of his countenance, to illuminate our contemplation of the sovereign light of his goodness, all the more surely should the good works he has given us serve thereto, which demonstrate that the Spirit of adoption has been given to us.'[132] This passage is indeed a surprising one. May it not confirm the opinion of those who think they can see in Calvin the germs of the future puritanism? In reality, the author of the *Institutes* admits the testimony of works only under the restrictions required by his theology as a whole, and as signs of a very inferior kind. 'The saints,' he writes, 'well understand that their integrity is not complete but is mixed with many imperfections and relics of the flesh.' So it is necessary to begin with an apprehension of the 'goodness of God, assuring oneself of this by the promises of the Gospel alone. For if they once begin to repute it according to works, nothing could be more uncertain and infirm; since, if works are valued in themselves, they will no less put the man in danger of the wrath of God by their imperfection than bear him witness of man's benevolence by their indifferent purity of intention.'[133] What assures us of our election,

---

[131] Sermon on Ephesians 1.3-4, *Opp.*, 51, 260. BUCER, *Enarrationes in Evangelia*, 1536, p. 579: 'Hanc autem gratuitam adoptionem tum demum sentiunt electi, cum Christum fide agnoverint, spiritu sancto, in quo Deum patrem per Christum invocent, donati.' However, Bucer's view was that each of the elect had hidden within him a 'seed of election' even before he had received the faith. Op. cit., p. 308 f.: 'Semper tamen sentias quoddam in electis semen Dei et veritatis studium, etiam tum, cum veritatem oppugnant, aut certe pugnantem cum illa vitam degunt.' And he invokes in support the example of St Paul before his conversion. Calvin reacted against this notion with some vehemence. *Inst.*, III, 24, 10 and 11.

[132] *Inst.*, III, 14, 18.

[133] *Inst.*, III, 14, 19. Upon this 'practical syllogism', which refers works back to election, cf. NIESEL, op. cit., pp. 164-73.

then, is first, our faith in Christ and our union with him, and secondly, the gifts that God grants in sanctifying us. We know that some disciples of Calvin took a much more affirmative position with regard to the testimony of works, and that for a number of his spiritual successors the abundance and the success of our works provided the manifest proof of our election and our salvation. But this tendency, it must be repeated, is contrary to authentic Calvinist thought.

It was again upon the union with Christ that Calvin relied for the definitive and unloseable character of the salvation conferred by election. He rejected the opinions of those 'who taught that the virtue and firmness of an election depended upon the faith'; the latter could only make the election manifest, but not give it efficacy.[134] 'To have the full firmness and efficacy of election, one must appeal to the Head, by whom the heavenly Father has joined his elect to himself, and has also bound them together in an indissoluble bond. Thus, by the adoption of the posterity of Abraham, God's liberal favour, which he withheld from all others, did indeed appear; but the grace extended to the members of Jesus Christ has quite another pre-eminence of dignity, for, being united with their head, they are never cut off from their salvation.'[135] Whether he is speaking of union with Christ, or of the immutability of the divine will, or of the Church and the promises made to her, Calvin always comes back to this idea that the elect cannot lose salvation whatever they do. Besides, their election includes the gift of perseverance, a free gift, independent of our will or our merits, since the grace of election is irresistible. 'The Spirit of God, being consistent with itself, nourishes and confirms the love of obedience in us.'[136] Calvin

[134] *Inst.*, III, 24, 3-4.

[135] *Inst.*, III, 21, 7. Cf. Sermon on Ephesians 1.4-6, *Opp.*, 51, 282: 'If we are his members and we hold him to be our head, as he allied himself with us, and that there is this holy union which can never be broken while we believe in his Gospel, it is there that we must go in order to be assured of our salvation.

[136] *Inst.*, II, 3, 11; cf. II, 5, 3; III, 24, 6 and 7; Commentary on I Corinthians 1.9 *in fine*, *Opp.*, 49, 313: 'When the Christian looks at himself, he sees only matter for trembling, or rather for despairing; but because he is called into the communion of Christ, he ought to have no thought of self when it is a question of his assurance of salvation, except as a member of Jesus Christ,

was trying to group all these things together when he defined as follows the foundations upon which our salvation rests: 'Firstly, it is founded upon the election of God, and could never fail unless his eternal providence were dispelled. Further, it is confirmed inasmuch as Christ must remain in his wholeness, and will no more suffer his faithful to be taken away from him than allow his members to be torn in pieces. In addition, we are certain that inasmuch as we dwell within the bosom of the Church, the truth dwells in us. Finally, we understand that those promises belong to us, in which it is said that there will be salvation in Sion: God will dwell for ever in Jerusalem and never depart out of the midst of it.'[137] In fact, if we ascribe any reality to predestination, it must indeed be admitted that the decree of election must be able to triumph not only over our initial resistances, but our permanent weaknesses and our liability to fall back into sin and disobedience. God must have the will and the power to apply it, otherwise we should be going back to the idea that the divine will was dependent upon the good will of man. Election has been decided once for all, it can no more be rendered out of date than the divine will can be changed. This had already been laid down by St Augustine in many passages of his anti-Pelagian writings and Bucer, following his lead, was never tired of repeating it.[138] Calvin, as early as the *Institutes* of 1536, was already taking some account of this idea which was afterwards to assume such great importance in his thinking: 'It cannot be,' he then wrote, 'that the true members of the elect people of God should in the end perish or be lost. Their salvation has such sure and firm supports that even if the whole machine of the world broke down, this could not fall. It rests upon the

---

in such sort that he ought to hold all [the Lord's] goods as his own. Thus he will conceive, beyond all doubt, a certain hope of final perseverance, as they say, holding himself to be a member of him who is in no peril of falling.'

[137] *Inst.*, IV, I, 3.

[138] See, for example, AUGUSTINE, *Contra Julianum*, Book v, chap. 4, 14, M. L. vol XLIV, 792; *De correptione et gratia*, 9, 23 and 13, 40, M. L. vol. XLIV 930 and 941. BUCER, *Enarrationes in Evangelia*, 1536, p. 716: 'Docet, omnia a divina electione pendere, eosque quibus semel datum fuerit oves esse, perire nunquam posse.'

election of God, and could change or disappear only with the eternal wisdom.'[139]

And yet the permanence of election is not strictly certain except in so far as the predestination of individuals is concerned. In order to take account of this fact, Calvin was led, especially in the last edition of his work, to distinguish two, or even three, sorts of election. Here he established a very clear difference between the election of the people of Israel in the person of Abraham, the election throughout Abraham's posterity of the truly faithful descendants of Jacob, and finally the election by Christ of 'those single persons to whom God not only offers salvation but also assigns such a certitude of it that its effect cannot be in suspense or doubt'.[140] The election of Israel in Abraham, whether this concerned the entire people or only the descendants of Jacob, is general; the election of the Christian is special. Four years earlier Calvin had already given expression to that idea in a sermon on Deuteronomy 7.7: 'What is spoken of here is the general election of all the people, inasmuch as they were adopted by God. And this is indeed noteworthy. For in calling Abraham, God extended the promise of salvation to all his posterity. He said to Abraham: I will be the God of your descendants after you. That is an election that we call general, of all the people, in so far as God has separated it from the rest of the world, and said that he was retaining it for his heritage and his Church. . . . But there is another, a second election which is stricter, so to speak; which is, namely, that God chooses out of that posterity those whom it pleases him . . . there is nothing contradictory in that. . . . But now, it is a gratuitous election by God, that we have his word purely preached to us, that we have the Gospel and the sacraments. . . . But nevertheless, he still keeps for himself such as he thinks fit, so that people should not put their trust in those outward signs, without faith and without obedience. But above all, when it pleases God to imprint the certitude of his promises in our hearts by his Holy Spirit, now that indeed is a more special adoption, when he assures us that we are of that little number whom he has reserved for himself.'[141] Thanks to this distinction between general election and particular election,

[139] *Opp.*, I, 73; *O.S.*, vol. I, p. 87.   [140] *Inst.*, III, 21, 5-7.
[141] *Opp.*, 26, 521-4.

Calvin thought he could explain how the people of Israel had been the object of an election in the proper meaning of the word, but had lost the benefit of that grace, while the believer who is the object of a special election cannot be deprived of it. It must be confessed that this is a purely verbal explanation; otherwise Calvin would have had to develop the idea that he no more than touched upon when he said, in the *Institutes*, that 'not all are effectually elected with an equal grace',[142] and insist upon the fact that the election of Israel is something very different from election to salvation in Jesus Christ.

The logical counterpart of election is presented by reprobation. Calvin was never content with the statement that God, in his goodness, elected to salvation a certain number of men taken from the mass of sinners; he thought that those who had not been chosen had also been the object of a special decree, that of reprobation. 'Election would be inconsistent,' he wrote, 'if it were not placed in opposition to reprobation. We are told that God separates those he adopts to salvation; it would be too crass a stupidity, then, to say that those who are not elected obtain by mere chance, or acquire by their industry, that which is given from on high to only a few people. Thus, those whom God leaves out of his election he is also reproving, and this for no other reason than that he wills to exclude them from the heritage that he has predestined to his children.'[143] On this particular point Calvin diverges from St Augustine, for whom the elect alone are the object of a special decision which withdraws them from the *massa perditionis*, while the reprobate are simply abandoned by God to the ruin that they have incurred by their sins.[144] The author of the *Institutes*, on the other hand, cannot admit that Christ would be unable to attract the recalcitrant souls to himself and so save them in spite of themselves. Neither could he admit that it was by an effect of natural laws that man was subject to

---

[142] *Inst.*, III, 21, 7.

[143] *Inst.*, III, 23, 1; cf. III, 21, 7. BUCER, *Metaphrases epistolarum Pauli*, 1536, p. 358: 'Atqui scriptura non veretur dicere, Deum tradere quosdam homines in sensum reprobum et agere in perniciem, quid igitur indignum Deo, dicere, etiam statuisse antea ut illos in sensum reprobum traderet et ageret in perniciem?' LUTHER, *De servo arbitrio*, W. A. 18, 712 f.

[144] AUGUSTINE, *De correptione et gratia*, 7, 12, M. L. XLIV, 923.

death: 'The Scripture says loudly and clearly, that all mortal
creatures have been made subject to death in the person of one
man. Since that cannot be attributed to nature, it must clearly
have proceeded from the wonderful counsel of God.'[145] Here we
have to do with an inscrutable secret of the divine judgment.
Reduced to his own resources, man is incapable of either accept-
ing or refusing the message of Christ. The reason why some
accept and others reject it is to be sought only in God, in a
decision of his will which is incomprehensible to us and which
we must not even seek to penetrate. Calvin finds no difficulty in
declaring: 'I confess that this decree ought to appal us.' At least,
that is how it is when we think of it according to human reason.[146]
But in reality that judgment cannot be unjust, because by definition every manifestation of the will of God is the expression of
righteousness itself. And thus, while fully maintaining the incomprehensibility of the decree of reprobation, Calvin is led to affirm
that the reprobate are condemned justly and by their fault.
'Since it is certain that they were not unworthy of being predestined to such an end, it is also certain that the ruin into which
they fall by the predestination of God is just and equitable.
Furthermore, their perdition proceeds from God's predestination
in such a manner that the cause and matter of it will be found
in them. The first man fell because God had judged that to be
expedient. But of why he had so judged, we know nothing. Yet
it is nevertheless certain that he had not done so had he not
seen that this would redound to the glory of his Name. But when
mention is made of the glory of God, let us think also of his
righteousness, for that which deserves praise must necessarily be
equitable. Man stumbles, then, even as God ordained that he
should, but he stumbles on account of his depravity. . . .'[147]
Attempts have sometimes been made to see this reasoning as an
originality on Calvin's part. It is no such thing, and one need

---

[145] *Inst.*, III, 23, 7.
[146] BUCER writes the same, op. cit., p. 359: 'Tum non potest non inhum-
anum iudicare, Deum vel permittere labi, quos solus a lapsu servare potest, et
crudele, poenas sumere de lapsis, qui ope eius destituti non potuerunt non
labi. Proinde iudicium rationis hic penitus reiiciendum est, et fatendum
iudicia Dei esse abyssum multam, esse imperscrutabilia.'
[147] *Inst.*, III, 23, 8.

only recall the parallel passages in Luther and in Bucer to find
that here again, the *Institutes* move along lines that had been
traditional since St Augustine.[148]

Reprobation is required to be just, so that, by the same right
as election, it may manifest the glory of God in the sight of the
faithful precisely by the mystery in which it is veiled; which also
serves to emphasize the omnipotence of the divine will, and not
only its omnipotence but also its mercy. 'The wicked are created
on the day of their perdition. For that does not come to
pass except in so far as God wills to heighten his glory. . . .
We have therefore to be resolved of this, that God had such a
care for our salvation that he did not meanwhile forget himself, but willed that the world should be as a theatre for his
glory.'[149]

Calvin was again drawing inspiration from the author of the
City of God when he explained how the reprobate, right up to the
Day of Judgment, lived side by side with the elect upon earth
and even within the Church. No sure means are at our disposal
which would enable us to discern the reprobate. At the most,
reprobation manifests itself by signs which may authorize us, in a
certain measure, to assume the presence of that eternal decree
of God. Even then, such an inference is possible only in the eyes

[148] AUGUSTINE, *Enchiridion ad Laurentium*, 25, 99, M. L., vol. XL, 278:
'Videt enim . . . universum genus humanum tam iusto iudicio divino . . .
damnatum, ut etiam si nullus inde liberaretur, nemo recte posset Dei vitu-
perare iustitiam'; *De anima*, IV, 11, 16, M. L., vol. XLIV, 533; *De dono perseverantiae*, 8, 16, M. L. XLV, 1002. LUTHER, *De servo arbitrio*, W. A. 18, 785:
'Hic tam lumen naturae quam lumen gratiae dictant culpam esse non miseri
hominis sed iniqui Dei, nec enim aliud iudicare possunt de Deo, qui hominem
impium gratis sine meritis coronat et alium non coronat, sed damnat forte
minus vel saltem non magis impium. At lumen gloriae aliud dictat, et Deum,
cuius modo est iudicium incomprehensibilis iustitiae, tunc ostendet esse
iustissimae et manifestissimae iustitiae.' BUCER, *Metaphr. epist. Pauli*, 1536,
p. 359: 'Fatendum itaque nobis est, Deum iuste exigere a nobis vitam sanctam
et virtutibus omnibus ornatum: iuste etiam quos vult indurare, excaecare et
tradere in sensum reprobum: iuste denique hos damnare et punire: nobis
autem omnem culpam nostrae perditionis adscribendam esse.'

[149] *Opp.*, 8, 293 f.; *Opusc.*, 1431. Cf. BUCER, *Metaphr. epist. Pauli*, p. 359:
'Propter se enim Deus, et in gloriam suam fecit omnia etiam impium ad diem
malum. . . . Et ubique in Scripturis gloria domini finis esse ultionis malorum
praedicatur.'

of faith, and therefore is not within the power of the reprobate themselves. Non-success in the preaching of the Gospel or the fact that it does not touch all men are signs of this sort; others can be found in the absence of sanctification: 'All those who are of the number of the reprobate, as they are instruments made for opprobrium, never cease to provoke the wrath of God by endless crimes, and to confirm by obvious signs the judgment of God that is decreed against them.'[150]   Nevertheless, the reprobate sometimes show signs analogous to those of vocation.[151] 'Experience shows that the reprobate are occasionally touched almost by a like sentiment as the elect, so that in their opinion they ought to be included in the ranks of the faithful. . . . Not that they understand what the virtue of the Spirit is, nor that they knowingly and vividly receive it, nor that they have the true light of faith; but because God, in order to keep them convinced and render them so much the more inexcusable, insinuates himself into their understanding.'[152]   Will not these, only apparently elect, sow confusion in the minds of true believers, who might be shaken in the certitude of their salvation by seeing that some of the reprobate share the signs of election with them?   To this Calvin replies somewhat briefly: 'Although there may be great similarity and affinity between the elect and those of a lapsed and transitory faith, nevertheless the trust of which St Paul speaks, namely, that dares to invoke God heartily as Father, is in full vigour only among the elect.   Wherefore, since God regenerates the elect alone in perpetuity by the incorruptible seed, and never permits the seed he has planted in their hearts to perish, so there is no doubt that he seals in their hearts, in a special fashion, the certitude of his grace.'[153]   Still, it is true that we may have beside us, in the Church itself, reprobates whose real condition is un-known to themselves, and all the more surely unknown to us. But there are cases where no doubt at all seems possible; for example, when we find ourselves in the presence of obstinate heretics, or again, of individuals whose conduct arouses scandal in the Church.   We have to believe, in these cases, that the signs

---

[150] *Inst.*, III, 23, 12; cf. III, 21, 7, *in fine*.   [151] *Inst.*, III, 24, 7.

[152] *Inst.*, III, 2, 11. Cf. AUGUSTINE, *De correptione et gratia*, 9, 20 and 13, 42, M. L., vol. XLIV, 928 and 942.

[153] *Inst.*, III, 2, 11.

of reprobation present unchallengeable evidence; and in fact, the Church must separate itself from these rotten members by excommunicating them. But even then, the disciplinary sentence of the Church in no way forestalls the definitive judgment of God. 'We ought never to expunge the excommunicated from the number of the elect or to despair of them as if they were already lost . . . and the more we perceive pride and obstinacy in them instead of humility, the more ought we to commit them to the hand of God and commend them to his goodness, hoping better for the future than we can see for the present.'[154] This is no more than an application of the principle that the judgments of God are incomprehensible and unfathomable to us, and that it is therefore impossible, in spite of all the 'signs' that may be given, for us at this present time to distinguish the elect from the reprobate. Although Calvin drew the practical consequences from his doctrine of predestination in what concerned the elect, he did not do the same with regard to reprobation. Undoubtedly, the knowledge we have of the latter is not merely theoretical, and striking examples may brutally convince us of its reality. But we have no right to inquire into its effects upon the plane of the Church or in our relations with other men. We have not to make ourselves the executors of the judgments that we may attribute with more or less probability to God. Predestination will be fully revealed to us only in the life beyond.

V. THE LAST THINGS

Book III of the *Institutes* concludes with a chapter upon the 'last resurrection', which is its crowning act, so to speak, designed to show the end that Christ's redemptive work has ever in view. 'I have put off treatment of the resurrection until now, so that the readers may learn, after having received Jesus Christ as the author of their perfect salvation, to raise themselves yet higher and know that he has been clothed with immortality and heavenly glory, in order that the whole body should be conformed to the head.'[155] The point he means to illuminate, then,

[154] *Inst.*, IV, 12, 9; cf. Commentary on Psalm 119.16, *Opp.*, 32, 153 and Commentary on I John 5.16, *Opp.*, 55, 371 ff.
[155] *Inst.*, III, 25, 3.

is how the faithful share in the life of Christ in the world beyond, and are 'conjoined with God'. The majority of the commentators who have studied this aspect of Calvin's theology have drawn attention to the restraint and sobriety he imposed upon himself in this domain, into which he never ventured without precaution or without the support of the Scriptural data.[156] We know too, that the author of the *Institutes* firmly refrained from publishing any commentary upon the Apocalypse and quoted from it only sparingly. This does not mean that he did not attribute a great importance to the future life and to the promises concerning the other world: on the contrary, he regarded meditation upon the latter as an essential element in the Christian life. He often repeats the Augustinian saying that believers are no longer, properly speaking, citizens of this world, that in any case they are only strangers and pilgrims upon earth, and that they ought to live with their eyes directed towards the life to come. Their meditation upon the future life makes them even now, in some measure, partakers in the heavenly life by hope and faith. 'Although the faithful are now like travellers through this world, yet by the trust and assurance that they have, they are moving through the heavens, to maintain themselves at peace in the future heritage as though they guarded it in their bosom.'[157] By its very object, faith is directed towards the beyond and the future, until the day when we shall know them in their reality. It is closely tied to hope and to the promises.[158] 'Faith, in apprehending the love of God, grasps thereby the promises of life present and future. . . . But wherever there is this lively faith, it cannot but bring always with it the hope of eternal salvation, or rather engender and produce it.'[159] Elsewhere too, Calvin identifies hope with perseverance or with constancy of faith.[160] However,

[156] Cf., for example, DOUMERGUE, vol. IV, p. 342; E. EMMEN, *De christologie van Calvijn*, p. 192.

[157] Commentary on Romans, 1.2, *Opp.*, 49, 89.

[158] P. BRUNNER, *Vom Glauben bei Calvin*, pp. 148 ff., has rightly insisted on this relationship between faith, hope and the promises. See also the interesting study by T. F. TORRANCE, *Kingdom and Church*, Edinburgh, 1956, pp. 90 ff.

[159] *Inst.*,'III, 2, 28 and 42.

[160] Commentary on I Corinthians 13.13, *Opp.*, 49, 515; and upon Hebrews 3.6, *Opp.*, 55, 38.

though the object of faith is situated in the life beyond, the believer is living by it now: 'Hope is not a dead thing, it is by no means some light fantasy conceived by us, but it is such an affection of the Holy Spirit that, although we are enclosed in this corruptible body . . . nevertheless God works oppositely by virtue of his Holy Spirit, so that we are still uplifted, and that we march onward, and aspire to this heritage that is prepared for us, never doubting but that we shall attain it, because our Lord Jesus Christ will then appear, and the life that is now hidden from us will be revealed to us.'[161]

The conditions of access to that life beyond are two: the immortality of the soul and the resurrection of the body. It is the second that presents the greater difficulties; this is 'a thing too high to attract human senses to it'.[162] Also we have need, in order to believe in it, of the two aids that the Scripture offers us; namely, the infinite power of God and the example of the Christ, 'who has so fulfilled the course of his mortal life in the nature that he took from us, that, being made immortal, he is a sure pledge for our immortality to come'. That transfiguration of our 'contemptible bodies' which is to take place on the Day of Judgment is 'a miracle which by the excellence of its greatness engulfs all our senses'.[163] It proceeds from the infinite power of God, so that there is no room to seek any other explanation for it. Calvin vigorously combats the opinion of 'those who imagine that the souls will not resume the bodies they are now clothed with, but that quite new ones will be fashioned for them'. To take too low a view of the body is to be in danger of falling into the error of the Manichaeans. Besides, has not God honoured our bodies by dedicating them as temples to himself, by making them members of the Christ, by ordaining that every part of them should be sanctified, and by associating them with the worship that we render him? A theological argument is adduced to strengthen this point of view. Bodily death is the 'accidental' result of sin; the restoration that Christ has obtained for us ought logically to abolish that consequence of the Fall.

As for the soul, since it is immortal we cannot speak of a resurrection of it. But then what becomes of it after death and

[161] Sermon upon Titus 3.4-7, *Opp.*, 54, 586. [162] *Inst.*, III, 25, 3.
[163] *Inst.*, III, 25, 4.

until its reunion with the revivified body at the Judgment Day? In his first theological work, the *Psychopannychia*, Calvin had already undertaken to refute the teaching of certain anabaptists who said that souls went to sleep during this period which preceded their definitive fate, and that meanwhile they were separated from the body. 'Our beatitude,' he wrote then, 'is ever on the way, until that great day which will put an end to every way: seemingly, the glory of the elect and the end of the last hope tend and look to this same day, that they may be accomplished. . . . There is no other perfection nor beatitude nor glory except in the perfect union with God.' The faithful who die before this last day do not sleep: they enter immediately into the Kingdom of God, that Kingdom which has already begun and will then be perfected.[164] He says the same in the *Institutes* of 1559: 'The souls of the faithful, after completing their term of combat and travail, are gathered into rest, where they await with joy the fruition of their promised glory; and thus all things remain in suspense until Jesus Christ appears as the Redeemer.' This rest is not a sleep; it is conscious, and the faithful are sharing in the Kingdom of God; but they will not be able to enter into the final glory until after the Judgment. 'As for the reprobate, there is no doubt but that their condition conforms with what St Jude says about the devils; that they are chained up like malefactors until the time when they are dragged to the punishment that is appointed for them.'[165] The intermediate state, therefore, is a period of waiting, but one that enables us already to foresee the final sentence.

With regard to the Judgment itself, now is the time that we must think about it, and draw the consequences that concern our present life. 'Nothing goads us more sharply than to be shown that we shall one day have to render an account. . . . Wherefore of necessity the announcement of the last judgment must thrill like a trumpet, summoning us to appear before the judgment seat of God. For then it is that we are truly aroused and begin to think of leading a new life.'[166] The day of Judgment will see the Lord's coming again and the separation of the faithful from the reprobate. 'He will descend in visible form even as he

[164] *Opp.*, 5, 211; *Opusc.*, 44 f. [165] *Inst.*, III, 25, 6.
[166] Commentary on Acts 3.20, *Opp.*, 48, 71.

was seen to ascend, and will appear to everyone in the unspeakable majesty of his kingdom, in the light of immortality, with the infinite power of his divinity, in the company of his angels. . . . He will separate the sheep from the goats, the elect from the reprobate, and no one either living or dead will be able to escape his judgment. For from all the ends of the earth will be heard the trumpet by which all men will be called and summoned to his throne, those still living no less than those who will have died before them.'[167] The last Judgment will be immediately preceded by the resurrection of all, both faithful and reprobate. Calvin has some difficulty in resolving a question raised by this general resurrection. 'We know that all were made subject to death in Adam; but since Jesus Christ has come, the resurrection and the life, is this to give life to the whole human race indifferently?' After recalling that 'the good that God does to those unworthy of it turns into a greater condemnation', he makes the resurrection of the body the condition of the judgment itself. 'One ought not to find this strange, that the resurrection should be common to the iniquitous also, by accident, to drag them against their will to the judgment seat of Christ. . . . For it would be but a very light punishment to be ravished by death without appearing before their Judge, from whom they have deserved vengeance without end, ceaseless and without measure, to receive the wages of their rebellion.'[168]

Concerning the fate that awaits the elect and the reprobate after the Judgment, Calvin observes great discretion and is very careful not to go beyond the Scriptural indications. 'Though the Scripture teaches that the Kingdom of God is full of light, joy, felicity and glory, nevertheless all that is said about it is far above

---

[167] *Inst.*, ii, 16, 17. A difficulty may arise from I Corinthians 15.36, concerning those still living at the Judgment day. Calvin skirts round this by saying that 'their mortal life will be abolished in a minute of time and transformed into a new nature' (loc. cit.), or again, that 'this flesh is reduced to nothing, inasmuch as it is now subject to corruption.' (Commentary on I Thessalonians 4.16, *Opp.*, 52, 166 f.) That would be, according to him, 'a kind of death'.

[168] *Inst.*, iii, 25, 9. st augustine had tried to explain the resurrection of the impious by the second death, and the bodily pains that were to be inflicted on them: *Enchiridion*, 23, 92, M. L., vol. xl, 274 f.; *De vera religione*, 27, 50, M. L., vol. xxxiv, 144.

our intelligence, and as though wrapped in imagery until the day shall come when the Saviour will explain himself to us face to face.'[169] The Bible can only use material comparisons which are more or less inadequate and in any case exclude all precision. The most we can infer from its accounts is that, although all the blessed participate in the heavenly glory, they do not do so in the same way or to the same degree. The graces that God grants in unequal measure to his faithful ones, here and now, are like an image of the glorification that awaits them in the life beyond. 'God will make one walk before and another walk behind, but we see that the one will be gifted with a greater excellence than the other, we shall see in one of them a greater perfection and saintliness of life than in the other: just as God works in this world in his faithful, so will he glorify them at the last day: that is why it is said, in particular of those who will have shown the way to others, that they will have a special glory.'[170] Obviously, all the elect cannot expect to be seated on thrones like the Apostles, or to receive a special crown like St Paul.[171]

The destiny of the reprobate is as little known to us in detail as that of the blessed. Here again, the Scripture has to content itself with images. 'Since no description could adequately express the horror of the vengeance of God upon the unbelievers, the torments they have to endure are symbolized to us by corporal things: namely, by darkness, weeping, gnashing of teeth, ever-lasting fire and worms incessantly gnawing at their hearts. For it is certain that the Holy Spirit intended, by such figures of speech, to denote an extreme horror invading all the senses; as when it is said that a profound gehenna is prepared for them from all eternity, which is glowing with fire, that there is always fuel prepared to maintain it and that the Spirit of God is like sulphur to inflame it.'[172] Calvin hesitates, however, to take these expressions literally. He wishes above all to see them as evidence of the misery of man separated from God, and of the terror aroused

---

[169] *Inst.*, III, 25, 10.

[170] Sermon on Daniel 12.2-4, *Opp.*, 42, 142. Calvin repeats, in this con-nection, that these degrees of glory are in no way whatever conditioned by human merits.

[171] *Inst.*, III, 25, 10.   [172] *Inst.*, III, 25, 12.

by the indignation of the celestial Judge. The passages that speak of the pains of the reprobate are not so much precise descriptions of anything as warnings addressed by God to his servants in this world 'in order to arouse them, under the burden of the cross, to make haste, until he shall be all in all'.

CHAPTER FIVE

The External Means

The fourth Book of the *Institutes* of 1559, which deals with the external means or aids employed by the Holy Spirit to put us in communication with Jesus Christ, is altogether centred in the problem of the Church. This is true not only of the first chapters, which endeavour to define the idea of the Church according to Biblical texts and in opposition to the Roman Church and to the negations of the spiritualists, but also of the chapters devoted to the sacraments, and even of the exposition of the theory of civil government which concludes the whole work, for the political ideas that Calvin develops here are envisaged in function with his conception of the Church and in comparison with it. However, any adequate treatment of Calvin's political doctrine, of its relations with the ideas contemporaneous with the reformer and its practicability in application, would raise a whole series of problems only distantly related to theology and would far exceed the scope of the present survey. Here it cannot possibly receive more than incidental treatment.

I. THE CHURCH

The function of the Church is introduced at the beginning of the first chapter, where Calvin states the problem as follows:

Because our crudity and ignorance, and I would add also the vanity of our minds, have need of an external aid by which faith may be engendered in us, grow and advance in us step by step, God has not forgotten to provide this for us, for the support of our infirmity. And in order that the preaching of the Gospel should go on, he has committed this treasure in trust to his Church: he has instituted pastors and teachers through whose mouths he teaches us; in short, he has omitted nothing whatever that might promote a holy agreement in faith and good order among us. Above all, he has instituted the sacraments, which as we know by experience are means more than useful to the nourishment and confirmation of our faith.[1]

The purpose of the Church is to be an instrument to our vocation and to come to the aid of our sanctification. The preaching of the Gospel and the institution of the teaching ministry are intended to awaken the faith and promote the collective sanctification of the members of the ecclesiastical community by establishing between them what Calvin calls 'the consensus of faith'; that is, a unanimous agreement in faith and in outward order. As for the sacraments, their principal function is to maintain the faith of believers and thus contribute to their individual sanctification.[2]

Even as God has had recourse to the means of the incarnation of his Son to re-establish the broken contact with fallen humanity, so must he make use of earthly means in order to proceed to the sanctification of those to whom he has given the gift of faith.

[1] *Inst.*, IV, I, I.

[2] See, upon the question as a whole, DOUMERGUE, op. cit., vol V; L. GOUMAZ, *La Doctrine du Salut*, pp. 312-36; WERNLE, op. cit., pp. 49-67, 355-90, 403 ff.; O. RITSCHL, op. cit., vol. III, pp. 221-9; NIESEL, op. cit., pp. 174-200; TH. WERDEMANN, 'Calvins Lehre von der Kirche in ihrer geschichtlichen Entwicklung' (*Calvinstudien*, pp. 246-338); A. LECERF, 'La Doctrine de l'Eglise dans Calvin' in the *Revue de Théologie et de Philosophie*, Lausanne, 1929, pp. 256-70; K. FRŒHLICH, *Gottesreich, Welt und Kirche bei Calvin*, Munich, 1930, pp. 48-74; P. BARTH, 'Calvins Verständnis der Kirche' (*Zwischen den Zeiten*, 1930); J. COURVOISIER, *La Notion d'Eglise chez Bucer*, pp. 135 ff.; A. GOEHLER, *Calvins Lehre von der Heiligung*, pp. 123 ff.; E. EMMEN, *De Christologie van Calvijn*, pp. 148-91; H. STROHL, 'L'Eglise chez les Réformateurs' in the *Revue d'Hist. et de Philos. religieuses*, 1936, pp. 296-315; W. NIESEL, 'Wesen und Gestalt der Kirche nach Calvin' in *Evangelische Theologie*, Munich, 1936; Munich 1936; J. BOHATEC, 'Calvins Lehre von Staat und Kirche', pp. 267-580; P. J. RICHEL, *Het Kerkbegrip van Calvijn*, Utrecht, 1942.

These earthly and human means consist of the different functions
and offices that have been vested in the Church. They have been
chosen by God as the most appropriate to the accomplishment
of the work of the Christ glorified upon earth; in which sense we
may speak of the Church as of divine institution, not only inasmuch as it is the body of the faithful, but also in its ministries and
the functions assigned to them.

Doubtless, God has no intention of being bound by the means
that he has chosen, and remains entirely free to communicate his
grace otherwise than by the pastors' preaching and the use of
the sacraments. But if God remains free because his will can
never be under constraint, we are no longer so: by the very fact
that the Church has been instituted we are bound to her, and to
the means of sanctification entrusted to her.

> St Paul says that Jesus Christ, in order that all things might
> be fulfilled, made some apostles, others prophets, others
> evangelists and others pastors and teachers for the perfecting
> of the saints and for the work of administration, in order to
> build up the body of Christ until we all should have attained
> to the unity of the faith and of the knowledge of the Son of
> God, to mature manhood, to the measure of the stature of
> the fullness of Christ (Ephesians 4.11-13). We see that God,
> although he could raise his own up to perfection in a moment,
> nevertheless prefers to make them grow little by little under
> the nurture of the Church. We see that the manner of this is
> made known; that is, inasmuch as the preaching is entrusted
> to the pastors: we see how all are under that rule, that they
> allow themselves with a docile and gentle spirit to be
> governed by the pastors created for that purpose. . . . Let it
> be no grievance on our part, then, to receive in all obedience
> the doctrine of salvation that they propose to us at his
> express command. For although his virtue is not attached
> to any external means, yet he has willed to constrain us to this
> common usage, and if one rejects it as some fantastic people
> do, one becomes enmeshed in many mortal ties.[3]

The preaching of the Gospel by the ministers of the Church is
therefore the ordinary means by which the faith is communicated

[3] *Inst.*, IV, 1, 5.

to us. But it is not on that account alone that we ought to have recourse to the Church. We depend upon it for the whole of our spiritual life and all our sanctification. Before this Calvin had already, in effect, declared:

> Because my present intention is to speak of the visible Church, let us learn, if only from her title of mother, how much the knowledge of this same is useful, and indeed necessary; seeing that there is no entering into the life ever-lasting unless we are conceived in the womb of that mother and she gives birth to us, feeds us at her breasts, and finally holds and guards us under her guidance and government until, being stripped of this mortal flesh, we become like the angels. For our weakness does not allow of our being with-drawn from school until we have been pupils for the whole course of our lives. It is also to be noted that outside the bosom of the Church one can hope for no remission of sins nor any salvation.[4]

Throughout this passage Calvin is using for his own purpose the well-known definitions of St Cyprian and St Augustine, and is repeating, in accord with general tradition and with Luther, that the Church is our mother and that apart from her there is no salvation.[5]

But the Church does not present itself only under its visible aspect as the Christian community;[6] it is also the communion of saints, the totality of the elect. In 1536, Calvin had hardly considered it except under this invisible and hidden aspect, and his point of view practically coincided with Luther's.[7] He modified it later during his contact with Bucer, who, though he accepted the Lutheran definition of the Church, took up a very positive attitude towards the visible community. As early as 1539

[4] *Inst.*, IV, 1, 4.

[5] CYPRIAN, *De catholicae ecclesiae unitate*, 6, M. L., vol. IV, 519; *Epist.*, 73, 22, ed. Bayard, vol. II, 275; AUGUSTINE, *Sermons*, M. L., XXXIX, 1512; *De baptismo*, liv. IV, 17, 24, M. L., vol. XLIII, 170; LUTHER, *Great Catechism*, third article of the Creed, at the beginning.

[6] This, however, is the only aspect of the Church taken into account by P. BARTH, *Calvins Verständnis der Kirche*, p. 217, when he writes: 'The Church, for Calvin, is nothing else but the Christian community.'

[7] Cf. H. STROHL, *L'Eglise chez les Réformateurs*, pp. 297 ff.

Calvin had developed this side of his ecclesiological conception, and the influence of Bucer is still more apparent in the edition of 1543. It was at that date, for instance, that he inserted in the *Institutes* the following passage, which has a thoroughly Bucerian resonance:

> [St Paul] is showing that the Church cannot maintain itself in its wholeness but by the help of the means which the Lord has instituted for its preservation: Jesus Christ, he says, ascended into heaven to accomplish and fulfil all things. Now, the means is that he dispenses and distributes his graces to his Church by his servants whom he has appointed to that office, and to whom he has given the ability to discharge it; and he even makes himself present to his Church by them alone, bestowing efficacy upon their ministry by the virtue of his Spirit so that they labour not in vain. So that is how the restoration of the saints comes about, that is how the body of Christ is built up, how we grow altogether into him who is the head, how we are united among ourselves, how we are all brought into the unity of Christ: namely, when prophecy takes place among us, when we receive the apostles, when we do not despise the doctrine which is given to us.[8]

The Church is not an institution situated outside us. We are parts of it: we are its members in the most literal sense. From the fact that we enter into communion with the Christ we form ourselves into a community which rests solely upon the action of Christ in us. That is what St Augustine was already saying in *The City of God*, when he affirmed that all who are animated by the love of God constitute one religious and social community; and Bucer, in his commentaries and his ecclesiological treatises,

---

[8] *Inst.*, IV, 3, 2. Cf. BUCER, *Enarrationes in Evangelia*, 1536, p. 595: 'Hinc itaque est, quod caput huius corporis Christus dat alios Apostolos, alios prophetas, alios Evangelistas, alios doctores et pastores, aliisve spiritus dotibus instructos. Nam quicquid huius donat, ad communem Ecclesiae suae utilitatem donat, ut per assiduam doctrinam et admonitionem sancti instaurentur, et illa, quae corpus suum est, incrementum sumat, donec perveniamus omnes in unitatem fidei et agnitionis ipsius filii Dei, et demum virum adultae aetatis Christi referamus.'

returned again and again with renewed emphasis to the ideas which assimilate the Church to an organism.[9] The Church is the body of Christ; it follows also that Christ alone is master of it and can therefore dispose of it as he pleases.[10]

Just like Bucer, Calvin taught—especially after 1543—that the supreme Church is indeed the invisible one composed of all the elect, living or dead, but that beside this is the Church with which we are directly concerned during our earthly life; that is, the visible Church formed by the grouping of Christians together in one and the same parish.

> We have said [he writes] that Holy Scripture speaks of the Church in two ways: sometimes it means by that word the Church which is such in very truth, no one being included excepting those who by the grace of adoption are children of God, and by the sanctification of his Spirit are true members of Jesus Christ. And then, not only is it speaking of the saints dwelling upon earth, but of all the elect that have been since the beginning of the world. But often, by the name of the Church, it means the whole multitude of men who, scattered over various regions of the world, make the same profession of honouring God in Jesus Christ, have the same baptism as evidence of their faith, who by the partaking of the Supper claim to have unity in doctrine and in charity, who accept the word of God and seek to protect the preaching of it in obedience to the commandment of Jesus Christ. In this Church there are some hypocrites, mingled among the good, who have nothing of Jesus Christ

[9] See, for example, *Enarrationes in Evangelia*, 1536, p. 593 f. 'Voluit arctissimam vitae inter suos societatem esse, ut alii aliorum membra, universi ecclesiam velut corpus unum constituerent,' or again, *De vera animarum cura* (1538), *Scripta Anglicana*, 1577, p. 267: 'Ecclesia Christi est congregatio et societas eorum, qui in Christo Domino nostro, ita e mundo congregati atque consociati sunt, ut sint unum corpus, et singuli aliorum membra; quorum unumquodque suum habet officium et opus ad aedificationem communem totius corporis, omniumque membrorum.' Cf. COURVOISIER, op. cit., p. 98 f.

[10] BUCER, *De vera animarum cura*, p. 272: 'ut in Ecclesia nulla alia quam unica Christi potestas purumque regimen sit et maneat.' This is the idea that Bucer was to develop to his satisfaction in the first part of the *De Regno Christi* of 1551.

but the title and the appearance. . . . However, as it is necessary for us to believe that the Church is invisible to us and known to one God alone, so we are also commanded to hold the visible Church in honour and keep ourselves in communion with it.[11]

The invisible Church which includes all the elect coincides exactly, then, with the body of Christ, which is not the case with the visible Church—that is, in so far as the latter is obliged to receive reprobates into its midst. But though the Church thus presents itself to us under two quite distinct aspects, of which one is an object of faith and the other an object of experience; or, if you will, one of which represents the Church as God sees it, and the other as it appears to us, it does not follow from this that there are two Churches.[12] Calvin knows of only one, distinguished by the fact that it has Jesus Christ at its head and is at his service. This unity of the Church authorizes one to pass a judgment upon the visible Church using the criteria of the Church invisible, it being of course understood that discrimination between the faithful and the hypocrites is beyond our competence. But how is one to recognize that a Church has Jesus Christ for its head and is at his service? It cannot be by the individual quality of its members, seeing that the visible Church becomes no less a Church for tolerating reprobates in its bosom. Just as Luther and Melanchthon did in the *Augsburg Confession* (art. VII and VIII), Calvin admitted two objective criteria for the discernment of a true Church: 'Wherever we see the Word of God purely preached and listened to, and the sacraments administered according to the institution of Christ, we must not doubt that there is a Church.'[13] It is not, therefore, by the quality of its members, which could only give occasion for a subjective judgment, but by the presence of the means of grace instituted by the Christ, that the Church is constituted and can be objectively judged. Calvin was well aware, as Luther and Bucer had been before him, that there could be no question of forming an ideal human community composed of the righteous and the saintly, such as the

[11] *Inst.*, IV, 1, 7. Cf. AUGUSTINE, *De baptismo*, liv. III, 19, 26, M. L., vol. XLIII, 152.

[12] Cf. A. LECERF, op. cit., p. 259. [13] *Inst.*, IV, 1, 9.

Anabaptists desired, for instance.[14] Seeing that we cannot clearly distinguish the righteous from the reprobate and that Christians themselves remain sinners throughout their earthly life, it would be presumptuous and practically impossible for access to the Church to be restricted to the perfect alone. Taking up an idea that he had expressed before, in 1536, Calvin concludes that by a 'charitable judgment' all may properly be held to be members of the Church who, by their faith, their conduct and their participation in the sacraments 'confess one same God and one same Christ with us'.[15] Conversely, we have to constitute the Church by basing ourselves upon our communion with Christ, and manifesting the same outwardly in the preaching of the Gospel and the administration of the sacraments.

But we have seen that the Church must not restrict itself to this; part of its duty is to guide and help its members in their sanctification. If the Church's preaching is not to be in vain and if the sacraments are effectually to confirm the faithful in their faith, the Church will have to practise constant self-examination in order to avoid all error and, in matters concerning its own members, it will have to use some ecclesiastical discipline towards them. The Church cannot exclude all those who are not of the elect, since they cannot possibly be discerned: but neither can it tolerate disorder or scandal, in questions either of doctrine or of its members' behaviour. The discipline that thus makes its appearance in Calvin is but a continuation of the ways opened up by Oecolampadius and Bucer as means of preserving the purity of the Church's teaching and the believers' efforts towards sanctification. But we must take care not to neglect yet another consideration that weighed in favour of discipline. The latter was made necessary, in effect, by the union of the faithful with Christ and his dignity as head of the Church. Whatever might produce disorder in the Church and be a scandal to its members thus reflected upon and affronted the Christ. This was par-

---

[14] BUCER, *Enarrationes in Evangelia*, 1536, p. 323: 'malos opera satanae, quam diu hoc seculum stabit, bonis suis, quorum ipse autor, fore permixtos, sed in fine seculi demum separandos, et in geennam abiiciendos. Hoc terreamus hypocritas, et consolemur nos ad tolerantiam malorum, quia aliter fieri non potest, dum hic vivimus, ferre hypocritas oportet.'

[15] *Inst.*, IV, 1, 8. LUTHER, *Enchiridion piarum precationum*, W. A., 10, 2, p. 394.

ticularly true of the Eucharistic community which implied the closest union with the Christ. Thus it was in respect of the celebration of the Supper that the notion of discipline had been carried as far by the leaders of the Churches of Basle and Strasbourg as it was by Calvin during his first period in Geneva.[16] 'In this our Lord communicates his body to us, so that he is made altogether one with us and we with him,' we read in the *Institutes* of 1543, which contains the most important of the Bucerian contributions. But 'since he has but one body of which he makes us participants, by this participation we too must necessarily be made all together one body. . . . None of the brethren may be despised, or rejected, violated or injured or in any way offended by us, without our similarly wounding, despising or offending Jesus Christ in him and doing him violence by our affront: we cannot have discord or division with our brothers without disagreeing with, and being divided from, Jesus Christ.'[17]

Under these conditions discipline is indispensable if a Church has any desire to preserve its character as the Church of Christ. As early as 1536 Calvin had distinguished three different and complementary aims of discipline. The first concerns the honour of the name of God. To prevent any possibility of Christ being blasphemed even in his Church, the Church should be able to take action against heretics and schismatics who are in open revolt against the Word of God and are putting the Church itself in danger of ruin. The Church must also suppress those who do it injury by their infamous conduct. 'For since the Church is the body of Christ it cannot be contaminated by dissolute members without a part of the shame being cast upon its Head. In order, therefore, that there should be nothing in the Church whereby the name of God might receive any ignominy, those persons must be expelled from it who by shameful conduct defame and dishonour Christianity.'[18] If it is necessary, by means of discipline,

---

[16] BOHATEC, 'Calvins Lehre von Staat und Kirche', p. 339 f, refers to the exchanges of views that took place betwen Calvin and the Strasbourgers in 1537. A. LANG, *Der Evangelienkommentar M. Butzers*, p. 183 f.

[17] *Inst.*, IV, 17, 38.

[18] *Inst.*, IV, 12, 5. It must be noted that here once again Calvin is adding, in 1543, a passage which shows the close relation between the administering

to maintain respect for God and Christ in the bosom of the Church, the other members must also be preserved from evil. That is the second purpose that Calvin assigns to the discipline: 'The second aim is that the good should not be corrupted by the conversation[19] of the bad, as very often happens. For accordingly as we are inclined to err, nothing is easier for us than to follow bad example. The usefulness of this was noted by the Apostle when he commanded the Corinthians to banish from their company one who had committed incest; a little leaven, he says, leavens the whole lump.' The example cited shows that Calvin had in view not only the strictly religious attitude but also the morality of the members of the Church; and this is abundantly proved by the orientation that he .gave to the Genevan Consistory. It is not correct, then, to suppose as some have done in recent times, that 'the ecclesiastical discipline was not intended to promote morality in the bosom of the Church.'[20] However, it of course remains true that, in contrast to the temporal jurisdiction, this discipline did not, in Calvin's mind, have what is properly called a juridical character. It was not purely repressive, nor intended only to safeguard public order. However it may have appeared, it was always a part of the cure of souls, as we can very clearly infer from the third purpose that Calvin ascribes to discipline: 'The third aim is that those who are punished by excommunication, being overcome by shame, may repent, and by such repentance come to amendment. And thus it is expedient for their own salvation that their wickedness should be punished, and that being stirred up by the rod of the Church they may acknowledge their faults.'[21] The function of the discipline was first and foremost to be educational.

One notices, however, that for all the vital importance that

---

of the Supper and the discipline: 'We must also, in this respect, have regard to the Lord's Supper, that it should never be profaned, by giving it indifferently to all. For it is certain that he to whom the dispensing of it is committed, if he admits anyone whom he should and could exclude, is guilty of sacrilege.'

[19] That is to say: by their conduct.

[20] NIESEL, op. cit., p. 189; cf. COURVOISIER, 'La discipline ecclésiastique dans la Genève de Calvin', p. 24.

[21] *Inst.*, IV, 12, 5. BOHATEC, op. cit., p. 551.

Calvin attaches to the ecclesiastical discipline he refrained from making it one of the marks of the true Church. This is a point of some importance upon which he did not follow Bucer. To the two *notae ecclesiae* of the Lutherans (the preaching of the Gospel and the administration of the sacraments), the Strasbourg reformer had finally added the ecclesiastical discipline—an element he regarded as indispensable to any true Church.[22] To Calvin the discipline was no less important, but not of the very essence of the notion of a Church; it was simply a measure of defence and a means of sanctification, and, as such, it belonged to the organization and not to the definition of the Church. Though the Church may remain imperfect as long as it exists upon earth, it must nevertheless labour unremittingly at its own sanctification and at that of each of its members at the same time. To the sanctification of the individual there corresponds, on the plane of the Church, a collective sanctification. The Church is indubitably the body of Christ, but because of the fact that its members are at present sinners, it must be ever striving to become that body of Christ.

> What St Paul says is very true: that Jesus Christ gave himself for the Church in order to sanctify it, and has purged it, washed it in the water of the Word of life, to make it his glorious bride without wrinkle or blemish. But this sentence is no less true, that the Lord is working from day to day to smooth out the wrinkles of the same and remove the stains, whence it follows that its holiness is not yet perfect. The Church is holy, then, in the sense that it is daily improving but not yet perfect, is daily progressing but has not yet arrived at its goal of holiness.[23]

For the organization of the Church, Calvin laid down a certain

---

[22] It was thus that he wrote about the ministry of the true Church in his *De regno Christi, Scripta Anglicana*, p. 36: 'Partes vero huius sacri ministerii, Doctrina Christi, Sacramentorum eius dispensatio, et disciplinae eius administratio.' Cf. G. ANRICH, *Martin Bucer*, p. 126; COURVOISIER, *La Notion d'Eglise chez Bucer*, pp. 65 ff., 125 ff.; STROHL, *L'Eglise chez les Réformateurs*, p. 284.

[23] *Inst.*, IV, I, 17; cf. Commentary on Ephesians 5.27, *Opp.*, 51, 224 f. See GOEHLER, op. cit., p. 125 f. Upon a similar passage of Bucer's, see R. STUPPERICH, 'M. Bucers Anschauungen von der Kirche' in the *Zeitschr. für system. Theologie*, 1940, p. 137.

number of rules in the *Institutes*, especially after the time when he had gained first-hand experience of the problem at Strasbourg and at Geneva. But here too, we find Calvin in close agreement with the views of Bucer, precisely in what was most peculiar to them. Whereas Luther regarded the ecclesiastical organization as dependent upon time and circumstances, both Bucer and Calvin deduced it directly from the lordship of the Christ over the Church and the gifts of the Holy Spirit.[24] Neither the individual nor even the community could intervene in order to modify or dispose of it. Moreover it was prescribed, even to certain details, by the Word of God. We must therefore keep strictly to the indications of Scripture, which were valid not only for the earliest Christian communities but reveal an order by the Holy Spirit which is of permanent validity. Calvin does not, however, advocate any servile imitation of the institutions of the primitive Church, so that he ends by coming to a point of view which, whatever may be generally thought about it, is not so very far from Luther's.[25]

> I do not mean to approve any other constitutions but those founded by the authority of God, and derived from the Scriptures, so that one may call them altogether divine. . . . As for the external disciplines and the ceremonies, he has not chosen to prescribe for us in particular, and as it were word for word, how we must be governed, forasmuch as that depended upon the diversities of the times, and one and the same form would be neither appropriate nor useful to all ages. . . . We have to conclude that these may be changed, new ones instituted, and that the previous ones may be

[24] Upon Luther, see among others J. KOESTLIN, *Luthers Theologie*, vol. II, pp. 274 ff. BUCER expresses his idea that the ecclesiastical organization rests upon an order willed by the Holy Spirit in several of his writings, e.g., in the Strasbourg Ordinance of 1534 (see A. L. RICHTER, *Die evangelischen Kirchenordnungen*, Weimar, 1846, vol. I, p. 233); in the Ziegenhain Ordinance of 1539 (ibid., p. 290) and in the Short Confession of Faith of 1548, *Scripta Anglicana*, p. 177.

[25] J. BOHATEC was one of the first to draw attention to the pliancy of Calvin's attitude in this domain, op. cit., p. 387. At the most he can only be reproached with having over-attenuated the difference which remains, in spite of everything, between Luther and Calvin.

abolished as may be expedient for the utility of the Church.[26]

Although the end of this passage seems in some measure to contradict the statement with which it begins, and to authorize an almost complete liberty, the ecclesiastical organization imagined by Calvin and his disciples is, as we know, distinguished by its fidelity to the Scriptural data, at least in comparison with the other Churches which had freed themselves from that consideration.

The diversity of ministries is founded upon the corresponding diversity of the gifts of the Holy Spirit, and upon the priesthood of all Christians. Calvin took great pains to deduce, from the fragmentary data in the Pauline epistles, a logical classification of the different ecclesiastical functions.[27] But he soon had to make a breach in his principle of the permanent value of the Biblical data. Among the ministries referred to in the New Testament there are in fact several which manifestly have no longer any reason to exist, or are no longer applicable: for example, the apostles, prophets and evangelists. We have also to distinguish between permanent and transitory ministries. However, Calvin never arrived at an absolutely rigid and definitive classification. Generally, as in the ecclesiastical Ordinances of 1541, he distinguished four ministries; those of the pastors, the doctors, the elders and the deacons. But a passage of the *Institutes* of 1543 which was maintained up to and in the last edition makes no mention of more than three ministries.[28] The most important ministries are those of the pastors and doctors, to whom are entrusted the teaching of the doctrine and the explanation of the holy books. Moreover, Calvin sometimes confuses these two ministries in one person, as they were in fact fused together in his own case, in Strasbourg and in Geneva.[29] Everything depends, after all, upon each person's capabilities.

[26] *Inst.*, IV, 10, 30.   [27] *Inst.*, IV, 3, 2-9.

[28] *Inst.*, IV, 4, 1: 'As we have said, that the Scripture tells us of three orders of ministers, so did the ancient Church divide all the ministers that it had into three kinds.' Cf. BOHATEC, op. cit., p. 466. Upon Bucer's influence, see also STROHL, 'Théorie et pratique des quatre ministères à Strasbourg au temps de Calvin' in the *Bull. de la Soc. de l'Hist. du Protest. français*, 1935.

[29] The distinction between pastors and doctors is made a little clearer in the commentary on Ephesians 4.11, *Opp.*, 51, 197 f.

The choice of those entitled to minister has to be made on dual grounds, heavenly and earthly at the same time. For it is the Christ who, by his Spirit, confers the gifts appropriate to each and who, in that sense, makes the initial and real choice. But those concerned have no right to set themselves to work of their own volition: an indispensable condition for being entrusted with any ministry is that we must have been regularly elected by the community,[30] an election which may, however, be reducible to a simple approval of the choice made by the pastors and the Magistracy. It should be noted that, on this point, there was no question in Calvin's mind of anything but a restricted electorate, and this was entirely consonant with his aristocratic tendency. Nor did even this circumscribed election correspond to current notions of an operation of that kind. In effect, the electors' choice was limited by the spiritual gifts of the candidates: 'No one must be elected who is not of sound doctrine and of saintly life.'[31] A properly-conducted church election confined itself, in fact, to ratifying or confirming the prior decision of the Holy Spirit.

Beside the pastors and the doctors Calvin ranges two purely 'lay' ministries (if the expression be allowable, for Calvin even more than Luther effaced all distinction between clergy and laity). These are the elders and the deacons. The principal occupation of the elders was the exercise of discipline in the name of the Church. Given the importance of discipline in Calvin's ecclesiastical system, the elders had a correspondingly important part to play. In 1536 they were not yet mentioned. But Calvin had been able to see 'elders' at work in the Church at Basle, as he did later at Strasbourg. And the example of Basle seems to have been decisive, seeing that from 1537 Calvin included the institution of elders in his Genevan Articles. However, it is only in the *Institutes* of 1543—that is, after his experiences at Strasbourg and after the adoption of the Ordinances in Geneva—that he tried to work out the theory of the presbytery. There is no need to return to this; we may simply note that elders had to be elected by the people, and that they, as well as the pastors, were required to superintend morals and discipline. But the sparse indications to be found in the *Institutes* and the Commentaries reproduce the ambiguities we have already noted in

[30] *Inst.*, IV, 3, 10, 11 and 15.   [31] *Inst.*, IV, 3, 12.

the distinction between pastors and doctors. Sometimes the elders are at the same time pastors and elders in the technical sense; sometimes on the contrary Calvin uses the term to denote the latter only.[32] With regard to the deacons he is more explicit. Named by election, in the same way as the other ministries, they are charged with 'the care of the poor'. Basing his opinion upon I Timothy 5.9-10, Calvin advises 'two kinds of deacons, of which the first are to serve the Church itself by organizing and dispensing the alms of the poor, the second by attending to the sick and the other poor'.[33]

Thanks to these four specialized ministries the Church is equipped to discharge its essential functions: preaching and the administration of the sacraments, the teaching of the doctrine, the maintenance of good order by discipline and the exercise of charity. But by virtue of what principle is the Church to impose its prescriptions upon the members? Here we come to the notion of the spiritual power which, according to Calvin, belongs to the Church even as the temporal power belongs to the State. This spiritual power, he writes, 'consists of three parts; which are, the doctrine, the jurisdiction and the faculty of ordaining laws and statutes'.[34] These three aspects of the spiritual power are complementary and support one another. The special interest that Calvin evidently takes in these is shown by the amplitude of exposition he devoted to them in the *Institutes*; but this must not lead one to think that there was any tendency to revert to the Roman doctrine of the ecclesiastical power. Calvin must have been aware that such an interpretation might occur to the minds of his readers: moreover, he took great care to define his own position in opposition to the Roman teaching.

This was no needless precaution, for Calvin did not shrink from making certain statements of which the meaning was all too easy to travesty. In reality, however, his expositions of the ecclesiastical power, and of the teaching power especially, gave him opportunity for forcible restatements of the principle of the unique authority of the Bible. Indeed, if the doctrinal power of the Church was to be prevented from growing into a tyranny like that of which the Church of Rome had become guilty, it had

[32] DOUMERGUE, op. cit., vol. v, pp. 153 ff.; BOHATE c,p. 464 f.
[33] *Inst.*, IV, 3, 9.   [34] *Inst.*, IV, 8, 1.

C.   *305*   U

to be kept within strict limits. The right to define doctrine must not belong to members of the Church as such, but to the Word of God alone. 'All that the Scripture attributes of dignity or authority, either to the Prophets or Priests of the ancient Law or to the Apostles and their successors, is attributed not to their persons but to the ministry and office to which they are assigned, or, to speak more plainly, to the Word of God which they were called to administer.'[35] The Word of God which the teaching of the Church cannot overrule is that which is written in the Scripture: 'We ought to take nothing in the Church to be the Word of God except what is contained in the Law and the Prophets and then, later, in the writings of the Apostles, and there is no way well and duly to teach in the Church, except to refer every doctrine to this rule.'[36] The Scripture alone is infallible in matters of doctrine; the Church is so only to the extent that it keeps strictly to the Scriptural data. The revelation offered us in the Scriptures is both certain and complete. Nothing that has been added to it, whether by the successors of the Apostles or by the Councils, can therefore presume to any divine authority. 'Such sobriety as God once recommended to his Church he wills that she should observe even to the end. But he has forbidden her to add anything to his Word or to take anything from it. That is an inviolable decree of God and of his Spirit, which our adversaries want to infringe, when they pretend that the Church is ruled by the Holy Spirit without the Word of God.'[37] There is no authority then, any more than there is inspiration, save in the Word of God as we can know it from the Scriptures. 'God takes away from men the ability to forge any new article, so that he alone may be our master and teacher in spiritual doctrine.'[38] The teaching power of the Church will therefore limit itself to formulating and explaining Scriptural doctrine and defending it against its adversaries.

As for the legislative power of the Church, Calvin's views are based upon its sociological reality, and are summed up in the following passage:

[35] *Inst.*, IV, 8, 2. The most complete exposition upon this point is that of BOHATEC, op. cit., pp. 516-29.

[36] *Inst.* IV, 8, 8.   [37] *Inst.*, IV, 8, 13.

[38] *Inst.*, IV, 8, 9.

If we see it to be necessary in all companies of men that there should be some police to keep peace and concord between them, if in all things there must be some order, to preserve a public civility and even humanity among men, then these things ought most of all to be observed in the Churches, which are maintained primarily by good order, and by discord are altogether disintegrated. Wherefore, if we would do our best for the preservation of the Church, we must diligently work so that all is done decently and in good order, even as St Paul commands. But since there are such great contrarieties of mind and of judgment between men, no police could hold together among them if it were not determined by certain laws, and no order could well maintain itself without some certain form. So far from rejecting laws that tend to this end, we indeed assert that, without them, the Churches would incontinently be dissipated and deformed. . . . Nevertheless, we must always take vigilant care in such observances, that they should not be held necessary to salvation, to bind men's consciences; and that the honour and service of God be not supposed to depend upon them, as though true piety resided therein.[39]

It is important, in regard to this passage, to note that there was no question, in Calvin's mind, of a secular legislation intended to regulate the state of the Church, as the Ecclesiastical Ordinances did, but only of ecclesiastical laws properly so called; that is, laws dictated by the Church itself. Doubtless he did not want that legislation to 'bind the conscience' as it did in the case of canon law. It remains no less true that Calvin was the founder of a real Protestant, ecclesiastical law, and was the defender of its autonomy.[40]

On the subject of ecclesiastical jurisdiction, Calvin repeats what he has just said about legislation, namely, that 'as no town nor village can be without a governor and without police, so also the Church of God . . . has need of a certain spiritual police

[39] *Inst.*, IV, 10, 27. Cf. WERNLE, op. cit., pp. 355 ff. BOHATEC, op. cit., pp. 529-39.

[40] This remains true even when we take into account the efforts in the same direction made by Oecolampadius or the theologians of Strasbourg.

which, however, is quite different from an earthly police.'[41] After referring to the Biblical passages which constitute the classic foundation for this jurisdiction by the Church, in particular to Matthew 18.17, he writes: 'But such admonitions and corrections cannot be made without full knowledge of the case. For all that, there must necessarily be some judgment and some order. Thus, if we do not want to break and do away with the promise of the keys, rejecting excommunication as well as remonstrances and all the rest that follows, we must necessarily give some jurisdiction to the Church.' Here Calvin shows much less originality than when he was discussing legislation. Memories of Basle and Strasbourg, and in particular of Bucer's insistent defence of the power of the keys and of an autonomous discipline within the Church, are evidently haunting his mind. He is especially careful to mark the differences that separate this spiritual jurisdiction from temporal jurisdiction: 'The Church has no sword for the punishment of malefactors, no power to constrain them, nor prisons, nor fines, nor any of the punishments that magistrates are accustomed to employ. Moreover, this is not what the Church is for, that whoever sins should be punished against his will, but that, by a voluntary chastisement, he should make profession of his repentance. So there is a great difference, so long as the Church does not attempt to usurp anything that belongs to the Magistracy, and the Magistracy cannot do what is done by the Church.'[42] What differentiates the juridical power of the Church from that of the Magistracy is, therefore, that the Church tries not to exercise a repressive and authoritarian power, but to safeguard good order among its members and perform an educational service in regard to them. But is not this also the end that every Christian magistrate sets before himself, at least in some degree? Calvin comes back again several times to this argument, which had been based on the thought that, under a Christian Magistracy, such an independent ecclesiastical jurisdiction would be unnecessary. Memories of what he had had to put up with from the Genevan Magistracy, when he was seeking to establish the jurisdiction of the Consistory, are present throughout this

[41] *Inst.*, IV, II, I. Cf. BOHATEC, op. cit., pp. 539-63; cf. in the present work, pp. 60-61, 72, ff, 143, 299 ff.

[42] *Inst.*, IV, II, 3.

discussion. Against the adversaries of such a jurisdiction, he loftily affirms that here we are concerned with a commandment of Christ which remains permanently valid. Moreover, the magistrate himself is answerable to the ecclesiastical jurisdiction: 'It very often happens that a magistrate is heedless, or even that he himself deserves to be punished, as in the case of the Emperor Theodosius.'[43] There is no question, however, of the Church's competing with the Magistracy. The two tribunals have separate domains and ought to assist one another. 'As the magistrate, by punishing evil here and now, should be cleansing the Church from scandals, so the minister of the Word, for his part, ought to be helpful to the magistrate by reducing the number of male-factors. That is how their administrations should co-operate, each relieving the other, not hindering it.'

It is clear from this text and a good many others that Calvin thought the two powers, civil and religious, ought to be comple-mentary.[44] Without doubt, the civil magistrate must see to it that the two tables of the Law are respected; but he is to do this in the sphere that is proper to him, just as the Church, for its part, will see that they are observed in the spiritual domain. Thus there was no question, as is so commonly supposed, of a theocratic regime in which the temporal power would be subject to the spiritual power. Calvin not only never succeeded in putting the Genevan Magistracy under the tutelage of the Church; he never even in theory announced the need for such a tutelage, which is precisely what characterizes a genuinely theocratic system. On the other hand he did recommend, and tried to put into practice, a system of close collaboration between the two powers, which committed them to reciprocal aid. The ministers of the Church were obliged by their function to con-tribute to the moral education of the citizens, and to explain to

[43] Ibid.
[44] Upon Calvin's political ideas and conception of the relations between Church and State, see G. BEYERHAUS, *Studien zur Staatsanschauung Calvins*, Berlin, 1910; H. HAUSHERR, *Der Staat in Calvins Gedankenwelt*, Leipzig, 1923; H. BARON, *Calvins Staatsanschauung und das konfessionelle Zeitalter*, Munich, 1924; P. MESNARD, *L'Essor de la philosophie politique au XVIème siècle*, Paris, 1936, pp. 269-308; BOHATEC, op. cit., more especially pp. 597-633; M.-E. CHENEVIÈRE, *La Pensée politique de Calvin*, Geneva, 1938, espec. pp. 243-71. This last study constitutes a useful summary and brings many texts together.

the members of the Magistracy the requirements of the Word of God, to which the civil legislation had to conform itself. The Magistrates, on their side, were in duty bound to protect the Church and promote respect for the open preaching of the Gospel. The theory of the relations between Church and State that Calvin elaborated is therefore as remote from the teaching of Zwingli, which led to confusion between Church and State, as it is incompatible with that submission of the Churches to the State to which things had come in Germany. On the other hand it comes sensibly nearer to Luther's personal ideas, and to the conceptions worked out by Bucer.

In his expositions upon the Church, Calvin developed above all his notion of the visible Church, and more especially that of a Church limited to one country or to a given territory. When speaking of the Church, what he has principally in view are Churches such as those of Geneva, Basle, Berne and Strasbourg, or else the different Churches that finally grouped themselves into the Church of France. This is not to say that the local Churches, taken as a whole, lie outside his horizon. On the contrary, he was much preoccupied with the unity of the visible Church. This unity existed between all the Churches that based themselves upon the pure Gospel, whatever differences there might be among them concerning customs, ceremonies and organization. Even divergencies of doctrine should not necessarily break this unity. One remembers that just after his first ministry in Geneva he had done his best to keep his own partisans within the communion of his previous Church in spite of the errors it had fallen into.[45] And when the Archbishop of Canterbury wrote to him proposing a meeting of the principal leaders of Protestantism in Europe, he replied: 'Would to God that we might have learned and serious men, taken from the principal Churches, come together to discuss the articles of faith and to hand down to those who will follow us the certain teaching of the Scriptures, as it is common to all. It must be counted among the worst evils of our epoch that the Churches are thus separated one from another, so much so that hardly any human society exists among us, still less that holy communion between the members

---

[45] Cf. letters to Pignée of 5th January, and to the Church of Geneva of 25th June 1539, *Opp.*, 10b, 309 f. and 351 ff.

of Christ which all profess but very few sincerely cultivate in reality.'[46] This initiative came to nothing, in spite of Calvin's warm endorsement.

The same concern for unity led him to combat the schisms that were rending the body of Christ. 'We ought not,' he wrote in the *Institutes*, 'to reject any assembly which entertains [the pure ministry of the Word and the pure manner of administering the sacraments] even though it be defective in several ways. What is more, there may be some defect either in the doctrine or in the manner of administering of the sacraments, which ought not in any way to alienate us from the communion of a Church. For not all the articles of the doctrine of God are of one and the same kind. The knowledge of some of them is so necessary that no one may doubt them, any more than the decrees or principles of Christianity: as, for example, that Jesus Christ is God and Son of God; that our redemption depends upon his mercy alone; and others like them. But there are others again that are in dispute between the Churches, without, however, disrupting their union.'[47] If Calvin was able to present himself as a champion of Church unity, it was by virtue of this doctrine of fundamental beliefs, which bears some analogy to Melanchthon's theory of the *adiaphora*. In this his Christocentric emphasis found opportunity to express itself anew and with a peculiar cogency; as when he wrote, for instance, that 'the fundamental doctrine, on which it is never allowable to compromise, is that we should learn Christ, for Christ is the one single foundation of the Church.'[48] The Churches, then, must never break their unity in dissensions over the inessential. Nor may the members of a Church, on their own account, separate themselves individually: 'Inasmuch as God wills that we should preserve the communion of his Church, by conversing in the company of the Church such as we see it among us, whoever separates himself from it is in great danger of withdrawing himself from the communion of the saints.'

[46] Letter to Cranmer, end of April 1552, *Opp.*, 14, 312 ff.

[47] *Inst.*, IV, I, 12.

[48] Commentary on I Corinthians 3.11. *Opp.*, 49, 354. Cf. DOUMERGUE, op. cit., vol. V, p. 28; H. CLAVIER, *Etudes sur le Calvinisme*, pp. 52 ff.

II. THE SACRAMENTS

At the head of the chapter on the general doctrine of the sacraments, Calvin declares that the sacraments are 'another aid, near
and similar to the preaching of the Gospel, to the sustaining and
confirming of the faith'.[49] Thus from the beginning the Gopels
and the sacraments are treated in parallel, which does not mean,
however, that Calvin puts them on the same plane. On the
contrary, throughout his teaching he insisted upon the secondary
and supplementary character of the sacraments, whereas the
Gospel could be sufficient of itself in case of need, and ought
normally to be so, were it not for our weakness which makes us
dependent upon cruder kinds of assistance.

He then gives two definitions of the sacraments in succession:

I think this definition will be right and simple, if we say
that the sacrament is an outward sign by which God seals
upon our consciences the promises of his good will towards
us, to confirm our feeble faith, and we give mutual testimony
before him and the angels no less than before men, that we
hold him to be God. One can still more briefly define what
a sacrament is, by saying that it is a testimony of the grace
of God towards us, confirmed by an external sign, with
mutual attestation of the honour we bear him. Whichever
of these two definitions one may choose, its meaning will
be in accord with what is said by St Augustine, that a sacrament is a visible sign of a sacred thing, or a visible form of
the invisible grace.[50]

[49] *Inst.*, IV, 14, 1. Cf. DOUMERGUE, op. cit., vol. v, pp. 320-7; GOUMAZ,
op. cit., pp. 337-46; WERNLE op. cit., pp. 85-93; NIESEL, op. cit., pp. 201-17.
Among special studies we retain J. BECKMANN, *Vom Sakrament bei Calvin*,
Tubingen, 1928, pp. 28-83; J. DE SAUSSURE, 'La notion réformée des sacraments' in the *Bull. de la Soc. de l'Hist. du Protest. français*, 1935, vol. LXXXIV,
pp. 243-65; A. LECERF, 'L'Election et le sacrement', in *De l'élection éternelle
de Dieu*, pp. 252-62; W. F. DANKBAAR, *De sacramentsleer van Calvijn*, Amsterdam,
1941 (a work distinguished by its qualities of method); R. S. WALLACE,
Calvin's Doctrine of the Word and the Sacrament, Edinburgh, 1953, conveniently
groups the principal texts relating to the subject.

[50] *Inst.*, IV, 14, 1. AUGUSTINE, *De Catechizandis rudibus*, 26, 50, M. L., vol.
XL, 34; *Epist.* 105, 3, 12, M. L. vol. XXXIII, 401.

Calvin has no hesitation here in avowing his dependence upon St Augustine, and the Augustinian imprint on his work is not limited to the sacramental definitions: it appears everywhere, and is indeed so obvious that the attempt has been made to derive the whole of Calvinist teaching from St Augustine's formulations.[51] Strong objections could be raised against that thesis, but it remains true enough that here as in other parts of his theology Calvin borrowed extensively from St Augustine, for whose formulas and expressions he is known to have shown an obvious predilection, although he sometimes gave them different meanings.[52] Luther on the one hand and Bucer on the other contributed to the formation of the Calvinist themes, and their interpretations of the Augustinian texts certainly guided Calvin towards the line that he took—a line which, in spite of such evident influences and perhaps because of their very diversity, was by no means without originality.

The existence of the sacraments depended, in his view, upon a prevenient divine promise; for the sacrament was no more than a confirmation of the promise, to give us additional faith in it. The sacrament, therefore, adds nothing to the promise as such, but is only a means of making us believe in it.[53] 'For our faith is so small and weakly that if it be not propped up on all

[51] In his monograph on Calvin's sacramental teaching, J. BECKMANN even went so far as to write in his conclusion, p. 163 f.: 'This doctrine of Calvin's is of a clearly Augustinian type . . . identifiable with what is most profound in Augustine's latest conceptions. This he has understood better than it could have understood itself. He has truly developed the Augustinian teaching upon the sacraments in its purity, clarifying it from all its Catholic fermentations.' This is a case of trying to prove too much and so proving nothing. To claim that Calvin understood Augustine better than the latter understood himself can mean only one thing—that Calvin's conception of the sacraments was different from Augustine's. And to talk about the purity of Augustinian doctrine when 'catholic fermentations' are extracted from it is to make oneself fair game for ridicule; it reminds one of the effort of certain sixteenth-century authors who wanted to make St Augustine a defender in advance of the *Augsburg Confession*.

[52] DANKBAAR, op. cit., pp. 225-40, has accurately pointed out the principal points of contact between Calvin's teaching and that of St Augustine, as well as those upon which they diverge.

[53] Upon this connection between sacrament and promise, cf. the commentary on Acts 7.8, *Opp.*, 48, 135: 'Only let us note this, that God promises

sides and sustained by every means it may suddenly become shaken to the depths, upset and irresolute. And forasmuch as we are so ignorant, so given up to earthly and carnal things and fixed upon them, so that we can neither think, understand nor conceive of anything spiritual, the merciful Lord accommodates himself in this to the crudity of our senses, so that by these same earthly elements he leads us to himself, and enables us even in the flesh, as in a mirror, to contemplate his spiritual gifts.'[54] The parallelism between the Scripture and the sacraments makes itself felt upon this point also: we have only to recall the numerous passages in Calvin's exegesis where he believes he can disclose proofs in the Biblical texts of the divine transcendence, coming to the aid of our incapacity by using figures and images.

He goes on to declare that 'the sacrament consists of the Word and the external sign'. Like Luther, of whose *De Captivitate Babylonica Ecclesiae* he makes much use, and whose conception of the sacrament he so largely shares, he shows that the Word has to be explained to the people, 'to teach us and make us know what the visible sign means'.[55] 'So when mention is made of the sacramental words, let us understand thereby the promise, which should be preached loudly and clearly by the minister, to lead the people whither the sign points.'

The usefulness and the nature of the sacraments being thus summarily defined, Calvin joins issue both with those who claim that 'the sacraments give us no evidence of the grace of God' and those 'who attribute to the sacraments I know not what secret virtues'—that is, against the Zwinglians and against the Roman Catholics. Summing up the view of the former, he makes

---

beforehand to Abraham the things which he afterwards confirms by the circumcision, in order that we may know that, unless the Word precedes them, the signs are vain and useless.' See GOUMAZ, op. cit., p. 339.

[54] *Inst.*, IV, 14, 3. BUCER, *Enarrationes in Evangelia*, 1536, p. 40: 'Ad haec cum Deus hoc ingenio nos condidit, ut promissiones et rerum invisibilium exhibitiones, sensibilibus signis factae, graviores sint ac plus moveant, visum est domino, et in promissione atque exhibitione redemptionis nostrae uti signis suis, quibus animos nostros in contemplationem bonitatis suae amplius attollat, fidemque in se pleniorem nobis reddat.' LECERF, op. cit., p. 261.

[55] *Inst.*, IV, 14, 4. Cf. LUTHER, *De Captivitate Babylonica*, W. A., 6, 516 ff. See also the Latin text of art. 24 of the *Augsburg Confession*.

them say that 'if our faith is good, it cannot make itself better; for it is not faith at all unless it leans and relies upon the mercy of God so firmly that it cannot be removed or distracted from it.'[56] To this Calvin replies that our faith remains ever imperfect, as is proved by the consciousness that we have of our sin. He also refutes the opinion that if we admit that the sacraments can confirm faith 'we do wrong to the Spirit of God' or show disrespect to the divine honour. Was it not God himself who instituted the sacraments? It is he who 'spiritually feeds and nourishes faith by the sacraments, which have no other purpose but to present his promises before our eyes, and even to be our surety for them.'[57] He finally rejects the argument that Zwingli had derived from the meaning of the word *sacramentum* in the ancient authors, by showing that the Christian writers gave a new meaning to the word 'by which they simply meant to designate sacred signs'.[58]

In opposition to the scholastic teaching about the sacraments, which affirmed that 'the sacraments of the New Law . . . justify and confer grace if we do not interpose some obstacle or hindrance of mortal sin,' Calvin declares that this is a pernicious and 'wholly diabolical' opinion;[59] 'for in so far as it promises righteousness without faith it throws consciences into confusion and damnation'. To this he opposes the thesis of the reformers: 'He who would have the sign with the thing, and not void of its truth, must apprehend by faith the Word which is there enclosed.'[60]

The conclusion to which Calvin comes at the end of this discussion is worth quoting:

[56] *Inst.*, IV, 14, 7. ZWINGLI, *De vera et falsa religione* (*Corp. Reform.*, vol. XC, p. 761).

[57] *Inst.*, IV, 14, 12.

[58] *Inst.*, IV, 14, 13. ZWINGLI, *De vera et falsa religione*, p. 758.

[59] *Inst.*, IV, 14, 14. LUTHER, *De Captivitate Babylonica*, W. A., 6, 533: 'Ita nec verum esse potest, sacramentis inesse vim efficacem iustificationis seu esse ea signa efficatia gratiae. Haec enim omnia dicuntur in iacturam fidei ex ignorantia promissionis divinae, nisi hoc modo efficatia dixeris, quod, si assit fides indubitata, certissime et efficacissime gratiam conferant.' Cf. R. SEEBERG, *Dogmengeschichte*, vol. III, p. 517.

[60] *Inst.*, IV, 14, 15. The scholastics required, however, at the very least, faith in the content of the sacrament.

God therefore accomplishes what he promises in the symbols and the signs are not without their effect in showing, so far as need be, that the author of them is true and faithful: but it is important to know whether God is at work by his intrinsic virtue, as they say, or whether he is resigning his office to the exterior signs. But I am resolved upon this, that whatever instruments he may make use of, it does not derogate in any way whatever from his own sovereign virtue. When any doctrine of the sacraments is given, their dignity is made clear enough, their use demonstrated and their usefulness recommended. Nevertheless a wise moderation is observed in all and everywhere, not to put more upon them than we ought, nor to take away anything that pertains to them. Meanwhile, that false imagination is abolished, which would keep the power to justify us and the graces of the Holy Spirit shut up in the sacraments as though they were vessels; and what has been omitted by the others is clearly expressed: namely, that they are instruments through which God works as he pleases.[61]

With whatever insistence Calvin underlines the usefulness of the sacraments, considered as instruments that the Spirit of God makes use of in order to reach us and bring us to Christ, still, the deepest requirements of his theology, which necessitate the rejection of any subordination of the divinity to earthly contingencies, compel him to exclude any essential union between the sacramental elements and grace.[62]

It should be noted, on the other hand, that the need for faith in the use of the sacraments takes on a peculiar emphasis in Calvin, because of the singular importance he attaches to predestination. Since the elect alone are able to receive faith, the efficacy of the sacrament is closely dependent upon election.[63]

[61] *Inst.*, IV, 14, 17.

[62] *Consensus Tigurinus*, art. 15, *Opp.*, 7, 740; *Opusc.*, 1701: 'All these claims of the sacraments need to be put on a lower level, so that no part of our salvation, however small, should ever be removed from him who is the author of it all, to be given to creatures or to the elements.'

[63] Ibid., art. 16: 'We teach that God does not exert his power indifferently in all those who receive the sacraments but only in his elect. And as he illuminates none but those whom he has already ordained to life eternal, so,

Calvin then goes on to speak of the relations between the sacraments of the Old Covenant and those of the New, and arrives at this conclusion, which could have been foreseen from his account of the relations between the Old and the New Testaments:

> Since the sacraments are like seals with which the promises of God are sealed, and it is certain that God has made no promise to man except in Jesus Christ, it follows of necessity that for our instruction and admonition in the promises of God, the sacraments must show us Jesus Christ. . . . There is only one difference between these old and new sacraments: that the former prefigured the promised Christ while we were yet expecting his coming, and our new ones testify and teach that he has already been given and made manifest.[64]

From the beginning Calvin retained no more than the two sacraments of Baptism and the Eucharist, believing that they alone are attested in the Scripture and 'clearly present Jesus Christ to us'. 'For baptism bears witness that we are purged and washed, and the Supper of the Eucharist that we are redeemed. By the water ablution is symbolized to us, and by the blood, retribution. Both these things are found in Jesus Christ, who, as St John says, came by water and by blood (I John 5.6)—that is, to purge and to redeem.'[65] For Calvin, therefore, the two sacraments sum up the work of the Christ, representing as they do the remission of sins and the redemption. In the passage that follows he briefly describes the part played by the Holy Spirit in the sacraments: 'The witness for this is the Spirit of God, or rather three together bear witness of it: the water, the blood and the Spirit. In the water and the blood, we have the evidence of our purgation and redemption; and the Holy Spirit, who is the chief witness,

---

by the hidden power of his Spirit does he give them enjoyment of the truth of that which is offered in the sacraments.' Unbelievers receive only the outward sign; cf. KOLFHAUS, *Christusgemeinschaft*, pp. 120 f.

[64] *Inst.*, IV, 14, 20. LUTHER, *De Captivitate Babylonica*, W. A., 6, 532. Cf. above, pp. 210 f.

[65] *Inst.*, IV, 14, 22.

certainly commends this evidence to us, makes us believe, hear and recognize it, for otherwise we could not understand it.' As in the case of the Word, so also with the sacraments, the Spirit intervenes to make us accept them, and to discover Jesus Christ in them. Furthermore, by means of the sacraments he initiates and deepens the union with Christ which is given us at the same time as faith: '[The sacraments] are aids and means to our incorporation in Jesus Christ, or, if we are already of his body, to confirm us therein more and more until he unites us wholly with himself in the life of heaven.'[66] And, turning to his own account of St Augustine's allegorical interpretation of John 19.34, Calvin writes: 'This high mystery was indeed shown to us when from the sacred side of Jesus Christ hanging on the cross there came forth blood and water: the side which, for that reason, was very well said by St Augustine to be the source and spring from whence our sacraments issued.'[67]

III. BAPTISM

The chapter on baptism, important parts of which date back to 1536, begins in a somewhat scholastic manner:

> Baptism is the mark of our Christianity, and the sign with which we are received into the company of the Church, so that being incorporated in Christ we may be reputed of the number of the children of God. But it was given us by God primarily to strengthen our faith in him; secondly, to serve as our confession before men, which, as I have already said, is common to all the sacraments. We will deal with these two ends and causes of its institution in due order. As for the first, baptism brings three things into our faith, and with each of these too, we shall have to treat separately. Firstly . . . etc.[68]

[66] *Defensio sanae et orthodoxae doctrinae de sacramentis*, *Opp.*, 9, 17; *Opusc.* 1705.

[67] *Inst.*, IV, 14, 22; cf. AUGUSTINE, *In Iohannem tract.*, 120, 2, M. L., vol. XXXV, 1953.

[68] *Inst.*, IV, 15, 1. DOUMERGUE, op. cit., vol. v, pp. 329-42; WERNLE, op. cit., pp. 93-105; J. M. USTERI, 'Calvins Sacraments und Tauflehre' in *Theologische Studien und Kritiken*, Gotha, 1884, pp. 417-56; BECKMANN, *Vom Sakrament bei Calvin*, pp. 84-102; DANKBAAR, *De sacramentsleer van Calvijn*, pp. 94-110.

And here Calvin combines the Lutheran and Zwinglian notions of baptism, as Bucer had done before him in his *Evangelical Commentary* and his treatise on infant baptism.[69] But though he never fails to recall that baptism is a profession of Christianity, what is of most importance to him, as it is to Luther, is to draw attention to the religious content of the sacrament of initiation.

Baptism appears to him first of all as the sign of the remission of sins: 'Those who have dared to write that baptism is nothing but a mark and sign, by which we profess our religion before men, as a man-at-arms puts on the uniform of his prince to show whom he serves, have not considered the principal thing about baptism—that is, that we have to take it with this promise, that all those who believe and are baptized will be saved.'[70] But in his customary manner, he immediately follows up this demonstration against what we might call the 'Left', with a warning against the extreme 'Right'. The power to purify us does not reside in the water of baptism itself, but in the very blood of Christ. 'We could find no better argument to refute the error of those who ascribe everything to the water, than by a reminder of what is the meaning of baptism, which withdraws us no less from the visible element that meets the eye than from all means of acquiring salvation, to make us rely wholly upon Jesus Christ.'[71] This corresponds fairly closely to the position taken up by Luther in his great Reformation writings. But it is probable that by insisting as he did upon the spiritual aspect of the sacrament and its foundation in Christ, Calvin wanted to raise his voice against not only the Roman theory but also some Protestant interpretations which ascribed to the consecrated elements a value too objective for his liking—such as Luther himself had put forward in his later writings, and his disciples had emphasized.[72]

On the other hand, Calvin again comes nearer to Luther in

---

[69] *Quid de baptismate infantium sentiendum*, Strasbourg, 1533.

[70] *Inst.*, IV, 15, 1. Cf. ZWINGLI, *De peccato originale declaratio* (*Corp. Reform.*, vol. XCII, p. 392). The fact that Calvin alludes to this opinion confirms the hypothesis that he knew this work; see above, p. 145, n. 31.

[71] *Inst.*, IV, 15, 2.

[72] LUTHER, *Shorter Catechism*: 'Baptismus non est simpliciter aqua, sed quae sit divino mandato inclusa et verbo Dei comprehensa.'

giving a permanent value to baptism. He is taking inspiration from the *De Captivitate Babylonica* when he writes:

> We ought not to think that baptism is given us only for time past, so that for the sins into which we fall after baptism we have to look for another remedy. I know that this error crept in in ancient times because some people did not want to be baptized until the end of their lives and at the hour of their death, so that they could obtain plenary forgiveness for their whole life—a foolish fantasy which is often revived by the bishops in their writings. But it must be known that whenever we may be baptized we are washed and purged once for all the time of our life. However, whenever we may fall again into sin, we must return again in memory to the baptism and thereby confirm ourselves in this same faith, that we are always certain and assured of the remission of our sins.[73]

But if he concludes from this that baptism and repentance are closely related, he none the less underlines—again like Luther—that the mercy of God is offered only to repentant sinners; and 'those who, on the contrary, expecting impunity, are seeking and taking herein reason and freedom to sin, are but provoking against themselves the wrath and the judgment of God.'[74]

But baptism is not only an ablution signifying the forgiveness of sins. Its second religious significance resides in the fact that 'it shows us our mortification in Jesus Christ, and also our new life in Him.'[75] In support of this, Calvin adduces Romans 6.3 and 4, of which he gives an explanation that strives to delve deeper and establish a connection with what he had been saying before about our union with Christ. '[St Paul] does not exhort us simply to an imitation (of Christ), as if he were saying that we are admonished by baptism so that, in some likeness and example of the death of Jesus Christ we might die to our concupiscences and by the example of his resurrection be revived in righteousness: he takes a much higher line, namely that Jesus Christ by baptism has made us partakers in his death, in order that we might be engrafted thereto.'[76]

[73] *Inst.*, IV, 15, 3. LUTHER, *De Captivitate Babylonica*, W. A., 6, 528.
[74] Ibid. [75] LUTHER, op. cit., p. 534. [76] *Inst.*, IV, 15, 5.

Thence we come to the third benefit that baptism confers upon our faith, which is that 'we are so united with Christ that he makes us sharers in all his goods.'[77] Here Calvin seems to be making union with Christ dependent upon reception of baptism, whereas almost everywhere else he says that this union is given at the same time as faith, and independently of the sacrament, which, on the contrary, presupposes the existence of faith and therefore of union with Christ. However that may be, the Christ is shown to be the true end of baptism, ' for everything that is held out at baptism concerning the gifts of God is found in Christ alone.'

Here Calvin interrupts his exposition, in order to affirm the identity of the baptism of John the Baptist with the baptism of Christ, in opposition to the Anabaptists who drew a distinction between the two baptisms on the basis of Matthew 3.11.[78] He rejects the arguments of St John Chrysostom and of St Augustine which tended in the same direction, and aligns himself with the exegesis of Bucer, who thought that since John the Baptist had confessed that the Christ was the Lamb of God, the apostles could have added nothing to his baptism. As we would expect, Calvin follows this up with a search for images of Christian baptism in the Old Testament, which once more enables him to assure his readers of the identity between the faith of the 'early Fathers' and our own.

He then attacks the Catholic doctrine of baptism, in so far as it claims 'that by baptism we are loosed and liberated from original sin and the corruption that is inherited from Adam by all his posterity, and that we are restored to an original righteousness and purity of nature, the same that Adam would have had

[77] *Inst.*, IV, 15, 6.
[78] Cf. BUCER, *Enarrationes in Evangelia*, 1536, p. 45: 'Neque enim audiendos puto, qui adeo alium Ioannis, et alium nostrum baptismum faciunt, ut exhibita remissio peccatorum baptismate Ioannis, oblata non sit. Baptizando Ioannes gratiam Christi offerebat, et Christi scholae consecrabat, idem fecerunt et discipuli, neque aliud nobis faciendum incumbit'; p. 46: 'Satis constat idem esse nostrum atque Ioannis baptismum. Quem cum ille instituerit, divinitus in hoc missus, ut sicut primus Evangelii praedicator extitit, primus Christi praeco, ita primus signi eius, quo Evangelii auditores insignirentur et Christo insererentur, usum inveheret: quid quaeso est, cur vel alium baptismum habere nos, vel per alium usum eius coepisse fingamus.'

if he had remained always in the integrity in which he had first been created.'[79] But then, what difference is there, after all, between this and the conception that Calvin has been expounding all along? It is not difficult for him to reply, however, that this would be a misunderstanding of the nature of original sin, original righteousness and the grace of baptism. Our whole nature is corrupted by original sin and by that fact 'it is hateful and abominable to God.' But baptism gives to the faithful the certitude 'that this damnation is taken away and driven out of them, since . . . our Saviour promises us, by this sign, that we have full and complete remission of sins, of the guilt that should be imputed to us no less than of the punishment which, for that guilt, we were to bear and suffer. And they also receive righteousness, but such as the people of God can receive in this life; that is, by imputation only, in that our Lord, of his mercy, regards them as just and innocent.'[80] In other words, baptism does not restore us to the state of integrity which was enjoyed by Adam, but it assures us that God has remitted our sin and the punishment which would normally have had to follow from it, and that he looks upon us as righteous by imputing the righteousness of Christ to us. The doctrine of baptism is thus logically connected with that of justification.

After having thus explained the properly religious content of baptism, Calvin turns to the second object for which this sacrament was instituted: that it might also serve as a confession towards men. This second aspect of baptism was, as we know, the only one that Zwingli had admitted. 'It is a mark and sign,' writes Calvin, 'by which we profess that we wish to be numbered with the people of God, by which we testify that we consent and agree to the service of one God alone, and of one religion with all Christians; by which, lastly, we publicly declare and avow what our faith is.'[81] The purpose of this public confession of the Christian faith is to promote the glory of God.

Finally, the *Institutes* discusses at some length the use that we ought to make of baptism, and undertakes to refute, upon this point, the principal theses of the Anabaptists. The Anabaptists repudiated the baptism that they had received at the hands of Roman Catholic priests, on the ground that the latter were

[79] *Inst.*, IV, 15, 10. [80] Ibid. [81] *Inst.*, IV, 15, 13.

322

unworthy and unable to confer true baptism. Calvin replies that what matters is that we should have been baptized in Christ, and that notwithstanding any errors or unworthiness in him who administers baptism the divine promise is fulfilled towards us. Incidentally, he denies that St Paul re-baptized the disciples who had already received the baptism of John the Baptist and are mentioned in Acts 19.3-5: 'the visible graces of the Holy Spirit were given by the laying on of hands, which graces are often enough called baptism in the Scriptures.'[82] This passage gives us a striking example of how adventurous Calvin's exegesis could be when he was using it in the service of his dogmatic preconceptions. To him, as to the other reformers, the anabaptists' arguments presented puzzles enough for all the ingenuity he could bring to bear upon them.

Still, this last was a small matter compared with the difficulties he had to surmount when he undertook, still against the Anabaptists, to defend infant baptism. Having taken up a position from which it was impossible to appeal to church tradition, he was obliged, at any cost, to find a scriptural warrant for this custom. 'It is said,' he acknowledges, 'that the baptism of little children is founded upon a decree of the Church, rather than upon any express commandment of Scripture. It would be a very poor and unlucky resource if, in defence of the baptism of little children, we were obliged to have recourse to the pure and simple authority of the Church; but it will appear . . . that this is not so.'[83] He was not, of course, the first to set himself to this task: Zwingli and Bucer had done so before him and had encountered the same difficulties. Luther, for his part, had taken up the defence of infant baptism, but he had invoked dogmatic rather than Biblical argument for it. He had sometimes, in fact, attributed an objective value to the sacrament, a value that would make it independent of the beneficiary's faith, but sometimes—and more often—had said it was not at all inconceivable that infants had faith (latent faith, of course), which would not manifest itself until later when they had attained a sufficient

[82] *Inst.*, IV, 15, 18.

[83] *Inst.*, IV, 8, 16. For further details, one may consult J.-D. BENOIT, 'Calvin et le baptême des enfants' in the *Revue d'Histoire et de Philosophie religieuses*, 1937, pp. 357-473; DANKBAAR, op. cit., pp. 110-27.

intellectual development. In some of his writings Luther had even admitted, though without insisting upon it, the argument that has been traditional since St Augustine, according to which the faith of the parents or godparents came to the aid of the children's faith.[84] Calvin had at first aligned himself with Luther's opinion that children are endowed with a faith of their own. He emphasized the necessity of faith for salvation, and children too, if they were to be saved, must have the faith; that was an absolutely general requirement from which children could not be excepted. 'This must not be understood as if I had said that their faith had always existed, from the mother's womb, whereas God calls adults themselves sometimes later and sometimes sooner; I am only affirming that all the elect of God enter by faith into eternal life, whatever the age at which they are taken out of this prison of corruption.'[85] But Calvin seems to have been not too sure of the validity of this argument, for he immediately adds that in baptizing infants we are obeying the will of God, who wished that they should be suffered to come unto him (Matthew 19.14).

The continual attacks from the Anabaptists, the discussions that Calvin had with them in Geneva and then at Strasbourg, and finally a more attentive reading of Bucer's writings, led Calvin to modify his exposition considerably, in and after the edition of 1539. He endeavours first of all to prove that infant baptism is of divine institution. In the New Testament there is certainly no proof of this as an external rite, but the outward observance has not the importance that people often want to attribute to it. 'The right understanding of the signs and sacraments that the Lord has left and recommended to his Church does not lie in their outwardness nor the external ceremony alone, but depends chiefly upon the promises and spiritual

---

[84] AUGUSTINE, *De Genesi ad litteram*, 14, 25, M. L. XXXIV, 418 f. LUTHER, *De Captivitate Babylonica*, W. A. 6, 538: 'Hoc dico, quod omnes dicunt, fide aliena parvulis succurri, illorum, qui offerunt eos; . . . ita per orationem Ecclesiae offerentis et credentis . . . et parvulus fide infusa mutatur, mundatur et renovatur'; *Greater Catechism*, 4th part, 53: 'Accedente aquae verbo baptismus rectus habendus est, etiam non accedente fide . . . (Baptismus) non fidei nostrae, sed verbo Dei alligatus est.' cf. W.A., 26, 154.

[85] *Opp.*, 1, 118; *O.S.*, 1, p. 136.

mysteries that our Lord wishes to represent by such ceremonies.
. . . There is no question of any insistence upon the water and
what is done outwardly; what is needed is to lift up our thoughts
to the promises of God which are given us in these things.'[86]

Already before this, in the chapter on the likenesses between
the Old and the New Testaments, Calvin had claimed that the
Chosen People knew the sacraments that we also have. He makes
use of this argument now, to draw a far-reaching parallel between
circumcision and baptism, as his predecessors had done, Bucer in
particular with his *Treatise on Infant Baptism*, 'When our Lord
ordained circumcision to Abraham, he prefaced it by saying that
he would be the God of Abraham and of his seed, declaring that
he was all-powerful, and held all things in his hand and would
be the plenitude and fountain of all goodness to him: under
which words we are to understand the promise of the life eternal.'[87]
Calvin goes on to demonstrate that God then promised Abraham
forgiveness of sins and instituted circumcision as 'a sign and
image of mortification'.[88] Christ is the foundation of baptism,
'and of the circumcision also'. Baptism and circumcision therefore convey the same promises: the differences belong solely to
'the outward ceremony'.[89] But he goes farther: 'It is certain
that the covenant that was once made by the Lord with Abraham,
saying that he would be his God and the God of his seed, applies
no less to Christians today than it did then to the Jewish people,
and that this saying is addressed to Christians today no less than
it was then addressed to the Fathers of the Old Testament.
Otherwise, it would follow that the advent of Jesus Christ would
have curtailed and diminished the mercy of God.'[90] The children

[86] *Inst.*, IV, 16, 2.

[87] *Inst.*, IV, 16, 3. BUCER, *Quid de baptismate sentiendum*, fo. 6a. 'Feodus vero
erat promissio, qua Deus promittebat Abrahae, se futurum illi et emini eius
Deum, hoc est, servatorem ac vitae aeternae largitorem'; *Metaphrases epist.
Pauli*, 1536, p. 154: 'Cuinam obscurum sit, circuncisionem ad hoc divinitus
institutam fuisse, ut Deus ea totius naturae nostrae ad imaginem suam et
participatum vitae aeternae innovationem polliceret, afferet et exhiberet?'

[88] BUCER, ibid., p. 296: 'Vates hanc promissionem, ut Dominus sit Deus
noster, per Christum contingere praedicant, continereque in se remissionem
peccatorum plenissimam.'

[89] *Inst.*, IV, 16, 4.

[90] *Inst.*, IV, 16, 6. BUCER, *Quid de baptismate sentiendum*, fo. 14a: 'Necesse est,

of the Jews who benefited from the old Covenant cannot be at an advantage compared to the children of the Christians. Quite the reverse: 'Our Lord Jesus, wishing to show that he had come rather to augment and multiply than to restrain the graces of his Father, benignantly receives and embraces the children who are presented to him.' But then, Calvin wonders, 'What similitude has this embrace of Jesus with baptism?' That was the objection commonly raised by the Anabaptists; and this is how he answered it: 'If it was a reasonable thing to bring the children to Jesus Christ, why should it not be allowable to receive them in baptisms which is the outward sign by which Jesus Christ makes known the communion and society that we have with him? If the Kingdom of Heaven belongs to them, why should they be denied the sign by which we are introduced, as it were, into the Church and declared to be heirs to the Kingdom of God?'[91]

Throughout this reasoning Calvin is following Bucer's line of argument. A detailed comparison of his chapter on infant baptism with the writings of the Strasbourg reformer would certainly show us in action just how Calvin used the work of his predecessors, and the degree to which he gave it the added imprint of his own mind. Most probably, too, it was in reliance upon the patristic evidences adduced by Bucer that Calvin felt able to write: 'We have no ancient history right back to the primitive Church which does not bear witness that even in those days the baptism of infants was in use.'[92]

After rapidly indicating the advantages that parents and chil-

cum Dominus baptizare iussit, qui in Evangelii doctrinam recipiunt, hoc est, omnium promissionum Abrahae facere participes, voluisse ut et horum infantes in foedus suum tingerentur. Nam nisi hoc voluit, non est gentibus tum baptismate collatum, quantum Iudaeis olim circumcisione, quod est impium dicere.'

[91] *Inst.*, IV, 16, 7. BUCER, ibid., fo. 10a: 'Accepit puerulos in ulnas, impositisque manibus benedixit, Quid vero obsecro haec erat benedictio? Quid pro illis oratio? Quid aliud tandem? quam redemptionis, quam humano generi perficiebat, communicatio, sine qua nihil non est noxium? nihil non maledictioni subiectum?'

[92] *Inst.*, IV, 16, 8. BUCER, op. cit., fo. 22 b f.: 'Sancti Patres ... non solum a baptismate infantes nunquam reiecerunt, sed etiam commendatam ab Apostolis hanc observationem diserte confirmant.'

dren derive from infant baptism, he proceeds to refute the leading arguments advanced by the Anabaptists. Here the question of children's faith makes a notable reappearance. 'How could this be, say the Anabaptists, seeing that faith comes by hearing, as St Paul says, and infants have no discernment of good and evil? But they do not see that St Paul is speaking only of the ordinary way in which the Saviour works to give faith to his own; not that he is unable to work otherwise, as in fact he has done in many whom, without ever making them hear a word, he has touched interiorly in order to draw them to the knowledge of his name.'[93] God therefore acts secretly in children, without our knowing how. 'It is a thing most uncertain and far from sure, to assert that the Lord cannot manifest himself in them some way.'[94] Calvin no longer speaks as in 1536 about the faith of children. To adversaries who asserted that baptism is a sacrament of repentance and faith, things that one could hardly find in a little child, he replies: 'That objection is resolved in one word, if we say that they are baptized for their future faith and penitence, whereof, although we see none in appearance, nevertheless the seed is here implanted by the hidden working of the Holy Spirit.'[95]

Yet although baptism is useful, indeed necessary, and though it has been recommended by Christ, Calvin does not go so far as to say that salvation is impossible without it. 'Our Lord,' he writes, 'says that whosoever believes in the Son has the life everlasting and will not come into damnation, but has already passed from death into life. Nowhere does he condemn those who have not been baptized. We do not mean to say this in any disparagement of baptism as though it could be neglected; we only want to show that it is not so wholly necessary but that a man might be excused for not having received it, if there had been some legitimate hindrance.'[96] The sacrament is only one instrument at the service of the Holy Spirit, who is not bound to use it, and who may effect our union with Christ without the baptismal rite. In common with almost the entire tradition Calvin also rejects

---

[93] *Inst.*, IV, 16, 19.   [94] *Inst.*, IV, 16, 18.   [95] *Inst.*, IV, 16, 20.
[96] *Inst.*, IV, 16, 26; Sermon on Daniel 9.19-20, *Opp.*, 41, 577. Cf. J.-D. BENOIT, op. cit., p. 468 f.

St Augustine's opinion that children who died without baptism were destined to hell, or at least to limbo.[97]

In conclusion, Calvin mentions one last argument which, in his opinion, tells in favour of infant baptism: that this custom enables us to perpetuate the Covenant we have with God. 'When the heavenly Father visibly testifies to us by the sign of baptism, that for love of us he wishes to take care of our posterity and be the God of our children, have we not good cause to rejoice after the example of David, at the thought of God's taking up the position of a good Father of a family towards us, extending his providence not only over us, but over our own after our death. In which rejoicing God is singularly glorified.' If we lost sight of this divine intention 'there would follow not only ingratitude and disregard for the mercy of God towards us, but neglect of the instruction of our children in the fear and discipline of his Law and in knowledge of the Gospel.'[98]

This last argument has in itself more value than all those that Calvin had been trying to extract from texts of Scripture. Since it was not possible for him to adduce a single New Testament passage containing a clear allusion to infant baptism, he had to be content with indirect inferences and analogies drawn from circumcision and Christ's blessing of the children. Calvin has been much reproached for the weakness of this reasoning, in such contrast to the more rigorous exegetical methods he usually employed, at least in dealing with the text of the New Testament: and he himself seems to have been aware of the defects of his exegesis upon this point. He was debarred, however, from using any other, from the moment when he undertook to defend on scriptural grounds an institution of later date than the New Testament writings, and to justify an ecclesiastical tradition after having proclaimed that all tradition, to be valid, must be based upon certain scriptural proof. By his having allowed for a degree of independence in the domain of external discipline and in ceremonies Calvin had, moreover, pointed to a way in which we may regret that he did not go farther.[99] For that would have enabled him to come to the conclusion that infant baptism was useful to the Church and for the piety of the faithful, while

[97] AUGUSTINE, *Contra Julianum*, IV, 11, 44, M. L. vol. XLIV, p. 809.
[98] *Inst.*, IV, 16, 32. [99] *Inst.*, IV, 10, 30.

frankly acknowledging that one cannot find an acceptable basis
for it in the Scriptures.

IV. THE LORD'S SUPPER

In everything concerning baptism Calvin limited himself, in a
general way, to harmonizing as well as he could the ideas and
the reasoning that he had found in St Augustine, in Luther and
in Bucer, the last of whom had reproduced Zwingli's argument
in all essentials, at least in so far as the main problem was how to
refute the Anabaptists. But when we pass on from the examination
of the Calvinist doctrine of baptism and begin to study his
conception of the Eucharist, we are soon struck by signs of a far
more determined effort to set up an original doctrine.[100] Not
that we forget how largely, upon this point also, he also borrowed
from the Fathers of the Church and from the reformers who had
preceded him: but the divergencies of their views, and in particular the quarrel that opposed the Lutherans to the Zwinglians,
made him want to elaborate a doctrine which, while it took full
account of these contentious opinions, would provide common
ground between the different Protestant interpretations. Bucer
before him had been haunted by the same desire, although his
efforts had amounted to little more than purely verbal recon-
ciliations and he had ended by adopting the Lutheran thesis
except upon a few points of detail. Calvin, who had never been
directly—or even very much—under Zwingli's influence, had
on the other hand closely studied the writings of Luther and
Bucer that were accessible to him, and it was from these that he
set out to construct something new. Moreover, he accentuated

[100] Studies of Calvin's Eucharistic teaching are particularly numerous and
of very unequal value. Let us name among the most important: WERNLE,
op. cit., pp. 105-14, R. SEEBERG, *Dogmengeschichte*, vol. IV, 2, pp. 605 ff.;
EBRARD, *Das Dogma vom Abendmahl und seine Geschichte*, vol. II, Frankfort, 1846;
J. BECKMANN, *Vom Sakrament bei Calvin*, pp. 103-62; E. EMMEN, *De christologie
van Calvijn*, pp. 170-85; H. GOLLWITZER, *Coena Domini*, Munich, 1937;
A. BOUVIER, *Henri Bullinger*, pp. 110-63; E. BIZER, *Studien zur Geschichte des
Abendmahlsstreits im 16. Jahrhundert*, Gütersloh, 1940. Specially indicated are the
very complete expositions of W. NIESEL, *Calvins Lehre vom Abendmahl*, 2nd edn.
Munich, 1935, and of W. F. DANKBAAR, *De Sakramentsleer van Calvijn*, which is
closely followed in the survey that ensues here.

his own system more and more after he had become aware that it was acceptable neither to Lutherans nor to orthodox Zwinglians. As we know, he ended by coming to an understanding with Bullinger on the question of the Eucharist, but this was at the price of repeated concessions on the one side and the other, so much so that it is unsafe to take the *Consensus Tigurinus* which embodied this agreement, as a basis for an objective study of the real Calvinist teaching. With the Lutherans, on the other hand, Calvin was unable to avoid a rupture which his polemics with Westphal rendered irreparable. And for all that, upon this point as upon everything to do with baptism, Calvin remained always much closer to Luther than to Zwingli.

The theological importance of the discussion between Calvin and the defenders of Lutheran orthodoxy has been often—and mistakenly—underestimated. For it was only by this quarrel that Calvin was brought to clarify his own position and give it its definitive character.

The increasing importance that Calvin himself attached to the question of the Lord's Supper can moreover be measured by the greater and greater space allotted to it in the successive editions of the *Institutes*. In 1536, what he was chiefly concerned about was to refute the Roman doctrine of the Eucharist; the few pages he then devoted to this polemic were destined to undergo successive amplifications until, in 1559, a whole chapter of Book IV was given up to exposure of the Roman errors. In this anti-Roman controversy, as in the positive exposition of the Supper, the edition of 1536 demonstrates above all the predominant influence of Luther. Calvin reveals himself here as an attentive reader of several Lutheran writings, in the first place of the *De captivitate Babylonica Ecclesiae*.[101] For instance, we find the Lord's Supper defined here as a testament and as a covenant, and we find the Lutheran explanations of the parts played by the promise and by faith.[102] From Luther's *Sermon upon the true and sacred body of the Christ* of 1519, which had appeared in Latin in 1524, Calvin borrowed his ideas upon union with Christ, and

[101] Cf. upon Calvin's borrowings, NIESEL, op. cit., pp. 23 ff.; H. GRASS, pp. 172 ff.

[102] *Opp.*, 1, 118 f.; *O.S.*, 1, 136 ff.; LUTHER, *De Captivitate Babylonica*, W. A., 6, 513 ff. and 517.

upon the unity of the Christians represented by bread which is
made up of a multitude of seeds.[103] Another Lutheran writing,
the sermon upon *Confession and the Sacrament* of 1524, which
appeared in Latin in the same year, and of which fragments are
to be found in the *Enchiridion piarum precationum*, was also laid
under contribution.[104] But Calvin knew hardly anything of
Luther's doctrine of the Eucharist except from sermons or
treatises dating back to the beginning of the German reformer's
career. Most of the writings composed by the latter during his
polemic with Zwingli were written in German and had not been
translated, doubtless because the most zealous translators of
Lutheran works had leanings towards the Zwinglian point of
view. This accounts for the peculiar character of the 'Lutheranism' in Calvin's *Institutes* of 1536, and also for the ease with which
he was able to borrow Lutheran ideas.

However, from 1536 onwards he had ceased to be a follower of
Luther upon at least one point of his teaching; that is, upon the
notion of the ubiquity of the body of Christ. On the contrary he
expressly refuted this idea at a time when he may not have been
aware that Luther had adopted it.[105] Indeed, in a passage which
he had meant to include in the preface to his *Commentary upon the
Epistle to the Romans*, Calvin had said that his polemic was aimed
at the scholastics and not at Luther. This passage, however,
written in 1539, at a moment when his conversations with Bucer
had given him a better grasp of the Lutheran point of view, did
not appear in the preface it had been written for; Melanchthon
persuaded the author against it, in order to avoid a quarrel with
Luther; but it was not therefore lost, for Calvin used it in the
Institutes of 1543.[106] In 1539, then, Calvin was evidently careful
to avoid any sort of conflict with the theologians of Wittenberg.
Otherwise, and apart from this question of the ubiquity,
the *Institutes* in its original form and even in its second
edition of 1539 shows a dependence upon Luther that is clear
enough.

[103] *Opp.*, 1, 119 and 126; *O.S.*, 1, 140-2. LUTHER, *De sacramento eucharistiae
contio dignissima*, W. A., 2, 743 ff., 748 f.
[104] See the passages collected in NIESEL, op. cit., p. 24, n. 10.
[105] *Opp.*, 1, 121 ff.; *O.S.*, 1, 140-2. Cf. NIESEL, op. cit., pp. 25-8.
[106] The references will be found in NIESEL, op. cit., p. 26, n. 22.

Besides the latter, it was Augustine and Bucer who contributed most to the formation of the Calvinist doctrine. With regard to Augustine, his influence on this point is but one aspect of his more general influence throughout the Calvinist doctrine of the sacraments. And as for Bucer's contribution, it can hardly surprise us: many examples of it could be cited. Thus the parallel that is drawn between the receiving of the elements and the nourishment of the soul by the body of Christ is already to be found in Bucer's *Evangelical Commentary*, expressed in terms very close to those employed by Calvin. The latter wrote in 1536: 'The corporal things presented to us in the sacraments ought to lead us to spiritual things by way of analogy. Thus when we see that the bread is presented to us as the sign of the body of Christ, we should at once recall this similitude: that just as bread nourishes, sustains and strengthens the life of our body, even so is the body of Christ the nourishment and protection of our spiritual life.'[107] And Bucer, for his part, declares in his *Commentary* that 'while offering the bread, he says, 'Take, eat, this is my body that is given for you,' meaning, Just as I give you this bread to eat by the corporeal mouth, so I give my body to your soul to eat. . . . Just as you eat with your mouth and take down into your stomach this bread that you have received from me, in order thus to sustain your life . . . , so ought you to believe from the depth of your soul that my body is given for you, so that your faith in God should be nourished and strengthened.'[108] Let us remember, on the other hand, that in 1537, during the Synod of Berne, Calvin wrote out a confession of faith in the Eucharist which reproduced all the essential features of Bucer's teaching and that Bucer did not hesitate to endorse.[109]

But though Calvin thus found in Luther, and still more in Bucer, a conception of the Supper with which he could sym-

[107] *Opp.*, I, 119; *O.S.*, I, 138.

[108] BUCER, *Enarrationes in Evangelia*, 2nd edn, Marburg, 1530, *In Evangelium Matthaei*, fo. 189a, quoted by A. LANG, *Der Evangelienkommentar*, p. 435. The passage in question was not included in the edn of 1536.

[109] Cf. above p. 139; we cannot adopt the opinion of H. GRASS, op. cit., pp. 175 ff.; who says that this text was imposed upon Bucer and thinks he can admit that Calvin had been hostile to the Concord of Wittenberg, whereas in fact his reservations applied only to the ambiguity he found in Bucer's attitude and in some of his formulations.

pathize, the same cannot be said of him in regard to Zwingli.[110] In the *Second Defence against Westphal* he gave one of the reasons for his hostility towards the Zurich reformer: 'I read in Luther that Oecolampadius and Zwingli had allowed nothing to remain of the sacraments but bare and empty figures (symbols); I was so set against their works, I confess, that for a long while I abstained from reading them.'[111] Perhaps we ought not to take such a remark too literally, especially since the *Institutes* of 1536 presuppose a knowledge of the *De vera et falsa religione* and perhaps of some other writings. But Calvin certainly had a poor knowledge of Zwingli's works, and was altogether ignorant of the latest of them which might have given him a more favourable opinion of Zwingli's sacramental doctrine. In a letter of May 19th, 1539, Calvin expresses satisfaction that Bucer had retracted his errors concerning the sacraments[112] and his regrets that Zwingli had not done the same; for, he says, 'his opinion on this point was false and pernicious.'[113] The people of Zurich long continued to reproach Calvin for this purely negative attitude, notably during a discussion which took place in Berne in 1555; he tried to justify himself for this in a letter to Bullinger, and went as far as to say in a rather curiously casual manner, that he 'did not remember having said, in a general sense, that Zwingli's opinion on the sacraments was false'.[114]

Be that as it may, Calvin had such a poor opinion of Zwingli that, during the time that he was writing the first two or three editions of his work, he took good care to avoid even the slightest direct borrowing from him. Although some have nevertheless thought they could detect expressions or phrases that remind one of Zwingli, it is to Bucer or even to St Augustine that the author was really indebted for these. On the other hand there is no lack of passages in which he is expressly refuting Zwinglian opinions. For instance: the author of the *De vera et falsa religione* had maintained that faith alone should be of importance to the Christian, and that the sacrament can give nothing more to anyone who possesses faith, for otherwise we should have to admit

---

[110] NIESEL, op. cit., pp. 30 ff.   [111] *Opp.*, 9, 51.

[112] He was therefore approving Bucer's reconsidered attitude, which was clearly Lutheran in tendency.

[113] *Opp.*, 10b, 346.   [114] *Opp.*, 15, 573.

that the Holy Spirit is tied down to the earthly elements.[115] Against this, Calvin avers that faith is indeed the work of the Holy Spirit, but that it is not without an object: it is directed to the Word and the sacraments.[116] Just as, in order to grasp the revelation contained in Scripture, we must have the interior witness of the Spirit, so does the Spirit make use of the sacraments to give us knowledge of Jesus Christ. They are of divine institution and we have no right to reject the means that God has chosen for our salvation. The sacraments, like the Word, are founded upon revelation and not upon arguments from human reason.[117] Besides, as we have had to note several times, Calvin denies that faith is perfect of itself; it is unstable and changeable, otherwise man would not continue to be a sinner as long as he lives on earth. But it is precisely because faith remains imperfect that man has need of sacraments, and in particular of the Eucharist. Again in 1559, Calvin said that Zwingli's conception was mistaken in its presentation of the sacraments simply as a testimony of faith.[118]

In his efforts to give the sacrament an objective content Calvin was, on the other hand, in opposition to all those who would allow nothing more than a purely spiritual communion with the spirit of Christ. It was not only with the spirit of Christ that the Christian had to enter into a relationship, but also with his body and his blood.[119] This idea, which is strongly emphasized in the *Confession on the Eucharist* of 1537, is also to be found in other writings of Calvin, and shows the persistence of his attachment to a conception of the Supper which would preserve all its reality. And yet it was precisely the spiritualistic attitude for which Westphal thought Calvin was to blame, when he accused him of emptying the sacrament of its real content and, notwithstanding all his protestations, of ascribing no more real value to it than Zwingli had done.

In the *Institutes* of 1559, which, here again, present the definitive phase of Calvin's thought, the developments upon the Supper

[115] ZWINGLI, *De vera et falsa religione* (*Corp. Reform.* vol. XC, 760 f.).
[116] *Opp.*, I, 118; *O.S.*, I, 137; cf. above, p. 000.
[117] NIESEL, op. cit., p. 39. [118] *Inst.*, IV, 17, 6.
[119] NIESEL, op. cit., p. 39.

But its instability cannot make predestined salvation unstable?

begin with an affirmation in which the authentically Lutheran accent is undeniable:

> When God has once received us into his family, not only to have us as servants but to maintain us at the status of his children so as to perform all that is befitting to a good Father who takes care of his posterity, thenceforward he takes charge of us, sustains and feeds us for the whole of our life. But further, not content with this, he has given us a pledge to certify this liberality towards us, which continues for ever. And that is why he has given to his Church, and by his Son's own hand, this second sacrament: namely, the spiritual banquet by which Jesus Christ testifies to us that he is the life-giving bread by which our souls are nourished and fed for an immortality of blessedness.[120]

In his analysis of the distinctive features of the Supper, Calvin distinguishes, as in every sacrament, the visible signs from the spiritual truth:

> I say then, as it has always been received in the Church, and as it is said today by those who are teaching faithfully, that there are two things in the Blessed Sacrament: namely, the visible signs that are given us in it for our infirmity, and the spiritual truth which is symbolized to us thereby and likewise exhibited. Now concerning this truth, when I want familiarly to show what it is, I say that there are three points to be considered in the sacrament besides the outward sign, which is not at present in question: namely, the signification; then the matter or substance; and thirdly the virtue or the effect which proceeds from the one to the other.[121]

It will be noticed at once that according to Calvin the spiritual truth of the sacrament is not only symbolized by the signs but is 'exhibited'—that is, presented and offered to the communicant.

---

[120] *Inst.*, IV, 17, 1. Cf. also art. 18 of the *Tetrapolitan Confession*: 'cum hanc coenam, ut ipse instituit, repetunt, verum suum corpus, verumque suum sanguinem, vere edendum et bibendum, in cibum potumque animarum, quo illae in aeternam vitam alantur.'

[121] *Inst.*, IV, 17, 11.

This does not mean, however, that it is contained in the signs. But we must try to see precisely what Calvin meant by the spiritual truth of the sacrament; and to do so we have to examine in succession what he means when he is speaking of the signification, of the substance and of the virtue of the sacrament. We may start from the very brief definition that he himself gives us in the following paragraph: 'The meaning is in the promises, which are imprinted upon the sign. I call Jesus Christ, with his death and resurrection, the matter or substance. By the effect I mean redemption, righteousness, sanctification, the life everlasting and all the benefits brought to us by Jesus Christ.' But he is prepared to meet the immediate objection, that we are already receiving all those good things by faith, and that the sacrament is therefore at least unnecessary. To this he replies: 'Those good things would never reach us if Jesus Christ did not first make himself ours. I say, then, that in the Supper, Jesus Christ truly is given to us, under the signs of the bread and the wine, nay, even his body and his blood in which he fulfilled all righteousness to win salvation for us. And that this is done, firstly, so that we might be united in one body; secondly, so that, being made partakers of his substance we should also feel his virtue, by communicating his benefits to all.'[122] This definition corresponds with the one he had given in the *Institutes* of 1536, in the *Confession of Faith in the Eucharist* of 1537, in his Little Treatise on the Lord's Supper of 1541, and he remained faithful to it all his life. It goes to the very heart of the problem.

The meaning of the Supper resides in the promises; these promises are as though included or enclosed in the sign. But in what do the promises consist? Like Luther, Calvin identifies them with the words of institution. It is there that we must look for the purpose of the sign, the reason for its existence. The elements in themselves have no value; they acquire their signification only by the promise.

---

[122] Ibid. Cf. the definition by Bucer in the XVI Articles adopted by the Strasbourg synod of 1533: 'In the Supper it is Christ himself, the food of the life eternal, who is offered to us primarily . . . but with the bread and the wine, as well as with the words, the true body and the true blood are symbolized and offered to us; that is, the true community of the Christ.'

Defensive

Those who amuse themselves with the bare signs and disregard the promises to which they belong do so to their confusion. By these words we mean no other thing than what has been so well said by St Augustine, and that everyone confesses to be true, namely that the elements are made into sacraments when the Word is added to them, not because someone merely utters it by mouth but inasmuch as it is received by faith. . . . To observe the external sacrament without paying attention to the promise—what can this be but pure illusion? Truly, if we bring to them no more than our speculative eyes while our ears are stopped against hearing anything of what God promises in them, then they are no different from the beautiful mysteries of the pagans. . . . In short, if the outward sign derives no taste and flavour from the promise, then it is all, as they say, without salt or sauce. For what could it profit one that a mortal and earthly man threw some water upon one's head to baptize one, if Jesus Christ did not announce from heaven that it was he who was washing and cleansing one by his blood, who was renewing one by his Spirit? Of what use would it be to us to eat a little piece of bread and drink three drops of wine, if that voice were not sounding from on high, saying that the flesh of Jesus Christ is the true food of our souls and his blood their true spiritual drink? Thus we have every right to conclude that we are not made partakers in Jesus Christ and in his spiritual gifts by the bread, wine and water, but that we are brought to him by the promise, so that he gives himself to us, and, dwelling in us by faith, he fulfils what is promised and offered to us by the signs.[123]

It is the words of the promise, then, that give the sacrament its meaning, that fortify the faithful and give them certitude: which assure them that the body and blood of the Christ have been given for us and are ours: but that is a mystery which we in our frailty would be incapable of grasping directly. It is to come to the aid of our tottering faith that the Christ makes use of the carnal elements.

Calvin takes up the same idea in a slightly different form in

[123] *Opp.*, 9, 21 f.; *Opusc.*, 1709 f.

his sermon on Luke 4.20-21: 'Truly, there is nothing here but some bread and some wine; these are perishable meats which, as St Paul says, are for the stomach. But in so far as we see [Jesus Christ] herein, just so far is it expedient for us, and according to our infirmity. For if Jesus Christ did not know that this was useful to us, he would indeed open the heavens and make us perceive his glory manifestly; but he knows what is right for us, and not without reason has he ordained the surety that we have here.'[124] Since we cannot contemplate the glory of Christ directly, we have to be put in contact with him by visible signs which are an image of the things invisible that are promised us. These visible signs are not to be confused with the reality of the spiritual content of the Lord's Supper; their function is 'to point to and to confirm this promise in which Jesus Christ tells that his flesh is meat indeed and his blood drink indeed, and that they feed us with eternal life'.[125]

Let us see now what Calvin means by the 'matter' or 'substance' of the Supper. We are invited, at this meal of communion, to eat the body and drink the blood of the Christ in order to partake of his substance. The promise contained in the words of the institution does not remain a mere promise; God really communicates to us what he has promised us:

We can infer from the sign having been vouchsafed us, that the substance is also given us in its reality. For unless someone wanted to call God a deceiver he would not dare to say that a vain and empty sign of his truth had been put forward by him. Wherefore, if the Lord does in truth represent to us the partaking of his body in the breaking of bread, there is no doubt but he grants it every time. And in fact, the faithful have always to keep this rule, that whensoever they see signs ordained of God, they also conceive it a certainty that the truth of the thing represented is conjoined therewith, and be firmly persuaded of it. . . . So, though it be true that the visible sign is vouchsafed us in order to seal the donation of the invisible thing, we must have this unshakable confidence that in taking the sign of the body we are likewise taking the body.[126]

[124] *Inst.*, IV, 17, 10. [125] *Inst.*, IV, 17, 4. [126] *Inst.*, IV, 17, 10.

What is promised us by the words of institution is therefore really given to us at the same time as the material signs of the promise. But nevertheless the material elements have to be carefully distinguished from the body and the blood of the Christ. In his *Treatise on the Lord's Supper* of 1541, Calvin explains his point of view on this subject with all the clarity we would desire:

> Now, if people nevertheless want to know whether the bread is the body of Christ and the wine his blood, we shall reply that the bread and the wine are visible signs which represent to us the body and the blood; but that the name and title of body and blood have been given them because they are as the instruments by means of which the Lord Jesus distributes these to us. There is good reason for this form and manner of speech. For seeing that it is a thing incomprehensible not only to the eye but to our natural judgment, that we should have communion with the body of Jesus Christ, it is here shown to us visibly.[127]

He then adduces as 'an example of a similar thing' the appearance, during the baptism of Jesus, of the Holy Spirit in the form of a dove. Although John the Baptist says he saw the Holy Spirit, all he was able to see was the dove, the Holy Spirit being invisible to him. But the Spirit 'was represented to him according to his capacity'. 'That is how it is', continues Calvin, 'with the communion that we have with the body and blood of the Lord Jesus. It is a spiritual mystery, one that is not to be seen by the eye nor understood by the human intelligence. It is therefore symbolized for us by visible signs according as our infirmity requires, in such sort however, that it is not just a bare symbol but is conjoined with its truth and substance.' According to Calvin, the spiritual reality of the body and blood of Christ does not identify itself with the material elements nor find itself in any way included in them. It is given at the same time as they are. This is neither the Roman transubstantiation nor the Lutheran consubstantiation, but neither is it the symbolization of Zwingli. If we want to find a historic precedent for the Calvinist conception of the relations between the Eucharistic elements and the body and blood of Christ, we shall come nearest to it in the teaching of

[127] *Opp.*, 5, 438 f.

Bucer—at least, in the form that this took from about 1530 to 1535.

But we must try to give still clearer definition to what Calvin meant by the body and blood of Christ being given to the faithful at the Eucharist. He had said, in a passage previously quoted, that the content of the Eucharist is 'the Christ with his death and resurrection'.[128] Now there is only one Christ and one body of Christ, that which died upon the cross and then was glorified. It is this same that we receive in the Supper of the Lord.[129] Our contact with God can be made only by the intermediation of the incarnate Christ. It is in his body and in his blood that we receive eternal life. The reality of this body of the Christ and its identity with the body of the Christ incarnate are forcibly affirmed in the commentary on I Corinthians 11.24:

> As for me, I acknowledge that we are sharing in the benefits of Christ when we possess him himself. But I say that we possess him when we not only believe that he was exposed as a sacrifice for us, but when he dwells in us, when he is one with us, when we are members of his flesh; in short, when we are incorporated with him in, so to speak, one and the same life and substance. Moreover, I consider and ponder what these words mean. For Jesus Christ offers us not only the benefits of his death and resurrection, but also his own body in which he suffered and was resurrected. I conclude that the body of Christ is given us really, as they say, that is, truly, to be a food healthful to our souls. I speak according to common parlance; but I mean that our souls are fed upon the substance of his body in order that we may in truth be made one with him.[130]

Leaving aside the particular question of the relationship between the body of the Christ and the elements, we can feel, in the passage quoted, an echo as it were of the formulations in the Confession of Augsburg and in the Concord of Wittenberg; and we can now understand why Calvin had no great hesitation in putting his signature to the documents of the Lutheran faith.

[128] *Inst.*, IV, 17, 11.
[129] Preface to the *Defence against Westphal* of 1555, *Opp.*, 9, 9; *Opusc.*, 1694.
[130] *Opp.*, 49, 487.

X A way of saying insubstantial?

But by this we do not mean to say, as some historians have said, that he was ever truly Lutheran in his doctrine of the Eucharist, even in his earliest days. Even without being aware of it, he was committed to a path which was to lead him very far away from the preoccupations of Luther and his disciples, while allowing him, right to the end, to accept certain aspects of the conception so vehemently defended by that adversary of Zwingli.

The third point about the spiritual reality of the Supper concerns its effects; namely, the benefits of the Christ or, one might also say, what the Christ with his death and resurrection communicates to us. This formulation enables us to verify what Calvin means to affirm when he says that our souls are fed upon the substance of the body of Christ. He is not using the word 'substance' with the meaning it had for the scholastics when they opposed the substance of a thing to its accidents.[131] There is no question of making Calvin say that in the Eucharist we receive a kind of invisible material substrate or, if one prefers, a kind of fluid, either material or of celestial essence, in which the body of Christ comes and melts into ours.[132] That is what Calvin very rightly emphasized as early as 1536, when he wrote in his first *Institutes*: 'For purposes of instruction we say that the body and the blood of Christ are presented to us truly and effectively, but not naturally. By that we mean that this is not the substance itself of the body, nor the true and natural body of the Christ that is given us there, but all the benefits that the Christ offers us in his body.'[133] In his remarkable analysis of the Calvinist notion of substance, H. Gollwitzer distinguishes three different acceptations of the term in Calvin:

[131] Cf. NIESEL, op. cit., p. 50, n. 103; KOLFHAUS, *Christusgemeinschaft*, p. 117 f.; H. GRASS, op. cit., p. 228 ff.

[132] Basing himself upon some declarations of Th. de Bèze which only reproduce Calvin's thought, H. GOLLWITZER, *Coena Domini*, p. 119, rightly observes: 'The substance of the body is here equivalent to the centre, to the particular property or, so to speak, the subject of the body, not to anything that would be identical with the notion of body but to something that transcends that notion . . . in short, Bèze is speaking only of a substance "for" the body, which is precisely the Christ himself, upon whom the body's being a "substance" depends. But from the Lutheran angle, we envisage the substance of the body itself, its own essence, which certainly consists of its matter.'

[133] *Opp.*, I, 123; *O.S.*, I, 142 f.

true and natural ≠ true

1. The 'substance or nature' of a thing, therefore the bodily substance; that is, 'the real and natural body of the Christ'; after 1536 Calvin never ceased to deny that this substance was given us; its function was to be the source from which flowed the life that was destined for us. . . . 2. Christ himself considered as 'the substance of the sacrament'. He is received by faith, in a personal union with him. 3. The substance of that which is given to us when we receive Christ; namely, the life, the benefits, the strength proceeding from his body. That is a spiritual substance. It is at the same time the 'spiritual substance of the body of Christ', whence it 'flows into our souls'.[134]

But it must be admitted that, by using the word 'substance' sometimes in its material and scholastic meaning, sometimes as equivalent to 'foundation', or again to spiritual gifts, Calvin himself helped to give an appearance of ambiguity to his doctrine which his adversaries were prompt to exploit.[135] One could even say without too much exaggeration that this defect in terminology was one of the reasons for the misunderstanding which severed him from the Lutherans, or was at least the direct cause of the accusations of dishonesty that were laid against him. Westphal, for instance, certainly did not see, or wish to see, that his adversary was using the word 'substance' with different meanings; and this enabled him to accuse Calvin of self-contradiction and of not admitting the real presence of Christ in the sacrament. In fact, though Calvin always rejected the transfusion of the natural substance of the body of Christ, he did affirm, on the other hand, the communication by faith of the Christ and his benefits, considered as the spiritual substance of the body of Christ present in the Supper. He was therefore logical with himself when he inveighed against the substantial union with Christ as it had been taught by Osiander, who, he said, had no right to speak of a mixture of the Christ's substance with our own. And on the other hand he himself could affirm the existence of a union with the

---

[134] GOLLWITZER, op. cit., p. 120 f. Upon the Calvinist notion of substance one should also consult the study, unequal though, it is by G. P. HARTVELT, *Verum Corpus*, Delft, 1960.

[135] Let us remember that on the subject of union with Christ also, Calvin had used the word substance with some imprudence; see above, p. 236.

substance of the Christ, but only by giving this term the meaning of a spiritual substance comprising the Christ himself and the benefits that he has won for us. Yet Calvin always protested that by this he never meant 'to put imagination or thought in the place of fact and truth'. While rejecting the material presence of the body of the Christ in the bread, he proclaims that the whole of the Christ is truly present, in his humanity and his divinity.

Nevertheless the Lutherans accused Calvin of professing a doctrine as vacuous and vain as that of Zwingli; and one of the arguments they advanced in proof of this must have been formidable: namely, that in 1549 Calvin had signed the agreement on the sacraments with Bullinger, Zwingli's successor. But it is only fair to recall that, upon the doctrine of the Eucharist, the formulations arrived at represented the maximum of what Calvin could admit, and one cannot take them as the basis for an equitable verdict upon his doctrine.[136] Westphal's allegation about these was, primarily, that they were evasive phrases meant to mark the spiritualism of their author. This seemed particularly clear to him in the interpretation of the words of institution: This is my body.

According to Calvin, what was in question here was a particular manner of expressing oneself, of which he thought he could find other examples in the Scriptures.[137] When they had to expound a mystery, the Biblical authors willingly made use of metonymy; that is, they often applied the name of the thing to the sign that served to designate it. But as we have seen, the signs that have been instituted by God are not simply symbols that do no more than represent the thing in question. They not only represent, but they present (exhibit) it, which implies that the thing itself necessarily accompanies the sign. Now, Westphal contested the idea that this was what Calvin really taught. The latter in turn reproached the Lutherans for failing to see what was fundamental to the question by clinging, as they did, to the literal sense of the copula 'is'. This, Calvin said, made them 'unable to conceive any other participation in the body and

[136] LANG, *Joh. Calvin*, p. 193; NIESEL, op. cit., p. 54, n. 1; for the contrary view, DANKBAAR, op. cit., p. 156 f.

[137] NIESEL, op. cit., pp. 56 ff.; GOLLWITZER, op. cit., pp. 28-39.

blood except by conjunction or local contact or by some crudely
conceived inclusion',[138] or, to quote the slightly different words
of the French version of 1560: 'True it is that they claim plenty
of fine things; but when all has been said, it turns out that they
have been beguiling themselves with a local presence. And how
comes that, unless they can conceive no participation in the body
of Jesus Christ other than holding him here below, as if to handle
him as they please.'[139] But Westphal could fairly retort that
Bucer and even Luther had always refused to teach impanation
or local inclusion of the elements. The remark was correct: the
sacramental union between the consecrated bread and the body
of the Christ that was taught by Luther in his confession of 1528
and that Bucer had admitted since before the Concord of Wittenberg could not be likened to impanation or local inclusion. And
Westphal, cleverly showing why the union between the body and
blood of the Christ and the consecrated elements does not necessarily imply identity or local inclusion, wrote in his *Apology* of
1558: 'Certainly, it sounds like "locally", when one says that
the body of Christ is, is given, and is received, in or under or with
the bread. But what then? Moses writes that God was present
in the ark, where he dwelt between the cherubim, and in Shiloh:
that too sounds as though it were locally: are we then to object
that Moses had enclosed God, or fixed him in the tabernacle?'[140]
The whole conflict upon this point can be shortly summed up
thus: Union between the Christ and the Eucharistic elements
meant, according to the Lutherans, that there was a real contact
between the body and the blood on the one hand, and the bread
and the wine on the other: according to Calvin, it meant only
that the believer received the body of Christ when he consumed
the consecrated bread. Westphal and the Lutherans therefore
maintained that there was a direct relation between the Christ
and the elements; Calvin, on the contrary, put the Christ and
the elements separately into direct contact with the believer.
The divergence is reducible, then, proportionately speaking, to
that which in the Middle Ages had set the Franciscans and Duns
Scotus in opposition to the traditional teaching represented by,
above all, Thomas Aquinas. For Franciscan doctrine, as for

[138] *Inst*, IV, 17, 16 (Latin text). [139] NIESEL, op. cit., p. 67, n. 41.
[140] Quoted by NIESEL, op. cit., p. 67, n. 41.

Calvin, there was a parallelism between the reception of the elements in the Supper and the action of the Spirit of Christ, but the elements and the Spirit remained distinct. The partisans of the opposing conception taught, as did Luther and his disciples, that there was a conjunction between the elements and the Christ[141] and that the Christ acted through and by means of the sacraments.[142]

But the interpretation of the words of institution was only one of the problems in dispute that set Calvin in opposition to the Lutherans. Equally the issue was the question whether the body of the Christ could possibly be substantially present in the elements. In other words, the problem was how to define the conditions of the real presence, and its ultimate limits. Luther had vigorously defended the ubiquity of the glorified body of the Christ; it was upon that basis that he thought he could explain the presence of this body simultaneously in every place where the Eucharist was being celebrated.[143] This is not the place to review all the modalities of that doctrine; but we must note that it soon became the distinctive sign by which orthodox Lutherans recognized one another. Westphal naturally turned it to his purpose, and all the more readily because Calvin had pronounced himself against it ever since 1536. The body of Christ, Westphal declared in effect, had by the fact of its glorification received a prerogative and a glory which it shared with no one, and thanks to which it is able to be present everywhere at the same time. However, that is a mystery we cannot understand; we must be content to believe.[144] Calvin, on his side, adopted an analogous point of view, but only to draw quite opposite conclusions. Like Westphal, he tried to define the conditions under which the real presence would supervene. But it was inadmissible, in his view, to refer back to the divine omnipotence in order to explain the presence of the body of Christ in several places at once. Nor was it possible by human reasoning to explain the union with Christ which is

[141] We are using a vague term intentionally, in order not to prejudge the way in which this union is to be conceived.

[142] Cf. R. SEEBERG, *Dogmengeschichte*, vol. III, pp. 510 f. and vol. IV, 2, p. 605.

[143] H. GRASS, op. cit., pp. 60-1. Cf. above, pp. 223 f.

[144] NIESEL, op. cit., p. 70.

effected by the Eucharist. One of Westphal's complaints bore precisely upon this point; and Calvin defended himself in an important passage in the *Institutes*: 'I am not reducing this mystery to the capacity of the human reason, nor am I subjecting it to the order of Nature. Did we, I ask you, learn from the natural philosophers that Jesus Christ feeds our souls upon his flesh and blood quite as well as our bodies are nourished and sustained by bread and wine? . . . Nor is this a thing any longer in accord with human understanding, that the flesh of Christ should enter into us to serve us as nourishment. . . . We say that Jesus Christ comes down into us as much by the outward sign as by his Spirit, in order truly to give life to our souls from the substance of his flesh and from his blood. Those who do not understand that such a thing cannot happen without several miracles are more than stupid, for there is nothing more contrary to the natural reason than to say that souls borrow the spiritual and heavenly life from the flesh, nay even from flesh that originated from the earth and was mortal. Nothing is more incredible than to say that things as remote from one another as heaven and earth are not only conjoined but unified, so that our souls receive nourishment from the flesh of Christ without its leaving heaven.'[145]

After having underlined the irrational and supernatural character of union with Christ, Calvin undertakes to refute the ubiquity, which seems to him a wholly unnecessary hypothesis. We do not need to talk about the omnipotence of God or to say that nothing is impossible to him; but only to say what God has willed. 'But,' Calvin goes on, 'it pleased him that Jesus Christ should be made like his brothers in all things except sin. What is our body? Is it not such that it has its own distinctive measure, that it keeps its place, that it is touched and is seen? And why, they say, should not God make one and the same body occupy several different places, so that it is not confined to any particular place, so that it has no form nor measure at all? O senseless man! what are you asking of the power of God; that it should make a body to be a body and not a body at the same time?'[146] That insult to the principle of identity is, in Calvin's eyes, not only a simple error in logic: it amounts to 'perverting the order of the

[145] *Inst.*, IV, 17, 24.   [146] Ibid.

wisdom of God'. As soon as the Christ had received a body identical with ours it had to have the same properties as our bodies. The glorification of the body of Christ has not changed anything of its own nature, which remains that of all bodies and does not transform itself into the nature of spirit. On this point Calvin was, after all, blaming his adversaries for what Zwingli had already complained of in Luther; that is, for effacing the absolute distinction between flesh and spirit.[147] They had put their finger on one of the fundamental peculiarities of Lutheran doctrine, which, in effect, had never admitted the strict dualism that Western theology had affirmed ever since St Augustine.

For Calvin the divine Spirit alone was endowed with ubiquity; but what was meant by this was not the omnipresence of God; what was in question here was the presence of the Christ, at once man and God, whose body had all the characteristics of the human body even when it was dwelling in heaven. 'It is not Aristotle but the Holy Spirit who teaches that the body of Christ, after being resurrected from the dead, keeps its own form and is received in heaven until the last day.'[148] When Westphal said that the saying of Christ, 'It is expedient for you that I go away,' (John 16.7), meant only that he was abandoning the things of this world,[149]; he replied that 'to go away and to ascend do not mean to make a show of going away or up, but actually to do what the words denote.' On the other hand, Christ promised that he would send the Holy Spirit; that, too, excludes any continuation of the corporeal presence of the Christ in this world. The Holy Spirit is indeed sent 'to fill the vacuum of his absence'. The controversy goes on in the same way with regard to the

---

[147] ZWINGLI, *De vera et falsa religione* (*Corp. Reform.* vol. XC, 787): 'Sic enim diversa sunt corpus et spiritus, ut utrumcumque accipias, non possit alterum esse. Si spiritus est, quod in quaestionem venit, iam certa relatione contrariorum sequitur, corpus non esse; si corpus, iam certus est, qui audit, spiritum non esse. Vnde corpoream carnem spiritualiter edere nihil est aliud, quam quod corpus sit, spiritum esse adserere.' The localization of the glorified body of the Christ is affirmed by Zwingli in numerous passages, for example in *Amica exegesis* (*Corp. Reform.* vol. XCII, 654 ff., 676 ff.); *Brevis ac distincta expositio fidei*, edn. Schuler and Schulthess, vol. IV, 51 ff. The argument had first been advanced by Oecolampadius in 1525, cf. W. KOEHLER, *Zwingli und Luther*, vol. I, p. 119 f.

[148] *Inst.*, IV, 17, 26. [149] NIESEL, op. cit., p. 74.

account of the Ascension. Whereas his Lutheran adversaries interpreted this figuratively and said that it signified that the Christ is no longer tied to the conditions of life upon earth and has become invisible, Calvin took the Biblical story literally. 'Does not the word "ascension" so often repeated mean that Jesus Christ moved from one place to another? This they deny, because it seems to them that what is denoted by this elevation is only the majesty of his empire. But I ask once again: What was the manner of his ascension? Was he not taken up on high before their eyes? Do not the evangelists clearly report that he was received into heaven?'[150] But although the body of Christ is in heaven, whence it will not return until the end of time, his reign is none the less extended over the whole world. Calvin did indeed localize the glorified body of Christ; he nevertheless interpreted the 'sitting at the right hand of God' as Luther did when he wrote: 'Although he has taken his flesh away from us and in the body has ascended into heaven, he is nevertheless seated on the right hand of the Father, which is to say that he reigns in the power, majesty and glory of the Father.'[151] Such importance does he attribute to the localization of the body of Christ in heaven that, in the *Second Defence against Westphal*, he advances it as the decisive argument against the material presence of the body of Christ in the host: 'For when we deny that Christ could be, as it were, hidden under the bread, this is not because, strictly speaking, he would [then] be shut up somewhere, but because, being raised above all elements, he dwells outside the world.' [152] Incidentally, this prompts us to wonder how far Calvin may have been led by his cosmological conceptions, and especially by his attachment to the ancient world-system, to put so much emphasis upon this localization of the body of the Christ above the visible sphere of the heavens and yet in a given portion of space.

He therefore rejects the doctrine of the invisible corporeal presence of the Christ in this world. In this he sees an evasion of the distinction between the two natures in Christ and, as Zwingli had taught it, an improper extension of the 'communication of idioms'. 'If we count among the qualities of a glorified body that

---

[150] *Inst.*, IV, 17, 27.   [151] *Inst.*, IV, 17, 18. Cf. LUTHER, W. A., 23, 133.
[152] *Opp.*, 9, 79; *Opusc.*, 1767.

it is infinite and fills all [space], obviously the substance of it will be abolished, and no distinction will remain between the divinity and human nature. Moreover, if the body of Jesus Christ is thus variable and of different sorts, to appear in one place and be invisible in another, what will become of the corporeal nature, which must have its limitations? And what will become of the unity?'[153] Calvin also sees in this a threat to belief in the resurrection of the body: 'All the hope that we have of going to heaven depends upon this, that Jesus Christ ascended thither and, as Tertullian says, took with him the payment for our resurrection. But, I ask you, how feeble a confidence would not this be, if the same flesh that Jesus Christ took from us had not entered into heaven?' True, the Acts of the Apostles says that the Christ was seen by St Stephen and St Paul; but he had not therefore come out of heaven; he gave 'supernatural sight to the eyes of his servant, by which he could see into the heavens'. Here Calvin ventures without much hesitation into an exegesis that is at least rather daring; and as much can be said of the way in which he tries to refute two other Scriptural arguments advanced by Westphal: the appearance of Christ in the upper room, and his sudden disappearance after the breaking of bread at Emmaus. Let this be judged from the following quotation: 'To enter into a room when the doors are shut does not mean that he pierced the wood, but only that he made himself an opening by his divine power, so that in a miraculous fashion he was found to be in the midst of his disciples although the doors were locked. What they advance, from St Luke, namely that he suddenly vanished before the eyes of the disciples who went to Emmaus, profits them nothing, but tends to our advantage. For in order to deprive them of the sight of his body he did not make himself invisible, but simply disappeared.'[154]

In defence of the ubiquity, the Lutherans finally quoted as evidence for their thesis, the saying 'I am with you, even unto the end of the world.' But Calvin of course contests the possibility that this could refer to a corporeal presence of the Christ:

[153] *Inst.*, IV, 17, 29.

[154] Ibid. Though the exegesis of this last phrase is disputable, we must not, however, be too hasty and deny that there is any real difference between 'invisible' and 'disappeared'.

'For if this were so, Jesus Christ would have to be dwelling in us
bodily apart from the observance of the Supper, since what is
there spoken of is a perpetual union. And thus they have no
cause to fight so bitterly to enclose Jesus Christ in the bread, since
they confess that we have him equally well without the Supper.
Moreover, the text shows that Jesus Christ is not speaking there
of his flesh, but is promising his disciples an invincible assistance
by which he will defend and maintain them against all the
assaults of Satan and the world.'[155] And Calvin goes on to speak
once again about the relations between the two natures of Christ,
which surely proves that at bottom the quarrel was of a Christological description and that the divergences on the subject of the
Eucharist were consequences of the positions they had taken up
towards the problem of the two natures.[156] 'Some people,' he
writes, 'are carried away by such ardour that they are not
ashamed to say that, because of the union of the two natures,
wherever the divinity of Jesus Christ is, his flesh, which cannot
be separated from it, is there as well. As though this union were
a fusion, to produce I know not what alloy, which would be
neither God nor man.' And this, as we have seen, was a horror
to Calvin. In his view, the two natures had to remain not
separated, but distinguished in such a way that 'each has its
property safely preserved for it.' In the Supper, Jesus Christ
'shows his presence in a special manner; nevertheless this is in
order to be present, not to bring to it all that he himself has;
seeing that, as for the flesh, that must be kept in heaven until he
appears in judgment.'

Definitely, then, Calvin did make, side by side, two distinct
affirmations that it is difficult to reconcile: on the one hand he
maintained that the body of Christ is present in the Supper and
communicates to us 'Jesus Christ with his death and resurrection';
that is, the benefits that his merits have won for us. On the other
hand, he declares that the body of the Christ has no local or
spatial relationship with the material elements of the Eucharist.
The Christ is corporeally in heaven, and therefore cannot, even
invisibly, be present in several places at once at the Supper. It

[155] *Inst.*, IV, 17, 30.
[156] The same had been true of the conflict that arose between Luther and
Zwingli.

was in a sermon which Erasmus had attributed to St John Chrysostom and had included in the edition of his works published at Basle in 1530, that Calvin found the idea that the Holy Spirit is the bond of our union with the Christ.[157] He had made use of this for the first time, it seems, in a passage in the *Institutes* of 1539,[158] the text of which remained unchanged to the end; and we read in the edition of 1559:

> Since we have no doubt but that [the body of Christ] has its limitations as the nature of a human body requires, and that it is contained in heaven, . . . we also think it is illegitimate to bring it down among the corruptible elements, or to imagine it can be present everywhere. And in fact, that is not really necessary for participation in it, seeing that the Lord Jesus extends this benefit to us by his Spirit, that we are made one with him, body, spirit and soul. However, the bond of this union is the Holy Spirit, by whom we are bound together, and who is like the canal or conduit through which all that Christ is or has comes down into us.[159]

There is an infinite distance between Christ who is in heaven and us who are upon earth: God alone can overcome that distance by the action of the Holy Spirit. The Christ comes down into us at the Supper and lifts us up, even to himself, uniting us with him body and soul. Calvin is very clear upon this last point. Westphal had accused him of over-spiritualizing the relationship between the Christ and the faithful in the Supper and leaving nothing of it beyond the Spirit of Christ and the soul of the faithful. In the *Last Warning* Calvin replied: 'I do not dispute that our flesh is restored by this spiritual food and drink, for we are communicating with the Christ in hope of the blessed resurrection, and that is why it is necessary for us to unite ourselves to him not only in the soul but also in the flesh.'[159b] While rejecting the local presence of the Christ in the elements, he admitted that between the Christ and ourselves there is a

---

[157] Cf. NIESEL, op. cit., p. 92.

[158] Until then, he had assigned this function, of acting as a bond, to the 'spirit of the Christ', both in the course of the Colloquy of Lausanne in 1536 and in the *Confession upon the Eucharist* of 1537, *Opp.*, 9, 884 and 711.

[159] *Inst.*, IV, 17, 12.   [159b] *Opp.*, 9, 208.

privileged relationship which is established only in the Supper. 'Although the body of Christ be in heaven,' he wrote to Bucer towards the end of his life, 'we nevertheless truly feed upon it here on earth because the Christ, by the unfathomable and omnipresent virtue of his Spirit, makes himself so much our own that he dwells in us without change of place. . . . I can see nothing absurd in saying that we are truly and really receiving the flesh and the blood of Christ, and that thus he is food to us substantially, so long as it is agreed that Christ comes down towards us not only in the outward symbols but also in the hidden working of his Spirit, so that we can ascend to him by faith.' [160] The Christ is present in the same measure as the Holy Spirit is making his presence felt by us, putting us into communication with him and with his benefits by drawing us towards him. The end of the Sermon on Luke 1.36-8 develops this theme further, and insists that the nature of the relationship formed between Christ and ourselves belongs to the domain of mystery and surpasses our understanding: 'We say that our Lord Jesus, dwelling in heaven, does not, however, cease to vivify us. And indeed, the sun, which shines on us from on high to give us energy and light, does it have to come down here to do its work? And yet that is a creature without sense. And how will it be then, with the Son of God? Moreover, the sun performs its office according to the order of nature; but Jesus Christ works a miracle, as I have said already.'[161]

It is of course the believer alone who can thus enter into communication with Christ by the intermediation of the Holy Spirit. For an unbeliever, to be brought into the presence of Christ he would have to be lifted up to him; but that would mean that he was no longer an unbeliever. To bring about communication with the Christ, the Holy Spirit builds upon faith. Union with Christ in the Supper ought then to be regarded as an effect of

---

[160] Letter of 27th December 1562, *Opp.*, 19, 603. It is not without interest to note that Calvin is here in close agreement with Oecolampadius, who as early as 1521 had written that, during the communion, one had so to behave 'ut videatur non modo Christus e coelis ad nos descendere, sed et nos vid eamur in coelos ad ipsum ascendere' (quoted by E. STAEHELIN, *Das theologische Lebenswerk J. Oekolampads*, p. 144).

[161] *Opp.*, 46, 98.

faith; of which, rightly considered, it is the fulfilment or completion. But this union with Christ, as we have seen, is given us from the very moment when we are incorporated in Christ by faith; it therefore does not originate in the Supper.[162] On the other hand, it does not come to an end with the end of the celebration, but is permanent, like the faith itself: 'The communion of which we are made partakers in the Supper is perpetual,' wrote Calvin in the *Last Warning*.[163] Prior to the Supper, and surviving it, union with Christ subsists therefore beyond the Supper itself and is always independent of it; since, according to Calvin, we may attain to it by other means, such as preaching, the reading of the Bible, or prayer. But here we are obliged to ask ourselves, what exactly does the Supper give us that we cannot obtain otherwise? Under these conditions, is there still good reason for the existence of the Supper alongside the preaching of the Word? This problem touches the very nerve of the notion of the sacrament as it was elaborated by the reformers; and the mere fact that it can present itself shows that they did not manage to integrate the sacrament organically into their theological system.

That problem did not, of course, escape Calvin's notice, and he made many efforts to justify the origins of the sacrament and its necessity. 'The sacrament,' he said in a sermon on I Corinthians 11.23-6, 'is to keep us still growing in the faith and to confirm us in it, so that at his coming Jesus Christ may show us the fruit of his death and passion and make us feel it.'[164] Before this, in the same sermon, he had declared: 'By the hidden and wonderful virtue of the Holy Spirit, Jesus Christ dwells in us, communicates his life to us and makes us share in his virtue. That is how the Supper serves us as a memorial, yet this is no mere memorial, not at all like a picture that we contemplate with the eyes, but it is a true and sure testimony that Jesus Christ is accomplishing in us what he symbolizes to us; that we do not come to the Supper imagining a vain thing, but to receive in truth all that is there pledged to us. Meanwhile we must be ever reaching upward, and let us remember . . . that the sacraments are not

---

[162] KOLFHAUS, *Christusgemeinschaft bei Calvin*, p. 117.
[163] *Opp.*, 9, 232; cf. NIESEL, op. cit., p. 95 f.
[164] *Opp.*, 49, 802.

instituted to detain us here below, but rather to draw us towards our Lord Jesus Christ.' Whenever the opportunity presents itself, Calvin places this emphasis upon the utility of the sacrament; but it is perhaps at the end of the sermon on Titus 1.1-5 that he expresses himself most clearly: 'The Supper too is a special assurance to us that we are being helped by our God, when we are as it were mid-way along the road that we are being made to go on, striving ever towards our God. Let us note also that the Supper is meant to correct and complete the things that are still defective. For our having made a beginning would be nothing unless God continued to make us feel his grace, and of that we have good assurance in the Supper.'[165] The Eucharist, then, is a means of sanctification for the elect who are already incorporated in Christ. It is an instrument that the Holy Spirit uses to confirm our faith and deepen it, by giving us the ever-renewed certitude of our union with Christ, and by reinforcing that 'holy union that we have with the Son of God by being members of his body, by having life in common with him, by being already through hope partakers of his glory, although we are living this mortal and corruptible life.'[166] It serves to complete or to double the action of the Word, with the aid of material or corporeal means appropriate to our frailty.

Yet, whatever may be the value of the arguments that Calvin adduces to justify his particular interpretation of the Eucharist, we must acknowledge that his doctrine leaves one with many obscurities, only imperfectly masked by an exegesis that is often peculiar, and by the appeal to mystery. In spite of the function he assigns to the Holy Spirit in establishing contact between the Christ and the believer, it is not easy to see how he could maintain that the faithful 'really' receive the body and blood of Christ in the communion. It may be that the decisive reason is not to be sought for in his doctrinal preoccupations but in his piety, which demanded very positive affirmations with regard to the presence of the Christ in the Supper.

From the more formal point of view, Calvin was more successful. The intervention of the Holy Spirit as the agent of union between the believer and the Christ does, in effect, establish a symmetry between the doctrines of baptism and of the Eucharist.

[165] *Opp.*, 54, 416.   [166] Sermon on I Corinthians 11.23-5; *Opp.*, 49, 778.

This, moreover, enabled him to make both sacraments dependent upon the preaching of the Word. 'Firstly, our Lord teaches and instructs us by his Word. Secondly, he confirms us by his sacraments. Thirdly, by the light of his Holy Spirit, he enlightens our understanding, and gives entry into our hearts to both the Word and the sacraments.'[167]   In both cases a similar function is assigned to the Spirit, which, however, is simply that of an intermediary, further emphasizing the central position that is occupied by the Christ throughout Calvin's theology.

[167] *Inst.*, IV, 14, 8.

CONCLUSION

When Calvin undertook the writing of the *Institutes of the Christian Religion*, his intention was to produce an exposition, as complete as possible, which would serve as an introduction to the reading of the Bible. His commentaries, and on a more popular and practical plane his sermons, had after all no other aim. Much more than Luther, and in a spirit more closely akin to Melanchthon's or Zwingli's in this respect, he endeavoured to systematize the scriptural data into a coherent whole. Remembering his lessons from the dialecticians of Montaigu no less than those of the jurists of Orleans and Bourges, he retained a liking for logic which neither religious meditation nor the experiences of life had been able to weaken. And yet his writings are not those of a logician, hardly those of a philosopher. His dogmatic system could not be compared, in rigour of reasoning, with the work of Spinoza, nor even of Aristotle or Thomas Aquinas. This, moreover, could not have been otherwise, from the moment that he had determined to base his work primarily upon the Scriptures. Just so far as it remained true to this Biblical foundation, Calvin's theology could not keep within a rigid framework of philosophical constructions built upon *a priori* principles freely chosen by its author. If we want to speak of a 'system' of Calvin, we must do so with certain reservations, owing to the plurality of themes that imposed themselves simultaneously upon its author's thinking.

It is because they have failed to realize this, that the majority of historians have tried to reconstruct the Calvinist dogmatic from the standpoint of one central idea supposed to dominate it as a whole. For a long while, as we know, predestination was held to be that idea. Some proposed to discard this in favour of the Glory of God; others exchanged it for the sovereignty of God, or even for eschatology. Still more recently the divinity of Jesus Christ has been presented as the central thesis of Calvinism, and perhaps some readers will think we have sacrificed a good deal to that opinion here. And it is true that a dominant—perhaps *the* dominant—preoccupation of Calvin was to present the divinity of Jesus Christ in the strongest light and guard it against the slightest depreciation. But this is not the central idea of his system from which all the rest of it could be deduced. If one wanted at all costs to find such a central idea, one would be more likely to find it expressed in this sentence, written one day by Luther: 'Omnia quidem habemus a Deo, sed nonnisi per Christum.' But every authentically Christian theology could claim this for itself. It would be better, we think, to confess that Calvin's is not a closed system elaborated around a central idea, but that it draws together, one after another, a whole series of Biblical ideas, some of which can only with difficulty be logically reconciled. As he developed them in turn, the author of the *Institutes* was doubtless striving to bring them into harmony by some sort of application of the formal method taught in the schools; that is, by expounding the opposed conceptions one after the other and showing that they are joined together in a higher principle. At other times the breach of logic, to which he himself takes good care to call attention by an 'as though', is passed off as merely apparent, as an effect of the contrast between the human and the divine points of view. That these attempts at reconciliation are sometimes superficial or contrived could be denied, we think, only by a partisan apologist. Often, however, they are ingenious, nay, even admissible. But they cannot do away with the dialectical opposites themselves. What have been called the 'paradoxes' of Calvin remain. These still present themselves in the unity of, and distinction between, the two natures of Christ, or in God's abiding love for his creatures and his wrathful attitude to fallen man, in the justification which leaves man still a sinner, or in the complete and immediate imputation of the righteousness of Christ while regeneration is slow and always imperfect, in man's greatness and his misery, in the Law's being abolished and yet persisting, in the value attached to earthly goods and the contempt for them, in the Church at once visible and imperfect and invisible and perfect, in the presence of the Christ in the sacrament and his seat at the right hand of God. It would be easy to extend the list. And every one of these contradictions was carefully examined by Calvin, with scrupulous fidelity to the Bible. One could even say that his fidelity is proved by the fact that he allowed them to remain.

But sometimes, for the sake of logical coherence or out of attachment to pre-established dogmatic positions, he also did violence to the Biblical texts. His principle of Scriptural authority then led him to search the Scriptures for illusory support, by means of purely arbitrary interpretations. The memory of his studies in law very likely played some part in this. The jurists, practising their exegeses upon the texts of Justinian, adopted much the same procedure. In this way they managed, by sheer ingenuity, to make their authorities say almost anything they wanted them to, sometimes things that had very little connection with the thought of the authority they quoted. Although Calvin showed himself capable of profiting by the methods of the humanists, and on many occasions gave proof of a sense of history that was rare enough in that epoch, he also knew how to adapt a text to the requirements of his doctrine. We have pointed out several instances of this, notably in regard to baptism. It would be ungracious of us to labour the point. But truth compels one to admit frankly that, despite all his fidelity to the Bible, he seems to have been searching the Scriptures more frequently for texts to support a doctrine accepted in advance, than to derive doctrine from the Scriptures.

But in this respect he was in line with tradition, for his predecessors, even since the Reform, had not done otherwise except upon a few points that could easily be indicated. The references we have adduced in evidence prove, moreover, how much he made use of the dogmatic tradition, even in fundamentals. Perhaps these references to St Augustine, to Melanchthon, to Bucer, may have been thought to show some lack of originality in Calvin. But in fact it would be rather unfair to look for his originality in the detail of his dogmatic affirmations, except in regard to certain points peculiar to his own teaching, such as the development that he gave to the doctrine of the Holy Spirit and his action, or the personal position that he took up in regard to the function of the Law. His desire to assert his unity with the tradition of the ancient Church would in any case have forbidden him to venture rashly upon unexplored ground. The imprint of his personality can best be seen in the emphasis that he put upon this or that doctrine, and in the practical consequences that he was concerned to draw from his notion of union with the Christ.

It was because he was the founder of a powerfully organized Church and at the same time the author of a body of doctrine which was able to rally around it an intellectual élite as well as the mass of the faithful, that Calvin made such a mark upon his age and, even beyond it, exercised an influence which does not yet seem likely to decline. Even more than a thinker, in the exclusive sense of the word, he was a leader of men.

Bibliography

Index

BIBLIOGRAPHY

ADAM, J., *Evangelische Kirchengeschichte der Stadt Strassburg*, Strasbourg, 1922.

AINSLIE, JAMES L., *The doctrines of Ministerial Order in the Reformed Churches of the 16th and 17th Centuries*, Edinburgh, 1940.

ANRICH, GUSTAV, *Martin Bucer*, Strasbourg, 1914.

Strassburg und die calvinische Kirchenverfassung, Tubingen, 1928.

AUGUSTINE, ST, *Opera omnia* (MIGNE, *Patrologia latina*, vols. XXXII-XLVI.

AUTIN, ALBERT, *L'Echec de la Réforme en France*, Paris, 1918.

L'Institution chrétienne de Calvin, Paris, 1929.

BAEHLER, E., 'Petrus Caroli und Johann Calvin' (*Jahrbuch für Schweizerische Geschichte*, vol. 29, 1904).

BAINTON, ROLAND H., 'Servet et les Libertins de Genève' (*Bull. de la Soc. de l'Hist. du Protest. franç.*, vol. LXXXVII, Paris, 1938.

Hunted Heretic; the Life and Death of Servetus, Boston, 1953.

BARNAUD, J., *Pierre Viret*, Saint-Amans, 1911.

'Jacques Lefèvre d'Etaples' (*Etudes théologiques et religieuses*, Montpellier, 1936).

BARNIKOL, HERMANN, *Die Lehre Calvins vom unfreien Willen und ihr Verhältnis zur Lehre der übrigen Reformatoren und Augustins*, Neuwied, 1927.

BARON, HANS., *Calvins Staatsanschauung und das konfessionelle Zeitalter*, Munich, 1924.

BARTH, PETER, 'Die fünf Einleitungskapitel von Calvins Institutio' (*Kirchenblatt für die reformierte Schweiz*, 1925).

'Calvins Verständnis der Kirche' (*Zwischen den Zeiten*, 1930).

'Calvins Lehre vom Staat als providentieller Lebens ordnung' (*Festschrift für P. Wernle*, Basle, 1932).

'Fünfundzwanzig Jahre Calvinforschung 1909-1934' (*Theologische Rundschau*, Tubingen, 1934).

'Das Problem der natürlichen Theologie bei Calvin' (*Theologische Existenz heute*, fasc. 18, Munich, 1935).

BAUKE, HERMANN, *Die Probleme der Theologie Calvins*, Leipzig, 1922.

BAUM, J. W., *Capito und Butzer*, Elberfeld, 1860.

BAUMGARTNER, A., *Calvin hébraïsant et interprète de l'Ancien Testament*, Paris, 1889.

BAUR, FERD. CHRISTIAN, *Lehrbuch der christlichen Dogmengeschichte*, 3rd edn, Stuttgart, 1867.

BECKMANN, JOACHIM, *Vom Sakrament bei Calvin*, Tubingen, 1926.

BENOIT, JEAN-DANIEL, *Calvin à Strasbourg* (*Calvin* 1538-1938).

'Calvin et le baptême des enfants' (*Revue d'Histoire et de Philosophie religieuses*, Strasbourg, 1937.

BENOIT, JEAN-DANIEL, (*cont'd.*)

    Calvin directeur d'âmes, Strasbourg, 1947.

    Jean Calvin, la vie, l'homme, la pensée, 2nd edn, s. 1., 1948.

BETH, K., 'Calvin als reformatorischer Systematiker' (*Zeitschrift für Theologie und Kirche*, Tubingen, 1909).

BEYERHAUS, GISBERT, *Studien zur Staatsanschauung Calvins*, Berlin, 1910.

BIZER, ERNST, *Studien zur Geschichte des Abendmahlsstreits im 16. Jahrhundert*, Gütersloh, 1940.

BLANKE, FRITZ, *Aus der Welt der Reformation*, Zurich-Stuttgart, 1960.

BOHATEC, J., 'Calvins Vorsehungslehre' (*Calvinstudien*, Leipzig, 1909).

    'Die Souveränität Gottes und der Staat nach der auffassung Calvins' (*International Congres van Gereformeerden*, 1934).

    Calvin und das Recht, Feudingen, 1934.

    Die Entbundenheit des Herrschers vom Gesetz in der Staatslehre Calvins (*Zwingliana*, vol. VII, Zurich, 1935).

    'Calvins Lehre von Staat und Kirche' (*Untersuchungen zur deutschen Rechtsgeschichte*, fasc. 147, Breslau, 1937

    'Calvin et l'humanisme' (*Revue Historique*, Paris, 1938-9).

    Budé und Calvin. Studien zur Gedankenwelt des französichen Frühhumanismus, Graz, 1950.

BOIS, HENRI, *La Philosophie de Calvin*, Paris, 1919.

BOISSET, JEAN, *Sagesse et sainteté dans la pensée de Jean Calvin*, Paris, 1959.

BORGEAUD, CH., *L'Académie de Calvin*, Geneva, 1900.

    L'Adoption de la Réforme par le peuple de Genève, Geneva, 1923.

    'La Conquête religieuse de Genève' (published in the collection: *Guillaume Farel*, Neutchâtel, 1930).

VAN DEN BOSCH, W., *De outwikkeling van Bucers praedestinatiegedachten voor het optreden van Calvijn*, Amsterdam, 1922.

BOSSERT, A., *Calvin*, Paris, 1906.

BOURRILLY, V. L. and WEISS, N., 'Jean du Bellay, les protestants et la Sorbonne' (*Bull. de la Soc. de l'Hist. du Protest. franç.*, vol. LIII, Paris, 1904).

BOUSSARD, JACQUES, 'L'Université d'Orléans et l'humanisme au début du XVIe siècle' (*Humanisme et Renaissance*, Paris, 1938).

BOUVIER, ANDRÉ, *Henri Bullinger*, Neuchâtel, 1940.

BREEN, QUIRINUS, *John Calvin: a Study in French Humanism*, Grand Rapids Mich., 1931.

BRUNNER, PETER, *Vom Glauben bei Calvin*, Tubingen, 1925.

BUCER, MARTIN, *Enarrationes perpetuae in sacra quatuor Evangelia*, 2nd edn, Marburg, 1530; 3rd edn, Basle, 1536.

    Bekandnusz der vier Frey und Reichstätt . . . Schriftliche Beschirmung und verthedigung der selbigen Bekantnusz, Strasbourg, 1531.

    Quid de baptismate infantium iuxta scripturas Dei sentiendum, Strasbourg, 1533.

    Metaphrases et enarrationes perpetuae epistolarum D. Pauli Apostoli, Strasbourg, 1536.

    Scripta Anglicana, Basle, 1577.

Bibliography

BUCHSENSCHUTZ, L., *Histoire des liturgies en langue allemande dans l'Eglise de Strasbourg au XVIème siècle*, Cahors, 1900.

BUISSON, FERDINAND, *Sébastien Castellion*, 2 vols., Paris, 1892.

BUNGENER, FÉLIX, *Calvin, sa vie, son œuvre et ses écrits*, Paris, 1862.

BUSSER, F., *Calvins Urteile über sich selbst*, Zurich, 1950.

CADIER, JEAN, *Calvin*, Geneva, 1958.

CALVIN, JEAN, *Opera omnia quae supersunt (Corpus Reformatoren)*, Brunswick, 1863-1900; here referred to as *Opp*.

    Opera Selecta (edition P. BARTH and W. NIESEL), Munich, 1926-36; referred to under *O.S.*

    Institution de la religion chretienne, Paris, 1859.

    Recueil des Opuscules, c'est à dire Petits Traictés de M. Iean Calvin, 2nd edn, Geneva, 1611; referred to as *Opusc*.

    Commentaires sur le Nouveau Testament, Paris, 1854-5.

    Institution de la Religion chréstienne, edit. critique, with notes and variants by J.-D. BENOIT, Paris, 1957 . . .

    Supplementa Calviniana, I, *Sermones de altero libro Regum habiti . . . ed.* HANNS RUCKERT, Neukirchen, 1936-61.

    Calvin, 1538-1938, Strasbourg, 1938.

    Calvinstudien, Festschrift zum 400. Geburtstage Johann Calvins unter Redaktion von Lic. Dr. Bohatec herausgegeben von der Reformierten Gemeinde Elberfeld, Leipzig, 1909.

    Calvin-Studien, 1959, *herausgegeben von J. Moltmann*, Neukirchen, 1960.

CANTIMORI, DELIO, *Eretici italiani del Cinquecento*, Florence, 1939 (German translation by W. KAEGI entitled *Italienische Haeretiker der Spätrenaissance*, Basle, 1949).

CAVARD, PIERRE, *Le Procès de Michel Servet à Vienne*, Vienne, 1953.

CHENEVIÈRE, MARC-EDOUARD, *La Pensée politique de Calvin*, Geneva, 1938.

CHOISY, E., 'Farel à Genève avec Calvin' (published in the symposium *Guillaume Farel*, Neuchâtel, 1930).

    La Théocratie à Genève au temps de Calvin, Geneva, 1897.

    Calvin, éducateur des consciences, Neuilly, 1926.

    'Calvin et la science' (*Recueil de la Faculté de Théologie Protestante*, University of Geneva, 1931).

    'Calvin et l'union des Eglises' (*Bull. de la Soc. de l'Hist. du Protest. franç.*, vol. LXXXIV, Paris, 1935).

CLAVIER, HENRI, *Etudes sur le calvinisme*, Paris, 1936.

CLOUZOT, H., 'Les amitiés de Rabelais en Orléans' (*Revue des Etudes Rabelaisiennes*, vol. III, Paris, 1905).

CORNELIUS, C. A., *Die Verbannung Calvins aus Genf im Jahr* 1538, Munich, 1886.

    Historische Arbeiten, vornehmlich zur Reformationszeit, Leipzig, 1889.

COURVOISIER, JACQUES, 'Bucer et l'œuvre de Calvin' (*Revue de Théologie et de Philosophie*, Lausanne, 1933).

    La Notion d'Eglise chez Bucer, Paris, 1933.

Bibliography

COURVOISIER, JACQUES, (cont'd.)
'Les Catéchismes de Genève et de Strasbourg' (*Bull. de la Soc. de l'Hist. du Prot. franç.*, vol. LXXXIV, Paris, 1935).
'Le Sens de la discipline ecclésiastique dans la Genève de Calvin' in the Symposium *Hommage et reconnaissance à Karl Barth*, Neuchâtel, 1946.

CRAMER, J. A., *Calvijn en de Heilige Schrift*, Wageningen, 1932.

DANKBAAR, W. F., *Calvijn, zijn weg en werk*, Nijkerk (undated).

De sacramentsleer van Calvijn, Amsterdam, 1941.

DELARUELLE, L., *Guillaume Budé, la vie, les idées maitresses*, Paris, 1907.
'De l'Election Eternelle de Dieu' (*Actes du Congrès international de Théologie Calviniste*, Geneva, 1936).

DELUZ, G., *Prédestination et liberté*, Neuchâtel, 1942.

DEMEURE, J., '*L'Institution chrétienne* de Calvin: examen de l'authenticité de la traduction française' (*Revue d'Histoire littéraire de la France*, vol. 22, Paris, 1915).

DIEHL, WILHELM, 'Calvins Auslegung des Dekalogs in der ersten Ausgabe seiner *Institutio* und Luthers Katechismen' (*Theologische Studien und Kritiken*, Gotha, 1898).

DOERRIES, H., 'Calvin und Lefèvre' (*Zeitschrift für Kirchengeschichte*, vol. XLIV, Gotha, 1925).

DOINEL, J., 'Jean Calvin à Orleans' (*Bull. de la Soc. de l'Hist. du Protest. franç.*, vol. XXVI, Paris, 1877).

DOMINICE, MAX, *L'Humanité de Jésus d'après Calvin*, Paris, 1933.

DOUMERGUE, EMILE, *Jean Calvin, les hommes et les choses de son temps*, 7 vols., Lausanne, 1899-1917; Neuilly, 1926-7.

Le Caractère de Calvin, 2nd edn, Neuilly, 1931.

DOWEY, EDWARD A., *The Knowledge of God in Calvin's Theology*, New York, 1952.

EBRARD, J. H. A., *Das Dogma vom Abendmahl und seine Geschichte*, vol. II, Frankfort, 1846.

EELLS, HASTINGS, *Martin Bucer*, New Haven, 1931.

ELSTER, L., 'Calvin als Staatsmann, Gesetzgeber und Nationalökonom' (*Jahrbücher für Nationalökonomie und Statitsik*, 1878).

EMMEN, EGBERT, *De christologie van Calvijn*, Amsterdam, 1935.

ENGELLAND, H., *Gott und Mensch bei Calvin*, Munich, 1934.

ERASME, D., *Opera omnia emendatiora et auctiora*, Leyden, 1703-6.

ERICHSON, A., *Die calvinische und die altstrassburgische Gottesdienstordnung*, Strasbourg, 1894.

L'Origine de la confession des péchés dite de Calvin, Dôle, 1896.

FAZY, H., 'Procès de Jérôme Bolsec' (*Mémoires de l'Institut national genevois*, Geneva, 1866).

'Procès de Gruet' (*Mémoires de l'Institut national genevois*, Geneva, 1886).

FEBVRE, LUCIEN, 'Le Problème de l'incroyance au XVIème siècle. La Religion de Rabelais' (*L'Evolution de l'Humanité*, vol. 53, Paris, 1942).

Bibliography

FEBVRE, LUCIEN, (cont'd.)
'L'Origine des Placards de 1534' (*Bibliothèque d'Humanisme et Renaissance*, vol. VII, Paris, 1945).

FENN, W., 'The Marrow of Calvinism' (*Harvard Theological Review*, 1909).

FICKER, JOHANNES, *Die Anfänge der akademischen Studien in Strassburg*, Strasbourg, 1912.

FRŒLICH, KARLFRIED, *Die Reichgottesidee Calvins*, Munich, 1922.
Gottesreich, Welt und Kirche bei Calvin, Munich, 1930.

GERBERT, CAMIL, *Geschichte der Strassburger Sectenbewegung*, Strasbourg, 1889.

GEROLD, THÉODORE, *Les plus anciennes mélodies de l'Eglise protestante de Strasbourg et leurs auteurs*, Paris, 1928.

GLOEDE, GÜNTER, 'Theologia naturalis bei Calvin' (*Tübinger Studien zur systematischen Theologie*, vol. 5, Stuttgart, 1935).

GODET, MARCEL, 'Le Collège de Montaigu' (*Revue des Etudes Rabelaisiennes*, vol. VII, Paris, 1909).
'La Congrégation de Montaigu' (*Bibliothèque de l'Ecole des Hautes Etudes: Sciences historiques et philologiques*, fasc. 198, Paris, 1912).

GOEHLER, A., *Calvins Lehre von der Heiligung*, Munich, 1934.

GOLLWITZER, HELMUT, *Coena Domini*, Munich, 1937.

GOUMAZ, LOUIS, *La Doctrine du salut d'après les commentaires de Jean Calvin sur le Nouveau Testament*, Nyon, 1917.

GRAF, C. H., 'Faber Stapulensis' (*Zeitschrift für historische Theologie*, 1852).

GRASS, HANS, *Die Abendmahlslehre bei Luther und Calvin*, Gütersloh, 1940.

GROBMANN, ALFRED, *Das Naturrecht bei Luther und Calvin*, Hamburg, 1935.

DE GROOT, D. J., *Calvijns opvatting over de inspiratie der Heilige Schrift*, Zutphen, 1931.
'Melchior Wolmar' (*Bullet. de la Soc. de l'Hist. du Protest. franç.*, vol. LXXXIII, Paris, 1934).

HARNACK, THEODOSIUS, *Luthers Theologie*, 2nd edn, 2 vols., Munich, 1927.

HARTVELT, G. P., *Verum Corpus: Een studie over een centraalhofdstuk uit de avond maalsleer van Calvijn*, Delft, 1960.

HAUCK, WILHELM ALBERT, *Calvin und die Rechtfertigung*, Gütersloh, 1938.
Sünde und Erbsünde nach Calvin, Heidelberg, 1939.

HAUSER, HENRI, 'A propos des idées, économomiques de Calvin' (*Melanges d'Histoire offerts à Henri Pirenne*, vol. I, 1926).
'L'Economie Calvinienne' (*Bullet. de la Soc. de l'Hist. du Protest. franç.*, vol LXXXIV, Paris, 1935.

HAUSHERR, HANS, *Der Staat in Calvins Gedankenwelt*, Leipzig, 1923.

HEPPE, HEINRICH, *Die Dogmatik der evangelisch-reformierten Kirche* (re-edited by E. Bizer, Neukirchen, 1935).

HERMINJARD, A. L., *Correspondance des Réformateurs dans les pays de langue française*, Geneva and Paris, 1866.

HERRLINGER, *Die Theologie Melanchthons*, Gotha, 1879.

HEYER, H., *L'Eglise de Genève*, Geneva, 1909.

HIRSCH, EMMANUEL, *Die Theologie des Andreas Osiander*, Göttingen, 1919.

Bibliography

HOLL, KARL, *Johannes Calvin*, Tubingen, 1909.

Gesammelte Aufsätze zur Kirchengeschichte, vol. 1, *Luther*, 6th edn, Tubingen, 1932; vol. III, *Der Westen*, Tubingen, 1928.

HOLLARD, A., 'Michel Servet et Jean Calvin' (*Bibliothèque d'Humanisme et Renaissance*, vol. VI, Paris, 1945).

HOLSTEN, WALTER, 'Christentum und nichtchristliche Religion nach der Auffassung Bucers' (*Theol. Studien und Kritiken*, Gotha, 1936).

HUGO, A. M., *Calvijn en Seneca*, Groningen, 1957.

HUNT, R. N. CAREW, *Calvin*, London, 1933.

HUNTER, A. MITCHELL, *The Teaching of Calvin*, Glasgow, 1920.

'The Education of Calvin' (*The Evangelical Quarterly*, London, 1937).

IMBART DE LA TOUR, P., *Les Origines de la Réforme*, vol. III; *L'Evangélisme*, Paris, 1914; *Calvin et l'Institution chrétienne*, Paris, 1935.

Internationaal Congres van Gereformeerden, La Haye, 1935.

JACOBS, PAUL, *Prädestination und Verantwortlichkeit bei Calvin*, Neukirchen, 1927.

JANSEN, JOHN FREDERICK, *Calvin's Doctrine of the Work of Christ*, London, 1956.

JOHNSON, TH. C., 'J. Calvin and the Bible' (*The Evangelical Quarterly*, London, 1932).

KAMPSCHULTE, F. W., *Johann Calvin, seine Kirche und sein Staat in Genf*, 2 vols., Leipzig, 1869-99.

KATTENBUSCH, FERDINAND, 'Arbitrium und voluntas dasselbe?' (*Theologische Studien und Kritiken*, Gotha, 1931).

KAWERAU, G., art. 'Westphal' in the *Realencyclopädie für protestantische Theologie und Kirche*, 3rd edn, vol. XXI, Leipzig, 1908.

KLINGENBURG, G., *Das Verhältnis Calvins zu Butzer untersucht auf Grund der wirtschafts-ethischen Bedeutung beider Reformatoren*, Bonn, 1912.

KOEBERLE, A., *Rechtfertigung und Heiligung*, 2nd edn, Leipzig, 1929.

KOEHLER, WALTHER, *Zwingli und Luther*, vol. 1, Leipzig, 1924.

Zürcher Ehegericht und Genfer Konsistorium, vol. II, Leipzig, 1942.

KOESTLIN, JULIUS, 'Calvins *Institutio* nach Form und Inhalt in ihrer geschichtlichen Entwicklung' (*Theologische Studien und Kritiken*, Gotha, 1868).

Luthers Theologie in ihrer geschichtlichen Entwicklung, und ihrem inneren zusammenhang, 2nd edn, 2 vols., Stuttgart, 1901.

KOLFHAUS, WILHELM, 'Der Verkehr Calvins mit Bullinger' (*Calvinstudien*, Leipzig, 1909).

Christusgemeinschaft bei Johannes Calvin, Neukirchen, 1939.

Die Seelsorge Johannes Calvins, Neukirchen, 1941.

KOOPMANS, JAN, *Het oudkerkelijk dogma in de Reformatie, bepaaldelijk bij Calvijn*, Wageningen, 1938.

KRUSCHE, WERNER, *Das Wirken des Heiligen Geistes nach Calvin*, Göttingen, 1957.

KUYPER, A., 'Calvin and Confessional Revision' (*Presbyterian and Reformed Review*, 1891).

Bibliography

LANG, AUGUST, 'Die ältesten theologischen Arbeiten Calvins' (*Neue Jahrbücher für deutsche Theologie*, Bonn, 1893).

LANG, AUGUST, (*cont'd.*)

Das häusliche Leben J. Calvins, Munich, 1893.

Die Bekehrung Calvins, Leipzig, 1897.

'Melanchthon und Calvin' (*Reformierte Kirchenzeitung*, Elberfeld, 1897).

Der Evangelienkommentar Martin Butzers und die Grundzüge seiner Theologie, Leipzig, 1900.

Der Heidelberger Katechismus, Leipzig, 1907.

Johannes Calvin, Leipzig, 1909.

Zwei Calvinvorträge, Gütersloh, 1911.

'Zwingli und Calvin' (*Monographien zur Weltgeschichte*, fasc. 31, Bielefeld and Leipzig, 1913).

'The Sources of Calvin's *Institutes*' (*Evangelical Quarterly*, London, 1936).

LENSON, GUSTAVE, '*L'Institution chrétienne* de Calvin' (*Revue historique*, Paris, 1894).

LECERF, A., *Le Déterminisme et la responsabilité dans le système de Calvin*, Paris, 1895.

'La Doctrine de l'Eglise dans Calvin' (*Revue de Théologie et de Philosophie*, Lausanne, 1929).

'Le Souveraineté de Dieu d'après le Calvinisme' (*Internationaal Congres van Gereformeerden*, La Haye, 1935).

'L'Eléction et le sacrement' (*De l'élection éternelle de Dieu*, Geneva, 1936).

Introduction à la Dogmatique réformée, Section 2: *Du fondement et de la spécification de la connaissance religieuse*, Paris, 1938.

LE COQ, JOHN P., 'Was Calvin a Philosopher?' (*The Personalist*, vol. XXIX, Los Angeles, 1948).

LECOULTRE, H., 'La Conversion de Calvin' (*Revue de Théol. et de Philos.*, Lausanne, 1890).

'Calvin d'après son commentaire sur le De Clementia de Sénèque' (*Revue de Théolog. et de Philos.*, Lausanne, 1891).

Mélanges, Lausanne, undated.

LEFRANC, ABEL, *La Jeunesse de Calvin*, Paris, 1888.

Histoire du Collège de France, Paris, 1893.

Introduction to: *Jean Calvin, l'Institution chrétienne*, original text of, 1541, Paris, 1911.

Grands écrivains français de la Renaissance, Paris, 1914.

LOBSTEIN, PAUL, *Die Ethik Calvins in ihren Grundzügen entworfen*, Strasbourg, 1877.

La Connaissance religieuse d'après Calvin, Paris, 1909.

Etudes sur la pensée et l'œuvre de Calvin, Neuilly, 1927.

LOOFS, FRIEDRICH, *Leitfaden zum Studium der Dogmengeschichte*, 4th edn, Halle, 1906.

LUETGERT, W., 'Calvins Lehre vom Schöpfer' (*Zeitschr. für system. Theologie*, Gütersloh, 1932).

Bibliography

LUTHER, MARTIN, *Werke, Kritische Gesammtausgabe*, Weimar, 1883 . . .
  Oeuvres, vol. II: *Les Livres symboliques*, transl. A. Jundt, Paris, 1947.

LÜTTGE, W., *Die Rechtfertigungslehre Calvins und ihre Bedentung für seine Frömmigkeit*, Berlin, 1909.

MANN, MARGARET, *Erasme et les débuts de la Réforme français*, Paris, 1934.

MARMELSTEIN, JOH. WILHWELM, *Etude comparatives des textes latins et français de l'Institution de la religion chrétienne*, Groningen, 1923.

MAURY, PIERRE, 'La Théologie naturelle d'après Calvin', (*Bull. de la Soc. de l'Hist. du Protest. franç.*, vol. LXXXIV, Paris, 1935).

MAXWELL, WILLIAM D., *John Knox's Genevan Service Book*, 1556, Edinburgh and London, 1931.

MAYER, C. A., 'Le Départ de Marot de Ferrare' (*Bibliothèque d'Humanisme et Renaissance*, vol. XVIII, Geneva, 1956).

MELANCHTHON, PHIL., *Opera quae supersunt omnia* (*Corpus Reformatorum*), Brunswick, 1834-60.
  Die Loci Communes Philipp Melanchthons in ihrer Urgestalt, edited by G. L. Plitt and Th. Kolde, 4th edn, Leipzig, 1925.

MESNARD, PIERRE, *L'Essor de la philosophie politique au XVIème siècle*, Paris, 1936.

MEYLAN, HENRI, and DELUZ, RENÉ, *La Dispute de Lausanne*, Lausanne, 1936.

MINGES, P., 'Der Gottesbegriff des Duns Scotus auf seinen angeblichen Indeterminismus geprüft' (*Theologische Studien der Leogesellschaft*, vol. 26, Vienne, 1906).
  Joannis Duns Scoti doctrina philosophica et theologica, 2 vols., Quaracchi, 1908.

MOORE, W. G., *La Réforme allemande et la littérature française*, Strasbourg, 1930.

MUELHAUPT, ERWIN, *Die Predigt Calvins*, Berlin, 1931.

MULLER, KARL, 'Calvins Bekehrung' (*Nachrichten der Gesellsch. der Wissensch. zu Göttingen*, Göttingen, 1905).
  'Calvin und die Libertiner' (*Zeitschrift für Kirchengeschichte*, vol. XL, Gotha, 1922).

MULLER, P. J., *De Godsleer van Calvijn*, Groningen, 1881.

VON MURALT, L., 'Uber den Ursprung der Reformation in Frankreich', *Festschrift Hans Nabholz*, Zurich, 1934).

NAEF, HENRI, *Les Origines de la Réforme à Genève*, Geneva, 1936.

NEUENHAUS, JOHANNES, 'Calvin als Humanist' (*Calvinstudien*, Leipzig, 1909).

NIESEL, WILHELM, 'Calvin wider Osianders Rechtfertigungslehre' (*Zeitschrift für Kirchengeschichte*, vol. XLVI, Gotha, 1928).
  'Calvin und die Libertiner' (*Zeitschrift für Kirchengeschichte*, vol. XLVIII, Gotha, 1929).
  'Zum Genfer Prozess gegen Valentin Gentilis' (*Archiv für Reformationsgeschichte*, vol. XXVI, Leipzig, 1929).
  Calvins Lehre vom Abendmahl, 2nd edn, Munich, 1930.
  'Verstand Calvin Deutsch?' (*Zeitschr. für Kirchengeschichte*, vol. XLIX, Gotha, 1930).

Bibliography

'Wesen und Gestalt der Kirche nach Calvin' (*Evangelische Theologie*, Munich, 1936).

Die Theologie Calvins, Munich, 1938; 2nd edn, Munich, 1957.

NIESEL, WILHELM, and BARTH, PETER, 'Eine französische Ausgabe der ersten *Institutio* Calvins' (*Theologische Blätter*, Leipzig, 1928).

NOESGEN, K. F., 'Die bei der Entstehung der Theologie Calvins mitwirkenden Momente' (*Neue kirkliche Zeitschrift*, vol. XXII, Erlangen, 1911).

'Calvins Lehre von Gott und ihr Verhältnis zur Gotteslehrer andere Reformatoren' (*Neue kirkliche Zeitschrift*, vol. XXIII, Erlangen, 1912).

NUERNBERGER, RICHARD, *Die Politisierung des französischen Protestantismus*, Tubingen, 1948.

OBENDIEK, HARMANNUS, 'Die *Institutio* Calvins als "Confessio" und "Apologie" ' (*Theologische Aufsätze Karl Barth zum 50 Geburtstag*, Munich, 1936).

OTTEN, HEINZ, *Calvins theologische Anschauung von der Prädestination*, Munich, 1938.

PACHE, EDOUARD, 'La Sainte Cène selon Calvin' (*Revue de Théologie et de Philosophie*, Lausanne, 1936).

PANNIER, JACQUES, *Recherches sur l'évolution religieuse de Calvin jusqu' à sa conversion*, Strasbourg, 1924.

Calvin à Strasbourg, Strasbourg, 1925.

Jean Calvin: Epître au Roi, Paris, 1927.

'Une Première *Institution* française dès 1537' (*Revue d'Hist. et de Philos. religieuses*, Strasbourg, 1928).

'Renée de France' (*Etudes Théologiques et Religieuses*, Montpellier, 1929).

Calvin écrivain, Paris, 1930.

Recherches sur la formation intellectuelle de Calvin, Paris, 1931.

'Notes historiques et critiques sur un chapitre de *l'Institution* écrit à Strasbourg (1539): De la vie chrétienne' (*Revue de l'Hist. et de Philos. relig.*, Strasbourg, 1934).

'Une Année de la vie de Calvin' (*Bull. de la Société Calviniste de France*, No. 45, p. 2).

PAUCK, WILHELM, 'Calvin and Butzer' (*Journal of Religion*, Chicago, 1929).

PETREMAND, J., 'Les Débuts du ministère (de Farel) à Neuchâtel' (in the symposium: *Guillaume Farel*, Neuchâtel, 1930).

DE PEYER, E., 'Calvin's Doctrine of Divine Providence' (*The Evangelical Quarterly*, London, 1938).

PFISTER, OSKAR, *Calvins Eingreifen in die Hexer- und Hexenprozesse von Peney 1545 nach seiner Bedeutung für Geschichte und Gegenwart*, Zurich, 1947.

PFISTERER, ERNST, *Calvins Wirken in Genf*, Essen, 1940; 2nd edn, Neukirchen, 1957.

POLMAN, A. D. R., *De Praedestinatieleer van Augustinus, Thomas van Aquino en Calvijn*, Franeker, 1936.

POLMAN, PONTIEN, *L'Elément historique dans la controverse religieuse du XVIème siècle*, Gembloux, 1932.

Bibliography

POTGIETER, FREDERICK J. M., *De verhouding tussen die teologie en die filosofie by Calvijn*, Amsterdam, 1939.

PRANTL, CARL, *Geschichte der Logik im Abendland*, vol. IV, Leipzig, 1870.

DE QUERVAIN, ALFRED, *Calvin, sein Lehren und Kämpfen*, Berlin, 1926.

QUISTORP, H., *Die letzten Dinge im Zeugnis Calvins*, Gütersloh, 1941.

DE RAEMOND, FLORIMOND, *L'Histoire de la naissance, progrès et décadence de l'hérésie de ce siècle*, Rouen, 1623.

RENAUDET, A., *Préréforme et humanisme à Paris pendant les premières guerres d'Italie*, Paris, 1916.

Etudes Erasmiennes (1521-1529), Paris, 1939.

RICHEL, PIETER J., *Het Kerkbegrip van Calvijn*, Utrecht, 1942.

RICHTER, AEMILIUS LUDWIG, *Die evangelischen Kirchenordnungen*, 2 vols., Weimar, 1846.

RILLIET, A., *Notice sur le premier séjour de Calvin à Genève*, Geneva, 1878.

RITSCHL, ALBRECHT, 'Geschichtliche Studien zur christlichen Lehre von Gott' (*Jahrbücher für deutsche Theologie*, vol. 13, Gotha, 1868).

Die christliche Lehre von der Rechtfertigung und Versöhnung, 4th edn, 3 vols., Bonn, 1895-1902.

RITSCHL, OTTO, *Dogmengeschichte des Protestantismus*, vol. III: *Die reformierte Theologie des 16. und 17. Jahrhunderts in ihrer Entstehung und Entwicklung*. Göttingen, 1926.

RODOCANACHI, *Renée de France, Duchesse de Ferrara*, Paris, 1895.

La Réforme en Italie, 2 vols., Paris, 1920-1).

SABATIER, D., 'La conversion de Calvin' (*Annales de Philosophie chrétienne*, vol, XXI, Paris, 1911).

DE SAUSSURE, J., 'La notion réformé des sacrements' (*Bull. de la Soc. de l'Hist. du Protest. franç.*, vol. LXXXIV, Paris, 1935).

SCHEIBE, M., *Calvins Prädestinationslehre*, Halle, 1897.

SCHERDING, PIERRE, 'Calvin, der Mann, der Kirche und die Bedeutung seines Strassburger Aufenthalts' (published in the collection *Calvin, 1538-1938*), Strasbourg, 1938.

SCHMIDT, ALBERT-MARIE, *Jean Calvin et la tradition calvinienne*, Paris.

VON SCHUBERT, HANS, *Johannes Calvin*, Tubingen, 1909.

Grosse christliche Persönlichkeiten, 3rd edn, Leipzig, 1933.

VON SCHULTHESS-RECHBERG, *Luther, Zwingli und Calvin in ihren Ansichten über die Verhältnis von Staat und Kirche*, Zurich, 1909.

SCHULZE, MARTIN, *Meditatio futurae vitae*, Leipzig, 1901.

Calvins Jenseitschristentum in seinem Verhältnis zu den religiösen Schriften des Erasmus, Görlitz, 1902.

SCHWEIZER, ALEXANDER, *Die Glaubenslehre der evangelisch-reformierten Kirche*, 2 vols., Zurich, 1844-5.

Die protestantische Centraldogmen, vol. I, Zurich, 1854.

SEEBERG, REINHOLD, *Die Theologie des Johannes Duns Scotus*, Leipzig, 1900.

Lehrbuch der Dogmengeschichte, vol. II, 3rd edn, 1923; vol. III, 4th edn, 1930; vol IV, 2, 2nd and 3rd edn, 1920, Tubingen.

Bibliography

SMITS, LUCHESIUS, *Saint Augustin dans l'œuvre de Calvin*, Assen, 1957.

VON SOOS, BÈLA, 'Zwingli und Calvin' (*Zwingliana*, vol. VI, Zurich, 1844-5).

SPRENGER, PAUL, *Das Rätsel um die Bekehrung Calvins*, Neukirchen, 1960.

STAEHELIN, ERNST, *Das Buch der Basler Reformation*, Basle, 1929.

Das theologische Lebenswerk Johannes Oekolampads, Leipzig, 1939.

STAEHELIN, R., art. 'Calvin, Johannes' (*Realencyclopädie für protestantische Theologie und Kirche*, vol. III, 3rd edn, Leipzig, 1897).

STRATHMANN, H., 'Die Entstehung der Lehre Calvins von der Busse' (*Calvinstudien*, Leipzig, 1909).

'Calvins Lehre von der Busse in ihrer späteren Gestalt' (*Theologische Studien und Kritiken*, Gotha, 1909).

STRICKER, EDUARD, *Johann Calvin als erste Pfarrer der reformierten Gemeinde zu Strassburg*, Strasbourg, 1890.

STROHL, HENRI, *l'Epanouissement de la pensée religieuse de Luther*, Strasbourg, 1924.

'La Théorie et la pratique des quatres ministères à Strasbourg avant l'arrivée de Calvin' (*Bull. de la Soc. de l'Hist. du Protest. franç.*, vol. LXXXIV, Paris, 1935).

'La notion d'Eglise chez les réformateurs' (*Revue d'Hist. et de Philos. religieuses*, Strasbourg, 1936).

'Bucer et Calvin' (*Bull. de la Soc. de l'Hist. du Protest. franç.*, vol. LXXXVII, Paris, 1938).

Bucer, humaniste chrétien, Paris, 1939.

'La Pensée de Calvin sur la Providence divine au temps où il était réfugié à Strasbourg' (*Revue d'Hist. et de Philos. religieuses*, Clermont Ferrand, 1942).

STUCKELBERGER, H. M., 'Calvin und Servet' (*Zwingliana*, vol. VI, Zurich, 1934).

'Calvin und Castellio' (*Zwingliana*, vol. VII, Zurich, 1939).

STUERMANN, WALTER E., *A critical Study of Calvin's Concept of Faith*, Tulsa, 1952.

STUPPERICH, ROBERT, *Der Humanismus und die Wiedervereinigung der Konfessionen*, Leipzig, 1936.

'M. Bucers Anschauungen von der Kirche' (*Zeitschrift für systematische Theologie*, Berlin, 1940).

TORRANCE, T. F., *Calvin's Doctrine of Man*, London, 1949.

Kingdom and Church, Edinburgh, 1956.

TROELTSCH, ERNST, *Die Soziallehren der christilchen Kirchen und Gruppen*, Tubingen, 1912.

TSCHACKERT, PAUL, *Die Entstehung der lutherischen und reformierten Kirchenlehre*, Göttingen, 1910.

UEBERWEG, F., *Grundriss der Geschichte der Philosophie*, vol. III, 12th edn, by M. Frischeisen-Koehler and W. Woog, Berlin, 1924.

USTERI, J. M., 'Die Stellung der Strassburger Reformatoren Bucer und Capito zur Tauffrage' (*Theologische Studien und Kritiken*, Gotha, 1884).

Bibliography

'Calvins Sakraments- und Tauflehre' (*Theologische Studien und Kritiken*, Gotha, 1884).

VAN DER LINDE, S., *De Leer van de Heiligen Geest bij Calvijn*, Wageningen, 1944.

VAN TIEGHEM, P., 'La Littérature latine de la Renaissance' (*Bibliothèque d'Humanisme et Renaissance*, vol. IV, Paris, 1944.

VIENOT, JOHN, *Histoire de la Réforme française*, vol. I, Paris, 1926.

VUILLEUMIER, HENRI, *Histoire de l'Eglise réformée du pays de Vaud*, vol. I, Lausanne, 1927.

WACKERNAGEL, RUDOLF, *Humanismus und Reformation in Basel*, Basle, 1924.

WALKER, WILLISTON. *John Calvin, the Organizer of Reformed Protestantism*, London, 1906.

WALLACE, RONALD S., *Calvin's Doctrine of the Word and Sacrament*, Edinburgh, 1953.
Calvin's Doctrine of the Christian Life, Edinburgh, 1959.

VON WALTER, JOHANNES, *Die Theologie Luthers*, Gütersloh, 1940.

WARFIELD, B. B., 'Calvin's Doctrine of God' (*Princeton Theological Review*, Princeton, 1909).

WEBER, HANS EMIL, *Reformation, Orthodoxie und Rationalismus*, 2 vols., Gütersloh, 1937-40.

WEBER, HERMANN, *Die Theologie Calvins*, Berlin, 1930.

WEISS, N., 'Arrêt inédit du Parlement de Paris contre *l'Institution chrétienne*' (*Bulln. de la Soc. de l'Hist du Protest. franç.*, vol. XXXIII, Paris, 1884).
'Calvin, Servet, G. de Trie et le tribunal de Vienne' (*Bulln de la Soc. de l'Hist. du Protest. franç.*, vol. LVII, Paris, 1908).
'Une Portrait de la femme de Calvin' (*Bull. de la Societé de l'Hist. du Prot. français*, 1907, vol. LVI pp. 222 ff).

WENDEL, F., *L'Eglise de Strasbourg, sa constitution et son organisation*, 1532-1535, Paris, 1942.

WERDERMANN, TH., 'Calvins Lehre von der Kirche in ihrer geschichtlichen Entwicklung' (*Calvinstudien*, Leipzig, 1909).

WERNLE, PAUL, *Calvin und Basel bis zum Tode des Myconius*, Tubingen, 1909.
'Zur Bekehrung Calvins' (*Zeitschr für Kirchengeschichte*, vol. XXXI, Gotha, 1910).
Der evangelische Glaube nach den Hauptschriften der Reformatoren, vol. III: Johann Calvin, Tubingen, 1919.

WILL, ROBERT, *Calvins Bedeutung für unsere Zeit*, Strasbourg, 1909.
'La première liturgie de Calvin' (*Revue d'Hist. et de Philos. religieuses*, Strasbourg, 1938).

ZANTA, LÉONTINE, *La Renaissance du stoïcisme au XVIème siècle*, Paris, 1914.

ZIMMERLI, WALTER, *J. Calvin: Psychopannychia*, Leipzig, 1932.

ZWINGLI, HULDREICH, *Opera*, edn of M. Schuler and J. Schulthess, Zurich, 1828-42.
Sämtliche Werke, ed. by E. Egli, G. Finsler, W. Köhler, O. Farner, F. Blanke, L. v. Muralt, Leipzig, 1905 . . .

INDEX

Index

Index

Index

Mair, John, 19

man, knowledge of, 114, 132, 151, 185-96

Manichaeans, 286

Marbourg, Colloquy of, 20, 39n

Marche, Collège de la, 18

Marguerite of Navarre, 23, 24, 40, 42, 64, 87n

Marot, Clément, 47

marriage, 52, 59, 65-6, 78, 112

means, external, 121, 291-355

Melancthon, 20, 33, 36, 46, 62-4, 97, 102, 103, 104, 114, 122, 133n, 134-5, 146, 189n, 198, 199n, 200, 203n, 205, 209, 236, 258, 264, 269, 297, 311, 331, 359

merits, 239, 251, 271, 273

millenarianism, 114

ministers, ministry, 75-7, 92, 143, 292-3, 303-5

monarchy, 30

Montaigu, Collège de, 18-20, 22, 46, 126-7, 176

Montmor family, 16, 19

morality, 72-3, 83-5, 245-55, 300

mortification, 242, 243, 244, 320

mysticism, 87n, 235-6

Necessity, 190-1

Nérac, 42

Nestorius, 220n

Neuchâtel, 57, 91

Nicaea, Council of, 125

Nicaean Creed, 54

Nicodemism, 39, 47, 82

nominalism, 127, 129

Noyon, 16, 17, 21, 25, 39, 42

Nuremberg, 235

Occam, William of, 33, 127, 128, 176

Oecolampadius, 20, 143, 298, 307n, 333, 347n, 352n

Olivétan, Pierre, 19, 20, 38, 161

On the Cure of Souls (Bucer), 114, 143

organization, ecclesiastical, 50, 59n, 60, 66, 71-81, 105-7, 117, 143, 301-6

Origen, 115, 124, 125n

Orleans, 21-3, 26, 43

Osiander, Andreas, 120, 175n, 235-7, 258, 259, 263, 342

Pagans, 155, 178, 192-3, 194, 207

Paraphrases (Erasmus), 31

Paris, 17-21, 25-6, 40-2, 48

Pascal, Blaise, 35, 248

pastors, 71-2, 75, 76, 81, 89, 91, 292, 293, 303, 304-5

penitence, 112, 114, 233, 242, 243-4, 248

Perrin, Ami, 66, 86-9, 92, 93, 97

perseverance, 245, 277, 285

philosophers, 34, 36, 45, 125, 136, 152, 153, 164, 174, 180, 193-4

Pighius, Albert, 81, 174-5, 264, 271

Placards (of 1534), 43, 112, 113

Plato, 115, 124, 173, 174

Platonism, 33n

Platter, Thomas, 112

police, ecclesiastical, 85

politics, 30, 58, 65, 67, 71, 79, 81, 100, 193-4, 291

Pont l'Evêque, 17

Postille (Luther), 133

power, civil, 55, 60, 71, 73-4, 79-80

power, ecclesiastical, 117

power, public, 30

power, royal, 30

power, spiritual, 305-6

prayer, 54, 80, 139, 233, 253-5

preaching, 266-7, 275, 283, 292, 293, 296, 305, 310, 353

predestination, 33, 44, 90, 92, 100, 114, 124, 127, 129, 134, 135, 137, 140-1, 178, 229, 231, 233, 263-84, 316, 357

presentiments, 174

pride, 187

promises, 209-12, 240, 252, 253, 254, 274, 276, 279, 313, 316, 324-5, 336-7

providence, 29, 114, 116, 121, 177-84, 267-8

psalms, 52, 60

381